EXPLORING THE
SOCIOLOGY
OF EUROPE

EXPLORING THE
SOCIOLOGY
OF EUROPE

AN ANALYSIS OF THE EUROPEAN SOCIAL COMPLEX

MAURICE ROCHE

Los Angeles | London | New Delhi
Singapore | Washington DC

© Maurice Roche 2010

First published 2010

Apart from any fair dealing for the purposes of research or private study, or
criticism or review, as permitted under the Copyright, Designs and Patents Act,
1988, this publication may be reproduced, stored or transmitted in any form, or by
any means, only with the prior permission in writing of the publishers, or in the case
of reprographic reproduction, in accordance with the terms of licences issued by the
Copyright Licensing Agency. Enquiries concerning reproduction outside those terms
should be sent to the publishers.

SAGE Publications Ltd
1 Oliver's Yard
55 City Road
London EC1Y 1SP

SAGE Publications Inc.
2455 Teller Road
Thousand Oaks, California 91320

SAGE Publications India Pvt Ltd
B 1/I 1 Mohan Cooperative Industrial Area
Mathura Road, Post Bag 7
New Delhi 110 044

SAGE Publications Asia-Pacific Pte Ltd
33 Pekin Street #02-01
Far East Square
Singapore 048763

Library of Congress Control Number 2009922161

British Library Cataloguing in Publication data

A catalogue record for this book is available from the British Library

ISBN 978-0-7619-4071-5
ISBN 978-0-7619-4072-2 (pbk)

Typeset by C&M Digitals (P) Ltd, Chennai, India
Printed in India by Replika Press Pvt. Ltd
Printed on paper from sustainable resources

For my son and daughter, Stephen Roche and Helen Roche,
and for the Europe I hope you get to live in.

CONTENTS

LIST OF ACRONYMS

AU	African Union
ASEAN	Association of South East Asian Nations
CAP	Common Agricultural Policy
DG	Directorate General (of the European Commission)
EC	European Commission
ECB	European Central Bank
ECJ	European Court of Justice
EEC	European Economic Community
EMU	Economic and Monetary Union
ESRC	Economic and Social Research Council, UK
EU	European Union
GAF	Global Adjustment Fund
GATT	General Agreement on Tariffs and Trade
GDP	gross domestic product
GNI	gross national income
ICT	information and communication technologies
IGC	intergovernmental conference (EU)
MERCOSUR	The Common Market of the South (the Latin American trade organisation)
NAFTA	North American Free Trade Association
NATO	North Atlantic Treaty Organisation
NRP	National Reform Programme
OMC	open method of coordination (EU)
SEA	Single European Act
TEU	Treaty on European Union
UN	United Nations
UNECE	UN Economic Commission for Europe
UNESCO	UN Educational, Scientific and Cultural Organisation
USSR	Union of Soviet Socialist Republics
WTO	World Trade Organisation

ACKNOWLEDGEMENTS

This book represents an attempt to outline some key elements of a sociology of Europe relevant to the contemporary period. It has been a long time brewing, too long indeed, but certainly time enough for a large number of people, whether wittingly or not, to have provided me with input and/or support. I would like to put my debts to them on record here. *En passant*, hopefully, some of the main contexts and interests which have generated and informed the book will be indicated.

The book is grounded in an historical and internationalist view of sociology, which I wouldn't have developed if it hadn't been for the period I spent learning, researching and teaching at the LSE in the 1960s and early 1970s. The intellectual climate formed there at that time by the mix of continental European *émigrés*, American exiles and British pragmatists was very special. My doctoral supervisor, Ernest Gellner, was the main influence, but other influences included teachers such as the philosophers of science Karl Popper and Imre Lakatos, the political theorists Michael Oakeshott and Maurice Cranston, the critical social analysts Ralph Miliband and Leslie Sklair, and departmental colleagues such as John Westergaard, Alan Swingewood, and the classicist Keith Hopkins. I was grateful for the support of Jürgen Habermas and Hans-Georg Gadamer for the work that came out of this stage of my career. Since that time people in and around British sociology who have been interested in and helpful to my work on various writing projects, including this one, include Gerard Delanty, Tony Giddens, Bob Jessop, Philip Schlesinger, Bryan Turner and John Urry, together with cultural analysts Franco Bianchini, Ian Henry and Mike Robinson, and of course my Sage editor Chris Rojek.

After moving to Sheffield University I worked for some years on the sociology and social policy aspects of citizenship. By the mid-1990s I began to develop an explicit interest in Europe, both as a context of diverse versions of national citizenship and also, in the form of the European Union, as potentially offering a new transnational dimension to the development of modern citizenship. This interest happened to coincide with an increased profile for citizenship as a policy theme on the part of the European Union. My view of the potential theoretical and practical importance of European aspects of citizenship was confirmed and encouraged by participation in seminars involving the European Commission in Brussels and the Federal Trust in London, which involved meeting, among others, the academics François Duchene and Elizabeth Meehan and the politicians and administrators ex-Irish Taoiseach Garret Fitzgerald, Andrew Duff MEP, and Giuseppe Callovi of the European Commission, Directorate General Justice and Home Affairs.

On the basis of this and with the support of Peter Leisink and particularly Rik van Berkel at Utrecht University and also the Economic and Social

Research Council (ESRC) I created a European network in 1995 to study the potential relevance of citizenship theories and practices for social policy in a European context. We gained support from the European Union for two projects in 1998–2000 under the Research Framework 4 programme and, among other things, we worked on a comparative study of social inclusion, work and citizenship policies. This and related work generated various publications, including Roche and van Berkel (eds) (1997a), Roche and Annesley (eds) (2004), and van Berkel and Moller (eds) (2002). It also provided a rapid and focused introduction to a range of European cities and countries I might otherwise have taken much longer to get to know.

The network gave me the privilege and pleasure of getting to know and exchange ideas with many interesting colleagues from around Europe. These included our leading partners Thomas Faist (Bremen), Laurent Fraisse (Paris), Marisol Garcia (Barcelona), Liana Giorgi (Vienna), Matti Heikila (Helsinki), Pedro Hespanha (Coimbra), Enzo Mingione (Milan), Iver Moller (Copenhagen), Tapio Salonen (Lund), and Jacques Vilrokx (Brussels). They also included other members of the network and participants in our cycle of seminars, such as Alberta Andreotti, Sabine Dreher, Aitor Gomez, Henning Hansen, Haka Johansson, Yuri Kazepov, Elsa Keskitalo, Angelika Kofler, Jens Lind, Carlos Machado, Ana Matos, Ilya Mertens, Ronald Pohoryles, Sylvia Portugal, Jan de Schampheliere, David Smith, Cyril Tholen, Ben Valkenberg, and Enid Wistrich. Vital support was provided by our Sheffield coordinating group, Claire Annesley, Joanne Cook, Colin Williams and Jan Windebank, and the project benefited greatly from the interest and support of Ronan O'Brien in DG Research at the European Commission. The conferences with which we concluded our network projects, and at which we disseminated their reports, enabled us to hear from and exchange views with Duncan Gallie, Anton Hemerijk, Siofra O'Leary and Ruud Muffels, among others.

Although our social policy network was extensive, it did not include Eastern Europe and the 2004/07 enlargement of the EU underscored this omission. In relation to this in recent years I have worked with the Soros Foundation's higher education programme and also the European Cultural Foundation, particularly in southeastern Europe and particularly in the fields of general sociology, the sociology of culture and cultural policy. I have been privileged to meet colleagues and students in the Balkan and Black Sea countries of Bulgaria, Georgia, Romania, Serbia and Ukraine, who have stimulated and supported my interest in understanding European society and culture. These include Alexander Kiossev and Valentina Gueorgieva, my good hosts at St Kliment university in Sofia, Bulgaria and their colleagues Boyan Knepolski and Martin Ossikowski, among many others, together with Predrag Cveticanin and his colleagues at the University of Nis, Serbia.

Our social policy network also had not addressed European cultural and cultural policy issues. So in addition to my southeastern European work and inquiries, I organised an international conference on the European Public

Sphere with a group of Sheffield colleagues in 2004. This provided an opportunity to meet some of the community of researchers and scholars in this field. These included, among others, Florian Oberhuber (Vienna), Barbara Pfetsch (Hohenheim), Karen Rosenwerth (Dortmund), Slavko Splichal (Ljubljana), Marianne van der Steeg (Florence), and Renee van Os (Nijmegen), along with British-based researchers including, among others, Barrie Axford, Richard Huggins, Peter Humphreys, Anthony King, Donald McNeill, Peter Millward, Katherine Sarikakis, Cornell Sandvoss, Damien Tambini, and Mark Wheeler. Some of the papers have been developed for publication in Harrison and Wessels (eds) (2009 forthcoming).

This and other related activities in the field of European social and cultural studies have been supported by a range of people in Sheffield University in recent years. These include, among others, Sir Ian Kershaw, Peter Ainsworth, Harvey Armstrong, Ian Bache, Micheline Beaulieu, Max Craglia, Matt Flinders, Andrew Gamble, Andrew Geddes, Stephen George, Mike Kenny, Edmund King, Bill Leatherbarrow, David Luscombe, Jon Nixon, Dominic Shellard, Martin Smith, David Shepherd, Paul White and Yorick Wilks. On the administrative front they include Helen Rana, Lada Trifanova-Price, and Steph Davy-Jow, who worked on our European Social and Cultural Studies Centre project, the staff of the University's South East Europe Research Centre in Thessaloniki, and Gill Wells from the University's European research office. From my own department and related units they include particularly Bob Deacon, Dave Phillips, Alan Walker, Tony Warnes and also Richard Jenkins, and my much-missed ex-colleagues Alan France, Sharon Macdonald and Nick Stevenson. I would like to thank my department and its current head Clive Norris for sustaining study leave, research travel resourcing, research time in staff workloads and other such supports. These are absolutely necessary for long-term projects of research and scholarship to be undertaken in British universities these days. They need to be defended against the threats posed by the long-term disease of under-funding, which has afflicted the UK's higher education system for the last decade or more.

On a lighter note, unlike the British, continental Europeans discovered many years ago the benefits of 'café culture' to counter-balance and compensate the monasticism required by writing. A number of people have helped keep café culture alive for me in Sheffield over the years. These are particularly my ex-doctoral students Jackie Harrison, Neil Sellors and Chris Fiddler, and my departmental colleague Bridgette Wessels. Their views, reading suggestions, company and encouragement have helped me greatly on this project, and thanks to them for that. Of course none of them, nor any of the other people mentioned above, is in any way responsible for the accuracy of the book's information or the adequacy of the views expressed in it.

Finally, thanks to Jan Roche, Stephen Roche and Helen Roche for their patience and support for me over the years on this and other European projects.

LIST OF TABLES

1

APPROACHING EUROPEAN SOCIETY

Introduction

This book aims to introduce, to develop and to explore the sociology of Europe and this chapter, together with Chapter 2, sets the scene for this project. The book as a whole aims to make the case that we need a sociological perspective on Europe, if only to counter-balance and contextualise dominant and often misleading political and academic conceptions of Europe and of the European Union in particular, which reduce them to being mainly economic or international legal entities. However, the ground on which to develop such a sociological perspective has not yet been secured by the discipline. It has certainly not been well trodden and it remains significantly unexplored.

Evidently, Europe, even in its EU form, is not a nation-state, which is the dominant form taken by societies in the modern period. So maybe, then, it is not a society either, in which case there would be no basis on which to set out to develop a 'sociology of Europe'. Perhaps this is why, by comparison with other social science and historical disciplines which have developed active specialisms addressing the EU in particular, there has been little comparable effort of this kind in sociology, the discipline devoted to the study of 'societies'.[1] The first section (below) reflects on this negative view.

The book is organised into three parts concerned with Europe's societal history (Chapters 3 and 4), its development of nation-state-based societies (Chapters 5 and 6) and contemporary social change, particularly with respect to welfare and the social economy (Chapters 7 and 8). These will be previewed later in more detail (third main section below). First, it is necessary to review some of the senses in which both Europe and the EU can be reasonably conceptualised and studied as forms of 'society', and this review will be taken further in Chapter 2. There are some ambiguities and dualities about understanding Europe as a society, and these are recurrent features of this field. They will be reflected on throughout our discussion and two of them need to be recognised from the outset. First, there is the ambiguity that contemporary Europe is not identical to the international organisations claimed to represent it, particularly the EU. Secondly, there is the important ambiguity that the EU can be seen either as an aggregate of nation-state societies and their differences, or as a sphere of commonalities, although it cannot easily be seen as both of these things simultaneously. The commonalities view provides some ground for seeing Europe and/or the EU as forms of society, but the aggregate-of-differences view appears to provide little ground for this. Before we go much further we need to try to clarify these two ambiguities.[2]

In relation to the first duality between Europe and the EU, it is worth bearing in mind that in 2005 the EU contained only 27 member states (as of 2008). This was fewer than the total number of nation-state societies occupying the area of the European sub-continent (among others, Norway, Switzerland and various Balkan countries remain outside the EU), and it is fewer than other relevant international organisations such as the Council of Europe (47 member states, as of 2008). That said, the EU remains the most organisationally developed and influential project Europeans have ever generated in the modern period to create a legally integrated and operational corporate European entity, an entity which has both international and also transnational features. Given this, and also given the fact that the EU possesses an expansionary dynamic which is likely to lead to the incorporation of many of the remaining non-EU states on the sub-continent over the coming generation, it is not unreasonable to view the EU as being significantly representative both of the sub-continent's societies and of Europe's society more collectively. So, while recognising the difference between Europe and the EU throughout this book, it is intended, and indeed is inevitable, that this difference will also be elided at various points in the discussion.

In relation to the second and more consequential duality noted above, Europe has always presented an enigmatic Janus face to those seeking to reflect on it and understand it, certainly throughout the modern period but also in preceding periods. That is to say, on the one hand Europe has appeared as characterised by its commonalities, as for instance in the recurrently influential concept that Europe is a 'civilisation'. Indeed, from some perspectives, both objective and 'Eurocentric' perspectives, it has been the world's most important civilisation.[3] However, on the other hand it has also recurrently presented itself as little more than an aggregate of a variety of differences, whether ethnic, religious or national. Indeed, throughout the modern period it has regularly been an arena of often violent conflict over the (assumed) deep differences between its nation-states and their associated ideologies and collective identities.

This fundamentally dualistic character of Europe does not provide secure ground on which to base a claim that Europe is a society. 'The Europe of commonalities' might provide such a basis, but 'the Europe of differences' does not. So from the outset we need to be aware that the project of developing and exploring a sociology of Europe, of the kind undertaken in this book, must involve a willingness not only to navigate between, but also to live with, both aspects of this duality, which is a fundamental characteristic of Europe and of Europeans' experience of 'the social' in the sub-continent over two millennia. With this in mind, in the following two sections we begin to consider the positive view that Europe *is* a society and also what this might mean.

The first section looks at commonsensical (that is, everyday and administrative) senses in which it is meaningful to speak about Europe as a society. It then goes on to consider some more general sociological and social theoretical discourses on European society, and in doing so it argues that the potential sociology of Europe needs to be intellectually located in the context of the broader challenges facing contemporary sociology.

Arguably, the discipline of sociology in general is in a period of radical overhaul and renewal of its mission and its theoretical and substantive research agendas. To face the challenge of developing the new field of the sociology of Europe involves engaging with this 'renewal agenda'. The second section outlines an analytic framework to help conceptualise the work in this new sociological field, which is opened up in more detailed and substantive ways in the main parts of the book. This framework is concerned with societies understood in terms of structure and change, that is structurally as social formations (of what will later be referred to as 'societal dimensions' and 'deep structures'), and in terms of social change (understood as transformations of these structures through processes of modernisation, globalisation and associated Europeanisation). This sociological framework is applied throughout the book both in terms of its general intellectual strategy and also in terms of the questions and debates to which its various parts and chapters are designed to be responses and contributions. As such it provides a basis for the preview and outline of the structure and content of the book, which is then provided in the third section.

In this book, then, we are concerned, among other things, with sociological aspects of historical and contemporary processes of 'Europeanisation' in European nation-state societies.[4] Some of these processes derive from the special and powerful contemporary dynamics of EU integration, and others derive from various sources, including those of history and globalisation, which influence both European and non-European societies. To weight the discussion towards Europeanisation processes is not to underplay the persistence of the consequential European duality noted earlier, that is the persistence of a Europe characterised as much by its differences as by the commonalities with which they coexist. As indicated above, overall the discussion in this book aims to navigate between the two sides of this duality. To begin with, then, we can encounter commonsensical and social scientific views of Europe as a potential society (first main section), before turning to outline the more developed sociological framework which will be employed to structure and guide the book's discussion (second main section).

Perspectives on European Society

The idea that Europe in general and the EU as its core contemporary expression can be seen as being in some sense a 'society' has some credibility in both commonsensical and social scientific perspectives. However, by contrast, sociology, the discipline which claims the remit to study 'society', has had all too little to say explicitly about Europe.[5] So in this section we will do two things. On the one hand, we briefly note the non-sociological ways in which Europe and the EU can be credibly seen as a society together with the limitations of these views. And on the other hand, we briefly rehearse and reflect on the curiosity of sociology's traditional apparent indifference to Europe as a form of society.

'Commonsense' views of European society: everyday and administrative perspectives

Two non-sociological perspectives, which we can refer to as 'everyday' and 'administrative' perspectives, provide some initial positive views of the idea that Europe and the EU in particular can be seen as a society.[6]

An everyday perspective

From an everyday perspective a great range of categories of people across the EU member states interact with, or take account of the existence and relevance of, the EU in practical, routine and everyday ways. This is particularly so for people working in farming, in the fishing industry, or in the tourism, travel and transport industries, or who live in areas dominated by these industries. Periodic crises in these industries (involving such things as contagious diseases among animals, or the decline of fishing stocks, or safety and environmental problems in the tourism and transport industries), together with EU-level policies and actions to manage them, can be covered in the media across Europe and provide for cross-European public debate. Such crises also serve to shine a light on the extent of the routine cross-European interconnections and interdependencies which operate unnoticed or at least uncommented upon in non-crisis times.

An everyday pragmatic perspective which routinely takes account of the EU as part of 'the furniture of the social world' clearly is present in the life-world of members of all of the EU states which are involved in the euro currency system.[7] Currencies are an ineradicable element of production, of consumption and of many of the transactions of everyday life in market-oriented and capitalist societies. Such a perspective is also present across Europe in such organisations as local and regional public authorities, large multinational companies, universities and law firms, employers' organisations and trade unions, social movements and lobby groups. Indeed, many of these kinds of industries and organisations, either themselves or through their associations, have established bases in the heart of the EU policy-making system in Brussels, or they have access to cross-European networks which, in turn, have such bases.[8]

People in these spheres interact with the EU in ways not dissimilar to the ways they interact with national states and governments in a national society. In summary, many people across Europe routinely organise their activities with reference to the existence of the EU as a broadly legitimate authority which contributes to and regulates a significant part of their social environment and which provides them with sets of rules and resources, constraints and opportunities to consider, use or engage with in the course of their activities and projects. They do this irrespective of whether they are politically opposed to or supportive of particular EU policies or indeed the EU as a whole, in the same way that people routinely orient their actions to the existence of their state as a governance system without reference to their political view of particular national governments. Having said this, the everyday view is clearly limited. It is pragmatic and largely unreflective beyond a limited instrumentalism. Also, it is essentially partial and fragmented, and thus at best it implies a picture of European and EU society as an umbrella for a bewildering mosaic of specific groups and their spheres of interest and activity.

An administrative perspective

From an administrative perspective EU agencies such as Eurostat gather and interpret comparative social data derived from a range of official surveys conducted on an annual cycle in the 27 current EU member states on such things as employment, unemployment, income, family structures and household composition, political attitudes, gender and age inequalities, and so on. In the course of communicating this to publics, users, and the media across the EU they often refer to this information as being about 'European society'. This is comparable to the ways that official statistical administrators in nation-states publicise their information as being about national societies.

The administrative view addresses national societies as self-contained units and provides us with a picture of the EU and EU society both as an 'aggregate' of these units and also as an artificial domain characterised by the 'averages' which can be constructed between national datasets. Beyond this, such a perspective, consistently maintained over time, can either reveal or construct social trends (depending on one's epistemology) among European national societies. These cross-European trends can be interpreted to have potentially problematic medium- and long-term implications for the continent's national societies; European citizens and policy-makers can come to see themselves as facing common social problems. This is the case, for instance, in relation to such trends as the decline in fertility and population replacement rates, or the general ageing of the population (both of which we consider further in our discussion of European welfare and social policy in Chapters 6–8 later). The identification of such trends in aggregate European society can provide common topics of public and political debate across Europe and also incentives for European states to coordinate their policy responses, particularly through the EU.

However, neither the everyday perspective nor the administrative perspective on Europe as a potential society provides for a perception and understanding of the EU as containing elements such as a common cultural identity, an integrated social structure, and an intra and intergenerational socialisation and social transmission system, which are among the elements typically taken, particularly in the discipline of sociology, to characterise what counts as a 'society'. Before we consider aspects of the sociological view of Europe further we can briefly turn to some of the various reflective but non-sociological views of Europe that are present in other social scientific and humanities disciplines.

Disciplinary perspectives on European society: humanities and social sciences

The sociological framework outlined later (second main section) recognises societies as having a number of dimensions, each of which can be the object of particular social science and humanities studies. Thus sociological perspectives on societies need to remain open to and informed by a range of disciplinary studies. Indeed, it can offer some elements of a more integrated perspective (a 'meta-perspective') capable of contributing substantially to the intellectual coherence of the multi- and interdisciplinary studies needed by multidimensional social complexes and processes in the contemporary period.

Humanities disciplines, such as history and also archaeology, have tended to present a picture of Europe as at least a long-evolving, continent-wide arena of interconnected social movements and institution-building projects, including religion-, nation- and empire-building projects. Europe's commonalities– differences duality is represented in history, on the one hand, by the differentiating and fragmenting visions of Europe which are dominant in the discipline and which are generated by national histories and event histories (e.g. wars). On the other hand, the commonalities view is represented by histories which take a Europe-wide view, by comparative history, and also by thematic histories of processes, which need to be tracked in their impacts and effects as reaching across many societies (e.g. plague, war, and technology).[9] With C.W. Mills, I believe that 'the historical imagination' is critical to any conception of 'the sociological imagination'.

While this is always an important aspect in the study of national societies, it is, for reasons to discussed later (Chapter 2), absolutely essential when approaching the study of European society and the EU. With this in mind, in Part 1 of the book we explore the historical territory in more detail by discussing the main forms, stages and factors in the long-term development of European society, both in its commonalities and its differences.

From a social sciences perspective, the disciplines of, for instance, political science and economics have generated substantial traditions of research and analysis of the EU as an economic system and as a political system, respectively.[10] In particular, political science has generated analyses which see Europe, particularly the EU, as an aggregate of national differences (e.g. 'intergovernmentalist' perspectives on the EU) as well as more integrative views which see Europe in terms of its commonalities and which see the EU in particular as one form or another of supra-national project (e.g. 'functionalist' perspectives). In recent years political science has reanimated the differences view of Europe by tracking the national state and citizenship-building of the post-communist societies of Eastern Europe.[11] And, together with legal studies, it has reanimated the commonalities view by taking seriously the challenges presented by globalisation and world regionalisation to European societies.[12]

Given that societies are composed at least of economic and political systems together with their interconnections, then it is reasonable to assume that these disciplines imply that an EU society exists even if they do not explicate this assumption. However, these social sciences and related views are, by definition, discipline-specific and tend to be intellectually disconnected. This produces a fragmented image of the EU as a set of decontextualised (economic, political and other) structures and processes. The social whole addressed by these perspectives is difficult to see as adding up to more than the sum of the parts. Compared with this, in principle, the discipline of sociology has as part of its mission to provide analyses which draw on and integrate a range of social sciences perspectives, including aspects of the political and the economic. It has traditionally done this for national societies, and in recent decades has done something similar for 'global society', but it has until recently had little to say about Europe in these respects, as we note next.

Sociology and Europe

From its inception in late nineteenth-century intellectualism and academy-building, one of the most important tools of the sociologist's trade could be said to be the concept of 'society'.[13] Against all of the disintegrative tendencies of our times, this concept appears to continue to make sense and to be applicable at local, national and even 'world' levels. Nonetheless evidently it appears to remain an enigma when applied to social organisation on the sub-continent of Europe, in spite of the social reality of the everyday and administrative experiencs and recognitions of European-level social organisation noted earlier. If nothing which can be defined as 'European society' can be said to exist, whether as fact or as potential, then there is little justification or incentive for sociologists to attempt to develop a sociology of Europe in general or a sociology of the European Union in particular.

However, against this, it might be argued that of course sociology has long been and remains committed to the study and understanding of European societies. For a start, every European nation-state has long been scrutinised and analysed at the very least by its own 'homegrown' sociological professionals and communities. Surely, then, it can be reasonably argued that, at the very least, the aggregation of all of these studies and professions constitutes a 'de facto', 'in principle', sociology of Europe? In addition, and more convincingly, there are the long-standing and well-developed fields of comparative empirical sociology and comparative social policy analysis.[14] Each of these has often taken European societies as its main field of study. Surely the comparative and empirical study of different forms of industrial and post-industrial state-capitalist, 'welfare-regime' and 'welfare capitalist' social formation among European countries amounts to a 'de facto' sociology of Europe and of 'European society' such as it is? In addition to this, what about the more qualitative and case study-based studies of particular urban, regional, migratory and national cultures in Europe, the studies of Europe's borderlands and its cosmopolitan cities and so on, which are collected by anthropologists, social geographers and other varieties of sociologically-relevant social scientist?[15]

No doubt there is something to be said for all of these kinds of activity amounting to a 'de facto' sociology of Europe. However, even if this is so, the field still awaits a clear conceptualisation and theoretical development (see below and later). And in any case it suffers from two notable weaknesses. First, it remains largely theoretically tied to the nation-state as the prime unit of analysis, and thus to an aggregative conception of 'European society' as a secondary unit of analysis. Secondly, and possibly with the exception of post-communist sociological interest in Eastern Europe's 'new nations' and their institutional 'policy culture' connections with the EU, it tends to minimise, and indeed often ignore altogether, the existence and impacts of the European Union as a social organisation, together with its integration and Europeanisation dynamics on European nation-states and national societies, within the EU, on neighbouring societies at its eastern and southern borders, and as a collective actor more widely in contemporary global society (see Chapters 2 and 8).

Unlike political science and economic analyses of the EU, which as we have noted have both developed strongly in recent years, the 'sociology of the EU' still barely exists as an enterprise and a field.[16] For instance, in the sociological community of at least one EU member state, namely the UK, research interest has been low in recent years. Compared with the plethora of variously constituted 'European Studies' higher education programmes, the UK has relatively few courses of study in the Sociology of Europe. In 1998–2000 the UK's main state-funded social sciences research agency ran a major interdisciplinary research programme studying Europe (namely the ESRC's 'One Europe or Many Europes?' programme). Compared with other disciplines, such as politics, the sociological interest in and contribution to this programme was minimal. Why this is the case is a bit of a mystery. Evidently it is not at all because sociologists are disinterested in life beyond the nation-state – witness their rapid colonisation of the study of the phenomenon of globalisation.[17] However, perhaps sociology's 'rush to globalisation' is part of the problem. Things that are 'in between' the national and global levels, things like Europe, tend to get bypassed. While the references to Europe and the EU in globalisation literature often sound interested and positive, they are also usually very brief and insubstantial – they are 'EU *en passant*'.[18] That said, clearly globalisation is of great significance for a sociological understanding of contemporary Europe and the EU, and we return to this later.

European public attitudes to the EU have evidently changed over time. Currently, there is Europe-wide public and political ambivalence, ranging from passively positive attitudes to indifference to scepticism – scepticism about the costs EU integration appears to bring, financial costs in particular but also the EU's much criticised democratic and legitimacy deficits. This has mounted in recent years to an unprecedented full-blown crisis for the EU in the 2005–09 period. French and Dutch publics rejected the proposed EU Constitutional Treaty in national referenda in 2005, and the Irish public did the same to the successor version, the Reform Treaty, in 2008. We will come back to this ambivalent public mood later (Chapter 9), however perhaps it has operated to undermine sociologists' interest in the field. In countries like the UK in particular, the long-standing and unrelenting anti-European prejudice of the bulk of the national press could possibly have added to academics' ambivalence. Or, less prejudicially, perhaps sociologists have come to acquiesce in some of the public perceptions of the EU as an impenetrably complex entity, most often distant and irrelevant but occasionally, and in unpredictable and excessive ways, intrusive into people's everyday lives.

Having noted contemporary mainstream sociology's traditional nation-state-centrism and its relative indifference to Europe, however, we can also observe that the field is slowly beginning to be recognised and developed both in particular areas, such as work, employment and the welfare state, and also more generally. Some of the new developments beginning to contribute to the sociology of Europe (noted above and see Chapter 9) draw in various ways from social theory, which can be understood as a broader intellectual tradition than that of sociology as such. This tradition includes, for instance, the reflection on, analysis and critique of Western (effectively at the time European) modernity and industrial capitalist society which was initiated in the late 19th century by seminal European intellectuals such as Karl Marx, Max Weber and Emile Durkheim, and developed both in liberal and in critical directions by successive generations worldwide in the 20th century. In this intellectual tradition, whether directly or indirectly, social formations beyond the nation-state (including world and European society), together with historical periods beyond the present (particularly in European history), have always received due attention. The recent sociologically-informed studies of Europe draw on this tradition in their various analysis of Europe as a complex social formation and as one which has been constructed and reconstructed by long-term forces of social change, and the discussion of Europe in this book aims to do the same.

Sociology's recent interest in the key phenomenon of social change in the contemporary period, namely globalisation, together with the reflection on its implications both for nation-state societies and for Europe, has developed in its interface with social theory. It is at this interface also that the challenges to mainstream conceptions of society and its analysis posed by the various 'post'- developments arguably associated with globalisation – namely post-modernism in culture, post-industrialism and post-Fordism in the economy, and post-nationalism in politics – have accumulated. Reflection on these challenges implies the need for a far-reaching 'post-societal' renewal of the field and enterprise of sociology (e.g. Urry 2000). This can be referred to as contemporary sociology's 'renewal agenda'.[19] The new sociologies of Europe noted above recognise and respond to this 'renewal agenda' to one degree or another. My discussion in this book concurs with this view and aims to approach European society in a similar spirit. Bearing in mind the resources of the social theory tradition and related intellectual traditions, we now need to turn to a more direct, if necessarily schematic, outline of some key concepts needed for understanding contemporary Europe as a society from a sociological perspective.

A Sociological Perspective on Europe: Elements of a 'Social Complex' Framework

Perspectives on Europe, such as the everyday and the administrative, and even the multidisciplinary and the '*en passant*' perspectives of much sociology encountered above, only take us so far. To adequately approach the task of understanding Europe as a society a general sociological perspective needs to be developed. This needs to have the capacity to grasp the historical and institutional commonalities, the differences and unavoidable complications, of a sub-continental social world crowded with nation-state societies, each of them highly self-conscious about their histories and collective identities. In this section, then, the particular framework of concepts to be deployed in this book, which can be referred to as a 'social complex' perspective, will be briefly outlined in general terms. In the following section, the particular selection of aspects of European society to be covered in the book's chapters will be outlined and the relevance of the perspective to this will be indicated. The potential of the analytic framework for understanding Europe and also the EU as a special social organisation attempting to orchestrate European society will be considered in Chapter 2 and its normative implications will be reprised in the final chapter (Chapter 9).

The 'social complex' perspective on my interpretation is one which derives in part from classical and mainstream sociology, but which is also intended to be sensitive to sociology's contemporary renewal agenda noted in the previous section.[20] It addresses society in terms of structure and change, accepting that structural analysis (cross-sectional, synchronic analysis) is an abstraction from the historical (diachronic) flow of social reality addressed in the study of social change. Also, in spite of its necessarily summary (and thus structure-emphasising) appearance, the perspective aims to be aware of the pervasive influence of agency and context in all social affairs.

Social structure: In relation to social structure, this perspective sees 'society' as a multidimensional social complex or 'social formation' of economic, cultural and political dimensions. Taking the concept of 'social formation' as the main unit of analysis enables sociology to engage not just with the forms of 'society' it is most familiar with, namely nationally organised societies, but also with the more complicated and looser structures which increasingly populate the international arena in our times, for instance networks of states and non-governmental organisations – whether at the level of 'global society', or, of particular relevance to understanding the EU, at the level of Europe. In addition, the concepts of social formation and social complex also aim to take account of some less routinely identified contexts and infrastructures involved in the existence and operation of societies and of individual and collective social agents, namely the social contexts (or what we will refer to as the 'deep social structures') of time, space and technology.

Social change: In relation to social change, the perspective takes the view that social transformation involves complex combinations and shifting balances of dimensional (economic, cultural and political) and contextual deep structural (time, space and technology) factors and dynamics. It also takes the view that social transformation is endemic in societies in the modern era. This is currently readily recognised outside sociology in the wider world of public discourse and international politics by virtue of the categorisation of societies as 'developing' in some cases, as 'post-communist' in others, and as 'transitional' in each case. However, going beyond this, the perspective suggests that it is useful to regard *all* societies throughout the modern era, and certainly in the contemporary period, as having been, and as remaining, in what amounts to being a permanent state of 'transition'. With this in mind, this book focuses on the influence of general and all-pervasive processes of modernisation and of globalisation on European social formations,' arguing for the usefulness and relevance of understanding Europe's nations and the continent's international configurations as forms of 'transitional society', not only because they are modern forms compared with pre-modern forms, but also because of their dynamics within the modern era.

Overall, then, this book's analysis aims to provide an outline understanding of the nature of, and interconnections between, on the one hand, European social formations (together with their dimensional complexes and deep structural contexts) and on the other hand processes of social transformation in contemporary Europe, particularly those of modernisation and globalisation. This develops a picture of European society in its differences and commonalities as both a complex of transitional societies and also as a transitional social formation as a whole. The rest of this section outlines these concepts and the framework further in general terms, first in relation to social formations (first dimensions and then contexts) and, secondly, in relation to social transformations.

Social formations: societal dimensions and deep social structures

Societal dimensions: economy, polity and culture

Classical and mainstream sociology and social theory developed by addressing and attempting to understand the nation-state-based forms of society and large-scale social organisation which were constructed in the course of the modernisation process, particularly from the mid-19th century, and particularly with respect to their economic or socio-economic aspects as industrial and capitalist societies. From these perspectives, societies were ultimately more or less well-integrated complexes of three key 'societal dimensions', namely economies, polities and cultures, typically contained within, and indeed significantly constructed by, nation-state societies. A societal dimension can be conceived as a particular sphere of institutions and interaction, together with a particular form of social inequality and division among people, and related forms of systemic interconnections ('divisions of labour') between them. In the economy, the institutions, interactions and inequalities take form in terms of economic production and consumption, property ownership and market exchange. In the polity, they take form in terms of power and authority, or the lack of it, within regimes or states, and particularly in modernity terms of the nation-state. In the culture, they take form in terms of meanings and identities, values and symbols, and generally in the media and forms of communication.

This kind of dimensional analysis of the institutional differentiations of modern social structure originated in the late 19th century in 'classical' era sociology and political economy, although the founding figures of the discipline no doubt had different interpretations of the nature of, linkage between and priority among these societal dimensions. Societal structures of identity and difference, and the social divisions and inequalities of the major social categories of class that they analysed, together with the social divisions of gender and ethnicity that subsequent generations of sociology analysed, can be conceived in terms of aspects of each dimension. For instance, social classes undoubtedly have political and cultural aspects, but may be analysed as particularly grounded in the economic dimension, while gender and ethnic groups, identities and relationships undoubtedly have political and economic aspects, but can be usefully seen as being grounded in a broad understanding of the cultural dimension (particularly the persistence in modernity of traditional familial and religious organisation).

Deep social structures: time, space and technology [21]

The concepts of social structure and social formation we are developing here need to be filled out with a concept of 'deep social structures' if we are to adequately address the particular and complex characteristics of Europe and European society. Faced with this task, sociological perspectives on Europe need to be kept open and oriented to the contributions of other and additional social sciences and humanities perspectives on Europe, not only those of economic studies, political studies and cultural studies, relating to the societal dimensions, but also as those of history and human geography, and of relevant studies of the social uses and impacts of science and technology. The concept of 'deep social structures', and the focus on time, space and technology contexts in particular, is intended to provide a basic framework for the development of the sort of multi- and interdisciplinarity needed by a sociological perspective on Europe, and is applied particularly in the historical sociological discussions of the development of European society in Chapters 3, 4 and 5.

'Deep social structures' refer to some of the basic general life-world conditions which make human social life both comprehensible and viable. For the purposes of our discussion of European society in this book we can focus on three core conditions, namely time, space and technology. These can be understood as being pervading influences on and conditions of humans' social existence at all social levels, from the interpersonal, through the institutional to the systemic and societal. At the interpersonal and institutional level they contribute to our understanding of the conditions and resources required for action, and for personal and collective agency in general. At the societal level, in combination with the analysis of societal dimensions, they contribute to what is required to understand both commonalities between national societies and also more developed multinational formations such as those referenced in sociological (rather than normative) conceptions of societal 'civilisation' (see later Chapter 3).

Deep social structures can be understood descriptively in objective, physical and 'material cultural' terms. Thus the contexts of time, space and technology can be illustrated for societies in the modern era by the environments and resources provided respectively by such things as cemeteries and clock-towers, border posts and railways, electricity generating stations and internal combustion engines – the multiplicity of such things are collected together in collective perceptions and understandings of landscapes and cityscapes as environments of social life and activity. In addition to pervasively constituting 'the furniture of the world' in this way, these basic social contexts and the materialities which exemplify them need to be understood as having both symbiotic and also symbolic relations with the structures and agencies of societal dimensions which they contextualise.

First, in terms of symbiotic relations, this is one way of understanding what might be meant by the common sociological view that basic social contexts such as time, space and technology are 'socially constructed'. That is, in addition to their pervasively constitutive role, key elements of them (and thus of the deep structural complex as a whole) are reciprocally continuously recon-structed by particular dimensional (political, economic and cultural) and inter-dimensional actions and effects (see 'social transformations' below). Secondly, in terms of symbolic relations, deep social structures can be seen as 'cultural constructs' of importance to societies' processes of producing and adapting versions of collective identity. That is, conceptions and versions of time, space and technology can be key elements of the overarching worldviews, dis-courses and ideologies with which sociological understanding has to engage and dialogue, and which are generated by elites and communities in the course of processes and struggles to reproduce, resist or change dominant societal self-understandings.

From a social perspective, *time* refers to the overarching context within which we can understand such things as the temporality of all action; social structuring and reproduction through events and calendars, intragenerational identity reproduction and the management of the succession of life-events in the cycle of ageing; intergenerational relations, cultural inheritance and trans-mission, and societal reproduction; and the consciousness and influence of history within and between long-term periods and eras.[22] From a social perspective, *space* refers to the overarching context for actors and their social organisations, in which the existential facts of human embodiment, mobility and locatedness are to the fore, and thus the real, imagined and virtual spaces and places which are necessarily associated with these facts. In terms of social construction, space refers to such things as familiar places (homes and home territories) and unfamiliar places; the built environments of cities; human-influenced but apparently 'natural' physical environments and landscapes; and the organisation of mobility within and between built and 'natural' environments.[23] It also refers to the human and social life-sustaining and life-threatening features of physical environments and habitats. From a social perspective, *technology* refers to a particular aspect of the social organisation and process of 'power', that is to the instrumentally rational social organisation of the means, the intellectual and material resources, which are required for effective actions and projects of all types, at all social levels and by all types of social agencies, in particular social complexes. Technology-as-power refers to the combination of the potential uses of material technologies together with the actual types of competences and uses associated with them and which are characteristic of particular human communities.[24]

Each of these deep structures can be seen to be relevant both to the characterisation and understanding of the three societal dimensions (i.e. particularly economically, or politically or culturally-oriented forms of the social organisation of time and space, and of the uses of technologies), and also to the understanding of the linkages and environments of their interdimensional relations (general, e.g. 'civilisational', aspects of social time, space and technology). In addition, the deep structures of time, space and technology are only analytically distinguishable; in concrete social and historical reality they can be understood as being interconnected in many ways. For instance, perceptions of time and space can be both interconnected by the nature of the contemporary technologies of transport and also of communication, and, without acceding to an over-simplistic technological determinism, we can acknowledge that such time–space connections can be altered by changes in transport and communications technologies.

Just as we need to understand the deep structural aspects of social formations in interconnected ways, as interstructural relations at the deep structural level of social complexes, we need to do the same with interdimensional relations for the institutional and dimensional level of social complexes. Interdimensional relations have been analysed from within mainstream sociological perspectives in mainly nation-statist ways ('methodological nationalism') and in functionalist ways. This can be seen fairly explicitly in a range of areas of sociology, not least in the sociology and social history of nationalism and nation-state and welfare states.[25] Interdimensional relations have also come to be analysed in sociology and social theory in more open and flexible ways, focusing on such topics and concepts as 'civil society', 'the public sphere', 'citizenship', and 'cosmopolitanism'.[26] Work which focuses on these sorts of interdimensional topic has tended to be more open, particularly to understanding social formations in terms which reach beyond the nation-state model and its assumptions, in particular in terms deriving from concern for the influence of global-level factors. The project to explore European society as, among other things, a complex social formation characterised by interdimensional dynamics and relations can benefit from reflecting on the work undertaken in recent sociology and related disciplines to apply such concepts in a European context, and we do this periodically throughout the book.

Finally, social complexes, as matrices of actual and possible relationships within and between social dimensions and deep structures, have been at times conceptualised in sociology (both in post-war sociology and also in recent sociology and social theory) in ways which go beyond the nation-state model and which take account of international and transnational levels and experiences. This is so, for instance, in studies of topics such as 'inter-societal systems', 'network society', 'the post-national constellation' and 'civilisations'. Each of these topics has been used to characterise and analyse Europe as a social formation, and we aim to refer to and draw on these kinds of analytical resources at appropriate points as we develop the discussion in the main body of the book.[27]

However, it remains the case that the analysis of social formations involves abstraction from the realities of the flow and change of real societies in history. The various social dimensions and social contexts connect with each other in social reality in these processes of social transformation. So, to develop the framework for exploring and developing a sociology of Europe further, we need to consider the nature of relevant forms of social transformation next in general terms.

Social transformation: modernisation, globalisation and transition

A sociological perspective which aims to understand Europe as a society, as we have indicated in the discussion so far, needs to develop a conception of society as both a complex social formation, involving key societal dimensions (of polity, economy and culture) and social contexts (time, space and technology), and also one which is continuously in the process of transformation. Before seeing how this perspective can provide a conceptual framework for the studies of European society covered in this book a little more needs to be said about the transformation aspect. Contemporary society, not least in Europe, can be seen as the product of two major transformations, namely those of modernisation and globalisation. The discipline of sociology was created in the late 19th century largely to address and comprehend the nature and implications of modernisation. And it is currently being challenged in comparable terms by the imperative need to understand and assess the social implications of the process of globalisation. So, to approach the analysis of Europe as a society, it is necessary first, drawing on an historical sociology approach, to briefly consider the general nature of social transformations, and then to look at modernisation and globalisation transformation processes in particular.

On the basis of the discussion of 'social formations' in the previous section, we can suggest that in general terms 'social transformations' can be said to involve complex combinations and shifting balances of dimensional (economic, cultural and political) and deep structural (time, space and technology) factors and dynamics. Social transformation is endemic in societies in the modern era. Outside sociology, in public and political discourse, this pervasiveness of change is currently recognised for some societies in the contemporary international order in their categorisation as being 'developing' and for others as being 'post-communist' societies, both thereby being identified as types of 'transitional' society. However, a sociological perspective which is adaptable to understanding European society would suggest that all societies throughout the modern era, and certainly in the contemporary period, have been and remain effectively in permanent 'transition'. So, first, sociology's general field of study is principally that of types of 'transitional society' and, secondly, this applies particularly to European society. This underlines the importance of an historical sociological approach to the development of the sociology of Europe.[28]

Modernisation [29]

The social transformations of 'modernisation' characterised the development of Western European societies from at least the 18th to the 20th centuries, and they continue to characterise Eastern European societies currently (not least in their recently renewed processes of sovereign nation-state institutionalisation and industrial capitalist economic development). As such it provided classical and mainstream sociology not only with its basic field of study, but also with its great challenge and stimulus as a phenomenon not only, analytically, to map and explain, but also, normatively, to critique and seek to influence.

Modernisation involved 'revolutions' (albeit 'long revolutions' to use Raymond Williams' useful expression[30]) in medieval and traditional social formations both within and between the three societal dimensions. Within the dimensions, long revolutions occurred in polities (to generate nation-states with increasingly influential legal systems and citizen communities), in economies (to generate, beyond subsistence agriculture, nationally organised mercantile capitalist and then industrial capitalist production and consumption systems), and in cultures (to generate common cultural worlds (mono-cultures) of language, literacy and value which would be open to the power of nationalist politics and industrial capitalist economic life). The implications of this for the relations between the societal dimensions was profound, in that they became significantly differentiated from each other in new legal and institutional ways, in addition to then being reconnected in new ways, in the course of the modernisation process in nation-state societies.

In addition, modernisation's dimensional 'long revolutions', both separately and taken as a whole, involved the transformation of medieval social contexts. The modernisation of social contexts conveyed a new nation-state-based social an organisation and cultural valuation of time, space and technology, an organisation and valuation which better reflected and facilitated the ideologies, aspirations and further development of such societies, particularly in economic and industrial capitalist terms. Modernity's national society-building projects involved the development of nation-centric and nationalistic versions of the societal contexts of time, space and technology, particularly those aspects of the contexts apparently within the control (real or aspirational) of nations (for instance, their own territories, their own histories, and their own material infrastructures and technological resources). While these processes of national cultural construction can provide insights into national societies, they can also obscure the way in which the contexts understood more generally have operated, have been perceived by other nations, and are relevant for the understanding of all of them in the transition to modernity. Further, they can obscure the extent to which, over the course of this transition, the deep structural contexts in general have been interpreted and influenced by international and now globalising forms of social action and social process.

Globalisation[31]
Globalisation can be seen as a particular form of modernisation, occurring in the 'late modern' or even 'post-modern' period and as involving developments which can either be regarded as taking modernisation trends to new levels ('hyper-modernisation') or as taking them beyond, and thereby undermining, the paradigm of modernity altogether ('post-modernisation'). Globalisation is argued to have begun to become a dominant vector of modern social development particularly in the late 20th century, although some would argue that it has been an underlying trend within the modernisation process from the very beginning, albeit one long unrecognised and only now becoming visible. Arguably, globalisation involves developments and transformations in the key societal dimensions and social contexts which theoretically differentiates it from, and practically takes it beyond, the social formations produced by the more familiar processes of 'modernisation'. These include developments in the societal dimensions, and also in associated aspects of the social contexts, which can be expressed both in positive terms and also in the more negative 'post'-modern terms of 'post-nationalism', 'post-industrialism' and 'post-modernism' in the political, economic and cultural dimensions, respectively.

More positively, then, globalisation has been associated in the political dimension with a ('post-national') willingness on the part of most nation-states to constrain and even subject their erstwhile 'sovereign' power and authority in relation to transnational forms of civil society and the rule of law (law emanating, for instance, from world regional international alliances, from global-level governance organisations, in particular the United Nations, and from the theory and practice of universal human rights). In the economic dimension, globalisation has been associated with a (post-industrial) development of a new kind of information and service-based economy in the context both of new communication and transport systems and of the new organisation of economic forces, resources and spaces of capitalism and markets at the global level which they make possible. In the cultural dimension, globalisation has been associated with the ('post-modern') cultural implications of (and also with anti-modern and reactions to and rejections of) such developments as, on the one hand, the spread of consumer culture associated with economic globalisation and new communications technologies, and, on the other hand, the moral and political secularism and universalism associated with political globalisation.

Expressed in terms of the transformation of social contexts, the modernisation process involved (and continues to involve) not only profound dimensional changes but also related changes in the social organisation and cultural representation of time, space and technology. Comparably, globalisation can be argued to simultaneously qualitatively intensify and extend modernisation's deep structural changes. Thus globalisation can be said to have impacts such as 'compressing' the personal and social experience of space and time, and accelerating the pace of technological innovation and its diffusion, in all of the world's societies in ways which are both historically unprecedented and also difficult to adapt to and to control.

Globalisation's ongoing impacts on nation-state societies and their familiar patterns of interdimensional and intercontext connections have been and continue to be potentially profoundly destabilising. National polities, economies and cultures, together with the national organisation of time, space and technology, all of which characterise nation-state societies and their core institutions, are under threat from the pervasive disintegrative influence of dimensional and contextual dynamics increasingly organised at, and reflecting interests and power at, the global level. In addition, interdimensional relations in the social formation at the global level are themselves relatively disintegrated, with economic globalisation currently proceeding at a faster rate than (and thus effectively 'out of control of') political globalisation and governance at a global level. This contributes extra destabilising aspects to the impact of globalisation on national societies.

Contemporary transformations and transitional societies: globalisation, 'glocalisation' and (world) regionalism

Globalisation cannot be understood without appreciating the degree to which it renders all established social formations and societies as 'transitionary societies' and indeed stimulates the construction of new social formations. This is particularly so in relation to the two globalisation-based processes of 'glocalisation' and (world)-'regionalism', each of which is relevant to understanding contemporary Europe as a field of social transformation involving transitionary societies at national, sub-national and continent-wide levels.

'Glocalisation'[32] is the other side of the coin of globalisation, understood as a standardising and homogenising force, and is a response to it. Glocalisation, as an aspect of globalisation, involves the reconstruction of national and sub-national societies as locally distinctive elements within the overall emerging global 'division of labour' and social formation. This local distinctiveness can take particularly economic and cultural forms. Economically, nations and sub-national regions, faced with the forces involved in the development of global-level markets and economic coordination, tend to seek to identify and develop their potential for corporate comparative economic advantage as productive and trading entities within this emerging environment, in terms of specialisation in particular economic sectors. Comparable with this, culturally (and also in terms of the cultural industry of international tourism), nations and sub-national regions tend to respond to conditions of cultural globalisation by doing something similar. That is they tend to renew and further develop the special and distinctive aspects of their cultural identities through social and economic investment in their place-specific material culture, involving such things as architecture, cityscapes and landscapes, and their history-specific public and performative culture, involving such things as commemorative and festive events. In these terms, glocalisation dynamics help to contribute to the contemporary forms taken by the 'Europe of differences' and the continuing processes of national and sub-national differentiation of societies within Europe.

On the other hand, there is the stimulus globalisation arguably gives to 'regionalism',[33] that is the formation of world regional international associations and organisations of states and other corporate actors. We have suggested that globalisation has destabilising and at least initially disintegrative impacts on nation-state societies. This generalisation might be qualified by adding 'other than for actual or emerging 'superpowers' (notably the USA and China, respectively)' which retain significant potential for unilateral action. Given this, and with the exception of superpowers, it is understandable that groups of neighbouring states might decide to explore the potential for agreements between them which might limit these forces and impacts. While some approaches see world regionalism as some sort of alternative process distinct from globalisation, in my view, and in the view of the perspective outlined here, it is better seen as an important version and expression of globalisation, albeit an ambiguous one containing the potential to interpret and channel globalisation geopolitically in terms of a possible 'multi-polar world order'.[34]

In terms of sociology's 'renewal agenda', then, key new sociological questions relate to the degree to which globalisation forces and factors have in fact generated and/or have the capacity to generate this new intermediate level and form of social organisation. This level is 'transnational' from the perspective of nation-state societies but is another, albeit grander, version of 'local' from a global perspective. 'World regional social formations', then, mediate between national and global social formations and share some of each of their characteristics. In the contemporary period, efforts are being made across a number of continents and world regions to create such organisations, for instance Africa (AU), Asia (ASEAN), Latin America (MERCUSOR), and North America (NAFTA). These efforts can be said to testify to the notion that there is a systemic logic in the processes of globalisation which makes it likely that sooner or later more substantial patterns of world regionalism will appear in the world social order.

The sociological perspective we have outlined here, and will develop further in Chapter 2 (also see Chapter 9), aims to contribute to developing a sociology of Europe. It is animated by the general contemporary interest in the discipline of sociology and relatedly of social theory to renew themselves in relation to the new analytic and normative challenges posed by contemporary 21st-century social realities and social change. Central among these challenges are those connected with the social transformational influences of globalisation, together with the related influences of disintegration, reconstruction and glocalisation. Europe is an important arena for engaging with these challenges. In particular, it can be argued that globalisation and its dynamics are being refracted in the European context through the influence of the European Union, and we will look further into these issues at various points throughout this book (particularly Chapters 2, 7, 8 and 9). The EU can be argued to operate both to filter and to steer the forces and dynamics of particularly economic globalisation on behalf of member states. In addition, in terms of the political dimension, the EU arguably represents a significant attempt to develop a new level of political organisation relevant to the new situation created by globalisation's economic power to overwhelm national economies. That is it represents an experiment to achieve a relevant degree of political and social organisation at a level intermediate between the national and global levels, namely at a world-regional or continental level. As such, the EU, understood as an experiment,[35] potentially carries lessons for nation-states in other world regions which are currently embarking on the exploration of albeit more speculative and embryonic forms of international association-building. Globalisation dynamics pressure national societies to become 'transitional societies' characterised by simultaneously ever more 'glocal' and also ever more 'world-regional' forms of adaptation. In European terms, this means the simultaneous intensification in the contemporary period, particularly through the EU and its Europeanisation pressures, of Europe's traditionally dualistic character as a 'Europe of differences' and a 'Europe of commonalities'. The sociological framework which has been outlined here is applied to the European social complex in the course of the discussion in this book, and we can now indicate the ground this discussion covers.

Exploring the European social complex: an overview of the book

The book is structured into three main parts, each containing two chapters. In addition, two introductory chapters (this chapter and Chapter 2 following) set the scene, and a final chapter summarises some of the main analytic themes and considers their normative implications (Chapter 9). The introductory chapters outline some relevant concepts and framework which, among others, can be used to analyse Europe sociologically. As indicated above, they include the concepts of the social complex and its dimensional and deep structural aspects, together with the concepts of social change and their global, glocal and regional dynamics. In Chapter 2 these are applied to European society and illustrated in terms of seeing the European complex as, on the one hand, a network society and, on the other, a new type of empire.

Part 1 is concerned with taking an historical sociological overview of the long historical development of the European social complex from the pre-modern to the modern era, in order to understand the origins and development of European society's dualistic character as a complex of commonalities and of differences. It begins by addressing the pre-modern commonalities of Greek, Roman and Christian forms of 'civilisation' and their imperial and feudal forms of social organisation (Chapter 3). It then moves on to begin to focus on understanding the European social complex in modernity and in terms of a Europe of differences, which occupies the following three chapters. This differentiated aspect of the modern European complex is initially engaged with by addressing the nature and development of nationalism and national citizenship (Chapter 4).

Part 2 takes the analysis of the development of the European social complex in the modern era as a 'Europe of differences' further. It addresses the growth in Europe of a system of distinct nation-states which were initially constructed around the waging of war (Chapter 5), and which were later organised to promote of welfare among their national communities (Chapter 6). It considers the relevance of war and also of cultural factors in particular national religions to the development of European welfare states. It also observes the development in Europe of distinct forms and aspects of national citizenship particularly connected with war and welfare.

Part 3 is concerned with understanding social change in the EU-orchestrated European complex and particularly in that aspect of it concerned with welfare. It first considers general contemporary social changes influencing Europe and promoting common kinds of social risks and problems, particularly socio-demographic, globalisation-based and post-industrial developments (Chapter 7). It then goes on to consider the nature of the common efforts to respond to these problems in the form of the development of an EU level of socio-economic and welfare policy (Chapter 8).

Given the preoccupation of the bulk of the book with analysis of the historical and contemporary aspects of the European social complex and analytic aspects of the sociology of Europe, the final discussion (Chapter 9) turns to consider normative aspects. It focuses in particular on cosmopolitanism, a common normative theme in the contemporary sociology of Europe. It proposes a view of European society as a 'civil complex' as a relevant way of interpreting normative cosmopolitanism and applying it to the understanding and assessment of contemporary European society.

Notes

1 For some significant developments in the sociology and social theory of Europe, see Beck and Grande 2007; Delanty and Rumford 2005; Favell 2008; Fligstein 2008; Rumford 2002; Outhwaite 2008; and the References section for other works by these authors together with the discussion in Chapter 9. Also see Bauman (2004) and sociologically influenced work on Europe and the EU, such as Christiansen et al. 1999; Medrano 2003; Risse 2004; Rodriguez-Pose 2002; Schneider and Aspinwall 2001; Shore 2000; and Walters 2002. For relevant multidisciplinary studies, see Dunkerley et al. 2002; and Sakwa and Stevens 2006.

2 Also see Calhoun 2001. Generally on the contested meaning and the nature of 'European identity', see Balibar 2004; Cederman 2001; Garcia 1993a, 1993b, 1997; MacDonald 1993, 2000; Moxon-Browne 2004a, 2004b; Shore 2000; and Strath 2002.

3 For an overview of changing ideas of Europe from the classical era to the EU, see Pagden 2002; and Wilson and van der Dussen 1996; and for accounts and critiques of 'eurocentrism', see Amin 1989; Blaut 2000; and Hobson 2004.

4 On the concept of 'Europeanisation', see Borneman and Fowler 1997; Delanty and Rumford 2005; Featherstone and Radaelli 2003; and Roche 2007; also Caporaso and Jupille 2001; Cowles et al. 2001.

5 Besides the sociological studies indicated in note 1 above, Therborn (1995) was an early major contribution. Also see papers by Mann (1998) and Outhwaite (2006a, 2006b).

6 It could be suggested that there is a third significant, albeit non-sociological, view of Europe as a society of some kind, namely that present in Europe's media. Media aspects of Europe are important and will be touched on periodically in the course of the book (for instance in Chapters 2 and 8). However, for the purposes of this introductory discussion they can be downplayed since they can all too often involve the attempt to ideologically influence public opinion and national experience in relation to Europe, and particularly the EU, rather than reflecting these things as social realities (for instance, see Anderson and Weymouth 1999).

7 On social aspects of the euro currency, see Dyson 2002; also Fiddler 2003.

8 On European society and networks, see Chapter 2 and also Fligstein 2008, Chapters 1, 6 and *passim.*

9 See references and notes in Chapters 3–5.

10 On Europe and the EU as economic environments and systems see, for instance, Dyson 2002; Schmidt 2002; and Thompson 2001; and on them as political

systems see, for instance, Dinan 2005; Nugent 2003; and Rosamund 2000. On EU integration, see Cram et al. 1999; Chrysochoou 2001; Farrell et al. 2002; and Wiener and Diez 2004.

11   On post-communist Eastern European countries, particularly in their relations with the EU and Western Europe, see Nugent 2004; and Schimmelfennig and Sedelmeier 2005; also Outhwaite 2008, Chapters 2, 3 and 5.

12   For instance, 'neo-functionalist', 'new governance' and 'regulationist' perspectives. See Hix 1998; and Rosamund 2000.

13   For relevant discussion of the concept of society in contemporary social theory and sociology, see Giddens 1984; Urry 2000, 2003; and Beck and Grande 2007.

14   On comparative social policy analysis relating to Europe, see the discussion, notes and references for Chapter 6 below.

15   For anthropological studies of Europe see, for instance, Bellier and Wilson 2000; and Borneman and Fowler 1997; for geographical and planning-based studies see, for instance, Jensen and Richardson 2004; Jonsson et al. 2000; and McNeill 2004.

16   Although it is beginning (see note 1).

17   The sociology of globalisation barely existed before the 1990s. Early contributions included Robertson 1992 and Sklair 1991. More recent contributions which have a general relevance for the analysis of Europe include, among many others, Albrow 1999; Beck 2000; Hirst and Thompson 1999; and particularly Scholte 2005. Also see Axtmann 1998; Lechner and Boli 2005; and Spybey 1999.

18   Some examples could be said to include the sections on Europe in Castells (1998) and Hirst and Thompson (1999).

19   On the renewal agenda particularly, see Urry 2000 and 2003 and the discussions in Chapters 2 and 9.

20   For alternative interpretations and discussions of the complexity theme which are of relevance to contemporary sociology and social theory, see particularly Urry 2003, 2005a, 2005b; also Castellani and Hafferty 2007; Chesters 2004; Chesters and Welsh 2005; Thrift 1999; and Walby 2007.

21   On the concept of human beings' intersubjective 'life-world' and some of its basic (here 'deep') structures, particularly in the experience of time and space and of the embodiment and instrumentalities (here 'technology') involved in human action, see the phenomenologically-derived analyses in Schutz and Luckmann 1974. Also see Roche 1973. The discussion here links this analysis to a perspective on temporal, spatial and technological phenomena and aims to see them also in material and spatial, institutional and historically changing terms. For a relevant sociological and social theoretical perspective on time and space, together with their linkage as social time–space, see Giddens 1981, Chapters 1 and 4, and 1984, Chapter 3.

22   The relevance of the deep structure of social time to the understanding of European society is indicated later in the long historical perspective taken in Chapters 3 and 4, and in the discussion of the mythologisation of origins and historical narratives in European nationalist ideology in Chapter 5. It is also indicated generally in the recognition of the intrinsic historicality of European society (Therborn 1995) and thus of the relevance of an historical sociological perspective. On the latter, see Hobden and Hobson 2002; Hobson 2004; Mahoney and Rueschemeyer 2003; and Skocpol 1984.

23   The relevance of the deep structure of social space to the understanding of European society is a key theme throughout the book, but particularly in the

discussion in Chapter 2 of the European social complex as historico-geographic 'common ground' analysable in terms of the social spatialisation processes associated with being a 'network society' or being a 'neo-empire'. For relevant discussions, see May and Thrift 2001; and Massey 2005.

24   The relevance of the deep structure of technology to the understanding of European society is a key theme throughout the book, including in relation to European 'civilisations' in the classical era and the influence of Eastern technologies on Europe's development in various pre-modern periods (Chapter 3), the importance of developments in military technologies and also the industrialisation of economic production in Europe's early and mature modernisation process (Chapter 5), and the importance of post-industrial information and communication technologies in understanding contemporary modernity and the dynamics of globalisation (Chapter 8). For relevant discussions of the 'techno-economic' aspect of modern social change, see Freeman and Soete 1987; Green et al. 1999; and Hull et al. 1999.

25   See the discussions in Chapters 4, 5 and 6.

26   See the discussions in Chapters 4, 6, and 9.

27   Sociological characterisations of European society as some version of a social complex include the following: as an inter-societal system (Parsons 1966, 1971); as a network society (Castells 1998, and also Chapter 2 below); as a post-national constellation (Habermas, 2001); as a civilisational complex (Delanty and Rumford 2005; and also Chapter 3 below); and as a set of social fields and arenas (Fligstein 2008); also see Outhwaite on (among other examples of European complexity) European culture as 'a complex mixture of elements of local and external origin' (Outhwaite 2008, p.14).

28   On historical sociology, see Burke 2005; Hobden and Hobson 2002; and Skocpol 1984.

29   The sociological analysis of modernisation involves a variety of long socio-historical perspectives relevant to the understanding of Europe, including among them such as those of Elias 1983, 2000; Gellner 1983, 1988; Giddens 1971, 1981, 1985; Mann 1986, 1993; and Parsons 1966, 1971. Also see the discussions in Chapters 3, 4 and 5.

30   Williams 1961.

31   On the sociological analysis of globalisation see note 17, particularly Scholte (2005), and Chapter 7 and 9 below.

32   On 'glocalisation', see Robertson 1992; Brenner, 2004; and Roche 2000a, Chapter 5.

33   On the analysis of world 'regionalism' in global society, see Gamble and Payne 1996; Schirm 2002; Scholte 2005; Telo 2001.

34   On the analysis of early 21st-century geopolitics as tending towards a new 'multi-polar world order' see, for instance, Grant and Barysch 2008; Katzenstein 2005; and Khanna 2008. See also the discussion of the 'new regionalism' in international political anlaysis in Larner and Walters 2002.

35   See Laffan et al. 2000; and Bauman 2004.

2

THE EUROPEAN SOCIAL COMPLEX: EUROPE AS NETWORK AND EMPIRE?

Introduction

A new complex and dynamic social formation appears to be emerging in Europe in the early 21st century significantly stimulated by the EU and processes of Europeanisation associated with it. However, even after a generation this development remains in its early stages. Its current outlines are complex and changeable, and its future outlines are difficult to discern and speculate about. Nevertheless this development needs to be given more attention and be better understood than it often is by a range of relevant social science and humanities disciplines, and not least by the discipline of sociology which has, on the whole, given it only marginal attention for far too long. Later we discuss some of the core areas where processes of reconstruction have been occurring. So we consider the changing balance of power and authority between nation-states and the EU in fields such as competition, employment and social policy, and the general emergence of a multi-form European welfare capitalism in Chapters 6–8. However, in this chapter (and also see Chapter 9) we aim to reflect more generally and theoretically on the nature of social change and reconstruction in contemporary Europe and the challenges it poses for the development of a sociology of Europe.

The development of the EU is an historically unprecedented process. Ex-European Commission President Jacques Delors is credited with referring to it as an 'unidentified political object' (or more colloquially here, a UFO, an 'unidentified flying object').[1] However, the UFO's progress is uncertain and its future is unclear. The challenges to be faced in developing a sociological perspective on and interpretation of this social formation are particular to its new and emergent complexity, dynamism and fragility. There is a need for a developed sociological specialisation in relation to Europe for a number of reasons: for its own sake, as a matter of intrinsic interest to a discipline concerned to renew itself in new times, to provide an integrative perspective and discourse to complement and help connect up the growing multiplicity of social science disciplinary angles in European studies, and also normatively and politically to inform growing national and cross-European political debates and policy-making in relation to the EU. Attempting to address these challenges is ambitious, even if (as in this book) we approach the field selectively, and even if we make the effort (which we must) to set our expectations about what can be achieved at a realistically low and provisional level.

The discipline of sociology, together with related social theory and social policy analysis, emerged from late 19th-century European intellectual culture in response to the theoretical and practical challenges posed by the development, institutionalisation and maturation of nation-state-based societies, particularly in Western Europe. As some have commented, it developed on the basis of a 'methodological nationalism'.[2] In considering the project of and possibilities for a sociology of Europe, it is perhaps some consolation to note that sociological progress can be made outside the traditional intellectual constraints of this mindset, for instance in the current sociology of 'global society' and 'globalisation'. This attempt to understand social formations and processes of even greater complexity than Europe has been engaged with much energy and some success over the last decade or more.[3] In addition, the academic caravan of the social scientific and sociological analysis of globalisation has also (albeit as an outrider) generated some useful contributions to the study of Europe, concerning the profound implications and accelerating impacts of globalisation on the EU and its member states.[4]

With this background and these provisos in mind this chapter can be ambitious. Indeed, it needs to be to do justice to the potential of the field of the sociology and social theory of Europe. Its primary aim is to identify and explore in outline some key aspects of the sociological imagination that are needed in, and underpin, the emergence of this field and that, in my view, need to be further developed in order for the field to make progress. As part of this aim it considers two useful models both for Europe as a social complex and for helping to 'identify' the EU UFO sociologically, namely those of Europe and the EU as a network society and as an empire (albeit a new and aspirationally benign type of empire).

Europe and the Sociological Imagination: Historical, Spatial and Ethico-political Aspects

As is well known, the seminal notion of 'the sociological imagination' was first introduced into sociological and general intellectual discourse by the post-war American sociologist C. Wright Mills in 1959 in his book under this title.[5] Mills' aim was to offer an alternative to the two views which dominated the mainstream sociology of his day. One view, which was associated with the social theorist Talcott Parsons, emphasised a view of society as a self-reproducing and self-equilibrating 'structural functional' system, populated by individuals understood as socialised role players. Its view of the kind of sociological perspective and discourse which was necessary to address these realities, was that it needed to involve abstract and complex conceptualisation, a view Mills criticised as 'grand theory'. Another view was associated with empirical social research traditions and emphasised the importance of methodological rigour in the commitment to data-gathering. This view was disinterested in theorising about large-scale social systems and Mills criticised it as 'abstracted empiricism'.

Mills' alternative view of sociology and sociological inquiry was theoretically pragmatic and methodologically 'realist'. It was concerned with the study of 'real world' social organisations, such as corporations, bureaucracies and elites, operating in particular national societies (in his case mainly the USA), by means of an array of research designs and methods to be determined by the intellectual craft and professionalism of the sociological researcher and analyst according to the situation. This view was also normatively relevant and engaged, and potentially politically critical, as much of the prejudices (literally pre-judgements) that were often built into traditional, mainstream and 'commonsense' attitudes to the social world, as of more explicit and ideological and politically powerful perspectives on society. In addition, and to support this version of sociology as realist and engaged, he emphasised the importance for the discipline of an historical perspective. Mills' views were highly relevant to the situation of post-war Western sociology. Sociology has undoubtedly changed over the decades but his advocacy of the 'sociological imagination' continues to retain some relevance for the discipline in the 21st century. This is particularly so, in my view, in relation to the development of a sociology of Europe.

The 'grand theory' problem he criticised, while it no longer takes a particularly Parsonian form, remains a problem in the influence of some philosophical, political and aesthetic discourses on sociological work, particularly in the late 20th-century moment of 'post-modernism'. Functional conceptualisations of social systems, while appearing to lose influence within sociology, tended to diffuse into other social sciences, and migrate on the one hand into critical and neo-Marxist perspectives, and on the other into governmental organisations' policy discourses and the operational reflexivity required by their managerial and democratic accountability processes. The 'abstracted empiricism' phenomenon he criticised remains a problem, now enhanced within and outside the academy by computerisation, the development of an 'information society', and the rise of data-gathering and analysis as key aspects of the operation of governmental organisations. These problems and Mills' promotion of a realist and engaged sociology remain relevant. So, too, does his advocacy of the historical imagination.

Mills' sociological imagination, in principle, aims to contextualise and guide a version of the practice of sociological research and analysis which is epistemologically realist, theoretically pragmatic, methodologically pragmatic and comparativist, and politico-morally engaged. The main components of this imagination in Mills' version are (explicitly) an historical imagination, and, more implicitly, an ethico-political aspect of the imagination. The former is a way of referring to a capacity to imagine particularly alternative polities to one's own in the present. This is a capacity which is promoted particularly by use of the comparative method, but which is absolutely imperative in relation to past societies. The latter refers to his advocacy of moral engagement and critique as a key dimension of his version of the sociological vocation, whether or not of the discipline *per se*. In my view, each of these elements of the sociological imagination is relevant to the development of a new sociology of Europe. This was indicated earlier in terms of the importance given to an historical sociology perspective in the framework developed for the discussion in this book (Chapter 1). This view also underlies the line of argument pursued in this chapter.

However, to make the theme of the 'sociological imagination' even more relevant to our contemporary concerns, I suggest that we also need to recognise a social spatial imagination and to use this in the context of considering the nature and potential of a sociology of Europe. This is very relevant to, first, the need to complement the historical imagination's address to the ontological category of social time with an equivalent address to the ontological category of social space. Secondly, it is relevant to the need to develop an integrative perspective and discourse in a renewal of the discipline of sociology in order to address what are claimed to be 'post-societal' social realities in a 'post-societal' era.

The relevance and use of the historical imagination will be illustrated throughout this book, particularly in the historical sociological approach to Europe taken in Parts 1 and 2. In addition, we will also touch throughout on aspects relevant to an exercise of spatial and ethico-political imaginations. Spatial aspects are involved in the discussions of Europe's continental 'common ground', Europe as a 'theatre of war', and 'Western' location in historical and global geopolitical and cultural relations in Chapters 3, 4 and 5.[6] Ethicopolitical aspects involving assessing Europe's possible commitment to common values and principles of 'social' or welfare rights or to 'cosmopolitan' values are discussed in Chapters 8 and 9 respectively.

To set the scene for this in this chapter we point to the relevance of the spatial imagination in the sociology of Europe by discussing why and how European society and the European complex might be in terms of such notions as spaces and places, networks and flows. Also we point to the relevance of the ethico-political imagination by discussing why and how the EU might be visualised as, among other things, a potential 'empire' and 'superpower'.

Imagining the European Social Complex 1: Networks and European Society

The concept of a network typically refers to a complex system composed of a multiplicity of hubs or nodes which are linked and between which a variety of particular kinds of things move or flow. Networks offer an imaginative visualisation of social space which is different from more familiar concepts and analogies, such as 'hierarchies', 'positions' and 'strata', traditionally associated, for instance, with the analysis of class and power relations. The latter imply 'vertical' and unidirectional relationships. The former, while not at all incompatible with 'verticality', tend initially at least to emphasise a more 'horizontal' and interconnective understanding. Networks can be said to require an understanding of society as socio-spatial to a greater degree than other analogies. First, their horizontality as well as their verticality, and the multidirectionality of the flows within them, imply a view of the society in which they exist as being a kind of (socio-spatial) container. Secondly, within their operation they can be said to create and reproduce space, in that they involve a differentiation and a structuring of space into a system of places, the places of the network's hubs, links and flows.

Generally, the concept and analogy of 'network' has grown in importance and use in contemporary sociology and social science in parallel to, and connected with, two major vectors of structural social change. First, there is the increasing importance of the role of computers and the internet – which is to say, intrinsically complex communicational networks – in contemporary social life.[7] Secondly, there is the need to model the increasing complexity in contemporary social formations due to the embedding of national societies within the process of globalisation (e.g. Urry 2003). Currently there are numerous different perspectives highlighting networks. These include 'actor network theory', which, among other things, pursues epistemological questions and concerns about the 'social construction of reality' originally derived from studies in the sociology of science across a great range fields. They also include 'social network analysis', which, among other things, is concerned to apply the visualisation and method of network mapping across a great range of fields.[8] Some of these are at too high a level of theoretical abstraction or methodological formalism to be particularly applicable to Europe *per se* (although of course in principle they can be adapted for use in this agenda as in any other field). However, some versions of network as an analytical tool and perspective could be said to be of particular relevance to the understanding of Europe. In addition, they illustrate the relevance of analysing social space into the three social dimension-based forms indicated above. There are at least three main relevant network concepts we can usefully consider here: urban and transport networks, political and economic networks, and communicational networks. Analyses of these networks have usually been developed in distinct disciplinary literatures. However, occasionally, as for instance under the banner of analysis of 'network society', they have either been juxtaposed or attempts have been made to link them in more coherent ways.[9] We should conceptualise and address each type of network as operating in and as producing 'environing', 'organisational' and 'communicational' socio-spaces and as having the full range of socio-spatial characteristics. We return to this integrative socio-spatial theme later. Nevertheless, analytically, different types of network have particular relationships to different forms of social space. They can be seen to illustrate and instantiate these different forms, as we can briefly observe here.

The category of 'urban and transport networks' refers to the territorial and material as well as social aspects of the localisation of populations, including residence, the pattern of interrelationships between population centres, and the systems of mobility operating within and between population centres. So they include the structures of cities and their zones and the pattern of interrelationships between sets of cities, together with the various transport systems operating to move people and things within and between cities. This category of networks, in both their personally used materiality and also their collectively objective materiality, illustrates the notion of the 'environing' form of social space noted earlier. Along with communicational space (below), they are particularly relevant to understanding societies' cultural dimension. In a European context they are the subject of various kinds of public interests and politics in planning and policy-making relating to a wide range of fields, such as housing, urban and regional development, transport and tourism, from local to EU levels. European Union 'spatial' policy relates to some of these fields and arguably this has both Europeanising (standardising and linking) aspects and also what can be called 'Euro-localising' aspects (differentiating and identifying places as locations within a specifically 'European' space). The EU's spatial policy has a Europeanising influence, for instance, in relation to such things as cross-border and trans-European air, road and rail transport systems, particularly major linking bridges and high speed rail systems.[10] The EU has a more 'Euro-localising' influence in relation to such tourism-related processes as the annual cross-Europe inter-city competition for 'European City of Culture' status.[11]

The category of 'political and economic networks' refers to systems of action within and between the spheres of governance and power on the one hand, and those of management and the market on the other. This category of networks illustrates the notion of the 'organisational' form of social space noted earlier, which is particularly relevant to understanding societies' political and economic dimensions. In the European context, analysts have proposed that the EU should be understood as a 'network state' and 'networked polity'.[12] Castells' analysis of the EU as a 'network state' is based on his conception of the dominating influence of globalisation in the contemporary period, which, because of the importance of information technology in it, he refers to as 'the information age'. Globalisation occurs through 'globally enacted networks of exchange of capital, commodities and information', this shapes Europe and European integration, which is both 'a reaction to the process of globalisation and its most advanced expression'.[13] In European societies, the EU and its associated Europeanisation tends to be perceived as a vehicle of economic globalisation and this provokes defensive reactions prioritising national and regional interests and identities as against a common European interest and identity. The EU's institutions and policy-making processes reflect these tensions in their 'growing complexity and flexibility'.[14]

Keohane and Hoffman (1991) proposed that the EU 'is essentially organised as a network that involves the pooling and sharing of sovereignty rather than the transfer of sovereignty to a higher level'.[15] Castells comments: 'This analysis ... brings European unification closer to the characterization of institutional neo-medievalism; that is a plurality of overlapping powers.' He argues that the EU institutions comprise a 'new form of state', 'the network state'. This is 'a state characterised by the sharing of authority ... along a network' (which) 'by definition, has nodes, not a centre'. The nodes include at least three leading EU member states – Germany, France and the UK – together with the various EU institutions. Although there are asymmetries between them, 'the various nodes of the European network state are dependent on each other'. 'The network state, with its ... variable sovereignty, is the response of political systems to the challenges of globalisation'.[16]

An alternative but closely related network-type concept is that of 'multi-level governance' (Bache and Flinders 2005). This concept attempts to register and understand new and more complex forms of governance emerging in contemporary political and economic systems. On the one hand, these developments involve, within nation-states, an increasing division of labour between state and non-state (civil society and private sector) actors. On the other hand, they involve, beyond nation-states, the increasing influence and penetration of international and supra-national systems of law and policy-making, including (and most particularly) the EU[17] in nation-state affairs. Marks' early understanding of multi-level governance in a European context explicitly visualised it in network terms as a situation in which 'supranational, national, regional, and local governments are enmeshed in territorially overarching policy networks'.[18] Commenting on this, Bache and Flinders implicitly acknowledge the relevance of socio-spatial as well as network conceptualisation when they observe that this concept of multi-level governance evidently 'contained both vertical and horizontal dimensions. "Multi-level" referred to the increased interdependence of governments operating at different territorial levels, while "governance" signalled the growing interdependence between governments and non-governmental actors.'[19]

Finally, the category of 'communication networks' refers to the socio-spatial imagination and visualisations produced and propagated in and between societies through the processes of discourse. In particular, the organisational network of politics provides the basis for the constructions of socio-spatial meanings in such fields as policy discourses, and more generally in the contextual phenomenon of 'the public sphere'. In addition, this category of networks also refers to information and communication technology, which we can refer to as the 'media-sphere'. As seen earlier, this figures strongly in Castells' analysis of the 'information age', 'network society' and Europe as a 'network state'. For the purposes of this discussion, the media sphere can be taken to refer to the material reality and personal usage of media technology. Thus it points us both to the complexity of this field in contemporary society and also to the profound transformations currently ongoing within it in relation to the diffusion and social penetration of digital technology and the internet in domestic, production and mobile social settings. This category of networks illustrates the notion of the 'communicational' form of social space noted earlier, and (along with environing space, above) is particularly relevant to understanding societies' cultural dimension. This aspect of European social space and network processes is the subject of various Europe-wide developments and EU-level policies. The Europe-wide development of the EU's single market project enables and incentivises both the mass diffusion of marketing images and consumption aspirations and also cross-border organisation of media and marketing industries. EU-level policies relating to such fields as 'television without frontiers', 'the information society' and 'the knowledge-based society' promote such communication-based versions of European social space as a common 'media space', a 'research area', and so on.[20]

Understanding the social realities of Europe, the EU and Europeanisation, as argued throughout this book, requires that main societal dimensions and their dynamics should not be addressed in isolation, but should rather be considered in their interrelationships, including in terms of their implications for and connections with deep structures such social space. The main types of network developing in Europe imply distinct social spatialisation structures and processes (see above). However, the same goes for them as for social dimensions. We need to attempt to visualise Europe in socio-spatial terms. That is, on the one hand, it is an intrinsically complex and dynamic social space, an overarching arena for the main networks, both for their intra-network elements of places, links and flows and their inter-network links. On the other hand, it is in not only a common space but in some respects a particular and singular social place. This socio-spatial way of experiencing and conceptualising European society is relevant to understanding, among other things, the nature, potential and limitations of European identity in the contemporary period. This theme recurs in recent studies in the sociology of such varied socio-spatial phenomena as the public sphere and also migration in Europe.[21]

Imagining the European Social Complex 2: Empire, Space and Power

The second major new paradigm or perspective for understanding Europe and the EU, which has been emerging in contemporary socio-political analysis, is that of 'empire'.[22] As with the network paradigm, the empire paradigm contains socio-spatial implications and, as a contribution to the development of a sociology of Europe and the EU, it also can be said to illustrate the spatial imagination.[23] The idea of seeing contemporary Europe as some kind of empire is a strange-seeming and potentially provocative idea. In the 21st century we are supposed to live in an era of modernity which, among other things, is decisively post-colonial and post-imperial. Contemporary nation-states typically define themselves constitutionally in ways which appear to make imperialism illegal, morally illegitimate and politically inconceivable. Of course it was not always so, as we will see in the historical sections of this book. And indeed, it is impossible to understand European society without reference to the role of empires in its history both in pre-modern and modern periods. This is not least in terms of the living legacies of empire represented by the presence in most European nations of a diversity of ethnic communities often originally deriving from intra-imperial and ex-colonial patterns of migration. Nevertheless, having gone through numerous often bloody and conflict-ridden processes of decolonisation and 'national liberation', many within living memory, the notion that the imperial still cannot be expunged from the characterisation of contemporary European societies and the social formation of Europe as a whole is, as Munkler, observes, a 'surprising return of empire in the post-imperial age'.[24]

In what follows the focus is on the sense in which the empire concept is particularly relevant to the socio-spatial imagination of Europe. Some types of and perspectives on empire are outlined and the ideas of some of the main contemporary proponents of the empire analogy are considered. The discussion concludes by considering the overlap rather than the distinction between empire and network. Is a convergent view possible and useful here in terms of contributing to and helping to guide the future sociology of Europe research agenda?

Empires: types and perspectives

For our purposes we can assume that there are three types of empire. Two of them we have noted earlier, namely pre-modern and modern empires. These can be differentiated in terms of the world regional location, periodisation and general societal characteristics of the modernisation process. Modern empires emerged on the basis of a platform of developed nation-states in Europe in the 18th and 19th centuries in particular. They used their colonies systematically to fuel the development of industrial capitalist economies in their imperial heartlands. They controlled their colonies politically by means of literate and rationalistic bureaucracies, and militarily by technologically enhanced oceanic and military power. They dominated them culturally and ideologically by complex combinations of religious, scientific and individualist worldviews. Pre-modern empires, by contrast, whether in Europe or elsewhere around the world, tended to be based on agricultural and trading economies, animal-based production and military power, and charismatic, dynastic or religious cultures and worldviews. The third type of empire, which it is claimed has developed in late modernity's otherwise post-imperial period, can be referred to as 'neo-imperialism'.

Views about the relevance of neo-empire models for understanding contemporary Europe no doubt draw on some aspects of each of the two main historical types. But, by contrast with these types, they tend to portray the neo-empire as a complex but benign and 'civilian' entity, which both integrates itself internally and also exerts influence externally through modern forms of politics and culture rather than through military force and domination. These views differ in terms of whether they emphasise the internal or external aspect, and we will consider each of them in turn.

Europe as a neo-empire: internalist perspectives

Some of the main writers relevant to an internalist perspective on Europe as a neo-empire are Beck and Grande (2007), Zielonka (2006) and Munkler (2007), and since Zielonka's analysis is more elaborate, more attention will be given to it here. Munkler takes an historical perspective on empires in Europe from the classical period to the present, whereas Beck and Grande's and Zielonka's main concerns are with the arguably neo-imperial character of the EU in the present and into the future. However, they have some common analytic interests. Each writer emphasises the profound difference between nation-states (and nation-state models for the EU such as that of a 'super-state') and empires, and argue that the EU is more like the latter than the former. Each is concerned about understanding the unfamiliar and non-nation-state character of the EU, in particular in relation to its borders, and thus implicitly as a new kind of territorial entity. Nation-state borders are clear and fixed, but the EU's borders are fuzzy (involving a number of different but overlapping jurisdictions) and flexible (i.e. changing, and mainly expanding).

Each feels that the notion of an empire, albeit in a new benign form, is a more useful model for understanding these aspects of the EU, particularly the border flexibility involved in EU enlargement processes, than any nation-state-based model. However, they take different views about further EU enlargement. Munkler is concerned to highlight the 'lessons from history' for the EU, regarding about the problems of 'imperial overstretch' attendant on pursuing an expansionary strategy.[25] He argues that 'If Europe is not to overstretch itself and eventually end in failure, it will have to take over (an) imperial model of boundary demarcation'. 'Europe's external frontiers (need to be made) at once stable and elastic' like stable imperial orders which have '"soft" boundaries, where the centre's regulatory claims gradually lose their force and where borderlands take the place of borders'.[26] By comparison, Zielonka takes the view that 'the EU may be compelled to carry out further enlargements on strategic grounds' and 'is unlikely to try to close its doors' to additional accession countries. However, like Munkler, he recognises that this carries risks and costs. Therefore it is likely that the EU 'will make the accession process longer and fill it with an ever longer list of membership conditions' and thus that it 'is likely to be more fuzzy and ambivalent'.[27]

Beck and Grande offer an analysis of the contemporary EU in terms of such dimensions as its political order, spatial structure, and societal structure, and in terms of the nature of its integration, sovereignty, political process and power in order to argue for the relevance of viewing it as an 'empire'.[28] Its political order is 'asymmetric'. That is, EU members have a range of kinds of status depending on which of a number of concentric zones of power they occupy. This runs from a central zone of complete integration out to more limited and loose forms of association, as in the case of accession candidate countries. Its socio-spatial structure is 'open and variable', involving processes of interweaving, transformation, border shifting, cultural pluralisation. Its societal structure is multinational and its integration as a multi-level governance system is simultaneously horizontal (between the nations) and vertical (between the nations and the EU). Its sovereignty is of a 'complex cosmopolitan' rather than nation-statist kind, and its political process is one which favours consensus-building and cooperation in law and rule-making, policy decision-making and conflict resolution. Following Ansell (2000), they argue that the power of this empire is exercised in and through its embodiment as a network.[29]

Zielonka's concept of the EU as a neo-empire emphasises the relevance of this notion to understanding its internal nature and structure both in analytic and normative terms. His main analytical tool in this context is that of the 'neo-medieval' character of the EU. This is an apparently historical (but actually effectively ungrounded and historically unspecified) concept.[30] It is intended to disconnect Zielonka's version of 'empire' (and EU-as-empire) from what we have referred to above as the 'modern' type of empire, which he sees as national states-turned-empires, and thereby as regimes committed to military conquest, territorial expansion and economic exploitation. In reality, most historical medieval empires both in Europe and beyond, whether or not based on nation-states, were just as committed to military conquest and the rest, albeit by different (non-modern) means, as were modern empires. However, Zielonka chooses to ignore this and to focus on aspects of medieval empires such as 'limited and decentralised government ... internal conflicts between a king or emperor and the lower aristocracy ... the persistent divergence of local cultures, religions and traditions ... [which] implied a highly divided political loyalty.[31] This interpretation provides a set of benign elements for his concept of a 'neo-medieval empire'. Applying this kind of concept to the EU suggests that the EU be seen as a regime characterised, among other things, by 'fuzzy borders and polycentric governance',[32] and the coexistence of 'multiple cultural identities' and 'diversified types of citizenship'.[33] Zielonka's line of analysis, as with Beck and Grande's, suggests that there are significant linkages to be made between neo-empire-based and network-based visions of the EU.

Europe as a neo-empire in a 'multi-polar world': externalist perspectives

In addition to perspectives which attempt to provide new models of the EU's internal nature and workings in neo-imperial terms, it is likely that studies of the EU as an actor in international relations and in the global order generally might also generate visions of the EU relevant to the neo-imperial perspective. The idea that the EU may be becoming a neo-empire in the context of its external actions and foreign policy has not yet been much articulated in explicit terms. For instance, for Khanna, the EU is a major world regional power, and its 'capital' is Brussels, 'the new Rome' (Khanna 2008). This might be because of the potentially negative normative associations of the concept of empire, even though contemporary usages of the concept 'neo-empire', such as those of Zielonka, as has been noted, are at pains to emphasise its benign or even normatively positive nature. Is the EU becoming a neo-empire in terms of its operations in the external context of international relations and global politics relations? The view that it is can be said to find some support in studies that focus on the EU's potential status as a new 'superpower', particularly in relation to the hitherto dominant, even singular, global superpower, the USA.[34] It can also be said to find support in analyses of the EU's character as a pole in an arguably emerging 'multi-polar world order', and, relatedly, as a region in a 'multi-regional world order'.[35]

In these analyses, characteristics of the EU that might have hitherto been assumed to be weaknesses are seen in a very different light, namely as strengths in the changing international and global contexts of the 21st century. For instance, the fact that the EU (at least currently) has not developed substantial or coherently organised military power, particularly when compared with the USA, might be taken to be a weakness. America's 'superpower' status since the Second World War derived significantly from its willingness and capacity to devote considerable economic and technological resources to its military 'hard power', to continuously enhance it, and to project it around the world. This strategy, and the 'arms race' involved in it, over the course of the Cold War, succeeded in draining the resources of the USSR, its only competitor. With the collapse of the USSR in 1990, the USA was left, for a decade or more, as the world's sole hegemonic power, a *de facto* modern empire exercising global influence through its economic as well as its military dominance.

America's period 'in the sun' has been a relatively brief one and arguably is beginning to pass as we enter the second decade of the 21st century as a result of the rapid onset of a number of types of challenge from other regions of the world – cultural ('civilisational') and military ('terroristic') challenges from the Islamic world, global economic and potential regional military challenges from a resurgent Russia and China, and economic competition from the European Union. This new and evolving geopolitical situation is a significantly unanticipated consequence of the economic globalisation processes promoted by the USA since the 1990s. No doubt it has much further to go in terms of developments and surprises as the 21st century unfolds, given such dynamics as the likelihood of continued economic and population growth in India, and the economic and military reassertion of the Russian Federation and its central Asian client states. It should be noted that at the heart of these developments are polities (China, India and Russia) which had imperial structures in the early modern period, which subsequently as modern (large-scale) 'nation-states' continued (and continue) to contain and organise empire-style multi-ethnic populations and multi-'national'/provincial structures, and which continue to exert an imperial-style influence on neighbouring nations and 'spheres of influence' in their world region.

The emerging global geopolitical situation involves changes which appear to be moving irrevocably away from a scenario of uni-polar American global hegemony and *de facto* imperialism and towards various possible scenarios. None of these alternative scenarios is yet clear or stabilised, but they all involve some version of a more polycentric, multi-polar world order. In the course of this transformation no doubt the possession of economic power will remain vital. However, as compared with the Cold War period, when this was significantly concentrated in the hands of the USA, it has for some time been becoming more dispersed around the world. This was initially, as we will see in Chapter 7, in relation to the EU, particularly from the 1970s, and Japan also emerged as a powerful global economic force in a more or less parallel development in the same period. Much more recently there has been the awesome phenomenon of China's rapid economic growth, and this could well be echoed in due course by India. The global economy is certainly more developed and interdependent than it ever has been, but it is also no longer a system run largely by and for the USA. By the early 21st century it has already become significantly polycentric, and it is likely to become much more so as the century unfolds.

Contemporary polities' military power and their capacity and willingness to use it to promote and project their interests is, and will remain, important in their relationships, as it ever has been in human affairs. All poles in the new world order, led by the USA and China, the old and new 'superpowers', but also even including the EU, are seeking to enhance their military power. However, the balance between 'hard' military power and the 'soft' power of cultural and political influence appears to be shifting in favour of the latter. The USA revealed a surprising degree of military ineffectiveness and associated political incompetence in getting its way in the second Iraq war, and also in Afghanistan in the early years of the 21st century. On the one hand, this provides some evidence to suggest that, in spite of its continuing superiority in military technologies (and the capacity to 'shock and awe' etc.), the USA is beginning to encounter the phenomenon of 'imperial overstretch' which has afflicted many previous modern and pre-modern empires (Munkler 2007). On the other hand, these displays of the limitations of military power were undertaken by a state with diminished moral and political legitimacy in the eyes of the international community, and also with a fading image as a social and cultural model. As such they could be argued to provide some evidence of the importance, even for exercises of 'hard' power, of the ability to influence other nations and the international community through cultural and political means, that is by means of 'soft' power. This shift in the balance between hard and soft power, whatever else it might also mean elsewhere in the emerging multi-polar world order, also increases the EU's potential status and influence, and shifts the balance within the two main 'Western' poles, the USA and Europe, more in favour of the latter.

From an externalist perspective, then, in terms of the EU in the wider world order (such as it is, and such as it might be becoming), the EU can be seen as a relatively benign neo-empire among a variety of kinds of extant and emerging 'great powers'. In externalist terms, the EU faces new challenges and opportunities presented by the process of globalisation *per se*, the emergence of the new multi-polarity and polycentrism in global geopolitics, and greater salience of 'soft' power in this situation. Arguments that the EU now has 'superpower' status (McCormick 2007) or that it is emerging as a new kind of 'civilian' power (Telo 2007) rest on its possession and use of 'soft' power. This includes the working model and experience it offers to other regional groupings of nations and/or to potential regional hegemons, of a long-term and largely successful project of regional international collaboration in the peaceful conduct of relations between culturally and politically different communities and in the pursuit of prosperity. The EU's soft or civilian power also includes the values and broader policies it pursues in support of, on the one hand, social responsibility and ecological sustainability in global economic growth and, on the other hand, respect for human rights and (UN-based) multilateral decision-making in the field of global governance (Telo), together with the economic resources and influence it can use to promote these values and polices. These kinds of characteristics not only enable the EU to be viewed as new kind of 'superpower' or 'civilian' power (McCormick, Telo). In effect, they also contribute to the general argument outlined here that the contemporary EU is analysable as a benign type of 'neo-empire', both internally in terms of the complexities of its structures, and also externally as an actor in the multi-polar world order emerging in the 21st century.

Earlier we identified three major 'visions' present in the contemporary development of the sociology of Europe and the EU, namely those of Europe as a 'network', as an 'empire' and as a 'cosmopolitan' social order. Each of them can usefully be understood as envisaging the European social formation in terms of the (socio-spatial) sociological imagination as a special kind of social and territorial space. Having considered the first two as new analytic perspectives, and given that the cosmopolitan perspective is significantly normative rather than analytic, we will postpone discussion of the latter to the final reflective chapter of book. In relation to the network and empire models, we have noted connections and overlaps between their visions of European society and its social spaces as well as differences. The empire model can be interpreted as a particularly politically weighted version of the network model. The 'neo-imperial network' concept enables internalist network-based views of the EU, which otherwise tend to stress cross-national forms and other forms of socio-spatial 'horizontality' in power relations, to restore socio-spatial 'verticality' and a recognition of multi-level hierarchy and inequalities in the analysis of power. It also requires that internalist network-oriented views recognise the relevance internally of EU's external situation and challenges, and that they pay due attention to the growing importance for the EU project both of the pressures of globalisation and also of its operation as a potentially influential actor in 21st-century international and global geopolitical settings.[36]

Conclusion

In this chapter contemporary Europe and the EU have been considered in general terms as together comprising a socio-political complex. The image of the EU in particular as a puzzling socio-political UFO has guided the discussion towards models which visualise Europe and the EU in socio-spatial terms as a network society and as a neo-imperial system. One of the core themes has been that of the EU's distinctive character as both an international and supra-national organisation, an organisation which has multinational and multicultural characteristics, and in which the governance system is multi-level and multi-form. The discussion reviewed a range of perspectives on the EU and on an EU-orchestrated Europe in this respect, noting in particular the inadequacies of the 'super-state' and nation-state analogies to adequately model it. The view of the EU which sees it as a 'meta-state' and a 'post-national state complex' was generally endorsed. In the course of this, the general sociological perspective involving notions of societal dimensions, deep structures and transformations, which was outlined in Chapter 1, was further developed in terms of the socio-spatial aspect of the sociological imagination, and this was applied in a preliminary way to the EU. These sociological concerns to understand contemporary European society and the EU will be taken further in more detail in later chapters. However, before we move forward and engage with this, it is necessary to pause and take a step back, a step into the historical, socio-temporal aspect of the sociological imagination, in order to take an historical sociological perspective on the development of Europe.

Sociology needs a continuing dialogue with history not only because modern societies are products of long-term and ongoing social change, but also because they, and the people within them, *believe* that they are. As we put it earlier, time is one of the 'deep structures' of society and human social organisation. Personal, generational, national and civilisational identities are founded in memories and beliefs about the past – including such things as 'origins', 'roots', 'defining moments', 'turning points' and so on – together with related practices of conservation and commemoration at all levels from the personal to the national. While this is true of all modern societies, it is particularly true for Europe as the continent and 'civilisational constellation' which led, and indeed often coerced, the rest of the world into the modernisation process.

Contemporary European society is characterised by changing balances, accommodations and conflicts within and between peoples differentiated by city-based, regional, national, religious and continental identities. This complexity provides both the social arena and ground for the EU and also generates the social and policy problems which challenge it and its member states. It cannot be understood in abstraction from an awareness of the real and perceived relevance of history for European society. So, in order to be able to return later to engage with the understanding of contemporary Europe and the EU on a well-grounded basis, it is necessary initially to step back into the history of Europe, not only in the modern period but also in pre-modern periods. This step is taken next in Part 1.

Notes

1 Cited in Zielonka 2006, p.4. For discussions relating to the analysis of the EU as a complex organisation or system, see Bache and Flinders 2005; Chrysochoou 2001; EC 2001; Jessop 2005; Hix 1998; Hooghe and Marks 2001; Marks and Hooghe 2005; Milward 2000; Rosamund 2000; Warleigh 2002; Wiener and Diez 2004.

2   See, for instance, Beck and Grande 2007; also Roche 1996, Chapter 2 on 'national functionalist' assumptions in social policy.

3   See note 17 above.

4   See, for instance, Axtmann 1998; Giddens 2007; and Giddens et al. 2006.

5   Mills 1959.

6   On spatial aspects, analogies and perspectives regarding society and social formations in general, see Benko and Strohmayer 1997; Brenner 2004; Crang and Thrift 2000; Lefebvre 1991; Thrift 1999; Tilley 1994. On the (implicitly socio-spatial) concepts of fluidity and mobility as characterising contemporary society, see Urry 2000, 2003.

7   See, for instance, Barney 2004; Benkler 2006; Castells 1996; Rossiter 2006; Sunstein 2007; Urry 2003, Chapter 4; and van Dijk 1999.

8   On 'actor network theory' see, for instance, Law 1992; on 'social network analysis' see, for instance, Crossley 2007; and White 2002.

9   See references in note 6 above.

10   On the EU's spatial policy, see Jensen and Richardson (2004), for relevant cultural geographic and social theoretic discussions see McNeill (2004) and Delanty and Rumford (2005, Chapter 7), respectively.

11   On the EU's transport networks policies and ambitions, see the seminal discussion in the Delors White Paper (EC 1993a); also Jensen and Richardson 2004. On the European City of Culture, see Palmer 2004; also Garcia 2005. On European tourist spaces, places and circuits in Europe and contemporary society more generally, see Shaw and Williams 2004.

12   See Castells 1998, Chapter 5. On Europe in terms of a network perspective, see Ansell 2000; Axford and Huggins 1999; and Leonard 1999.

13   Both quotations, Castells 1998, p.318.

14   Castells 1998, p.331.

15   Quoted in Castells 1998, p.331.

16   All quotations in the preceding paragraph from Castells 1998, pp.331–332.

17   See Featherstone and Radaelli 2003; also Marks and Hooghe 2005; George 2005; Bache 2005.

18   Quoted in Bache and Flinders 2005, p.3.

19   Bache and Flinders 2005, p.3; also see Jessop 2005 on the EU as a case of 'multi-meta-governance'.

20   On the European information and knowledge economy see, for example, Axford and Huggins 2007; Mansell and Steinmuller 2000; and Rodrigues 2002. On European media and communications spaces and places see, for example, Bondeberg and Golding 2004; De Vreese 2003; Gripsrud 2007; Harrison and Wessels 2009 forthcoming; Harrison and Woods 2000; Morley 2000; Morley and Robbins 1995; Schlesinger 2003; Silverstone 2005; and Williams 2005. On EU cultural policy see, for example, Shore 2000.

21   Contemporary sociological interests in exploring the European dimension of the public sphere lies in Habermas's work (1989, 1992). For some notable contributions see, for instance, De Vreese 2007; Eder and Giesen 2001; Eriksen 2007; Fossum and Schlesinger 2007; Koopmans and Erbe 2003; Peters and Sifft 2003; Peters et al. 2005; Risse 2003; van de Steeg 2005. For sociological and related studies of migration in Europe and EU, see Favell 2008; Fligstein 2008; Geddes 2003. On the social theory of social space and identity in Europe, see Beck and Grande 2007, Chapter 4; Delanty and Rumford 2005, Chapter 7; Rumford 2006; also Axford 2006; Axford and Huggins 1999; and Jonsson et al. 2000. On European socio-spatiality in terms of borders, see Balibar 1998;

Delanty 2006; Eder 2006; Ferrera 2005a; Rovisco 2007; Rumford 2008; and Walters 2002.

22 See, for instance, Beck and Grande 2007, Chapters 3; Munkler 2007; Zeilonka 2006. As Beck and Grande and other writers on neo-empire indicate (e.g. Hardt and Negri 2000), neo-empires are importantly embodied as networks and usefully understood in terms of them.

23 See, for instance, Munkler 2007, pp.96–101, on 'the construction of imperial space'.

24 Munkler 2007, p.139.

25 Munkler 2007, pp.111–119, 166–167).

26 The quotations in this part of the paragraph come from Munkler 2007, pp.166–167.

27 The quotations in this part of the paragraph come from Zielonka 2006, pp.174–176.

28 Beck and Grande 2007, pp.64–67.

29 Beck and Grande 2007, pp.69–70.

30 See Zeilonka 2006, p.18.

31 Zeilonka 2006, p.12.

32 Zeilonka 2006, p.18.

33 Zeilonka 2006, Introduction and pp.98, 120, etc. Zeilonka is only the most recent of many writers who have viewed Europe and the EU in 'neo-medieval' terms. See also Friedrichs 2001; Burgess and Vollaard 2006; also more generally Gamble 2001.

34 See McCormick 2007; Telo 2007.

35 See Telo 2001; and Grant and Barysch 2008. On versions of the multi-polar world order concept connected with concepts of world regionalism and poly-centrism, see also Gamble and Payne 1996; Mouffe 2005; and Scholte 2005. Katzenstein's study of 'a world of regions' retains a concept of America's relation to the world as being a central and neo-imperial one. But his interpretation of the world order being one of 'regions embedded in an American imperium' (2005 p.1) has some relevance and lends some support to the emerging multi-polar world-order views.

36 See, for instance, Bretherton and Vogel 1999; Rifkin 2004; McCormick 2007; Telo 2007.

PART 1

The Development of the European Social Complex: Civilisations and Nation-states

3

ORIGINS OF THE EUROPEAN SOCIAL COMPLEX: PRE-MODERNITY, COMMONALITIES AND EUROPE AS A 'CIVILISATION'

Introduction

To understand the contemporary duality and complexity of Europe as a social formation it is necessary turn to the socio-historical aspect of 'the sociological imagination', and to explore Europe's history and development. In historical perspective, Europe's pattern of commonalities-in-difference can be addressed in part through an interest in understanding Europe as a 'civilisation' and interpreting the meaning of its 'heritage' from pre-modern to modern times.[1] These are current issues for both Europeans and non-Europeans. For Europeans, they relate to questions about 'European identity'. For non-Europeans, they relate to the everyday, political and academic processes of reviewing the claims and contributions of the civilisations and heritages of all world regions which has been triggered by contemporary globalisation. The nature and value of 'European civilisation' is an open question for our contemporary generation, something to be questioned and subjected to scrutiny rather than anything to be simply assumed and thoughtlessly defended in a 'Euro-centric' fashion.

In this chapter, then, we focus on outlining some commonalities in the historical experience of Europe, particularly in the pre-modern era. This aims to provide essential food for thought for questioning assumptions about the nature and value of 'European civilisation', and for developing an understanding of the phenomena of Europe's duality and complexity. Also, it helps prepare the way for the topic to be addressed in later discussions, particularly in Chapters 4 and 5, namely the emergence of nationalistic differences over and above civilisational commonalities as the dominating theme of European experience in the modern era. There are four steps in the discussion. First, we consider Europe as a 'common ground'. This refers both to the sub-continent as an environment and territorial space, and also as an arena of human action and interaction. Secondly, we consider Europe as a common 'civilisation' both in the form of a common condition influenced by external cultures and civilisations, and also in the form of a common culture and cultural dynamic, particularly that associated with Christianity. Thirdly, we consider some common societal structures and changes in the fields of politics and economics, not least those associated with the pervasive role of cities, war-making and external factors in the feudal medieval period. Finally, we consider the transitionary period around the 15th century in which some of the key factors influencing Europe's modernisation process began to emerge.

Europe as a Common Ground[2]

Differences of everyday culture, tradition and social experience, not to mention linguistic differences, have always characterised Europe as a diverse and complex social formation. Although much reduced in the modern era, these socio-cultural differences remain significant in our times. This is consistent with the notion that Europe has provided a common mobility space over the millennia. Without acknowledging any dubious assumptions about environmental determinism, we can, nonetheless, recognise that to a significant extent (and leaving the linguistic differences to one side), in the premodern era Europe's socio-cultural differences derived (and continue to some extent to derive in the modern era) from the different physical environments and habitat conditions which prevail across the sub-continent and to which human communities have adapted themselves in differing ways over the millennia.[3]

These different habitat conditions relate to universal human needs for shelter (housing and clothing) and nutrition, and require long-term and robust forms of social organisation to service them from generation to generation. In Europe these conditions have been significantly imposed on humans (at least until the late modern period) by the fact of the sub-continent's global location as a region positioned in high northern latitudes. At least for central and northern European societies, this location has significantly affected their access to the key human resources of warmth and daylight. There are also the differential climatic impacts, on the one hand, of the Atlantic on Western Europe and, on the other hand, of the Eurasian land mass and its climatic systems on Eastern Europe. Europe's global location in terms of latitude and it relationship to oceans and land masses has had evident and major implications for the differentiation of Europe's climatic zones (e.g. cold north and warm south). This in turn has had major implications for differentiation across Europe in the traditional and 'characteristic' forms of socio-cultural adaptation to the particularities of these climatic and environmental factors.

These differential adaptations are readily visible across Europe's societies, in their different material cultures, including differences in the nature and traditions of housing and architecture, of clothing and textile production, and generally of food and drink production and consumption. They also include the differential agricultural fertility and access to material resources of major geographic regions. These major regions include the north European plain, the various chains of mountains in south, central and eastern Europe, and the long coastal belts which surround the sub-continent. Human communities which settled in these very different sub-regions of the European sub-continent were inevitably going to develop different material cultures and traditions relating to dress, food and domestic architecture because of their need to adapt to the different limitations and opportunities provided by these different climatic and geographic conditions in what came to be their 'homelands'.

So far we have suggested a picture of European society as inherently complex and diverse, a mixture of differences ultimately deriving in part from differential adaptations to the sub-continent's environmental characteristics. However, this should not be understood to detract from the notion that Europe also was always, and remains to this day, a 'common ground' in various other more recognisably social ways. The concept of 'common ground' refers to both environmental and territorial space, on the one hand, and also to social space, arenas of human perceptions and assumptions, actions and interaction on the other. Perceptions and assumptions may or may not be accurate, and may be based on variously adequate experience, from observation to hearsay. Nevertheless, every regional society in Europe has long-held 'commonsense' assumptions and stereotypes about its neighbours across the sub-continent, and about how Europe as a whole constitutes a distinctive and specific environment when compared with other neighbouring continents and world regions, such as Central Asia, the Middle East and North Africa. In addition, in terms of actions and interactions, Europe has long been a 'common ground' in the sense that from the earliest periods of human settlement its regions and the sub-continent in its entirety have been incessantly crisscrossed by intra-regional and inter-regional flows of ideas, goods and technologies, and also by flows of people and migrations of peoples for reasons of trade, war and pilgrimage, work and welfare, and tourism or settlement.[4]

In this connection it is important to recognise that, compared with most other continents and world regions, Europe is a relatively small physical territory and, with the exception of the mountain chains, it is readily traversable in every direction. As itself a peninsula of the Eurasian land mass, it is composed to a significant degree of subsidiary peninsulas bounded by seas around most points of the compass. In addition, it is deeply penetrated inland from all directions by major river systems, and also by the sea in strategic areas, such as the Atlantic reaches of the north European plain. So, even for the most basic forms of human mobility, namely by walking (as in the case of armies from Rome to Napoleon), using horses and/or using coastal and river-based boats, from the earliest times the European sub-continent, unlike many other world regions, has always been very accessible both in principle and in practice. In practice over the centuries, in spite of the changing claims to exclusive territories by empires, kingdoms and nation-states, in spite of the drawing and redrawing of borders, and the changing politico-legal conditions affecting people's and groups' abilities to move, it has been a common ground in the concrete sense of being a relentlessly traversed space. We can refer to it as historically operating as ultimately a singular 'mobility space'.

Europe's ease of access provided the environmental opportunity and resource for its major civilisation-shaping developments and their mass mobilisations: in the classical period for both the relatively rapid cross-continental expansions and then the long-term maintenance of the classical imperial systems of the Hellenic world and of Rome; in the medieval period for the process of Christianisation, including the waves of conversion of 'barbarians' in the north and east, and the Crusades in the south and east; and in the early modern period for the continent-wide communication of the new ideas and values of the Renaissance, the Reformation, and the scientific and industrial revolutions. The common ground also provided the opportunities and resources in every historical period over three millennia, on the one hand for Europeans' strong and fateful commitment to inter-regional and international trade, and on the other hand for their equally strong and fateful addiction to inter-regional and cross-European war-making. Throughout its history, because of its basic environmental accessibility, Europe has been a common ground which has been relentlessly criss-crossed in all of these respects. Its cities, towns and ports have long constituted hubs in widely distributed socio-spatial networks. In this chapter regarding the pre-modern period, and more generally in the subsequent chapters covering the stages of the development of European modernity, we note that this mobility served the purposes of trade and of ideological and cultural communication, although all too often it also served the purposes of war-making, whether for defence or domination. Some key spatial, historical and sociological aspects of Europe as a common ground and mobility space are summarised in Table 3.1. We now need to consider the factors involved in these patterns of mobilisation in a little more detail.

Europe as a Common 'Civilisation': External and Internal Factors

The idea that Europe, recognising its complexity and diversity, nevertheless developed as common 'civilisation' can be said to refer to two sets of factors. One set relates to 'external' influences deriving from outside the European sub-continent, and the other relates more to factors 'internal' to Europe. On

Table 3.1   Pre-modern European 'common ground': main cross-continental communications and habitats

HABITATS	
Main European regional environments	• Scandinavia • Atlantic coastlands (and coastlands of related seas) * • North European plain • Major mountain chains (South Central and Eastern Europe: Iberian plateau, Pyrenees, Massif Central, Alps, Balkans, Carpathians) • Mediterranean coastlands (and coastlands of related seas)
SEAWAYS Access to navigable seas	• *Peninsulas*: Scandinavia, Danish, Iberian, Italian, Balkan • *Island systems*: Danish/Swedish islands, British Isles, Balearics, Sardinia, Corsica, Sicily, Crete, Cyprus, Greek island systems, etc. • *Seas*: Baltic, North, Atlantic, Mediterranean, Adriatic, Aegean, Black

WATERWAYS	Rivers draining to:	River systems + deltas:	Main coastal + inland hubs + ports:
Access to major navigable (and canalisable) river syatems	Baltic Sea North Sea + Atlantic Sea Mediterranean + Aegean Seas Adriatic Sea Black Sea	– Oder, Wista – Elbe, Rhine, Meuse, Thames, Seine, Loire – Ebro, Rhone, Nile – Po – Danube, Dneiper, Don	– Konigsberg/Danzig – Hamburg, Bremen, Amsterdam, London, Paris – Avignon, Lyon, Athens, Alexandria – Venice, Ravenna – Regensburg, Vienna, Budapest, Belgrade, Kiev, Rostov, Constantinople

COMMUNICATIONS	Cross-European + cross-Mediterranean routes:	Eurasian routes:
Pre-modern trade + transport routes	*Roman empire roads*: Rome to/from all provinces, enabling Imperial armies access throughout Britain, through France, the Alps and Balkans to the Black Sea, particularly to defend the empire's borders on the Rhine and the Danube *Roman empire sea-routes*: Rome to/from North Africa and Asia Minor, etc., via Naples, Athens/Piraeus, Syracuse, Corinth, Thessalonica, Constantinople, Alexandria, Antioch (Syria), Tripoli, Narbonne, etc. *Medieval European inter–national + inter-regional trading centres + circuits*: *Flanders* (Bruges, Ghent, Antwerp, Brussels, Utrecht, also linked to London) *Champagne* (Paris, Lagny, Provins, Troyes) *Lombardy* (Milan, Bologna, Parma, Verona, also Florence and Pisa; linked to northern Italian international trade empires of Venice and Genoa)	*'Silk' roads*: From Chinese empire (Beijing), through Mongolian empire (Anhsi, Kashgar, Samarkand), either via Persia (Merv, Isfahan, Herat) and Arabia (Baghdad, Damascus, Antioch), or via Turkish/Armenian territories (Tabriz, Trebizond), or via Mongol/Russian territories (Sarai, Tana) *'Spice' routes*: From East Indies and India through Persian Gulf or Red Sea to Mediterranean at Antioch, Acre or Alexandria, and on to Rome, Venice, Genoa, etc.

Sources: Information compiled from various sources; see endnotes for this chapter, including note 1 and in particular notes 4 and 5.

the one hand, it can be argued that important aspects of Europe's commonality as a civilisation, a way of life, derived from the fact that throughout the pre-modern era it constituted a 'common condition' profoundly influenced, both positively and negatively, by non-European cultures and civilisations. On the positive side, most European communities in this period competed with each other to achieve the perceived and real benefits of international trade from the East. On the negative side, throughout this period they were effectively 'in the same boat' in relation to recurrent and serious threats of invasion and domination from North Africa and Eurasia. Secondly, arguably what most identified Europe's 'civilisation' as a whole and distinguished it from other world regions and their civilisations in the pre-modern era was the 'internal' cultural dynamic associated with the religion of Christianity (originally of course an 'external' import from the Middle East). Some of the main internal and external factors are summarised in Table 3.2. We will look first at the external factors.

External factors

For centuries through the first millennium and well into the second millennium with few exceptions all European societies, whether settled in the north, central and west regions, or in the south and eastern regions of the sub-continent, which were most exposed, were nonetheless all powerfully affected, whether for good or ill, by the activities of both neighbouring and also far-distant cultures and civilisations. European civilisation developed later than a number of other major world civilisations, and related religious worldviews, notably those of China and Confucianism, and of India and Hinduism. In the vicinity of Europe, the civilisations of Egypt, Israel and Mesopotamia each influenced Mediterranean Bronze and Iron Age European cultures, particularly early Greek culture. Europe's neighbouring societies in the East always included the 'barbarian' tribes of Eurasia and from the seventh century AD they came to include from the south and east the Islamic cultures of Arab North Africa and Asia Minor. The long-distant cultures included those of the Far East, in particular the relatively transient regimes and empires of Central Asian nomadic tribes, particularly the Mongols, and also the successive and enduring imperial regimes of China.

Trade

The main external influence which can be argued to have been generally positive and progressive for Europeans was participation in international trade. From the classical period onwards Europeans, particularly Greek, Macedonian, Roman and other Mediterranean-rim cultures, exchanged such things as precious metals, woollen textiles, furs and slaves for such things as silk textiles from China and spices, dyes and precious stones from India and

Table 3.2 Pre-modern European historical development: main periods, events, factors and dynamics

Pre-modern periods	'Internal' cross-European factors and dynamics	'External' cross-European factors and dynamics
Ancient Empires (4th Century BC-5th Century AD)	• 'Hellenic world' 'empire' • Roman empire • Germanic invasions + migrations (Goths, Burgundians, Franks, etc.) • Romanising of Europe • Christianising of Rome and empire	• Barbarian invasions + migrations (e.g. Vandals, Goths) • Early Christianity in Middle East provinces
Early Middle Ages (5th to 11th Centuries)	• Christian kingships + Western 'empires' (Carolingian + Germanic) • Invasions and migrations (Vikings, Normans, etc.) • Feudal military + agricultural system (v. invasions) • Split of West + East European 'Roman' empires + 'Christendoms'	• Barbarian invasions + migrations (Huns, Slavs, Bulgars, Magyars, Mongols, etc.) • Islamic Invasion of Western Europe (Iberia) • Crusades • Eurasian overland trade (silk, slaves, via Samarkand, etc.)
Late (High) Middle Ages (12th to 15th Centuries)	• Development of national + absolutist states • Development of West European Christianity + Papacy • Development of feudal system (and of military + agricultural technologies) • Migrations from land to towns • Development of town-based capitalist economy + society (burghers + guilds)	• Barbarian + Islamic invasions of East Europe (Mongols + Turks) • Blockage of Eurasian trade • Beginnings of oceanic exploration of sea-routes to India + Asia

Sources: Information compiled from various sources; see endnotes for this chapter, including notes 1, 7, 10 and 11.

South Asia. These commodities came to be highly prized as markers of lifestyle, status and power by Europe's governing political and ecclesiastical elites, and in most cases could not be produced within Europe. For centuries, through to at least the middle centuries of the Middle Ages, Europe was a relatively minor regional player on the periphery of this world trade, which was most highly developed in circuits linking China, India and Arabia.[5] A range of land-based and sea-based trade routes, together with developed commercial and transport organisations, laws and systems was developed to provide the necessary socio-economic infrastructure for these long-distance trading circuits. The main 'silk roads' were land-based and linked northern China to the eastern Mediterranean through the Mongolian steppes, Persia and either Arabia or the Black Sea. The main 'spice' routes included sea and land-based systems from the East Indies and India through the Persian Gulf or Red Sea to the eastern Mediterranean (see Table 3.1).

Until the middle of the Middle Ages Europe was relatively undeveloped economically compared with the main participants in the world trade circuits. In addition to whatever economic benefits European trading cities and their mercantile and financial classes received from world trade, it can be argued that more broadly Europe benefited disproportionately in many ways from it. It benefited culturally in general because of the information flow enabled by trade flows, and which involved different and challenging moral-religious and scientific ideas and worldviews. In particular, it benefited from the service to world civilisation as a whole provided by Islamic literate culture's retention of ancient Greek philosophical, scientific and literary texts. This was against the background of post-Roman fragmentation and incessant conflict and instability across continental Europe. The rediscovery of these texts in the 13th and 14th centuries as part of Europe's trade links with the Arab world helped to fuel the Renaissance.[6] Politico-economically, Europe benefited disproportionately from this trade, among other ways, in terms of the powerful models of societal organisation (for instance of international economic systems, large-scale cities and poly-ethnic empires) that it provided, and also the flow of military and economic technologies it supplied, and we return to this theme later.

War and invasion
However, other external influences, although equally powerful and pervasive in their impacts on European society and civilisation, were much less positive. Some of the main external factors which need to be recognised when understanding pre-modern Europe's development in the late classical and early medieval period were almost wholly threatening to Europe, which was seen as the Romanised but post-imperial sphere of 'Christendom'. Europe's 'common ground' and its common condition in these pre-modern periods, among other things, was its vulnerability to these external threats. However, this very vulnerability was effective within Europe in stimulating and communicating technological and organisational development, particularly politically and militarily. For over a millennium the external threats involved the recurrent possibility of the destruction of European cities and societies, and the mass killing or enslavement of Europeans by invading armies from outside the sub-continent.

On the one hand, Europe experienced recurrent waves of invasion from the 'east', from Eurasian and Central Asian tribes and empires that were often seen by Europeans as 'barbarians', through much of the classical period, throughout the first millennium and through much of the second millennium.[7] Persian threats to invade and control Greece in the classical period, particularly in the 5th century BC when they were decisively defeated, could be said to have resulted in a strengthening of the Greek system of city-states, arguably the cradle of European civilisation. The Roman empire was not so fortunate with its eastern invasions. In the first millennium Central Asian and Eurasian Huns invaded European lands throughout the 4th and 5th centuries AD, including much of the by then Christianised Roman empire, in both its Western and Eastern versions. In turn, Hun invasions drove the north and eastern European 'barbarian' tribes, such as Vandals and Goths, bordering the Roman empire, to enter and challenge it militarily. The capital of the Western Roman empire, Rome, was sacked by Goths and then by Vandals in the 5th century. The Western empire fell and Gothic kingdoms were created in post-Roman Italy and Spain. Post-Roman early medieval Europe more or less immediately faced further invasion from the East. Eurasian Bulgars and Magyars invaded and occupied Eastern European kingdoms and the Eastern Roman empire (Byzantium). These threats were in turn soon followed by invasion by Central Asian armies of the first and second Mongol empires in the 13th and 14th century, respectively. The military power of European Christian feudal knights of Germany, Hungary and Poland was decisively defeated on European soil by armies of the first Mongol empire during the 13th century. The northern Black Sea lands of modern Ukraine and southern Russia were occupied and controlled successively by Eurasian and Central Asian invaders, Scythians in the classical period, the Bulgar empire in the early medieval period, and the khans of the first and second Mongol empires in the 13th and 14th centuries.

On the other hand, from the post-Roman early medieval to the early modern period, Christian Europe also experienced continuous threats from what no doubt appeared to it as a different version of 'barbarianism', namely that of an alternative and equally authoritative monotheistic religion, Islam. Militant and empire-building Islamic powers invaded Europe in two major waves which have both left their mark on European history and identity through to the contemporary period. The first wave was that of Arab Islam from the 7th century. The expansion of Arab Islam and its caliphates after the death of Muhammad in 632 was rapid and occurred on many fronts simultaneously. Three fronts were of relevance to Europe and its Christians – Jerusalem, Byzantium and Spain. First, Christian access to the Holy Places of their religion in Jerusalem, previously controlled by them, was lost as Arabs took control of the city in 638. Secondly, Islamic armies and navies attacked the Byzantine empire and attempted to take its capital Constantinople on two occasions (668 and 717), ultimately unsuccessfully. Finally, from 711 Islamic armies invaded the Iberian peninsula, defeated its Visigothic kingdoms and installed Arab Islamic control and caliphates throughout Iberia. An additional attempt to invade and conquer France for Islam was defeated by Frankish feudal knights at Poitiers in mid-France in 732. Islamic control of Spain flourished for a number of centuries but was ultimately driven out after a long series of campaigns by the end of the 15th century. The long-term persistence of the Islamic military threat and cultural presence in Iberia contributed directly and indirectly to the identity and development of at least three European nations – France, Spain and Portugal. The initial period of military threat and the need to define and defend French culture and territory strengthened the power of the Frankish king Charlemagne and his development of the first extensive European Christian empire in the post-Roman/early medieval period. Later, the long-term project to 'reconquer' Iberia for Christendom, led from the 12th century by successions of alliances of Iberian kingdoms, created the context in which the Spanish and Portuguese states could be constructed and their national cultures could begin to be defined and popularised.

The second wave of Islamic invasion of Europe that left its mark on European modernity occurred when the Ottoman Turks surrounded the Byzantines in the 14th century. Constantinople, which had successfully fought off Islamic attacks for centuries, finally fell to the Ottomans in 1453. The Turkish Islamic empire invaded and took control of much of the Balkans and southeastern Europe, from the 14th century onwards, defeating a Serb-led alliance at the battle of Kosovo in 1389. Periodically, the Ottomans invaded the Hapsburg empire and attempted, unsuccessfully, to take its capital Vienna on two occasion in the early modern era (1529 and 1683). Islamic control of southeastern Europe endured until the revival of nationalism and Orthodox Christianity in Greece, Serbia, Bulgaria, among others, in the 19th century. Nationalist struggles against Turkish rule ensued, followed by the dismemberment of the Turkish empire after the First World War in the 20th century and the (re)construction of the nation-states of southeastern Europe.

Internal factors

In addition to the external 'barbarian' and other influences on European civilisation and state formation there were also important internal factors and dynamics. These were both the allegedly 'civilising' influences of the Hellenistic world, the Roman empire and the Christian church, and also the influence of Europe's own allegedly 'barbarian' cultures. Each of these internal factors generated distinct flows of cultural, political and economic influence across the sub-continent, experiences of culture-contact and communication, and elements of standardisation in ways of life. Each appeared to undermine and superimpose itself on the factor which preceded it. However, in reality the later factor of Christianity, which most clearly characterised Europe as a distinct civilisation in the medieval period, tended to retain the imprints and build on the contributions of the earlier factors. We can now look at them briefly in turn.

European 'barbarians' and European civilisation

European 'barbarian' cultures generally provided the context for the development of waves of cross-European 'civilisation-making' in the classical period. Three of the main waves were those of Romanisation, the Christianisation of the Roman empire, and post-Roman/early medieval Christianisation. Celtic and Germanic (Gothic) tribal culture provided the main continental context both for the wave of Romanisation which rolled out east and west from Italy (the 3rd century BC to the 2nd century AD) with the construction of the Roman republican and then imperial regime from Scotland to the Black Sea. Together with the Slavs in central and eastern Europe, they also provided the context for the primary wave of Christianisation of the patchwork of cultures incorporated within the empire in both its western and eastern versions, in the period of fragmentation and decline of the western empire (5th century AD). Viking and Slav 'barbarian' cultures provided the main context for the secondary wave of Christianisation which rolled out beyond the ex-Roman lands through north and eastern Europe until the 11th century and beyond.

Cross-European cultural influences and the emergence of some significant forms of commonality, a common European civilisation, were evident in the pre-Roman period (e.g. c. 600BC–100BC). In this period, the 'Iron Age' cultures and religions of the various major northern and central European 'barbarian' tribal and civilisational groups were widely distributed, overlapped and influenced each other. The term 'barbarian' referred to the fact that these tribes, particularly the Celtic and Germanic tribes, had either undeveloped writing systems or none at all, and spoke languages other than Greek and, subsequently, Latin. Thus Greeks and Roman colonisers and empire-builders found it difficult to communicate with them in the course of their only partially successful attempts to conquer and enslave them.

However, cultures such as that of the Celts had a civilisational presence and progressive influence, not least in spheres such as metal-working and the creation of weapons and jewellery. This influence was felt all the way across Europe, from the British Isles to the Black Sea, including by the Greeks and the pre-imperial Romans.[8] Generally, 'barbarian' cultures' influences on the long-term development of European society and civilisation in the classical and early medieval periods, both direct and indirect, both destructive and constructive, were important and are often wrongly underestimated and marginalised.

Barbarian cultures provided the context, in this period, for the development of the Greek city-states and, through their creation of colonies and alliances, for the development of a distinctively Hellenic world in the lands bordering the Aegean and eastern Mediterranean. The Greeks created the first great intensively and extensively recorded version and stage of 'European civilisation' in their innovations in alphabetic literacy, arts (e.g. sculpture and architecture), sciences (medicine, astronomy, mathematics), politics (e.g. democracy, law, and constitutionalism) and much else. In addition, in the early 4th century BC the Macedonian king Alexander extended the reach of this civilisation by leading a pan-Hellenic empire-building project into Persia and beyond, temporarily unifying an empire which covered what is now the territory of Greece, Egypt, Turkey, Afghanistan, Iran and Pakistan.[9]

Roman empire-building and European civilisation

In its turn, the Roman empire, when it had forcibly incorporated the Hellenic world by the 3rd century BC, imposed an even stronger and more standardised cultural uniformity on much of the European continent. The empire's 'Europe' was bounded to the north by the great rivers of the Rhine and the Danube and to the east by the Black Sea and Asia Minor, and it incorporated North Africa to the south. This turned the Mediterranean into an 'inland' Roman–European sea and waterway for a number of centuries, rather than being the 'natural' borderline between continents and civilisations that it appears as today. The cross-European influence of Rome continued in later centuries and eras in the influence of Roman law, Roman architecture ('Romanesque' church building in the early medieval period, 'classical' architecture in the modern period), the status of the Latinised literate heritage in all subsequent education systems up to the contemporary period, and the status of Roman power politics as models and its political titles as high status names for rulers. The titles of 'Kaiser' and 'Tsar' for the office of political leader in the German and Russian polities in the modern period derive from 'Caesar' and generally the title of 'emperor' taken by post-Roman European rulers from Charlemagne to Napoleon is an acknowledgement of the continuing status and influence of the Roman empire. The influence of Rome and Greece continued through the period of European modernity from the 19th century onwards when the search for Graeco-Roman heritage, connections and legitimacy, fuelled by the discoveries about Greece and Rome of the new science of archaeology, was important to the education systems and self-images of German, French and British nation and empire-builders.

The Roman empire and the 'Romanisation' of Europe that it involved became the crucial social mechanism for the early pan-European dissemination of Christianity – effectively a new revisionist Judaism, in the 100–400 AD period. With the later rise of the idea of Europe as 'Christendom' (and in international law as 'republica Christiana') particularly in the post-Roman early medieval period, Christianity was to associate itself during the medieval period and beyond with the identity of the whole continent of Europe for over a millennium. This was both for 'insiders' and also for 'outsiders', crucially the aggressive 'outsiders' of Central Asia and Islamic North Africa, and later from the 16th century onwards the colonised 'outsiders' of 'pagan' and 'barbarian' South America, East Asia and Africa.

The extension of the Roman empire to Asia Minor, its takeover of the Greek world, and the relocation of its capital under Emperor Constantine to the new city of Constantinople in the 4th century precipitated a division of the empire into Western and Eastern halves. The Latin language-based Western 'Roman' empire was by this time militarily weak and increasingly vulnerable to the incursions of powerful 'barbarian' Germanic tribes, in particular the Franks and Goths into what is now France, Italy and Spain. The Greek language-based Eastern 'Roman' empire, was for many centuries after the fall of the Western empire, relatively speaking, much more secure. In a form later referred to as the Byzantine empire, it continued for another millennium to be the dominant power in the eastern Mediterranean and Asia Minor until overthrown by the Islamic Ottoman Turks in the 15th century. The Byzantine empire was partially re-Latinised after being retaken by the Venetians during a crusade in the 13th century, and was a declining regime by the time of its overthrow. Nevertheless Byzantine civilisation continued to influence world history through the extension of orthodox Christianity through the Balkans and in particular to Russia, where it blossomed into a major defining characteristic of Russian ethnic and national culture and identity, an identity which is newly resurgent in our times.

Christianity and European civilisation

The 'Christianisation' of the Roman empire occurred against the background we have sketched above and this had a number of important consequences for European history and culture. First, it led to a major 'schism' between the Latin language-based Western church and the Greek language-based Eastern church, which helped to structure the continent into Western and Eastern zones from that time to this. The split developed over a number of centuries in the early medieval period and was formalised in the 11th century. Secondly, the political and military weakness of the Western empire gave the Western church based in Rome a number of incentives to develop itself in particular ways, which we can now consider in a little more detail.

On the one hand, lacking political and military power, if it was to survive and to exert its influence and authority, it needed to do so mainly through culture. That is to say, it needed to do so through the media of ideas and ideals, of faith and doctrines, and through the related Europe-wide institutionalisation of church-building. This cultural system was organised through a hierarchy of bishoprics, culminating in that of the Pope, the 'Bishop of Rome', and the Papacy. Originally there had been five Christian Patriarchs. Three of these were engulfed by the rise and spread of Islam in the 7th century, namely the Patriarchs of Alexandria, Antioch (Syria) and Jerusalem. The remaining two, the Patriarchs of Rome and Constantinople, provided the organisational focal points for the subsequent East–West schism in Christianity.

Western Latin Christianity became an actively missionising church, attempting to convert the incoming 'barbarian' kings and their kingships to the official Roman imperial religion. In this respect, beginning with the conversion of Clovis, king of the Franks, in the mid-4th century, it was largely successful. The missionising church swept steadily through Europe in the early medieval period with the Scandinavians, Poles and Russians converting to the doctrines of the European Christian faith community by the 11th century. However, the missionising church also led to the great extra-territorial anti-Islamic 'crusades' and 'holy war' ('just war') projects of the 11th–12th centuries. The European 'crusading church', with its project to 'save souls' and its doctrine of 'just war' against heretics and infidels, left a disastrous legacy of violence in the Middle Eastern Islamic world on the routes to the holy city of Jerusalem in this period, a legacy which of course survives and indeed is resurgent to this day.

From the 11th century, the institutionalisation of Christianity involved the creation and propagation of standardised and high-status Europe-wide monastic orders and the Europe-wide building of great high-status cathedrals in Europe's towns and cities. The Christianisation of Europe in the post-Roman early medieval period also led to a strong defensive attitude to what it was in Europe that needed to be defended against threats, invasions and migrations by 'barbarian' insiders (e.g. 8th/9th-century Vikings) and 'outsiders' (Islamic Arabs in the 8th–12th centuries, East Asian nomads (from Huns to Magyars, Turks and others) from the 5th–13th centuries, and Ottoman Turks from the 13th–17th centuries). What needed to be defended was what now defined Europe as a religiously inscribed environment, as Christendom, namely the network of sacred places, churches and the relics of the saints, and the places and territories of the sacralised cities, princedoms, kingdoms and empires, and the places and routes of mass pilgrimages.[10] Fatefully, of course, the sacralised environment extended beyond Europe's continental territories to include Jerusalem and 'the Holy Land', which was under Arab Islamic control.

Within Europe, Christianity was successful in exerting direct cultural influence and authority, together with indirect political power, through the medium of the propagation of faith and doctrine, through the governance of its institutions and through the mobilising power of its missionising and crusading projects. In this way, the Western church and the Pope as its leader could aspire to some direct, albeit limited, political and economic control of territories in Italy and also to much more widespread indirect political influence across Europe. The latter could be achieved by providing religious legitimation for the rule of princes, kings and emperors in Europe's emerging proto-states and proto-nations. The Pope and the Papacy became a central, integrative and legitimising power and authority in a Europe that was never wholly or permanently 'captured' and controlled by any of the continent's more diverse secular powers, although it was often threatened by them, particularly by the emperors of the Holy Roman Empire in the 11th–13th-century period. They governed the Eastern, Germanic section of Charlemagne's 9th-century

Frankish-Germanic empire. Indeed, they effectively represented Europe and attempted to play the role of power-brokers between Western European states and empires, on the one hand, and the Orthodox Christian Byzantine empire (11th–15th centuries) on the other hand. Later, in the form of the Hapsburg empire, they represented Europe in relation to threats from the Ottoman Turkish empire (from the 15th century onwards).

Commonalities of Societal Organisation and Change in Pre-modern Europe: Factors in the Rise and Fall of Feudalism[11]

Early European society and change

In the classical period the main economic basis for the survival of Europe's peoples and societies was settled farming, crop cultivation and animal husbandry (semi-nomadic pastoralism), supplemented by hunting and by the acquisition of resources (including slaves) generated by raiding neighbouring communities. This was particularly so in the northern, central and Atlantic European regions occupied by Nordic, Germanic and Celtic 'iron age' tribal communities. The process of clearing the great European forests to create farm land began in this period. In the form of 'assarting', this process gathered pace throughout the medieval period using slave or serf labour. This extension, together with more intensive forms of agricultural production, provided key dynamics in the development of localised, militarised and ultimately Christianised forms of feudalism in east and northern Europe in this period.[12]

In southern Europe in the period of the Alexandrian Hellenic empire and then in the Roman empire, more advanced forms of urban and imperial organisation permitted larger-scale economic production and long-distance distribution systems. These involved plantation production and large-scale use of slave labour, together with inter-city and inter-regional specialisation, transport and trade. In both 'civilised' and 'barbarian' society, iron age mining (of metal ore, semi-precious stones, rock salt etc.) and metal-working industries supported the production of military technologies such as weapons, armour and chariots; (the metal elements of) economic and urban technologies such as tools, carts, buildings and trading ships; elites' domestic food and drink utensils; and elites' status ornamentation and jewellery.

Roman imperial expansionism fuelled the need to finance and supply the empire's formidable military machine through organised and empire-wide tithes, taxation and tribute in order to dominate and incorporate new colonies, to maintain the *pax Romana* across all of its colonies and provinces, and to defend the empire's long and distant Rhenish and Danubian borders against invasion by the 'barbarian' tribes of the north, west and east. This in turn generated a powerful economic dynamic, enhancing economic organisation, growth and general living standards in the empire, attracting incoming migrant barbarian communities until the empire was finally eroded and defeated by Frankish, Gothic and other barbarian tribal societies and proto-nations in the 5th century.

In the main Germanic and Scandinavian tribes, leadership was by warrior chieftains and warlords, and there were usually traditions of election of the bravest and most charismatic to 'kingship'. The inheritance of kingship by rights of descent (dynasticism) became important later in the development of European states, particularly in the late medieval and early modern periods of so-called 'absolute' monarchy and state formation. However, in this early period any such rights were balanced by the perceived effectiveness of kings to defend and benefit their peoples, and to command loyalty from warriors and nobilities. European political institutions were shaped by varying combinations of the legal traditions inherited from Roman imperialism and the mixtures of elective and dynastic traditions inherited from European tribalism.[13]

Medieval European society and change 500–1500: the rise and fall of feudalism

The rise of feudalism

In the early medieval period a localised feudal agrarian economy developed. This was based on an unequal social contract between peasants and landowners. Peasant serfs were provided with access to land and thus the ability to grow food to feed their families and communities, in return for obligations to work for, and to produce a surplus to pay for protection by, warrior elites and nobilities. The expansion of this system across Europe continued to be driven throughout the medieval period by the process of forest-clearing noted earlier. In addition, it was fuelled by agricultural technology improvements imported from the middle East and beyond, which substantially increased the productivity of both land and labour. These included crucial innovations such as windmills and watermills, heavy turn ploughs and breeds of heavy horses to pull them, together with horseshoes and collar harnesses to make the system work.[14] Feudalism resulted in a degree of fragmentation of European social formations which tended to develop in ways which were more politically decentralised, economically productive and self-sufficient, and also more locally militarily defensible than had been the case in the preceding imperial era.

Politico-military and political-economic dynamics in Europe changed in the post-Roman early medieval period from the expansion and defence of a cross-continental imperial system to the expansion and defence of a complex system of localised agrarian settlements. In this context, there was initially something of a general decline in the relative political and economic role of towns and cities across Europe. This situation ultimately altered in favour of

European towns and cities as political and economic hubs and distribution centres in the high medieval period as a result of a number of factors. Among other things, agricultural production continued to grow, to differentiate regionally, and to seek wider markets. International trade developed, politico-military changes enhanced the urban location of monarchical and ecclesiastical authority, and investments were made to fortify towns and cities against European and non-European military threats.

Stereotypes of feudal agriculture might imply a picture of an inflexible economy involving the political control and spatial fixing of labour. However, the system always had some dynamic elements, as already indicated. This increasingly included, in Western Europe at least, the freeing up of labour and the development of labour markets as well as produce markets. The traditional mobility of labour around the countryside and between town and countryside in response to seasonal patterns of production became qualitatively enhanced as problems in the supply of labour deepened over time. The factors influencing these developments included the increasing use and recurrent loss of manpower in warfare, and the occasional decimation of populations because of plagues (such as the Black Death of the 1340s which killed possibly half of Europe's population).[15] Ironically, such plagues were spread, among other reasons, because of the growth of cross-continental and inter-world regional trade, and in turn, through the boost they gave to labour demand, wage levels and labour productivity, they ultimately can be said to have contributed to economic growth in Western Europe.[16]

There is a tendency when considering feudal Europe to assume that it was above all else an economic system. Sociology, in particular, has no doubt been influenced in this direction by Marxism's economistic 'historical materialist' approach and its view of modernity focused on capitalism as an economic system, and on modern social classes mainly in terms of the relations of production. However, it needs to be emphasised that feudalism and Europe's transition from feudalism to capitalism in the course of modernisation cannot be understood in mainly economistic terms, nor in the mainly internalist terms (of class relationships) they imply. To understand both the rise and the decline of feudalism requires that the other dimensions of societal analysis, namely the political (particularly the politico-military) and the cultural (particularly the religious), together with external factors, be fully taken into account.

The incessant external politico-military threats to pre-modern Europe noted earlier had a profound effect on stimulating the rise of feudalism. They promoted processes which we can refer to as the 'hardening' of European societies' defences. They did so in two senses. First, there was the physical hardening of habitations, by the walling of kings', warlords' and nobles' courts and great houses (castles and forts), and ultimately the walling of towns and cities. Secondly, there was the defensive 'hardening' during the late classical and early medieval periods, given the decline and ultimately the absence of Roman imperial power, of local communities through the feudal system of social organisation itself.

Contrary to the view that sees feudalism as a mainly economic system, it was in reality just as much a politico-military-based system. It effectively involved new social contracts between peasant farmers and local warrior nobility for the latter to provide military protection to the former in return for tithes, taxes and military service from the peasantry. In addition, it effectively involved new power balances and social contracts between empowered local nobilities and all putative centralising authorities and state-builders, such as claimants to kingship. The latter could only qualitatively improve and entrench their ascendancy and purchase the support of their nobles by campaigns of external raids, wars and other such military adventures, whether against neighbouring societies and states or against Europe's various enemies and 'others', particularly in the Islamic world during the period of the Crusades (11th–13th centuries).

The external military threats were significantly reduced after Europe's gunpowder-based 'military revolution' in armament technology. This began in 14th century and came to a head in the 16th century, and we explore its social impacts on the development of the European complex in greater depth later (in this chapter and in Chapter 5).[17] As a result of this revolution, the relationship between world regions and civilisations turned dramatically in Europe's favour. From the 16th century onwards Europe was able to develop and deploy a massive military technological superiority as compared with all other civilisations on land and sea. Also as a result of this revolution, Europe's feudal system of class relations had been substantially undermined, revealing the system's essential politico-military character. The social power and authority of feudal nobilities rested on their specialist military skill in the arts of heavily armoured cavalry-based warfare. This could not ultimately survive the advent of firearms deployed by large-scale infantry-based armies. The possession of firearms had the capacity, in principle, to equalise and empower their possessors as individuals without respect to class. Simultaneously it also created new possibilities for the monopolisation of the means of force, which was a precondition for kingship achieving ascendancy over feudal nobilities, as well as for the centralised control, defence and expansion of the territorial states which marked the modernisation process in the early modern period in Europe.

The decline of feudalism and the rise of modernity [18]

The decline of feudalism in Europe was not historically inevitable, as 'historical materialist' perspectives might imply. Nor was it a unitary and once-and-for-all process. It receded unevenly over time across different regions of Europe, more rapidly in the north and west, and much more slowly in the east. Its recession was associated with a number of interconnected internal (intra-European) and external factors. Ultimately, feudalism (at least in its European variants[19]) proved to be incompatible with the economic, political and cultural characteristics and dynamics involved in the growth of capitalism and of modernisation in general in Europe. The 15th century was a 'tipping point' in European social change. Key factors involved in the decline of feudalism and the concomitant rise of capitalism and early modernity can be seen in this period in high profile. These factors included the major external 'event' of the advent of a hostile and Islamic Ottoman Turkish empire on Europe's southeastern border and indeed on Europe's territories in this region in the 15th century. We briefly review this period and the factors involved in it in the following section. First, however, it is useful to set the scene somewhat by considering the relevance and development of towns and cities in Europe in the medieval period.

Even if the main political and economic structures of medieval Europe were feudal and thus based in the countryside, around landed power and agricultural labour, nevertheless towns and cities were very significant components of medieval culture and economy. Culturally this can be seen in the mid/high medieval (11th–14th centuries) heritage of Christian religious buildings, cathedrals, churches and monasteries, which still mark towns and cities across contemporary Europe.[20] In terms of economic activity, mid-medieval towns and cities continued to undertake and develop their intra- and inter-regional role and, in the leading cases (particularly Venice, and also Genoa and others), their international trade.

In this period we can see the beginning of the development of modern Europe's central 'city-belt' from northern Italy, around the Alps, through the Rhineland to the low countries of northwestern Europe.[21] Later, the international trading cities, particularly Venice but also other Italian cities, developed from Roman and Byzantine sea-going experience. These cities built trading empires involving the exchange of, among other things, precious metals and slaves from Eastern Europe for silks, spices and other luxuries for Europe's ruling elites. These were transported to and from India and China via the Black Sea and the overland 'silk route' to China, and in relation to India and the 'spice trade' via a mixture of land and sea routes through Alexandria, the Byzantine empire based in Constantinople, and also the Islamic world of Mesopotamia and the Persian Gulf.[22]

In the post-Roman early and mid-medieval periods, Europe's towns and cities were useful to the rising rulers and kings of Europe's migrant barbarian proto-states and empires because they provided the capital base for them to mount their many military campaigns and adventures. These were undertaken for their own material interests in raising resources through raiding and pillaging, for their political interest in extending the productive land and serf labour under their control, to reward their often querulous and rebellious circles and counsels of feudal nobles, and sometimes, at least ostensibly, for religious reasons, as in the Crusades of the 11th–13th centuries.

In the later medieval period, cities became increasingly important and powerful and we can see the emergence in embryo in this period of the new economic system of capitalism in the development of cities and their economies, particularly the international trading cities of northern Italy (especially Venice and Genoa), the bases of the European Renaissance.[23] Cities were relatively free from involvement and smothering by the feudal system, particularly so in Western and Central Europe which had the strongest networks of cities, and many conceived of and constructed themselves as city-states. To enhance their position further networks of inter-linked trading cities and city-states occasionally banded together in formal leagues and federations (for instance, the Hanseatic League in the Baltic and the Lombard League in northern Italy). They provided a non-feudal base for capital accumulation via trading, finance and production. They specialised in politically important crafts and trades, such as iron-working and weapon manufacture for military purposes and precious metal and jewellery-working for political and religious elite luxury consumption and status display. They enabled distinct non-feudal economic classes and institutions to develop (e.g. finance capitalists and banking institutions) and attendant social organisations (e.g. the craft guilds). The rise of towns and cities in European society over the course of the medieval period was both an indicator and condition of the decline of feudalism both as an economic and also a politico-military system, a decline which was particularly apparent by the 15th century, to which we now turn.

Beginning the Transition to European Modernity: The 'Long' 15th century [24]

The 15th century in Europe represented a major period of change and transition towards modernity. This was particularly so in the dimension of European culture, where three cultural revolutions occurred. First, there was the advent of printing, which transformed the continent's communications and cultural transmission system. Secondly, there was the long process known as 'the Renaissance', in which art and humanistic culture reached new heights. A 'long century' interpretation of the 15th century incorporates the early decades of the 16th century. This allows both the origins as well as the first manifestations of the third revolution, the Protestant Reformation, to be taken into account. Each of these three cultural revolutions can be said to be significantly 'internal' to Europe, were massively influential and have left their marks on contemporary Europe, and we return to them later. In addition to these changes, and no doubt interconnected with and assisting them, a number of momentous political and economic transformations began to get underway in this period. These were of an interconnected internal and external kind, and they include technological revolutions in military and transport systems and major changes on the geopolitical situation and fate of Europe in relation to its East and West border zones. A number of these factors and events, which made the 15th century such a transitionary period, are summarised in Table 3.3 and will be commented on in this section. 'Eurocentric' assumptions might predispose the discussion towards a focus on 'internal'

Table 3.3 Early modern Europe: the transition period 1300–1550 and the 'long' 15th century

	CULTURE		POLITY			ECONOMY		External factors + influences
	Religion	Architecture, art, etc.	War	Military technology	Power aspects	Social aspects		
14th century Years 1300– 1350	Crises in Catholic Christianity: 1307–77	Italian Renaissance: e.g. Giotto's 1334–59 Bell Tower, Florence	1337 Hundred Years War begins: England v. France	1326 First Cannon (Florence/ England) Longbow/ crossbow undercut the power of European Feudal nobility	1339 War bankrupts English king (Edward III). Crisis for Florence + Europe's banking system	1348 Black Death halves Europe's population, leading to a rise in labour mobility + incomes v. feudalism	Late 13th century Chinese gunpowder + cannon technology to Europe by early 14th century Black Death via silk + spice trade routes Second mongol empire (Tamerlane) takes control of Persia, North India, South Russia, and threatens China, etc.	
1350– 1400	Papacy returns to Rome + 'Two Popes' Schism 1378–1414		Mercenary armies invade northern italy; inter-city wars	1450–1550 First gun powder revolution: 'bronze age' guns		1357 + Peasants' Revolts across Europe	1354 Ottoman Turks take Gallipoli 1389 Turks defeat Serbs at Kosovo 1402 Mongols defeat Turks and block East	
15th Century 1400– 1450	1453 Gutenberg's Bible + seeds of Reformation	1419–36 Brunelleschi's dome for Florence's cathedral			1492 Columbus to Americas (Spain)		1421–23 Chinese navy to West Africa (+ possibly to North & South America), but then China totally withdraws	
1450– 1500	1478 Spanish Inquisition 1494–8 Savonarola's pre-'puritan' coup in Florence 1492 Spain ejects last Islamists and also Jews	1450 Gutenberg's press + the spread of print technology + literate culture	1453 Hundred Years War' v. England ends French victory + boost to French nation-statehood	1453 Turks use cannon against Con-stantinople New field artillery + naval use of cannon	1493 Pope 'divides world' for Portugal + Spain 1498 Da Gama to India + spice trade (Portugal)		1453 Turks take Constantinople + Byzantine (Eastern Christian) empire 1456 Turks defeat Hungary + take Belgrade 1492 Tamerlane dies; end of Mongol threats (except to Russia)	
16th Century 1500– 1550	1517 Luther's articles + Reformation 1530 Northern German 'Protestant' states v. Hapsburg. emperor. 1533 English king excom-municated + boost to Protestant English nation-statehood	Michaelangelo: The 'David' statue in Florence (1501), Sistine chapel paintings (1512) Leonardo: 'Last Supper' (1497) 'Mona Lisa' (1505) Papacy: St. Peter's long + costly rebuilding begun in Rome	1495–1525 France invades Northern Italy 1525 Spain ejects France from Italy. Religious wars in northern Europe	1550–1650 Second gun powder revolution: 'iron age' cannon + muskets Arms race New military organisation training of mass infantry armies	Spain's Americas empire, gold/silver to Europe Europe to Africa/Asia Control of spice trade + new Atlantic slave trade	Scientific + factory-based weapons production European population recovers to pre-Black Death levels	1529 Turks threaten Hapsburg empire + lay siege to Vienna 1536 Turks ally with France v. Hapsburg empire	

Sources: Information compiled from various sources; see endnotes for this chapter.

factors. However, this analysis aims to take full account of the influence of external factors, both positive and negative, as well as internal factors.

A shattering geopolitical and military event occurred in the mid-15th century, which reverberated around Europe creating long-term after-shocks and reactions which helped to shape the Europe we are familiar with today. The event was to result, for at least two centuries afterwards, in both conflicting and cooperative politico-military projects across Europe to promote continental political interests and cultural identities both on the continent and outside it. This event was the fall of the great capital city of the Christian Byzantine empire, Constantinople, to the Islamic Ottoman Turks in 1453.

The capture of this strategically key city represented a great leap forward in the power of the Ottoman empire. It enabled the empire to decisively consolidate its previously slowly growing influence over Eastern Europe, and it underscored the long-term geopolitical and cultural threat the empire posed to the rest of Europe. From the 14th century the Turks had successfully raided, invaded and dominated major regions of Eastern Europe, in particular the Balkans, the lower Danube plains and the western borders of the Black Sea. They in their turn were being pressured and threatened in their Eurasian and Anatolian lands by Mongols and Russians and felt pressures to move west. The city of Constantinople that they captured was by the mid-15th century the engulfed core of the long-diminished eastern half of the classical-era Roman empire. However, this was a very significant event for Europe for at least two reasons, one connected with warfare and the other with trade and Europe's capacities for economic growth.

In terms of warfare, the Turks achieved the capture of Constantinople through, among other things, a demonstration of the effects of an early version of the 'gunpowder revolution' in new military technology. This led to 'the military revolution' we need to discuss at greater length in the following chapter. Gunpowder technology had entered the Middle East down the trade routes from China. As with agricultural and other technologies in the medieval period, it ultimately found its way to Europe and greatly affected Europe's political, economic and cultural development.[25] The Ottoman Turks were the first to construct new large-scale cannons and they deployed them in overwhelming force in their successful siege of Constantinople. Gunpowder-based armament technology was rapidly taken up and further developed across Europe's societies even more than with other Chinese and Middle Eastern technological innovations imported throughout the late medieval and early modern periods, to a significant extent because of the recurrent fear of Ottoman invasion. This in turn led to qualitative transformations over the succeeding centuries in the intensity and destructiveness of European societies' war-making capacities and practices, (incessantly rehearsed and perfected within their own world region, via mobile field and siege cannon whether between city-states, kingship states or empires), and also to the recurrent need to achieve power balances between them. It also led to mobile naval cannon and thus impacts in the world outside the European world region. Possession of this military technology was the necessary material condition for the Atlantic European states and polities (principally Portugal, Spain, the Netherlands and England) to be able promote their self-interests, project their power and enforce their will initially through colonial trade and later through imperial projects.

In terms of trade, the city of Constantinople held the key strategic position controlling sea trade between the Mediterranean and Black Seas, and its consequent political links with Venice and other Italian city-states and their colonies and trade networks. This had long given it a pivotal position in medieval Europe's long-distance international trade with China and India, the silk route and the spice trade. Its capture by the Ottoman Turks meant that these lucrative and important trade routes were now subject to Turkish taxation and control, and in any case could be cut off at will. This effectively created a major political and economic crisis situation across Europe's international trading system, but particularly for its roots in the Italian city-states, the trading empires of Venice and Genoa, and the associated financial centre of Florence. Europeans now rapidly needed to react and to search for alternative routes to the East if they wished to retain control over international trade in and out of Europe and to develop it further. They spent the later half of the 15th century, after the fall of Constantinople, urgently investigating alternatives.

The countries of Europe's Atlantic borderlands, particularly Portugal and Spain, later to be followed by the Netherlands and England, were best positioned to explore these alternatives, with the assistance of finance from the Italian city-states. A period of great oceanic explorations and navigations ensued, on the one hand south and east around Africa and through the Indian ocean, and on the other west to south, central and north America. The routinisation of long-distance oceanic travel required new technological developments. These included new navigational and astronomical instruments, improvements in ship building and engineering, and the incorporation of the gunpowder revolution in military technology into naval architecture in the form of naval cannon and the development of ships as weapons platforms. These developments opened up the world and the future to Europe. It gave Europeans both the incentive, given the Turkish control in Eastern Europe, and also the military and transport tools, to extend and defend their trades, and to dominate and ultimately to colonise other societies and civilisations around the world from the 16th to the 19th centuries.

Thus these largely externally-induced 15th-century changes paved the way for the later development by European societies from the 16th century onwards of such things as long-distance oceanic trade routes in spices and silks to India, Indonesia, Japan and China, the pillaging of South American gold and silver, the European colonisation of the Americas, and the horrific trans-Atlantic slave trade. In doing so they also prepared the way for the emergence in European society in general, from the 16th century onwards, of a post-feudal and also a post city-state world. This was a world of large-scale centrally organised and commercially adventurous and competitive national states, particularly in north and west Europe, in England, the Netherlands, France and Spain, with developed and capital-accumulating capital cities and city networks, states which, as we consider further in Chapter 4, were increasingly capable of and recurrently committed to making war with each other.

So far we have considered largely externally induced but major changes which helped to make the 15th century a 'tipping point' in terms of the decline of feudalism and the onset of modernisation. From this we can now briefly turn to the kind of more internal-seeming factors which are more conventionally cited as being relevant to understanding this process. As noted earlier, they are the distinct but connected cultural processes referred to as the Renaissance and (on a 'long' interpretation of the 15th century to include the early 16th century) also the Reformation.

Each of these cultural developments arose in response to opportunities and problems presented by the Western Christian Church, which had been institutionalised under the Roman patriarch or Pope from the 11th century onwards. In the absence of a Byzantine-style empire to enforce it, the Western Church, unlike its Eastern counterpart, as we saw earlier in the discussion of the Roman and post-Roman waves of Christianisation in Europe, relied on a culturally-based strategy involving the sacralising of monarchs' authority and the mass conversion of populations. By the 13th and 14th centuries and the rise of the Italian trade-based city-states, whose leaders and elites required religious legitimation, a new cultural dynamic emerged in connection with the Church. This involved the civic elites' competitive sponsorship and display of ostensibly religious innovative art, sculpture and architecture. This dynamic created the resources and space for the creative and humanistic talents of the Italian Renaissance, and it served to enhance the cultural centrality and political prestige of simultaneously both the civil elites and the Church. However, it did not guarantee the ethics of either.

In the case of the Church, to modify the old saying, those who 'live by the word' risk 'dying by the word'. The mid-medieval church was the custodian and exclusive interpreter for its community of believers of the Christians' 'word of God', both in the literary form of the meaning of the Bible text as well as in the form of prayer. The Church as an organisation depended both on the powerful and their wealth, and also, in relation to the ordinary communities of the faithful, on tithes and the selling of spiritual services (for instance, prayers, relics and rituals). This situation of unaccountable cultural power and economic dependence offered too many possibilities for exploitation, corruption and conflict. These processes duly ensued, affecting all levels in the hierarchy of the Church's organisation from the Papacy down, and they included a schism (1378–1416) in which multiple popes competed for recognition by European states. The Papacy had limited direct control of provinces and territories, but it attempted to aggrandise its power and wealth in its heartland in Rome. In particular, it engaged in a hugely expensive, grandiose and long-drawn-out effort to associate itself with the cultural innovativeness of the period. This was a project, begun in 1505 but only completed in the 17th century, to rebuild the Vatican and in particular St Peter's basilica as new symbols of the Church's cultural and political status and power. It notably included securing the artistic, sculptural and architectural work of the Renaissance master Michaelangelo, among many others.

The general corruption problems, together with the financial burdens placed on the community of the faithful by the Vatican project, generated critical responses and calls for Church reform across Europe. Powerful challenges to the Catholic Church had began to emerge and take root as early as the 14th century and throughout the 15th century. An early wave of criticism was from radical 14th-century Tuscan and Umbrian re-interpreters of Catholicism, such as Francis (in Assisi) and Savonarola (in Florence), and other waves included calls in the 15th century for reform by clerics in England (John Wycliffe) and Bohemia (Jan Hus). However, the main wave built up in Germany in the early years of the 16th century in campaigns against the selling of spiritual services and against the burdens of the Vatican project.

This wave was based in a German cultural context which had begun to be revolutionised in this period by the radical opening up of the public's access to 'God's word' in the Bible, signalled by Gutenberg's publication of the Bible in 1455 using the new technology of moveable type printing. From the late 15th century onwards, printing enabled, among other things, the growth of a radical new personal and mass access to the 'Word of God', through the popular extension of literacy skills and personal reading.[26] This was not only in editions published in the Church's elite language of Latin, but also through those published in most of Europe's major 'national languages', an issue of considerable significance for the formation of European nation-states in early modern Europe, and one we return to in the following chapter. The cultural fires of what came to be called the Protestant Reformation were lit by Martin Luther's criticisms of the Catholic Church's sale of indulgences (remission for penances for believers' sins) in 1517. His criticisms of Catholic Christianity were rapidly published and read, debated and often taken up, across many German states and princedoms, and by people in all social classes, from peasants, to burghers, to princes. This cultural revolution of the Protestant Reformation rapidly spilled over into political and military conflicts across Europe, not least between Protestant states and the Catholic powers of Spain and the Holy Roman (German) Empire. It spelled the end for the apparent unity of medieval Christendom (at least in Western Europe), together with the feudal social and military system associated with it.

The 'long' 15th century, interpreted in terms of this cultural revolution, as well as in terms of the political economic and politico-military revolutions inaugurated and marked by trans-oceanic colonialism, began an historically unprecedented process of modernisation in Europe. This process was to be characterised, among other things, by the development of nationalism, nation-state differences and war-making, and we need to consider these aspects further in the following two chapters.

Conclusion

In this chapter we have charted some key aspects of the pre-modern European social complex, mainly in terms of its commonalities, but also in terms of its differences. The pre-modern commonalities included the following. They included the common ground represented by the European sub-continent as a set of habitats and as a readily traversable and commonly traversed territory. They included interconnected forms of Graeco-Roman and tribal 'barbarian' civilisation which provided the basis for the emergence of a Europe-wide faith community of Christians, and of Europe as 'Christendom' from the Christianisation of the 4th–5th-century Roman empire onwards. In the medieval period, we observed that Europe as Christendom divided into East and Western versions, and later in the early modern period, into Northern Protestant and Southern and Central Catholic versions.

The pre-modern differences included Europe's diverse and pluralistic experience of forms of polity (political community and organisation), particularly empires and city-states. Each of these types of political organisation were notably pluralistic in many ways. Empires were pluralistic because of their military reach and because they were thus poly-ethnic and incorporated many languages and religious groups (for instance, Alexandrian Greece and also Rome in the classical period, and the Holy Roman Empire in the medieval period). At a much smaller level, because of their inter-regional and international trading role, city-states were often similarly cosmopolitan (for instance, Athens in the Hellenic period and Venice in the medieval period). It is important to appreciate this diverse pre-modern context as the background to the development of Europe's medieval and early modern proto-states, and states, and thus ultimately of the sovereign nation-states of modernity.

In pre-modern periods the commonalities and cross-continental connections might be said to have somewhat overshadowed the differences in the European complex. They provide the context for understanding the continent's modernisation process and they have left their marks on European modernity. In Europe, as the modern era got underway, arguably differences began to overshadow commonalities, and we start to consider this next.

Notes

1   Historical sociologists, such as Geary 2002; Gellner 1988; Hobson 2004; Mann 1986, 1993; Tilly 1992, 1993; and Wallerstein 1974, 1980, 1989; also Elias 1983, 2000; Goody 2000, and of course 'long-view' historians, such as Braudel 1993; Davies 1997, 2006; McNeill 1974; and Roberts 1996, point towards an analysis of Europe in terms of its commonalities. That is they tend to treat pre-modern and early modern Europe, at each of its stages of development, as effectively comprising a single societal system. The system is usually visualised as a complex and differentiated one with components changing at different rates and with much internal competition and conflict alongside other more positive processes such as communication and emulation. For relevant discussions of Europe as a civilization, see Delanty 1995; Delanty and Rumford 2005, Chapter 2; and Elias's interesting but controversial studies of Europe's alleged 'civilising process' (Elias 1983, 2000; Fulbrook 2007). Also see the 'long-view' historians indicated above, and Hobson 2004. For contemporary views and debates about Europe as a place of particular values and solidarity, see Michalski 2006.

2   On the deep historical reality of Europe as a succession of versions of 'common ground' and common 'mobility space', see note 4 below. Also see general historical overviews such as those of Davies 1997, Chapter 1; and Roberts 1996, Chapter 1.

3   On the influence of different world regional environments and habitat conditions on different world civilisations, including those of Europe, see Fernandez-Armesto 2001.

4   On these issues see, for instance, Kristiansen 1998 and Oppenheimer 2006 on the prehistoric period; Cunliffe 1997 on the classical period; and McCormick 2002 on the early medieval period. For the early modern period see later Chapter 4.

5   See Abu-Lughod 1989; and Hobson 2004.

6   See Brotton 2002.

7   On 'eastern' invasions, generally, see Davies 1997, Chapter 4; and Roberts 1996, Chapter 4; on Persia, see Holland 2005; on Huns, see Kennedy 2002; on Mongols, see Man 2004; and Marozzi 2004; on Turks, see Goodwin 1999; Lewis 2002; Roxburgh 2005. On Byzantium, see Norwich 1998.

8   See, for example, Eluere 1993; and James 1999.

9   See, for example, Briant 1996.

10 On Christian institution-building in the context of the development of medieval Europe see, for instance, Koenigsberger 1987, *passim*; Le Goff 2005, Chapter 1; also Davies 1997, Chapters 5 and 6; and Roberts 1996, Book 2. For an architectural history perspective on Christian cathedral and church-building see, for instance, Sutton 1999, Chapters 3 and 4, also Chapters 5 and 6 *passim*.

11 On the history of medieval and feudal Europe, see Bartlett 1994; Bloom and Blair 2001; Halsall 2003; Jordan 2002; Koenigsberger 1987; and Le Goff 2005. On this period in relation to the central role of religion and religious conflict, also see O'Shea 2006; and Wheatcroft 2004.

12 See, for example, Jordan 2002.

13 See, for example, the assessment of the early modern political relevance of medieval constitutionalism in Downing 1992.

14   See Hobson 2004, p.102.

15   On medieval European plagues, see McNeil 1998.

16   See Abu-Lughod 1989.

17   For some key discussions of the European early modern military revolution, see Downing 1992; McNeill 1983; Parker 1996; Roberts 1967. As Hobson (2004) reminds us, many of these military technologies were ultimately derived from innovations which reached Europe from elsewhere, particularly from China. However, the European exploitation and transformation of these influences was of qualitative order and was historically decisive.

18   On the decline of feudalism see the seminal discussion by Dobb 1963, Chapter 2; also Mann 1986; and Elias 1983, 2000.

19   Japanese feudalism survived into the 19th century under the Tokugawa shogunate. Its overthrow and restoration of the Meiji emperor provided a context for a rapid process of modernisation, under the external pressure of European and American imperialism and the imperative of national economic development and militarization in order to resist this. For a brief account see Braudel 1993, Chapter 15.

20   On European international trade, trade fair processes and the towns, cities and regions in which they developed, see Abu-Lughod 1989.

21   For sociologists' observations on the history and social significance of the European city belt, see Crouch 1999; Therborn 1995; and Tilly 1992.

22   See Abu-Lughod 1989; and Brotton 2002.

23   See Mann 1986; and Tilly 1992.

24   On the early modern period in Europe, see Brotton 2002; Cameron 2001; MacCullough 2004; and Strathern 2005; also Davies 1997, Chapters 7 and 8; and Roberts 1996.

25   See Hobson 2004 and above. On the historical significance for the development of early modern Europe of the Ottoman Turkish empire and its military and cultural contest with the Hapsburg empire for the mantle of inheritor of the Roman empire, see Wheatcroft 2008.

26   On the revolutionary impact of print literacy in the early modernity see the seminal analysis by Goody and Watt 1975; also Eisenstein 2005.

4

DEVELOPING THE MODERN EUROPEAN COMPLEX: NATION-STATES, CITIZENS AND DIFFERENCE

Introduction

This chapter, together with the following one, is concerned with the emergence of the modern European social complex. In this complex the kinds of commonalities discussed earlier in Chapter 3 tend to play a background role, and differences connected with distinct nation-states present themselves as having a higher role both in ordinary people's perceptions and also often in academic analysis. The following chapter focuses in particular on one key dynamic, which drove the development of a Europe of national differences, namely war. This chapter provides a broader context for understanding what it was that war acted on as a catalyst, namely the three key factors of nationalism, statehood and citizenship. The sections of the chapter deal with each of these factors in turn. We begin with the ideology of nationalism and the myths about it, which were developed in the 19th century. Although this was an early phase in a period we can refer to as 'mature modernity', conceptually, it often reached back into Europe's pre-modern and early modern history. In addition, the discussions in this and the following chapter ultimately aim to enable a fuller picture of the linkages between modern and pre-modern Europe to be pieced together, particularly in respect of the major significance of early modernity and of the 15th-century transitionary dynamics and bridges to modernity which we began to encounter in Chapter 3.

European Nationalisms: Myths and Realities of Identity and Difference[1]

The modern understanding of Europe as characterised largely by its differences refers in particular to the coexistence of the numerous distinct nation-states which parcel up the territory of the sub-continent. Nation-states as social realities have two aspects which concern us here, namely their existence in collective consciousness and discourse and their existence as institutions and practices of self-government. The latter aspect refers to their organisation as 'states' and will be considered in the following section. The former aspect refers to ideologies of and myths about 'nations'. This came to be a popular way of thinking in and about European societies in the early 19th century, and periodically since then. Currently, in the early 21st century, it has become notably visible and politically important again in post-communist Eastern European states, where it often takes a particularly ethnic or ethno-nationalist form. Such nationalist forms of consciousness and discourse are often (but not always) connected with states, and are used to legitimate them, and this is the focus of this section. First, some features of nationalism as an ideological system involving myths about such things as ethnic origin and homeland are considered. Secondly, nationalism's mythic discourse is criticised with reference to some of the historical and social realities of European nations, namely as being ethnic mixtures within politically constructed territories. Finally, some differing perspectives on how and why nationalism arose in the context of European history and modernisation are considered.

Nationalism and myth

Nationalism, as a form of collective consciousness and as a 'movement' in popular politics connected with distinctive cultural identities and the desire for self-government, has been argued to be a distinctly 'modern' phenomenon, developed in the 19th century in particular.[2] The late 18th century saw the 'modern' European political ideals of individual liberty, equality and citizenship institutionalised in the revolutionary and constitutional aspirations of the nation-based states of the USA and France, and also seeded in 'national liberation movements' and state formation in Central and South America.[3] The 19th century saw successful military struggles for national unification and state creation in Italy and Germany. And the same period saw nationalist movements develop across Europe in resistance to dominating empires such as those of Napoleonic France, Russia, Britain, Austro-Hungary and the Ottoman Turks, albeit with variable degrees of success, from Ireland, Belgium and Poland in northern Europe, to Greece, Serbia and Bulgaria in southern and eastern Europe.

Nineteenth-century nationalist ideologies were often initially a political and cultural 'invention' of elite groups.[4] Nonetheless they were propagated relatively rapidly through the evolving mass communication system of popular literacy and a popular press to become a form of popular and mass consciousness. The ideologies involved narratives and beliefs about the identity of a 'people' or 'nation' and its distinctive and special characteristics[5] and also about the personal characteristics of 'nationals'. These former characteristics often included beliefs about a range of special elements and experiences allegedly shared among a community – a language and literature, an origin, history and destiny, a religion, a homeland, and so on. The latter characteristics referred to the fact that 'nationals' could be seen by others, and could see themselves, as having selves and personalities which were importantly influenced by features which were understood to be typical for their distinctive 'nationality'.

Within such ideologies, the more that such essentially socially constructed elements could be re-presented (effectively, disguised or mythologised) as 'given' realities (i.e. not humanly or socially constructed) the better, and the stronger the community's claim on them as identifiers. There were three main ways to do this. This first emphasised the 'natural' (nature-given) character of the community. The second emphasised its 'religious' (God(s)-given) character (e.g. as in notions of God's 'chosen people', or the sacredness of national monarchs or religious leaders). The third offered a mixture of these two, that is, natural characteristics and identifiers which were understood to be both 'natural' and God-given. A key factor which promoted both the religiously-based and 'nature'-based forms of nationalistic myth-making, and which also promoted their mixture into even more potent ideological brews, was that of European states' empire-building in the 18th and 19th centuries.

Modern Western European imperialism promoted a renewal of traditional Christian religiosity, particularly of the individualistic and self-improving Protestant variety, to legitimate it and to provide it with a high moral purpose – the missionary purpose being to bring 'the Word' and 'civilisation' to non-European peoples of various kinds who were presumed to lack both.[6] Relatedly, the 19th century also saw the invention of the notion of allegedly 'natural' 'race' differences and inequalities among human individuals and communities, both as a pseudo-scientific theory and also as an ideological rationale for political domination and exploitation. Nationalist ideologies became connected with racial beliefs in two ways, which we can briefly review.

On the one hand, as European nations competed to acquire colonies and empires around the world, there was an administrative imperative to categorise non-European peoples of various kinds in Asia, Africa and elsewhere in order to better control and use them, and also to legitimate invasion and control. Claims about the superiority and 'civilising' influence of European and national 'civilisations' in relation to colonised societies were often mixed with claims about the alleged 'racial' differences and superiority of Europeans and European nationalities over colonised 'races'. In the context of empire-building, the development and diffusion of evolutionary thinking, together with the new 'science' of anthropology, whether wittingly or not, provided a fertile intellectual environment for assumptions about the racial distinctiveness of contemporary European nationalities.[7]

On the other hand, 19th-century European nationalists, whether drawing on the development of other new 'sciences', such as those of archaeology, historiography and philology, or on traditional legends and myths, or both, where possible also sought to link their contemporary 'people' or 'nation' to some particular ancient European culture or 'race'. Such 'origin myths' functioned both to attribute to 'national peoples' a Romantic particularity and exclusive identity within Europe and also, outside Europe, to indicate their racial priority and superiority in social evolution terms over whatever tribal and/or other peoples they happened to be colonising and controlling at the time in their empires. Irish, German and English 19th-century nationalist ideologies developed and reanimated such 'origin myths' in their historiographies and education systems, respectively about the Atlantic Celts, Germanic tribes and Anglo-Saxon 'gothic' heritage. In addition, the practice of origin myth-making had a substantial dimension in the impressive marks (and now 'cultural heritages') it has left in many modern European countries in the neo-Gothic architecture of their central urban environments and material culture.[8] This ideological strategy was undertaken in direct and indirect ways.

A direct way of developing the nature-given ideological strategy of nationalism was by associating contemporary 'nations'' self-images and their aspirations and claims for self-government with beliefs and myths about the 'nature'-based phenomena of time, 'blood' and 'soil'. Thus nationalist discourses typically involved claims for the legitimacy and authority of time in the form of a community's long and continuous history and identity. This might be symbolised by the contemporary construction of buildings in styles which aimed to make reference to assumed features of the originary ethnic community/ies, as for instance in the rise of 'neo-gothic' architectural style in 19th-century England. The discourses involved claims for the legitimacy and authority of 'blood' and 'soil' in nationalist identities and cultures. 'Blood' refers to the biological connection provided by long continuities of descent among a community's families, particularly its aristocratic and elite families (sometimes including claims about such linkages even to legendary 'founding' figures or originary generations). Also they involved claims for the legitimacy and authority of 'soil' in the form of the long and continuous occupancy of a particular territory.

It is worth noting an irony in the 'blood'-based element of nationalist ideology. On the one hand, the core of this element, particularly in the late medieval and early modern period, was the bloodline of kingship, and the continuity and symbolic focus it appeared to offer to emerging nation-states. On the other hand, while the monarchical bloodline could not be 'contaminated' through inter-marriage with fellow-nationals who were 'commoners', the need for inter-state alliances generated by Europe's volatile and violent inter-state environment promoted inter-marriage between the members of the monarchical and aristocratic family systems of different countries. The result of this process was effectively to significantly 'Europeanise' or at least 'multi-nationalise' these family systems over time. A significant example of this multinationalisation, which had implications for the evolution of some nation-states into empires in Europe in the 16th and 17th centuries, was that of the Hapsburg family. The networks and bloodlines of this family recurrently entwined and connected up the governing elites in what are now the distinct nation-states of Austria, Hungary, Spain, and the Netherlands, periodically turning them into the dominant class of a singular European multinational state complex. Nineteenth-century nationalists might have successfully propagated myths about the distinctive racial character of their 'peoples' and 'nations'. However, the persistence of monarchs as focal points for nationalism inserted some inevitable ambiguity into such ideology. For example, 19th-century English nationalism may have attempted to cultivate a sense of continuity with England's 'gothic', Anglo-Saxon 'racial' and ethnic origins, but the modern German (Hanoverian and Saxon) origins and cross-European family ties of its main monarch and dominant symbol, Queen Victoria, introduced a discordant note into this kind of narrative. Similar observations could have been made a century earlier in relation to the 'national' identities apparently promoted by the Russian and French monarchies, given the discordant fact of the non-national (again German) descent of, respectively, Catherine the Great and Marie Antoinette.

More indirect and self-consciously 'cultural' ways of developing the nature-given ideological strategy of nationalism were by nations claiming some special affinity between themselves and the ancient Greek and Roman civilisations and empires of Europe's classical era. This was particularly popular among the more powerful and richer European nations, in particular Britain, France and Germany, which could then promote themselves as the 'new Greece' or 'the new Rome', standard bearers carrying ancient European civilisation forward into a new age.

Nation-state building was associated with processes of modernisation and the institutionalisation of a new post-traditional and post-religious 'modern' form of 'civilisation', a new civilisation which appeared to value such things as 'enlightenment' and 'progress' through rationalism, science and technology. Nation-state builders and ideologists could simultaneously associate their projects with modernistic civilisation and also generate elite and popular recognition and legitimation for this process by claiming links to originary European civilisations. This kind of claim was made substantial in the form of the international fashionability and popularity across many European countries and capital cities in the 19th century of neo-classical architecture, particularly for new state-related and high-status buildings. It was also made institutionally substantial in the participation by nation-states and the cultural leaderships, for nationalistic reasons, in international cultural events and related movements, such as the Olympic and the Expo movements, movements which provided creative performative bridges between ancient and modern European civilisational forms and achievements.[9]

These links to Greece and Rome in some cases were mediated by historical linkages through particular variations of the European civilisational experience of Christianity. For instance, modern Greek nationalism could draw on the cultural and identity resources provided by the institutionalisation of Hellenic civilisation within Christianity in the form of the Eastern Orthodox

Church, organised under the auspices of the Byzantine empire, as well as on the resources provided by classical Greece. Similarly, modern Italian nationalism could draw on the cultural and identity resources provided by Roman Catholic Western Christianity and its association not only with the city of Rome but with the history of the late Roman empire. In each of these cases, ethno-nationalism could place these non-ethnic and civilisational influences alongside their claimed common European Christianity and classicism and weave both themes into their more particularistic ethno-nationalist histories, narratives and discourses. We will return to this cultural and religious aspect of European nationalism in a moment. Next, we need to consider the 'nature'-based aspects a little further, particularly in relation to the realities of 19th-century and contemporary European nations.

Nationalism and the reality of Europe's multi-cultural complexity

Two of the core 'nature'-based beliefs within modern nationalist ideologies, as indicated, are those relating to 'blood' and 'soil', namely the allegedly exclusive linkage of a modern people to a particular ethnic even racial origin, and to a particular 'homeland' or 'fatherland'. However, the work of contemporary historians makes clear not only the 'invented', culturally constructed, nature of these myths, but also the way in which they obscure and misrepresent the historical and social realities of modern European nations. As Norman Davies puts it in relation to post-Roman early medieval Europe: 'There is no reason to suppose that Celts, Germans, Slavs and others did not overlap and sometimes intermingle. [And] The idea of exclusive national homelands is a modern fantasy.'[10] And as Patrick Geary puts it in his study of the 'myths of nationalism' and the 'medieval origins of Europe': 'The flux and complexities of (European) Late Antiquity belong to a different world from the simplistic visions of (modern nationalist) ideologues.'[11]

To understand Europe as a collection of distinct and different nation-states which developed particularly in the modern period we need to bear in mind the discussion of Europe's commonalities, common ground and civilisation already undertaken in Chapter 4. From this, two points about the pre-history of European nation-states and national identities can be made clear from an objective rather than ideological perspective. They relate to 'nature'-based 'blood' and 'soil' beliefs in nationalist ideology and they point to the political and cultural construction of such myths. These points can be expressed in the form of two general propositions.

First, all major European nations are mixtures of successive waves and layers of culturally distinct invaders, or migrants, or both (proposition 1). Thus they are essentially multi-ethnic or multicultural, and constitute themselves as more or less successful compositions and blends of culturally diverse influences. The national heritages of archaeology, buildings, writings, oral traditions and so on, which help to identify nations and peoples, are invariably multicultural mixtures and combinations of cultural products rather than testaments to any ethnically singular or racially 'pure' culture. Modern nations may no longer propagate beliefs about 'pure' blood lines connecting them to originary races, as was the case in fascist ideologies in the early 20th century. They might attempt to propagate apparently less controversial and more reasonable claims to having mono-cultural, culturally-integrated identities through their institutions of national cultural production and reproduction (particularly their school systems and media systems). However, such culture-oriented claims are just as mythic as the nature-based ones. The distinct identities of, and differences between, modern nations arise from the particularity of the socially organised mixtures that make them up, not from other more 'natural' or 'purer' versions of particularity.

Second, the borders and 'home' territories of all contemporary European nation-states are essentially contingent and changeable products of political power and decision (proposition 2). Thus national territories have always been to a significant extent flexible and capable of alteration and reconstruction in principle, and they have been so in historical reality. The distinct identities of, and differences between, modern nations in relation to territory arise from the particularity of the politically organised changes they have experienced in their borders, not from other more 'natural' or simpler versions of homeland and territorial particularity. These two propositions inevitably overlap to a significant extent in that Europe's modern nation-states and their peoples have the varied and mixed cultural background and makeup that they do because of the changing and varied occupation of what is now regarded as the nation-state's rightful territory. They can be illustrated schematically as follows.

The multicultural reality and distinctiveness of contemporary nation-states is not only a product of contemporary migration flows. Proposition 1 suggests that 'blood', biological descent, is irrelevant to understanding the cultural particularity of 'nations'. Rather, national particularity derives from the mixtures of peoples in a given nation's history of invasion and/or in-migration. The social and cultural complexity of nations and their cultural heritages and identities can be indicated by listing some of the main peoples and cultures which, over the long run of historical time, once occupied and claimed the territory now referred to as 'belonging' to any given modern nation-state. In the case of France this includes Celts (Gauls and Britons), Romano-Italians, Germanic tribes (e.g. Franks and Burgundians), Danish Vikings (Normans), Catalans, Basques and others. In the case of Germany this includes Germanic tribes, Celts, Vikings and Slavs. In the case of Spain this includes Celtic/Iron age tribes (e.g. Basques), Romano-Italians, Germanic tribes (Visigoths), Arabs and Berbers, and Franco-Hispanics (e.g. Catalans). In the case of Italy this includes Etruscans, Romans, Germanic tribes (Lombards and Ostrogoths) and mixed inhabitants of the island of Sicily (which for many centuries was disconnected from Italy and existed as a separate culturo-political entity, occupied and ruled successively by Greeks, Romans, Arabs, Normans, Byzantines and Turks). In the case of Great Britain with its constitutional multinational character, this 'nation' includes Celtic tribes (Britons, Welsh, Picts and Scots), Germanic tribes (Angles and Saxons), Vikings (Norwegian and Danish), and Normans (French, originally Danish Vikings). In the Balkans, which in our contemporary period is a hot-bed of 'nation construction' and state-building, the multi-ethnic heritage and reality of modern nation-states is just as clear, arguably even more so. To take just one example, what is now the Bulgarian nation-state was built up from layers of different invading and incoming ethnic communities, including Thracians, Macedonians, Greeks, Slavs, Bulgars, Turks and Romanies, among others.[12]

Later we go beyond nationalist ideology to look at states themselves. To anticipate that discussion we can note at this point that states became unified and centralised in the early modern period by incorporating numerous subsidiary kingdoms and princedoms and independent cities and other such territories and political entities. Most international peace treaties during Europe's modern history over four centuries (from the 16th-century wars onwards) had this kind of effect.[13] National states expanded or diminished their territories (indeed came into existence or went out of existence) according to the political power balances prevailing at any given time. In relation to proposition 2, the political and changeable character of national territories not only points to the mythic character and objective irrelevance of nations' 'soil', but also had effects in terms of the size and cultural composition of national populations. Episodes of expansion of nation-states' territories and borders usually involved the incorporation of extra and often culturally different peoples. It should be emphasised that from a sociological perspective this was effectively a form in-migration, adding to nations' cultural mixes by the movement of borders rather than of people. This kind of change, resulting in new multicultural configurations, remains of significance in 21st-century Europe, particularly in the post-communist East given the new prominence there of national borders, the recognition of their lack of fit with ethnic settlement areas, and the occasional felt need to change state structures and borders (as in the Czech and Slovak case).[14]

Understanding nationalism: modernist and continualist perspectives

How is the rise of nationalist ideologies of identities and differences in Europe in the modern period to be understood or (more ambitiously) explained? Some interpretative and explanatory perspectives have already been implied in the preceding accounts of nationalist myths and realities, and so it will be useful at this stage to make them more explicit. However, it should be emphasised here that the ultimate purpose of our discussion is to enlighten the rise of 'nation-states' in Europe, and not merely the consciousness of 'nationhood'. So the question about the rise of nationalism has problems with it. At the very least, it is inherently limited in what it can offer to a broader understanding of 'nation-states'. This broader issue cannot be usefully addressed without a consideration of social realities beyond those of nationalism, namely those connected with the rise of the 'state'. It requires a parallel analysis of this phenomenon and this will be considered in the following section. So, although we can reflect further, if briefly, here on the question of how to understand the rise of nationalism, this not only remains an open and much debated question in academic research, but it is also one which, in any case, needs to be supplemented with additional questions and analyses from inquiries in other fields, which will be considered more directly later.

Approaches to European nationalism

A range of different approaches has been taken to the analysis of the nature and role of nationalism in understanding modern Europe. In what follows we select two of the main approaches from this range, which can be called 'modernism' and 'continualism', and briefly focus on them. They differ not only in terms of the substance of their analysis of the rise of nationalism, but also in terms of what they regard as paradigm cases of nationalism. The modernist perspective tends to focus more on the modern period, particularly the cases of 19th-century nationalism, some of which we have already noted (e.g. Germany, Italy, Greece, the Balkan countries). By contrast, the continualist perspective tends to focus either on the pre-modern period of the high middle Ages (10th–15th centuries) or the early modern period (15th–17th centuries) and emphasises the cases of England (although not Britain) and France.

The modernist perspective is associated in particular with the seminal studies of Gellner, Hobsbawm, Anderson and others.[15] This sees nationalism as a rather artificial and mythologising process of social construction which occurred mainly in the period of mature modernity – a process connected with the 'invention of traditions' and the 'imagining of communities' and of peoples. This is assumed to have occurred mainly in the early to mid-19th-century period and is understood in largely functional sociological terms as an adaptive response to the industrial revolution and the rise to dominance within modernising societies and social formations of the industrial capitalist economy. The nationalist adaptive response led over time to the creation of what I have elsewhere called 'national functionalist' nation-state societies by the early 20th century.[16] This was conceptualised and promoted as a new integrative ideology among the new urban-industrial masses and classes by the new industrial capitalist power elites of modernity and their aristocratic allies.

The 'continualist' perspective is associated in particular with the work of Hastings, Armstrong and, to a certain extent, Smith, among others.[17] While this perspective accepts that some nationalism may be of the modern kind, nonetheless it sees some of the most important and paradigmatic European nationalisms, for instance those of England and France, as being very different. In these key cases and others like them, collective understandings and practices of 'nationhood' and of 'peoplehood', which can in principle be seen in 'ethno-national' terms, are argued to have evolved more organically over a long period of time, from the high medieval period (10th–15th centuries) and boosted by developments in the early modern period (15th–17th/18th centuries). In principle, this approach can be said to lend more credibility to 'ethno-nationalist' views of the nature of modern nationalism than does the former 'modernist' and social constructionist view. We can now consider each of these perspectives a little more closely.

Modernist perspectives on European nationalism

Gellner and the modernists tend to situate nationalism in a functionalist analysis of the process of modernisation in European societies, which gives priority to the political and economic dimensions rather than the cultural dimension of social formations. According to this perspective, the societies of industrial modernity needed (and contemporary developing and modernising societies continue to need) something like nationalism as a cultural glue to promote social cohesion and social order in the face of the revolutionising, conflict-generating and disintegrative impacts of their political and economic transformations. Nationalism is thus seen as a cultural process which is institutionalised in and transmitted through the development of nation-state-sponsored mass schooling systems as well as mass communication systems. As such, it is generated by and explicable in relation to the functional needs of modernising societies.

In particular, modernism tends to focus on the invented character of nationhood in the context of the modern decline of traditional empires (Russia, Turkey, Hapsburg) in Central and Eastern Europe and the rise of modernisation processes there. From the experience of inter-war Fascism, they tend to be both analytically and normatively very critical of nationalism in relation to any claimed ethnic basis, that is ethno-nationalism. And from both analytical and normative points of view we might say that there is some justification in taking this perspective in the current period, given the various problems of ideological obscurantism, racism and jingoistic militarism associated with the rise of ethno-nationalist versions of nationalism in post-communist societies and nation-states, particularly manifested in the Balkan wars of the late 20th century.

Greenfeld has recently provided a useful modification of the modernist line of argument with her alternative analysis of the role of nationalism in modernisation. It has been conventional in this perspective to see the economic dimension, in particular capitalism and, connected with it, the industrial revolution, as the driving force, virtually as an independent *sui generis* causal variable, which called forth the modern nationalist cultural and political response, among other things. Marxist analyses have often taken this line. Efforts to explain capitalism in its turn, where they are not blocked by this line of analysis, have included the well-known Weberian inquiry into the role of the cultural factor of religion, specifically the Protestant Reformation version of Christianity. However, Greenfeld reveals the independent importance of nationalism as a cultural and political factor, and the key role it played in mediating and indeed stimulating and shaping economic modernisation and the rise of capitalism, from the early modern period onwards in Europe and beyond.[18]

Continualist perspectives on European nationalism [19]

A major contribution to what can be called the 'continualist' perspective was made by Hastings in his work on 'the construction of nationhood' and the role of 'ethnicity and religion' in the course of this. Hastings recognises the modernity of fully-fledged nationalism, nationalist mass movements and nationalist ideology. However, he sees the fledgling versions of these things in a very long historical perspective, which involves clearly distinguishing between the collective consciousness and discourse of nationhood and the institution-alised form of the nation-state.

In terms of the long historical perspective, Hastings argues that the mod-ernist approach underplays, in fact largely ignores, the history of pre-modern and medieval periods, particularly for Western Europe, particularly for the Atlantic sea-board states, and particularly for England. In all of these kinds of cases, he argues that historical reality points to the development of 'old continuous nations' in the pre-modern period (hence 'continualism'). In the course of these developments, typically, a dominant ethnic community came to be connected with a state. In this context, we can thus speak of the exis-tence of (pre-modern) nations and nation-states. Also, his analysis reminds us that we need to recognise that states not only had the potential to develop separately from nations and nationalism, but also to predate and stimulate the development of nationalism.

He argues that the main factor (among a mix of factors) in the real historical development of nation-states in Europe is the development of a vernacular literature, and particularly a religious literature in the cultural context of the development of societies defined and permeated by religion, communities of faith organised significantly around religious institutions and mass religiosity. As we saw in Chapter 3, Europe in the late Roman and early post-Roman centuries had gradually become Christianised and had come to be identified as 'Christendom' and with Christianity as a 'civilisation'. It defended this self-definition on a pan-European basis against the incursions of Arab Islam in Iberia, in France and around the Mediterranean from the 7th century. In turn, this provided a mobilising focus for the pan-European projects of the Crusades in the 11th and 12th centuries. So the development of vernacular literatures related to the processes of particularising and localising the Bible and Christian religious texts and manuals from the assumed universalism of

Latin, through translations, into some of the main various spoken languages of European societies. These literary forms, even in largely illiterate societies, were subject to popular diffusion by their use in often obligatory church attendance and participation, both in the pre-Reformation and Reformation periods. This was particularly so for Protestantism and Protestant societies in the 16th century, and was associated with the coterminous (Gutenburg) revolution in printing technology which matured and diffused massively in this period. But these processes were also evident in the pre-Reformation and pre-print period in some cases.

Biblical imagery contained strong references to the paradigmatic nation, Israel. It portrayed a world divided into nations, each with their own legitimate leaderships and governments. In particular, it contained a striking repertoire of powerful nationalistically-relevant and locally adaptable images, narratives and discourses relating to such notions as the Holy Land, the Chosen People, their exile, and their liberation from oppression. Hastings suggests that nationalism emerged in the pre-modern period through this cultural dimension, and the process of the development of a vernacular literature in the context of mass religiosity. For him, the prototype pre-modern nation was England. Hastings argues that England had a consciousness of nationhood and organisation as a nation-state as early as the 10th century, under the Saxon kings. This process survived the Norman conquest and re-emerged strengthened by Norman political power and organisation in the 13th and 14th centuries by which time the nation-state of England had been largely established, and centuries earlier than would be anticipated from the modernist account.

However, while this interpretation of the history of English nationhood might be arguable, Hastings makes this case more strongly for the fully-fledged existence of the nation-state of England in relation to the 16th century. The Protestant religious influence exercised by Henry VIII and Elizabeth I, their state-building achievements in establishing the Tudor dynasty and state military power through the navy, and the successful defence of England against the threat of Catholic Spain set the stage for the subsequent powerful development of England in terms of its nationalism and its nation-statehood. The Elizabethan political moment, in particular, led first to the export of Protestant Englishness and nationhood ideas to the American colonies, which in turn seeded a nationalist process which was to erupt into a strongly citizen-oriented form of nation-statehood two centuries later. It also, secondly, set the stage for the dynamic differentiation of dynastic monarchical authority as distinct from national mass religiosity, and thus for England's Civil War, which erupted in the 17th century. This involved the first major European, indeed world, effort to construct a citizen-oriented nation-state, which in turn was an additional influence on the nurturance of this paradigm of collective self-government in the American colonies. However, it might be argued that Hastings' 'continualist' analysis is not wholly incompatible with that of modernism. To some extent its strongest arguments are more about the need to extend the meaning of 'modernity' to take full account of the early modern period. This version of continualism is not a rejection of the very concept of modernity *per se*.

Constructing European Identities and Differences 1: European States

The emergence of a Europe of differences in the modern period is clearly intimately connected with the rise of nation-states, with their distinct identities and organised differences. But also, as has been indicated, this process, on the one hand, involves comparable processes of modernisation and thus commonalities in European nation-states' social formations (their complexes of social dimensions and deep structures), and, on the other hand, arguably the key differences and commonalities across Europe may be those between *types of nation-state* and national experience rather than between each and every individual nation-state. From this perspective it is the emergence of intra-family resemblances and inter-family differences between types of nation-state and national experience which are the more important issues needing to be recognised and understood. In part, this might be taken to refer to the geographic factor of proximity, and the familiarity and communication this makes possible. So in terms of this aspect it is commonsensically understandable that Scandinavian nation-states are likely to have developed family resemblances to each other, Mediterranean nation-states similarly, and the two sets of states, distant from each other in different physical and climatic environments, thereby developed significant differences between each other.

However, the differences between types of nation-state might also be said to relate to *the social elements of nation-statehood*. So far we have considered one of these social elements, namely the collective consciousness of *nationalism* and the associated cultural factors of religion and relevant differences here also. So, for instance, there are type differences across Europe between Protestant- and Catholic-influenced experiences of nationalism, and thus between more individualist and liberal as opposed to corporate and hierarchical versions of nationhood, and this is an additional factor which needs to be taken into account in seeing family resemblances and differences between, say, Scandinavian and Mediterranean nation-states.

In addition to nationalism, there are two further elements of nation-states which need to be taken into consideration, both in understanding their individual identities and differences and also in understanding their family resemblances and differences. These are the organisational elements of *statehood* and *citizenship*. Later (Chapter 5) the focus will need to turn to one of the major catalyst factors, namely *war*, through which the three elements of the nation-state were energised and synthesised into particular experiences of nationhood in the course of Europe's modernisation processes. At that point it will be necessary to look again and in more depth at the development of the state and of citizenship. However, for the moment these two elements of statehood and citizenship need to be introduced and mapped out in general terms in the context of European development in the modern period. States and citizens are, to some extent, two sides of the same coin, namely that of the organised polity, the legally and politically organised community. They can be said to need each other in various ways, and to relate to each other typically through understandings on each side of each other's (particularly formal, but also informal) rights and duties. Nevertheless, we can consider them in turn, and first look briefly at the state.

European nation-states: similarities and differences – an initial overview

It will be useful at this stage in the discussion to briefly map out some of the main and most visible commonalities and differences among Europe's numerous contemporary nation-states. Later, the issue of the nature of these differences and of how they developed will need to be addressed (Chapters 5 and 6). The most basic and 'obvious' observation about Europe as a whole, which can be made on the basis of this information, is not only that it is both a record of difference and of commonality, but also that distinct types of state can be recognised which can be differentiated according to some basic criteria. Thus Table 4.1 gathers together information about the creation, interruption and termination of European (and neighbouring) states over the course of the modern period, categorising it historically and also with reference to the size and type of state.

As we saw in Chapter 3, the commonalities of pre-modern Europe were compatible with the existence of very different forms of political organisation and governance from city-states to empires. This diversity of political form continued to be visible throughout much of the modern period in Europe. For instance, it was powerfully present at various times in the empires of Hapsburg Austria-Hungary, of Russia, Germany, the Ottoman Turks and the British. It is also present in what are effectively city-states in the cases of the micro-states of Monaco, San Marino and their surviving peers. Nevertheless, over time the empires succumbed to fragmentation and transformation into nation-states and this particular source of difference was very much attenuated. Besides being a record of the long emergence of a contemporary Europe of national differences, then, Table 4.1 also records the increasing commonality of the sovereign state, and mainly of the nation-state (whether constitutional monarchy or republic), as the dominant and standardised form or 'container' for political power and social organisation in Europe over the course of modernity.

Table 4.1   European states in modernity: the birth and death of states 1500–2000

Types of state	Early modernity period (1450–1750)	Mature modernity period (1750–1989)			Late modernity: post-communism (1989 +)
		High modernity (1750–1914)	World wars period (1914–45)	Post-war period (1945–89)	
'Great power' states	UK 1707 Spain 1516	German empire 1871 France 1792 + 1871	Russia 1917	(W. Germany 1949) (Spain 1976)	(Germany 1990) (Russia 1991)
Intermediate states	Denmark 1523 Netherlands 1648 Portugal 1640 Sweden 1523 Switzerland 1648	Albania 1913 Belgium 1830 Bulgaria 1878 Greece 1829 Italy 1860 Norway 1905 (Portugal 1910) Romania 1877	Turkey 1923 Armenia 1918 Austria 1918 Belarus 1918 Croatia 1941 Estonia 1918 Finland 1917 Georgia 1918 Hungary 1918 Ireland 1922 Lithuania 1918 Latvia 1918 Poland 1918 Slovakia 1939 Ukraine 1918	(Austria 1945) (Bulgaria 1946) Cyprus 1960 (Greece 1973) (Hungary 1946) (Ireland 1949) (Italy 1946) (Romania 1947) Yugoslavia 1945	(Armenia 1991) (Belarus 1991) Bosnia 1992 (Bulgaria 1989) (Croatia 1992) Czech 1992 (Estonia 1991) (Georgia 1991) (Hungary 1989) (Latvia 1991) (Lithuania 1991) Macedonia 1992 Moldova 1991 (Poland 1989) (Romania 1989) (Slovakia 1992) Slovenia 1992 (Ukraine 1991)
Micro states	Andorra 1278 Monaco 1297 San Marino 1631	Liechtenstein 1866 Luxembourg 1890	Iceland 1944 Vatican State 1929	Malta 1964	
'Interrupted history' states (states with temporary loss of statehood)	Bohemia (Czech) 1526 Hungary 1526 Lithuania 1569 Livonia 1561 Poland 1569 Portugal 1580	Ireland 1801 Moldavia 1859			

Terminated states (usually incorporated within larger states)	Aragon 1516 Burgundy 1579 Castile 1516 Florence 1532 Mongol/Russian Khanate 1502 Milan 1535 Navarre 1516 Teutonic State 1525	*1750–1914 period*		*1914–45 period* Ottoman empire 1920
		Crimea 1783 England 1707 France (Kingdom) 1792 Genoa 1797 Georgia 1801	Holy Roman Empire 1802 Muscovy 1721 Scotland 1707 Naples 1860 Papal States 1870 Venice 1797 Wallachia 1859	

Sources: Adapted from Davies 1997, *passim* and Appendix III; Tilly 1992, *passim* and Ch. 6, from C. Tilly, 'European states in modernity: the birth and death of states 1500–2000' in *Coercion, Capital and European States, 990–1990*, Wiley-Blackwell reprinted with permission.

Note: Brackets indicate new constitutions, e.g. mainly post-war or post-communist.

Given the reality of this standardisation, Table 4.1 nevertheless also indicates some preliminary factors in terms of which European national political experiences can be argued to have differed substantially and which thus can contribute to an analysis of types of European nation-state and their family resemblances and differences. These factors include those of: (i) the duration and scale of nationhood; (ii) the collapse of dominant regimes and empires together with the impact of major wars; and; (iii) the lack of fit between nations and states.

Duration and scale of nationhood

Duration: The duration factor refers to the simple fact of the intergenerational longevity or lack it in the experience of statehood and/or nation-statehood, and thus to the status of states as differing in terms of their place on an historical axis running from 'old continuous' to 'new'/'modern' types. Numerous examples of this polarity can be seen in Table 4.1. For instance, the political experience and identity of the Netherlands and its people as a nation-state is inevitably going to be different in quality from that of Macedonia. The political experience of the Netherlands as a self-governing constitutional state has accumulated in a substantially uninterrupted way over the course of four centuries. Macedonia provides a sharp contrast with this. On the one hand, there is the fact of Alexander's Macedonian empire in the 3rd century BC, and the originary national myths connected with this. On the other hand, nation-statehood, together with a written constitution and international recognition, was only achieved over two millennia later, as recently as 1992. As part of this durational differentiation there are the apparently unavoidable factors in European experience of major wars and their effects, and also of the role of empires, and we will return to these in a moment.

Scale: A further simple fact differentiating the standardised container of the contemporary European nation-state into types of state is that of scale. For instance, it is evident that over the course of history, and through to the present day, there are major differences of scale (which can be readily seen in comparisons of territorial extension and population, for example) and thus of type between nation-states. This has created, at least among the biggest and most powerful nations, namely those which have periodically played roles as 'great powers' (or 'super-nations', see below), networks of alliances and dynastic inter-marriages as well as shared experiences and memories of conflicts. Thus perceived hierarchies of European nation-states, albeit periodically changing ones, have always existed through the centuries of Europe's modernisation. These ran, and continue to run, from 'great power' core states, through the ranks of medium-sized secondary states (allies or associates of one or other of the core states), through to small states and microstates. The latter were usually of marginal strategic significance in European geopolitics. Whether or not they communicated much with each other, it is reasonable to assume that at least they were aware about the common rank they occupied in the hierarchy of the continent's multi-state formation.

'Post-imperial' and 'post-event' nations

Nation-states which formed in the aftermath of distinct and major historical episodes of repression as components of empires, or of war, civil war or social strife, are unavoidably differentiated in their political identities and experiences by the particularity of the 'event' that formed their origin. They may be 'post-imperial/post-colonial', or 'post-First World War', or 'post-Second World War', or 'post-communist' states. Nevertheless, the national political cultures of many of Europe's contemporary nation states have been permanently marked, even 'branded', by the particularity of their 'post-event' status and experience.

Nation-states may derive from a great variety of sources, and retain this derivation in the collective memories attaching to their identities. They may have derived from pre-existing large-scale empires, from provinces or principalities within empires, from independent national states of some early kind, or from small-scale city-states. Contemporary Spain and Andorra are both equally nation-states, but evidently not only are they vastly different in scale and geopolitical importance, but their contemporary political identities and experiences are also vastly different because of their history, respectively, as a 'once-transcontinental empire', on the one hand, and as 'ever-a-small-principality' on the other.

The commonality of the standard nation-state form, far from implying and enabling political differences and identities to be clearly represented, also masks other important collective differences in political experience. Societies which are now nation-states differ significantly between those which can claim some long continuity in their self-government and those which were incorporated, even suppressed and otherwise 'interrupted' for long periods by stronger regimes. Such suppression and interruption has been a common experience in east, central and south and east European societies, where for many centuries the shifting presence of the Hapsburg, Tsarist Russian, Ottoman and Soviet Russian empires smothered what had earlier claimed to be national states, as in the case of countries like Hungary and the Czech Republic (see Table 4.1).

In addition, there is the historically very recent phenomenon of the neo-imperialism of the USSR in east, central and south east Europe and the profound effects of its collapse in the early 1990s. A major wave of creation and re-creation of 'new' European post-communist nation-states was triggered among the ex-USSR's neighbouring satellite regimes. This major neo-imperial regime collapse has come to be seen as a process of 'velvet revolution' rather than of violent international and civil war, with the notable exception of the Balkan wars of the mid-1990s. Nonetheless, episodes of state violence and counter-regime violence were interwoven in this process. Of course some nations had a double helping of imperial repression throughout much of the modern period. For instance, most of the southeastern European and Balkan nations (Bulgaria, Romania and Serbia) went straight from either Ottoman Turk or Russian imperial domination to USSR domination, subsequently becoming post-communist nations in addition to having a relatively recent preceding post-imperial history.

Finally, Table 4.1 records the huge impacts of post-war peace-making, particularly after the First World War, and to a lesser extent after the Second World War, on the one hand on the unmaking of empires and imperial regimes (e.g. those of Ottoman Turkey, Tsarist Russia, Austria-Hungary, Imperial Germany, Nazi Germany and Italy) and on the other on the making and remaking of numerous European nation-states. We must return to this factor in more detail later in this chapter.

Stateless nations

In addition, given the distinction made earlier between 'nation' and 'state', it is clear from Table 4.1 that the European sub-continent is populated by many stateless 'nations'. These are peoples which either were never able to achieve full statehood in earlier periods, or which, having once achieved full statehood, subsequently ceded it or had it taken away from them. They now exist as sub-national regions and/or provinces with more or less ability to influence their own affairs, but incorporated within states which were built around different and more dominant 'nations'. Examples of stateless nations include the 'nations' of the Scots and Welsh in what is now the nation-state of the UK, the 'nations' of the Basques and Catalans in what is now Spain, the 'nations' of the Bretons, Normans, Burgundians and Corsicans in what is now France, the 'nations' of the Sardinians, Sicilians and Lombards in what is now Italy, and so on. For the contemporary nation-states of the UK, Spain, France and Italy, the persistence of these intra-state national differences and subordinations remains an important factor in national cultural politics, constitutional politics and public life in general. In this chapter our main emphasis when considering modern Europe is on the fact of differences between nation-states, and thus between nations which have been formally institutionalised as states. But the persistence of stateless nations within nation-states should not be overlooked. It is at least relevant to understanding the contemporary challenge European nation-states face when attempting to re-conceive themselves as multicultural political communities.

Constructing European Identities and Differences 2: European Citizenship

The two nation-state elements of nationalism and the state singly and together carry implications for a third element, namely that of citizenship. Citizenship refers to an identity-conferring status of membership of a polity, and the formal and informal rights and duties typically associated with this status. European nation-states differ from each other not only as individual entities, but also, as has been suggested, in terms of the types of nationalism and the types of state they involve. The descriptive richness and analytic utility of this picture of type differences (and, by definition, of intra-type commonalities) can be added to by considering the element of citizenship. To introduce this element we can briefly consider its linkages first with the state and then with nationalism.

Citizenship and the state

The connection of citizenship with the development of European states can be indicated in summary form in the following sorts of ways. It was historically connected, from the classical period through to the Italian Renaissance, with elite participation in the social life and governance of cities and city-scale states.[20] In the medieval period, the status spread to wider elite networks in kingship-based and territorially extended states and empires. These larger-scale socio-political formations typically encompassed numerous cities. Their central states required both the economic resources and political acquiescence of their elites, both land-owning aristocrats and urban capital-owning citizens, often through institutions of 'council' or 'parliament'. Citizenship, then, was connected with more than the status of being a 'subject' under the authority of kings or the law of the land. Through the evolution of constitutional contexts of and limitations on kingship, the status of citizen became a focal and indispensable one, involving the civil economic power to contribute resources to a state, through taxes and levies, and also the civil and political power to contribute legitimacy to a state by influencing and licensing law, or even by making it more directly. Subsequently, as the modern era began to unfold through the popular influence of the Renaissance and Reformation, among other factors, citizenship, and its promise of participation in the life and shaping of the state, came to be a status aspired to and struggled for by a widening range of people and of social classes both old and new.

Citizenship and nationalism in Europe

Citizenship was connected to the development of the ideology of nationalism initially through notions of duty and later through notions of individual and collective rights. Ideologies of nationalism carried within their discourses, either explicitly or implied in their 'logic', both an address to and also a reference to the idea of the individual person as 'national' or 'member of the national society'. Such a member was understood to have personal and collective identity through their 'belonging' to the nation. This identity-conferring belonging involved in the status of citizenship originally was understood and enacted through notions of various sorts of 'duties' 'owed' to the nation, to its central state representative, typically a king or emperor, and also its local state representatives, including local nobility. Through the associated notion of 'patriotism', the belonging and identity of citizenship came to include not only the primary duty of military service to defend or extend the interests of the nation-state, but also such things tax-paying and faith in the national religion, and/or faith in the nation itself as a secular religion.

However, systems of national citizens' duties presuppose the existence of nationalisms which had already become operational communities of national citizens, and which had been established organisationally as nation-states. Prior to such establishment, nationalist ideology offered to individuals and collectives (and continues to offer in our contemporary period in parts of Europe and around the world) powerful and appealing notions of rights, particularly the notion of the collective right to self-governing statehood on the basis of common nationality. This in turn provided, and continues to provide, the basis and motivational context for personal, elite and mass movement mobilisation and politico-military campaigns and conflicts. These typically aimed at the unification of fragmented domains, or at the incorporation of dispersed and diasporic communities of nationals, or at 'national liberation' from the denial of recognition and the repression endured within larger, often imperial-type, regimes, or at some combination of these goals.

Citizenship, rights and duties

As has been indicated, citizens were originally connected to the medieval state and its embryonic conceptions of nationhood initially more through duties than through rights, for instance the duties to obey the law, to pay taxes, and to offer military service. Citizen duties implied state rights. However, the reverse was also true. Citizen rights implied state duties. Citizen rights in the medieval period were limited to such things as an expectation of protection of life and property, and of justice and fairness in relation to the operation of the law. As modernisation began to unfold and progressed, these conceptions of rights developed into more complex and demanding forms in relation to such things as claims for individual freedoms and law-making powers. Through contest and struggle they diffused more generally in the form of the growth and spread of democratic ideals and aspirations.

A particular ideological and institutional form which encouraged the development of citizenship rights in the early modern period was that of the theory and practice of contract, both between the state and its citizens and also among citizens. The contract form began to pervade political life in city-states during the Italian Renaissance, given their need to employ mercenary armies to defend themselves.[21] It influenced the subsequent development of the standing armies and navies and professional military organisations which grew in the larger-scale northern and western European states. In these contexts states developed formal and informal contractual approaches (the offer of pay in cash or in kind, the offer of the rewards of piracy and the spoils of war) to managing the problem of recruiting and motivating the nations' citizens and proto-citizens to provide military service. Even more substantially, the contract form began to pervade the economic life of all European societies and inter-citizen relations in the early modern period, through such things as the development of market- and profit-oriented production, particularly of textiles, intra-national and inter-national as well as national inter-regional trade in such commodities, and labour markets. These political and economic drivers in the development of contractualism in early modern European societies provided some of the main sociological conditions and changes which helped provoke and explain the diffusion of the status and ideal of citizenship by the 18th century in western European societies. The emergence of influential intellectual and political notions of 'social contract' and 'civil society' in the 18th century with all of their implications for the theory and practice of citizenship, for the nature of its rights, of its community, of its links to the state and so on, added to this development. They helped provided the conceptual and discursive context for both the American and French revolutions, and thus for the radical step-change in the development of the modern era of nation-states, in Europe and beyond.

Citizenship rights and their growth in Europe

The increasingly mass diffusion of the ideal and for some also the status of citizenship from the 18th century onwards in European societies, including through such cultural developments as the growth of literacy, contributed a key cohesive element in the development of the modern nation-state in general. National citizenship and its rights made it clear, in terms of the benefits they offered, why individuals might rationally want to perform their duties within these emergent polities, and also what the principled and legitimate limitations of those nationalistic and state-authorised duties might be. A number of types of citizens' rights were struggled for and were developed among European nation-states over the course of three centuries of mature modernisation from the early 18th century to the present. These have been argued to consist of three main categories – 'civil', 'political' and 'social' rights of citizenship[22] – and also to have developed in the course of Europe's modernisation in more or less that sequence in most nation-states.

Civil rights consist mainly of the protection, within the state and its law, of public and private spaces for citizens in terms of individuals' basic freedoms of expression, communication and association. Political rights consist of rights to democratic participation, including the ability to vote for effective legislatures while social rights consist of rights to the educational, health, employment and income conditions needed to fully use and participate in the community, afforded by civil and political rights. Most European nation-states have ended up in the contemporary period developing all three types of citizenship to more or less the same degree. However, they have had very different experiences along the way and have taken very different trajectories in terms of which of these rights they tended to prioritise, and also the sequence and pace at which they developed them. In the same way that they can be differentiated in terms of their types of nationalism and of statehood, European nation-states can also be differentiated in relation to these various forms of development of citizenship rights and duties, and of the prioritisation and combination of citizenship rights. These issues can be illustrated in the information presented in Table 4.2.

Table 4.2 is organised in terms of the three main types of citizenship rights and the sequence in which they developed in a range of European nation-states. It is based on T.H. Marshall's seminal analysis of citizenship and later developments in the sociology of citizenship, particularly Janoski's work (1998). The indicators for the civil rights of citizenship are the dates at which courts were first willing and able to defend male and also married women's property rights, and at which religious freedom and free speech were first protected in a constitution or the equivalent. The indicators for the political rights of citizenship are the dates at which various categories of people (male property holders, all males, women, and all ethnic groups) first achieved the vote in national elections. Finally, indicators for the social rights of citizenship are the dates at which programme rights were first achieved for old-age pensions, health and sickness, unemployment insurance, and family allowances.

The twelve nation-states are grouped into three main types, namely 'social democratic', 'traditional' and 'liberal/mixed'. This is a categorisation of family resemblances and differences which is derived from studies in contemporary comparative social policy analysis. This analysis will be explored in some depth when we consider European 'welfare capitalism' in Chapter 6. However, for the moment and for the purposes of mapping out some type differences and similarities between European nation-states in respect of their experiences and versions citizenship here, the categorisation is a reasonably sound and useful one.

With some caveats and modifications Table 4.2 confirms T.H. Marshall's implied general schema of the historical sequencing of citizenship rights – first civil, then political and then social rights – as being relevant to wider European experience than his main case, Britain. However, the schema appears most clearly with reference to the 19th and 20th centuries rather than, in Marshall's analysis, requiring inclusion of 18th-century experience. Civil rights seem to be earliest in a relatively liberal group of northern European countries (Netherlands, Denmark, Sweden, and also the UK, (although it is notable that, in spite of this, ethnic rights were achieved last in Denmark). In terms of political rights, it is notable that they were achieved last for women in the traditional (corporate and Catholic-influenced) nation-states of Austria, France, Germany, Belgium and Italy. Social rights developed earliest in traditional states (notably Germany) and also in some northern liberal states (notably the Netherlands).

Table 4.2 European national citizenship in modernity: the growth of rights 1700–1950

Countries (by regime type)	Civil rights				Political rights				Social rights			
	LM	LS	LR	LW	PE	PM	PW	PR	SO	SH	SU	SF
Social democratic:												
Denmark	1788	1849	1849	1925	1901	1915	1915	1950	1922	1933	1907	1952
Netherlands	1581	1581 *1867	1815	1957	1887	1917	1922	–	1909	1909	1916	1939
Sweden	1695	1776	1809	1921	1909	1918	1918	1918	1913	1891	1934	1948
Norway					1898	1913	1913	1913	1936	1909	1938	1946
Finland					1906	1906	1906	1906	1917	1963	1937	1948
Traditional												
Austria	1867	1945 *1867	1945 *1867	1945	1955 *1918	1955 *1918	1955 *1918	1955	1927	1912	1920	1948
France	1815	1815 *1791	1815	1965	1884 *1790	1884 *1790	1944	–	1946	1930	1967	1952
Germany	1815	1949 *1871	1949	1977	1949 *1870	1949 *1919	1949 *1919	1949	1889	1883	1927	1963
Belgium	1815	1949			1919	1919	1948	–	1924	1912	1912	1930
Italy		*1871			1945 *1919	1945 *1919	1945 *1919	1945	1912	1946	1919	1912
Liberal/Mixed:												
UK	1689	1795	1795	1883	1832	1918	1928	–	1925	1911	1920	1945
Ireland					1919	1919	1922	–	1920	1911	1945	1944

Codes:
NB * indicates previously created right, sometimes overturned for a period

LM – Courts defend male property rights
LS – Religious freedom protected in constitution or equivalent
LR – Free speech protected in constitution or equivalent
LW – Courts defend married women's property rights

PE – Male property holders have vote in national elections
PM – All males have vote in national elections
PW – Women have vote in national elections
PR – All ethnic groups have vote in national elections

SO – Old-age pensions programme rights
SH – Health and sickness programme rights
SU – Unemployment insurance programme rights
SF – Family allowance programme rights

Source: Adapted from Janoski 1998, tables 7.5, 7.6, 7.7, pp. 202–9, from T. Janoski, *Citizenship and Civil Society*, 1998, reprinted with permission from Cambridge University Press and the author.

Conclusion

In this chapter we have reviewed the nature and role in the development of the modern European social complex of the three key factors of nationalism, statehood and citizenship. In passing, we have mentioned the special relevance of war as a catalyst in relation to these factors. We now need to turn our attention to this catalyst in the process of European modernisation. In spite of being a version of 'barbarism' rather than civilisation, and of 'diswelfare' rather than welfare, arguably war has been a key catalyst for the development of both societal dimensions and also deep structures in the formation of the modern European complex. In Chapter 5 we consider war as a key factor in the general development of European modernisation and nation-state-building, and also in particular in relation to the differences and commonalities between types of European nation-state in the wider European complex. In the course of this, war's characteristic social conditions and social effects in Europe will need to be explored. The social conditions include developments in the political and cultural societal dimensions as well as in the economic dimension, and related developments in the deep structures of space, time and technology. The social impacts include influences on the development of social categories, divisions and inequalities between classes, genders and ethnic groups, as well influences on population growth, empire-building and ultimately even on welfare-state formation in Europe, which is the major theme we move on to address more directly in Chapter 6 and in Part 3.

Notes

1   On the historical sociology of nationalism and nation-states, some key contributions include Elias 1983, 2000; Gellner 1983, 1998; Giddens 1985; Hastings 2003; Mann 1986, 1993; Parsons 1966, 1971; and the work of Anthony Smith, 1995, 1998, 2004, 2005, 2006. Also see contributions to collections in this field, particularly Delanty and Kumar 2006; and Guibernau and Hutchinson 2001. For a notable sociological perspective on the 'national revolution' in the emergence of modern Europe, see the discussion of Rokkan's analysis in Flora et al. 1999; and Flora 1983. Tilly (1992) was influenced by Rokkan's work and a contemporary application of Rokkan's analysis to European welfare states is given in Ferrera 2005a.

2   Reference to the '19th century' here indicates what is sometimes called the 'long 19th century' from the late 18th-century creations of the two main models of 'modern', popularly legitimated state regimes through the American and French Revolutions, to the end of the First World War, the end of European continental empires and the first 20th-century wave of creation of nation-states. See, for instance, Bayly (2004), Hobsbawm (1992) and Zimmer (2003) for discussions of this periodisation and studies of national and other forms of political regimes over these periods.

3   See Anderson 1991. A wave of anti-colonial struggles and nation-state formation occurred across much of Hispanic Central and South America in this period, influenced by Simon Bolivar. Also at this time waves of slave and popular, potentially 'national', rebellions against imperial control occurred among the Caribbean island colonies of Britain and France, often brutally repressed. The most visible and successful case was that of the Haitian revolution in 1793, which led to Haiti achieving independent nation-statehood in 1804. In spite of the repression (and probably because of this), these rebellions generally sowed the seeds of nationalism in this region. See James 1980; and Sherlock and Bennett 1998, Chapter 16.

4   On 19th-century nationalist ideologies as a political and cultural 'invention' of elite groups, see Anderson 1991; and Hobsbawm 1992. In the 19th and 20th centuries, nationalist politics were often led by cultural and religious elites in the countries of southeast Europe influenced by the Ottoman empire and later the Soviet empire. On this see Kolsto 2005; and Schopflin 2000.

5   On such ultimately 'ethnic' characteristics, see Smith 2004, 2005 and 2006.

6   On the links between imperialism and religion in general, see Bayly 2004, Chapter 9. In the British case, in which Christianity was linked to the new secular religion of national and international sport, see McIntosh 1968; and Roche 2000a, Chapter 4.

7   On the links between imperialism and racism in general, see Bayly 2004, Chapter 6; and in relation to Jamaica and the Caribbean, see Sherlock and Bennett 1998. Also see studies of the international and imperial 'expos' of the late 19th and early 20th centuries where alleged 'racially' different groups from the hosts' colonies were often presented in 'native village' and 'human zoo' ways to white European and American audiences (Roche 2000a, Chapters 2 and 3).

8   On European nationalist origin myths in general, see Geary 2002; and Hobsbawm 1984. On the connection between 19th-century nationalisms and origin myths in the case of German nationalism, see Mosse 1975; and in the case of English nationalism, see Colley 2003; and Hobsbawm and Ranger 1984.

9   On European neo-classical architecture, see Sutton 1999, Chapter 7. On Hellenistic culture in 19th-century European international event expos and Olympics, see Roche 2000a, Chapters 2 and 4.

10 Davies 1997, p.217.

11 Geary 2002, p.156, my inserts.

12 On the ethnic origins and mixtures of modern European nations (France, Germany, Italy, Britain) see, for instance, Davies 1997, 2006; Geary 2002; Oppenheimer 2006; and Cunliffe 1997, 2005.

13 See Tilly 1992.

14 On European peace treaties and border changes, see Tilly 1992, Chapter 6. On East European ethnic zones and national borders, see Schopflin 2000.

15 For 'modernist' perspectives, see Gellner 1983; Hobsbawm 1992; and Anderson 1991; also Geary 2002; and Greenfeld 2003, 2006. For analyses of the economic modernisation processes which created the capitalist context for such nation-state developments, and ultimately also the industrial context for the development of the welfare state (see Chapter 6) see, for instance, Mann 1986, 1993; Parsons 1966, 1971; Rimlinger 1993; Polanyi 2001; and Wallerstein 1980, 1989.

16 See Roche 1996, pp.40–42.

17   On 'continualism' (or 'historical ethno-symbolism' as Smith and his colleagues refer to it), see Armstrong 1982; Hastings 2003; Smith 1995, 1998, 2004, 2005, 2006; also Gorski 2006.
18   See Gellner 1983, 1998; Hall 1998; and Greenfeld 2003.
19   For work from a 'continualist' perspective, see note 17 above.
20   On the history of citizenship, see Heater 1990; Janoski 1998; and Turner 1986.
21   See McNeill 1984, Chapter 3; also Saunders 2004 for a particular case study.
22   This three-dimensional analysis was first proposed by T.H. Marshall (1992) in his seminal contribution to the sociology of citizenship. On this field, also see Barbalet 1988; Bendix 1964; Habermas 1994; Isin and Turner 2002; Turner 1986, 1993 (ed); Roche 1996; van Steenbergen 1994. The idea that there might be a fourth dimension of citizenship, namely culture and cultural rights, is explored in Isin and Wood 1998; and Stevenson 2000.

PART 2

The Modern European Complex and Social Change: A Europe of Nations, Warfare States and Welfare States

5

THE MODERN EUROPEAN COMPLEX: WAR AND PEACE

Introduction

It is a sociologically significant fact (as well as a morally sobering fact) about Europeans that, with the notable exception of the period since the Second World War, they have killed each other on behalf of their states for generation after generation throughout the entire modern era. The possibilities and risks of violent death and destruction through warfare have pervaded the continent's political history and permeated the ordinary lives of its inhabitants. European society, the European complex, as we have seen in Chapter 4, developed in the modern period around the themes of national state-building and thus around the emergence of a Europe of differences more than of commonalities. In the course of introducing the nation-state theme, three of its key aspects, namely nationalism, statehood and national citizenship, were discussed. We observed in passing that these three aspects were interconnected and also that there was a key catalyst factor which helped not only to interconnect them, but also, more generally, to drive their development in the long term. This factor was the persistent involvement of European states, empires and nation-states with war, particularly international war but also intra-national ('civil' and/or 'revolutionary') war. Later, we aim to explore the nature of and possibilities for European society in the 21st century in terms of such things as Europe's commitment to a welfare-oriented 'social' version of capitalism (Part 3), and also to the peaceful coexistence of ethnic and national differences according the values of cosmopolitanism and citizenship (Chapter 9). However, these issues cannot be sensibly engaged with without first understanding where contemporary Europe (as it is said) is 'coming from'. Europeans built 'warfare states' before they ever built 'democratic states' or 'welfare states'.

Contemporary European publics and the European Union have interests in and abilities to promote such values as welfare, peace, tolerance and rights. However, these interests are completely misunderstood sociologically if they are attributed, under the influence of an absent-minded Eurocentrism, to the contemporary working out of some idealistic and unitary notion of 'European civilisation'. On the contrary, as we have seen in Part 1, Europe's civilisation-building and civilisation-destroying experiences have been historically complex. More to the point, they have also been intertwined over the course of pre-modern and modern millennia with the 'barbarism' of xenophobic intolerance of difference and with mass violence and slaughter, the recurrent dialectic of the history of what Mazower has called a truly 'dark continent'.[1] Europe's interest in and capacity to promote its values in the 21st century are dynamic factors which derive from its memories of the unleashing of barbarism as well as the building of civilisation, and from its plentiful experience of failing as well as periodically succeeding in controlling the barbaric in human affairs. To appreciate the scale of Europe's timeworn engagement with the barbaric it is necessary, at the very least, to recognise the centrality of war to Europeans' experiences of the building of nation-states and of a Europe of national differences in the modern period. This is the issue we explore in this chapter.

In Chapter 3 we observed how important war-making was to social structure and change in pre-modern Europe, in both the classical and medieval periods. Arguably, it is even more important when attempting to understand the reasons and causes for the development of nation-states, which, in world historical terms was pioneered in Europe in the early modern period (15th–17th centuries). War-making permeates the whole of Europe's modern history, and it underpins the emergence of modern Europe as a complex of nation-states and associated differences.

My argument in this chapter, then, is that incessant war-making in Europe, generation after generation, century after century, was the main catalyst and field through which the nation-state formed both in individual national cases and also as an interconnected international system and context of competitive social units.[2] It was through the experience of continually preparing for wars, frequently actually having to fight them, and then having to manage their positive or destructive consequences internally and the diplomatic consequences externally, that European states developed their national identities and differences, and some of their most emotional and deep memories, symbols and rituals of collective suffering and achievement. In addition, it was in part through this 'warfare state' process that Europe both distinguished itself from other world regions and civilisations and also 'took off' politically and economically to dominate the world by the 19th century.

In spite of the prominence of organised inter-national violence as a factor in the history of modern societies and in their 20th-century and contemporary experiences, particularly in Europe (and with due recognition of their albeit limited and internalist interest in the sociology of violence noted earlier), war has not been given as much attention as it has warranted by sociology and social theory, with some notable exceptions.[3] Of course these disciplines, in both their classical and contemporary phases, cannot be said to have wholly ignored the topic of violence in modern society or in the course of the modernisation process. They have addressed it in such topics as the rise of the modern state as involving the attempted monopolisation of violence (Weber) and of surveillance (Foucault). They have also addressed it in their concern for - the persistence in modern societies of the potential for individual and collective violence relating to such spheres as the abusive exercise of patriarchal power in family contexts (feminist sociology), crime and related policing and punishment systems (criminology), public assembly and the potential for civil disorder and riot (political studies), and class conflict and the potential for rebellion and revolution (sociology). They have also recognised the relevance of military institutions and orders to the structuring of elites and power both in developed and modernising societies.[4] However, these perspectives tend to take state-based societies for granted and to look within them into their internal structures and dynamics. There is limited utility in this internalism and 'methodological nationalism' in attempting to understand the nature and development of European societies. Rather, it is necessary to look beyond any given state-society, into its multi- and inter-state environment and into the dynamics of this environment. In particular, what might appear as development internal to state-societies can often be shown to be profoundly influenced by such aspects as the territorial settlements they could achieve and defend through the mobilisation and engagement of their societies in inter-state war, whether with their neighbours or with distant continental empires and 'great powers'. This chapter aims to explore this insight and line of analysis.[5]

The chapter aims to discuss and analyse the sociological nature and significance of the factor of war in understanding European social structure and change. The conceptual framework we are using, here as before, involves considering the modernisation of European society in terms of changes in the *deep structures* of time, space and technology, in the *societal dimensions* of economy, polity and culture. The chapter is divided into two main sections. The first section begins by descriptively outlining the scale of the phenomenon of war in Europe over the course of the modern period. It then steps back to take an analytic perspective on European society in terms of the ways in which war can be interpreted as embodying changes in Europe's deep social structures. The second section outlines the social relevance of war for the modernisation of European society understood as simultaneous and interconnected changes in the three main social dimensions. It proceeds in three stages looking in turn at the economic, cultural and political dimensions. It looks at the development of Europe as a complex of warfare states, and thus at the relevance of war in terms of European states as respectively contexts of capitalism, Christianity and political difference.

One way to organise such a summary discussion is by using the abstract and arguably over-simplified analytical notions of social cause and effect. In this kind of discourse we might visualise the phenomenon of war, on the one hand, as an effect of underlying societal causes and conditions, and, on the other hand, as itself a cause of social effects. Less paradoxically and more realistically, we can conceptualise social causal and effect factors operating through feedback loops, cycles and iterations over time. We can thus visualise war as a dynamic mediating and catalytic element in these feedback processes, here providing both a practical and symbolic vent and expression for broader social forces, there creating major social impacts and challenges which, in turn, come to enable and motivate further cycles of war-making. In all societal contexts in every European nation-state and society – whether here acting more as a cause, or there acting more as an effect – the commitment to war-making manifested itself both in high-status, state-based and specialised social institutions and traditions, and also in widely generalised public experiences and collective memories.

The emergence of a European complex in the form of a Europe of different nation-states has no doubt been mediated and driven by particular wars. But it has also been mediated and driven by the commonalities involved in the priority which all European countries, as warfare states, have chosen to give (and often have had no choice but to give) to war-making and its requirements and consequences. This emergence has been marked by *the common paradoxes and dialectics of war*, namely that positive and constructive things can sometimes develop alongside and even on the basis of this sphere of destruction and negativity. Achieving the status of *warfare states*[6] has typically carried political and structural implications. Common and consequential implications in many European societies include those of also (and we might add, thereby) achieving the interconnected statuses of being both *citizen states and welfare states*. We have noted some of the distinctive European patterns of and preoccupations with the development of citizenship earlier. Later we need to explore the connected theme of Europeans' varying commitments to welfare and 'the European social model' (Chapter 6 and Part 3). Each of these developments in modernity can be analysed socio-historically and be shown to be connected with the influential role of warfare in the experience and shaping of European societies. This chapter thus helps to prepare the way for the discussion of these issues in Part 3.

War in the Development of Modern European Societies

Warfare as a factor in European development

The discussion so far has provided some elements of a preliminary and provisional understanding of the nature of war's relevance for understanding modern society in general and the modernisation process in Europe and the European social complex in particular. We will return to these analytic concerns in a moment in relation to understanding the long-term social causes and effects of war in Europe. For the moment it is appropriate to take a step back into a more descriptive orientation to war in Europe. So, first, we will review some key aspects of the nature and scale of Europe's involvement with war.

The military needs of European societies and regimes have been onerous and incessant throughout recorded history. The need to service the military imperative was felt as keenly and as frequently in the Alexandrian and Roman empires in the classical period as it was in vulnerable proto-states and principalities of the early medieval period, and as it was in the centralising dynastic monarchical states in the late medieval and early modern periods. However, the need became increasingly costly and central to state activities as military technology increased in sophistication and expense following the 'gunpowder revolution' of the 14th–16th centuries, and the oceanic explorations of 15th century, and as highly trained and costly state-based standing armies and navies were developed from the 16th century. The vast bulk of most states' expenditures in the centuries of the early modern period, together with the regularisation of taxation and the organisation of state borrowing and national debt to finance it, were determined by the needs of war.[7] Table 5.1 gathers together information which gives some elements of a picture of Europe as a 'theatre of war' and of European states as 'warfare states' over the course of modernity from at least the 16th century. The table gives an overall picture of the extent of the commitment of European peoples and states to war-making and to some of its more visible consequences, namely violent death and peace-making.

The number and duration of major wars, and by implication the small proportion of time that the major European states spent at peace rather than at war, is indicated in Table 5.1 (column 2). In the formative centuries of the 'early modern' period, for instance the 17th century and including (on a flexible interpretation) the 18th century – the period some analysts regard, as we noted earlier, as comprising one long 'civil war' within Europe as a whole – the proportion of time spent at war was enormous.[8] Political regimes often fought long intergenerational and mutually exhausting military campaigns and wars. These may not quite have matched the 'Hundred Years War' between England and France in the high medieval period (1337–1453), but wars raged on for over a generation in a number of cases. For instance, the revolt of the Dutch Republic against the Spanish Hapsburg empire came to be referred as the 'Eighty Years War' (1568–1648). Similarly, the intra-Christian war of Protestants versus Catholics in Germany involved, besides the German principalities, the Protestant states of Sweden, Denmark-Norway, England, Scotland and Bohemia, against the Catholic states of Spain and the Holy Roman Empire (including Austria and Bavaria), and came to be referred to as the 'Thirty Years War' (1618–48). In this war, Germany, (the German princedoms of the Holy Roman Empire) suffered a massive loss of life

Table 5.1   European war and peace in the process of modernisation: 'Great Power' battle deaths and peace treaties 1600–1950

Century	War	Battle deaths (Great Powers)	Main peace treaties
17th century	Thirty Years' War (1618–48)	2,071,000	Westphalia (1648)
	Franco-Spanish War (1648–59)	108,000	
	Ottoman War (1657–64)	109,000	
	Franco-Dutch War (1672–78)	342,000	
	League of Augsburg (1688–97)	680,000	
	Total	*3,310,000*	
18th century	Spanish Succession (1701–13)	1,251,000	Utrecht (1713)
	Austrian Succession (1739–48)	359,000	
	Seven Years' War (1755–63)	992,000	
	Ottoman War (1787–92)	192,000	
	French Revolutionary War (1792–1802)	663,000	
	Total	*3,457,000*	
19th century	Napoleonic War (1803–15)	1,869,000	Vienna (1815)
	Crimean War (1853–56)	217,000	
	Franco-Prussian War (1870–71)	180,000	
	Russo-Turkish War (1877–78)	120,000	
	Total	*2,386,000*	
20th century	First World War (1914–18)	7,734,300	Brest-Litovsk (1918) and Versailles (1919) Paris (1947)
	Second World War (1939–45)	12,948,300	
	World Wars Total	*20,682,300*	

Source: Data are adapted from Tilly 1992, pp.165–6, 170, from C. Tilly, 'European war and peace in the process of modernization: 'Great Power' battle deaths and peace treaties 1600–1950' in *Coercion, Capital and European States, 990–1990*, Wiley-Blackwell reprinted with permission.

Note: The data excludes both civilian deaths and also wars involving less than 100,000 deaths. The core of the group of 'Great Powers' here are France, England, Austria (Holy Roman Empire, Hapsburg), Spain, Russia, Ottoman Turkish empire. But the group also periodically included Sweden, Portugal and the Netherlands.

due to battle deaths and the effects of war on civilians, which some estimates put as being between a third and a half of their populations.[9]

States involved in war often waged it on foreign territory, as for most involved in these two cases. Their armies, artillery and supply trains and camp followers criss-crossed Europe like travelling cities, periodically transforming many regions of Europe into a spatial network of 'theatres of war'. Geopolitically and strategically, this incessant war-making constructed

Europe and its space in general as a potential continent-wide 'theatre of war', although it was only to fulfil this fearful destiny in more substantial ways later in the Napoleonic Wars (1803–15) and in the unconstrained mass destruction visited upon it by the two world wars of the 20th century.

The centuries of modernity from the 17th to the 20th centuries are otherwise optimistically describable as periods of 'enlightenment' and 'progress', and generally as periods of development, at least in continental Europe. However, the scale and overall long-term increase of the destructive impact of European war-making over the course of these centuries, in terms of the numbers of battle deaths through the major wars in each century, is indicated in Table 5.1 (column 3). The destructive impact of war increased most dramatically in the most 'modern' period, the 20th century. Of course, this discordance with Europe's 'progress' and 'modern civilisation'-building narratives would be even more emphatic had the civilian deaths associated with this era of 'total war' and genocide been included.

Europe's long cycles of war have also engendered recurrent bursts of peacemaking and (relatively short) periods of peace and reconstruction. Some of the main post-war peace treaties in each century are indicated in Table 5.1 (column 4), although it should be emphasised that these represent only a small selection from the numerous conclusions which needed to be negotiated to European wars over the course of these centuries. Peace treaty-making has consequences for nation-building both in theory and in practice, and also for Europe's potential role in international law and geopolitics in the contemporary world. On the one hand, in terms of the practical creation of new nation-states, the treaties concluding the Napoleonic Wars and the First World War, as we have seen in Chapter 4, were profoundly influential in either directly creating new European nation-states or in stimulating their development. On the other hand, in terms of the theory and ideal of nation-statehood, Westphalia in 1648 was particularly significant. The treaty settled both the Eighty Years War and the Thirty Years War noted above. In addition contemporary analysts have credited it with providing an early and influential assertion of the notion of national sovereignty and the legal equality of nation-states (irrespective of the actual differences between them in terms of size and power) in international law, often referred to as 'the Westphalian state' model.

In practice the Treaty of Westphalia[10] produced a positive outcome for the Dutch and their republic, securing its independence from the Spanish Hapsburg empire. It can also be credited with securing a certain degree of tolerance for religious differences within Christianity, although this also legitimated the development of national churches which would serve to support the power and often authoritarian control of national dynasties and related state systems. However, the treaty was signed by and created new international legal arrangements for a variety of types of political regime beyond that of the 'Westphalian state' model. These ranged from princedoms to empire. Indeed, it served to restore peace and power balances within the Holy Roman Empire of the Austrian Hapsburg dynasty, and thus the legitimacy and operation of a multi-level governance system which permitted only limited sovereignty for the German princedoms.

In general, Europe's long engagement with the dialectical and cyclical character of war and peace had at least one arguably positive outcome. European state leaderships and their diplomatic representatives gained valuable professional experience, a tradition and expertise in international diplomacy, peace treaty-making and international law-making, relative to political and legal elites in other world regions. This intra-continental experience, together with their 19th-century extra-continental experience of 'export' of European legal systems worldwide as a dimension of empire-building, continues to have implications in the 21st century in terms of the EU's potential 'soft power' around the world in the promotion of the United Nations, multilateralism and peace.[11]

War, modernisation and Europe: deep structures and social change

Social and political change and development, particularly in early modern Europe (15th–17th centuries), principally revolved around the long-term rise of versions of the modern state and its institutions, particularly as revenue-raising and spending systems, and involving new power balances between monarchs, classes and publics. However, as Paul Kennedy observes, 'all such remarks remain abstract until the central importance of military conflict is recalled',[12] since the vast bulk of states' spending for centuries in Europe was to prepare for wars, to wage them and to deal with their effects. The transformation of Europe into a continent of nation-states, a Europe of differences, in the course of the long modernisation process from the 15th to the 20th centuries cannot be understood without reference to the innumerable successive periods of war-making between variable combinations of greater and lesser European states. Many of the periods might have been relatively short, a few (albeit usually cataclysmic) years, particularly as military technology increased in destructive power. However, as we have seen, some were a generation-long and a few were many generations-long. The longstanding and recurrent practice of making inter-national war and then subsiding into an exhausted peace, or even actively 'making' peace, together with periodic and often related bouts of civil war, had a great range of impacts across the societal dimensions of European proto-states and nation-states, and also in relation to their deep structures and the deep structures of European society in general.

From a general sociological perspective on modernisation and modernity, war is both produced by and interacts upon societies in ways which can be seen to be mediated through societies' multiple societal dimensions (of economy, polity, culture) and their multiple deep social structures (time, space and technology). In addition, war carries profound implications for the main social divisions (class, gender, ethnicity and age) in modern societies. At this point it is also worth noting that focusing on war as a central social process within the context of the modernisation of European societies carries general implications for some familiar classical sociological and social theoretical perspectives concerned with understanding the emergence of industrial capitalist society with its associated structures of class and power, as the core social system in modernity. These include Marxist 'historical materialism', the Weberian emphasis on the role of ideas (including religion) and rationality (including rational-legal authority structures), and the Durkheimian emphasis on individual and institutional functional differentiation within an integrated legal and moral context. We will return to the social divisions aspects and also to these general perspectives on modernisation later. We can now briefly map out some of the main dimensional and deep structural aspects relevant to understanding Europe and its development in the modernisation process.

War and social deep structures in European modernisation

So far we have seen that inter-national and also 'civil' war have had profound implications for the main societal dimensions of the European complex. However, they have had comparable implications for the deep structures of social life and the social world in Europe. This refers to the implications of war for social time (e.g. societies' historical self-consciousness), for social space (e.g. for the meanings and values of their national territories, spaces and places), and for the nature of their engagement with scientific and technological development. In the European social complex, military organisation and war and peace-making have been of considerable importance in producing recurrent processes of what can be referred to as social temporalisation and spatialisation, temporal and spatial ordering and reordering of cultures and environments. These processes have left their marks on European societies and their identities over the course of the modernisation process.

Time: Socially organised time in European societies is inconceivable apart from the events of war and the succession of wars across the continent. They have profoundly structured the narratives of national identity within every European nation-state, and the histories of the international relations between them. In every nation the collective experiences of wars, the great events of suffering and sacrifice, the successes and failures, have been repressed in official secrets, or etched into collective memory through commemoration and ritual, statuary and architecture, parade grounds and cemeteries. On the one hand, war-related events can remain highly valued and relevant to the symbolising of contemporary national identities. Some examples here include, for instance, for the British, the end of the First World War (commemorated as Remembrance Day), and for Serbs, the 14th-century defeat of Serbian resistance to the Ottoman Turkish invasion at Kosovo (commemorated on

St Vitus Day (Vidovdan)). On the other hand, they can also be sources of collective guilt, shame and denial, as for example, for the British, the mass destruction bombing raids against Dresden and other German cities in the Second World War, for Serbia, the massacre of Bosniaks, including children, at Srebrenica in 1995, and particularly for Germany, but perhaps more broadly and indirectly for much of European society, the Holocaust genocide against Europe's Jewish community in the Second World War.

Space: A similar and related case to that of social time can be argued in relation to the social organisation of space in European societies. European nations' collective perceptions, constructions and valuations of homeland and heritage, of borders and heartlands, of networks of cities and travel routes, that is, of societal space and place, is inconceivable without reference to their histories of war – the struggle for space, the defending of borders, the marking of places of battle and death, and the building of the architectures of defence and power. Earlier we saw, for instance, that major European wars such as the Thirty Years War in the 17th century and the First and Second World wars in the 20th century – particularly through the international peace treaties and settlements which concluded them, from Westphalia 1648 to Paris 1947 – had major impacts on the very existence as well as the territories and shapes of European nations and states (Chapter 4).

Technology: Finally, something similar can be argued about the relevance of war to the deep structure represented by the social organisation and development of technology. The commitment to war-making by states typically involves mass production and supply systems for armaments and military technologies of various kinds, together with special distribution, surveillance and communication systems to deploy, locate and coordinate them within the space of the nation and often beyond it. It typically generates a competitive 'arms race' between states, in which the search is constantly on for tactical and strategic advantages which might be provided by developments in the science and technology of destruction.

The exploratory uses and opportunities cultivated by the continuous production and availability of innovative new military technologies can be understood in relation to the other deep structures (spatial and temporal) in terms of their joint influences on the societal dimensions of the societies which surrounded them. Without endorsing a technological determinism, it is possible to summarise these technology-related uses and opportunities in ways which picture them as relatively independent factors with their own logics of development and influence, both within the sphere of war and beyond it, on the fortunes and natures of their host societies. This is well illustrated in the argument that the 'long 16th century' saw a politically and socially influential 'military revolution' in Europe.

According to one its main proponents, Geoffrey Parker, the military revolution involved innovative and advanced applications of gunpowder-based weaponry, particularly cannon artillery, and their incorporation into the three interconnected sectors of the design of ocean-going capital ships, siege strategy and fortress architecture.[13] The uses of new weaponry in these sectors led, among other things, to a shift away from field warfare and wars of manoeuvre to siege warfare focused on fortresses and walled cities. The intensified destructive and killing power of these artillery and firearms applications required such things as long-term growth trends in the size, training needs and costs of navies and infantry-based standing armies. Correlatively, it led to a decline of the scale and use of medieval-era cavalry and accelerated the relative social decline (e.g. in relation to urban merchants and financiers) of the military and political power of the land-based knightly class which organised it.

The military revolution also periodically required major developments and investments in both offensive and defensive military technologies and facilities, that is, respectively, the power and mobility of the weaponry on the one hand, and the design and arming of fortifications on the other. This changed the landscapes and cityscapes of European societies in the early modern period. Towns and cities across Europe became fortified to a degree and in ways they never had been in the medieval period. In addition, the military revolution helped create the foundations and infrastructures for the emergence beyond the continent of Europe's world-spanning colonial and imperial systems. States with access to the Atlantic ocean and with the opportunity for long-distance trade now had available to them new and unprecedented powers to dominate foreign peoples in military encounters both at sea and on land, to defend whatever military and trading enclaves and holdings they might acquire in foreign lands, and to attract and manipulate foreign allies.

Generally, military technology dynamics cannot be sustained without a broader institutionalisation of science and technology in national educational and research systems. This provides a base not only for military applications, but also for broader applications of technology, particularly into mainstream economic production, which in turn has implications for societies' capacities for economic development and growth. In addition, the power and prestige of the 'social technology' of effective military organisation in societies has ramifications for the nature of national education and training systems, the nature and power of political elites, and the nature of states' authority and legitimacy in general. In terms of technology, as we have seen in this chapter, war-making, warfare state-building and the inter-state arms race competitiveness associated with it can involve, and indeed require, major technological change at least in fields such as weapons production. The evident possibility that this can often carry significant implications for the wider economy is something we can reflect on a little further next.

European Warfare States and Social Dimensions

The historical survey undertaken so far suggests that Europe's war-making dynamics, and thus its nation-state-forming dynamics, are best understood as an outcome of a combination of three factors. The three factors are 'revolutions' or vectors of transformation, in the three major societal dimensions of culture, polity and economy, particularly in the early modern period, and we consider them in this section. This combination of factors is not to be understood in terms of a notion of historical determinism or any 'cunning of history' inevitability about the ultimate global ascendancy of Europe; things could have happened differently if any one of the factors had been missing. Changes in the economic dimension were of course very important. Nonetheless political and cultural transformations can be argued to have had an equivalent, at times arguably greater, influence in the overall mix of factors contributing to the development both of modern Europe in general and also of warfare as a catalyst and a field of inter-factor connections in this process.

The European economy: war and the rise of capitalism[14]

The contemporary European complex of interconnected states and societies and the EU as a whole are organised as capitalist market-based economies and related social formations. Western European societies have organised and grown their economies on a growth-oriented capitalist basis since the onset of modernisation in the 15th and 16th centuries. They experienced a long-term and accelerating structural shift away from feudal forms of economic and social organisation from this period, developing capitalist and market-oriented economies, initially in the city-states of northern Italy and subsequently in the expansion of the system to larger societies in northwest and Atlantic Europe. The building of interlinked capitalist economies across Europe involved the construction and institutionalisation, the extension and intensified use, of markets – both intra-societal and inter-national markets in capital, raw materials and commodities, and currencies and credit, even in labour (both formally free and slaves). It involved regional production specialisation (e.g. English wool production), the development of transport infrastructures (e.g. canal and dyke construction in England and the Netherlands) and also the trans-oceanic trade and transport systems of colonialism and ultimately imperialism.[15] The original forms of agricultural, mercantile and financial capitalism developed into industrial capitalism, which was linked to the international capitalist system particularly strongly from the 19th century. East European societies had a more undeveloped and intermittent engagement with capitalist economic organisation prior to their recent post-communist experience.

Given this relatively common historical and economic experience across Europe, it is understandable that sociological and related forms of social and historical analysis, from liberal individualist to Marxist perspectives, has traditionally tended to focus on the economic dimension of European societies when attempting to understand nations, states and modernisation. However, the analytic perspective taken here is that the capitalist structuring and development of the economic dimension in European societies cannot be understood without reference to war, particularly in the context of its links to religion and nation-state-building. So the claim is not that war-making and military preparedness for it were the only factors influencing the development of European societies as capitalist economies. Neither is it denied that the war–capitalism relationship was one of interaction and feedback over time; on the contrary, they helped to generate, condition and change each other over the course of European modernisation. But the long reign of liberal functionalist and Marxist versions of economism and relatedly of (what claims to be) 'materialism' in the historical sociology of Europe needs to be ended. In the perspective taken in this book, they need to be replaced by a realistic recognition of the multidimensional complexity of this history. In this context, war, together with its political and cultural linkages, needs to be restored to the analysis alongside the economic factor of capitalism. This is so even if we were only to aspire to achieve an adequate understanding and account of European capitalism itself.

The capitalist character of early modern European warfare

War in early modern Europe often took capitalistic forms. In the 14th and 15th centuries officers as well as soldiers were often involved in armies and navies on a periodic and transitory basis, and were motivated by the pillaging, looting and hostage-taking they could undertake as a reward for success. More formalised commercial systems developed in Renaissance Italy, where the leaderships of city-states came to rely on professional mercenary armies to lead and supplement their citizen armies. Commercial contracts were often drawn up between the state and the condottiere providing military services.[16] By the 16th century mixed systems began to evolve in which states were willing to tolerate and even encourage military and naval 'privateering' alongside the deployment of governmental forces.[17] In addition, the 'military revolution' began to significantly raise the costs of war-making to states which now had to equip and resupply large standing armies, to construct a new generation of fortifications, and to organise large-scale artillery and infantry-based siege warfare. The periodic but recurrent costs of war-making and the continuous costs of war-preparedness in 'peace' times remained the largest and most urgent claim on most European states' expenditures throughout the early modern periods. European capitalism's development of economic institutions and class roles provided the key economic, financial and production conditions necessary for this development of European states as warfare states.

Those countries which pioneered and promoted the development of capitalism (such as the Netherlands and England in the case of 16th- and 17th-century mercantile capitalism, and later the United Kingdom in the case of 18th- and 19th-century industrial capitalism) were most able to cover the costs of their growing military requirements, and in this sense to fund their growth as 'warfare states'. On the other hand (and paradoxically because of this), they were also most able to keep in check the risks that their 'warfare states', the military and autocratic aspect of their political cultures, might pervade and dominate the governmental and 'civil society' elements of their social formations, as happened in other European countries, notably Prussia, but also France at various times (also see below). It should be emphasised that this line of argument does not have to assume that the development of capitalist economic organisation in European modernisation made war probable, let alone necessary, merely that it made it possible. We can now consider the influence of war on European capitalism and economic modernisation.

Warfare states' influence on the development of European capitalism

In the longer term and from an analytical rather than a normative perspective, the destructiveness of war could be argued to have had some economically and socially positive aspects for the warfare states which engaged in it. Wars created needs and provided incentives for regimes at least to rebuild and renew their buildings and infrastructures and to improve their defences. It also created incentives for them to plan ahead and seek for new military technologies and military organisational innovations which might give them an advantage in wars to come, and to invest in the capacity to do this themselves rather than allowing themselves to become dependent on potentially untrustworthy foreign powers and their military industries. In addition, warfare states institutionalised and propagated disciplined, rule-following approaches to social action and organisation, which in Weber's view contributed to modernisation and to what he elsewhere famously referred to as the 'spirit of capitalism'.[18]

European states developed their military capacity incessantly from early modernity onwards to promote the power of rulers and dynasties, to defend themselves against takeover (whether reactively or pre-emptively) and for status reasons. In terms of the latter, large standing armies and technologically sophisticated armaments had powerful political symbolic and legitimating functions internally in nation-state-building as well as practical military utility externally against enemies. As we have seen, economic resources and economic growth were a critically important condition to enable these warfare-state projects to proceed. So rulers had long-term and growing strategic interests in using state power to construct and promote national commercial and financial institutions, and national production and distribution systems in weaponry and associated military goods and technologies.

The military needs and demands of political regimes in both the high medieval and early modern periods provided increasingly powerful incentives for the development of and investment in mass production techniques, technological innovation and international trade in strategically important economic sectors, such as those involving metal-working industries, shipbuilding, and instrument and machine-making. The impacts of these demands on proto-industrial production systems grew with the military advent of gunpowder and particularly after its exploitation in Europe's 16th-century 'military revolution' in fields such as the design and mass production of ocean-going ships, naval cannon, mobile field cannon, fortress cannon, and muskets and firearms. In addition, these demands promoted the development of centrally coordinated agricultural production and distribution systems, together with state-based institutions and employment connected with tax-raising and procurement.

War often had some demonstrable economic function and rationale, for instance to defend trade routes, sources of raw material and markets from competitor states or to claim new ones in the course of intra-continental and inter-continental imperial expansion. And it embedded competitive, accumulative, strategic and instrumentally rational attitudes and motivations in the organised life of states and societies which could be readily transposed from destructive military purposes to more productive economic purposes, not only in times of peace but on an ongoing basis between what could be seen as parallel and complementary channels of societal activity.[19]

The finance required to pay for the armed forces and the general expenses involved in each military campaign typically tended to exceed revenue-raising possibilities for the relevant years. So this induced the motivation, even the desperation, in state governments to seek credit in the private, national and international banking system. This demand helped to promote the development of that system, which in turn was a key element in the early growth of capitalism. Also it induced states to start acting like private corporations in the sense of selling shares (or bonds) and creating new or additional state-market finance systems in the form of bond markets.[20]

Overall, then, it is clear that the development of the military revolution and of warfare states in the early modern period was both conditioned by the development of Europe's capitalist economic system, and also had significant effects on it. More generally, it can be argued that powerful connections began to be developed in this period between, on the one hand, the economic impacts of these cycles and dynamics of war-based destruction and, on the other, the emergence of the modern capitalist economic order within and between European states. This was an order which carried the mark of war in a number of respects. The capitalist economic order at the inter-state level, in its cycles and dynamics of techno-economic innovation and growth, could be said to have institutionalised its own processes of socio-economic competitive conflict and capital 'destruction', albeit processes substantially less violent than those of war.[21] However, within each nation-state it also involved versions of the development of state-economy linkages which, as we have observed, could be seen (to use a later expression) as 'military-industrial complexes'.[22]

European culture: war and Christian 'Reformation'

War was inextricably interconnected with developments and conflicts in the cultural dimension, particularly those involving Europe's Christian faith communities, which often provided the ideological rationales and motivational fuel for military conflicts. Indeed, although much of the war-making in Europe was of a demonstrably inter-national character, from an analytical perspective it is arguable that it can as well be conceptualised and interpreted as being effectively 'civil war', 'internal' to a Europe seen as an evolving inter-state social system.[23] This is particularly so given the crucial role played by the dimension of religious conflict in European wars in the early modern period, which could often be interpreted as civil wars within Europe understood as 'Christendom'.[24]

There were three key religiously defined fault lines which repeatedly generated wars in addition to ideological and political conflict. These were, first, the fault line between Western Catholic Christianity and Eastern Orthodox Christianity running from the high medieval period into early modernity as the rising Russian empire took over the institutional and political leadership of Eastern Orthodoxy from the declining Byzantine empire. Secondly, there was the cleavage between Catholic Christianity and the modernising thrust of Reformation Protestant Christianity which dominated the 16th and 17th centuries across Europe. Finally, and contextualising the intra-Christian conflicts, there was the long-established fault line, from the era of Iberian Islam and the Crusades, between Christianity as a whole and Islam. In the early modern period, Christian–Islamic conflicts were reanimated by the growth of the Ottoman Turkish empire, its final defeat of the Eastern Orthodox Byzantine empire and takeover of Constantinople in 1453 and its subsequent aggressive expansion into southern and eastern Europe.

In particular, full account needs to be taken of the cultural dimension and of the cultural revolution in European Christendom marked by the emergence and course of the Reformation in the 16th century. We need to bear in mind that most of the wars undertaken in Europe in the crucial two to three century period from the late 15th to the mid-17th centuries were 'religious' wars between champions of Protestant and Catholic versions of Christianity. The religious factor was both distinctively European and also critical in the process. It is a commonplace since Weber, albeit a still-debated commonplace, to observe that Protestantism had an important influence on the rise and 'spirit of capitalism', for instance in arguably promoting a new popular rationalistic individualism among Europeans which was compatible with capitalism's cultural and psychological requirements. What is entirely missed in this analysis is the greater importance of Protestantism in relation to nation-state formation (and thus, in turn, through the economic imperatives associated with nation-state-building, for the growth of capitalism).[25] It did this through enabling the creating of 'national' Christian churches (e.g. the churches of England, Scotland, Ireland, Sweden, etc.). On the one hand, this helped to generate a national 'people' and a 'public' through the impetus it gave to popular literacy in the vernacular language among the now nationally defined Christian faith community. On the other hand, this gave a new religious status and legitimation to nation-states, state authorities and (through the sacraments and rituals of coronation) to kings. In addition, through the risks, suffering and achievements in the religious wars with the state champions of Catholicism (e.g. Spain, the Hapsburg empire and France) that the Protestant states got involved in, the newly religiously sanctified kings could create new deep 'national' bonds with their newly religiously defined 'national' 'peoples'. It was in the crucible of war-making for inspirational Christian reasons and legitimations (the mortal body sacrificed for the sake of the transcendent 'realities' of immortal souls, entry to Heaven, and so on) that the institutions of government and the popular identities of nations were first properly forged.

So in addition to Weber's well-known and much-debated 'Protestant ethic' thesis about 'Protestantism and the rise of capitalism', arguably also we need to take account of a rather different kind of 'Protestant ethic' thesis, namely that concerning 'Protestantism and the rise of the nation-state'. Of course this is not irrelevant to the rise of capitalism, since European nation-states directly promoted capitalism through mercantilism and colonialism. It is rather that Protestantism's impacts on capitalism in this case need to be understood as being generated through different social psychological and institutional routes than in the initial Weberian analysis.[26]

Finally, as an aspect of the cultural (religious) conditions for European modernisation (albeit one with strong connections to aspects of the politico-military and economic dimensions) we should note the relevance of Islam, via the Ottoman Turks, to processes of change in Europe in early modernity. First, the Turkish overthrow of the Byzantine empire and of Eastern Orthodox Christianity in the 15th century led to the fragmentation of Eastern Christianity into nationally defined churches in a strange parallel to the Protestant states. However, in Eastern Europe this meant, on the one hand, the repression of the Greek nation and their Greek Orthodox Church under Turkish rule and, on the other hand, the migration of the centre of Orthodoxy to Russia through the newly nationalised Russian Orthodox Church. Russia remained outside Turkish control but was permanently 'on guard' against it. Because of this, it was thus never as open as Western Europe to political developments associated with legalism, constitutionalism, citizenship and parliamentary democracy. Secondly, the Turkish attack on Vienna and the Habsburg empire in 1529 distracted the Hapsburg emperor from attempting an immediate military response to and repression of the Protestant princes in the German lands of the empire. This enabled them to buy crucial time, popular legitimacy and international legitimacy for the Protestant cause at a critical moment in its development.

The European polity: war, state formation and the European complex [27]

So far we have considered how changes in the economic and cultural dimensions of European society in their connections with the factor of war contributed to European modernisation. Capitalist competitiveness and intra-Christian cultural conflict linked with war-making to generate both commonalities as well as differences in the historical experience and development of European societies. In the course of this discussion we have inevitably also touched on the political dimension, not least in the notion that the political containers of early modern Europe's economic and cultural dynamics can be understood, among other things, as warfare states. Relatedly, the configuration of European society which emerged and became institutionalised by the 19th and 20th centuries, whatever else it might have been and have aspired to be, was nothing if not at least that of a complex of warfare states. This provides the socio-historical basis for understanding major developments in the 20th century, such as the growth of welfare states and the advent of the European Union, which we will turn to in Part 3. In this section, given our previous emphasis particularly on the commonalities involved in the development of European states as warfare states, we will look a little further at some of their political differences and at the role of war in this.

The European social complex emerged in the course of modernisation as a fragile and volatile inter-state system of warlike nation-states. The long-term historical changes involved in this developmental process can be analysed in a variety of ways. Most analyses acknowledge a minimal distinction between types of state, namely at least between 'great powers' and the rest. However, they also tend to assume that these processes of development either continuously refer to, or ultimately converge upon, a common and otherwise undifferentiated 'modern' version of European nation-statehood which developed on the basis of the 17th-century 'Westphalian state' model, noted above. In addition, they all recognise some version or another of the common 'military revolution' process referred to earlier, which generated what amounts to a recurrent arms race and military competitiveness between Europe's developing state societies from the 16th century onwards.[28]

This long-term inter-state and military-oriented competitive environment led to states developing institutionally in comparable stages. However, European states experienced these common processes and stages of modernisation differently according to the (albeit limited) different political routes they took, and the (albeit limited) different political outcomes they reached. The result of these processes in terms of the 20th century and contemporary European complex was a set of formally comparable nation-states with some social structural similarities which nonetheless contained some deep and consequential political differences. The main relevant differences, apart from those of national particularism, were those to do, on the one hand, with the degree of state control exercised over markets, the economy, and the welfare of citizens and, on the other hand, the degree of state control exercised over citizens politically and the space permitted for the operation of processes relating to the rule of law, citizens' rights and democracy. These axes of difference from the relatively liberal to the absolutely authoritarian in each sphere no doubt overlapped. We will focus on the economic and welfare-related differences between European states and societies later (see Chapter 6). It can be argued that these kinds of difference are likely to continue to be consequential for contemporary EU-led Europeanisation among European nation-states in the fields of social and economic policy going forward in the 21st century. However, for the moment we can give more attention to the emerging differences among European states and societies relating to democracy, which marked their history up to and in the 20th century.

The inter-state differences between liberal democratic polities and authoritarian fascist and communist polities have evidently been massively important in structuring the destinies and fates of European societies in the 20th century. In the 21st century the memory and heritage of such democratic–authoritarian differences remains important both for older and for newer EU member states. In addition, major differences along this axis remain between the EU as a whole and important political aspects of its world-regional 'neighbourhood', from Morocco to Russia. However, the fact remains that the contemporary EU prohibits authoritarian politics and polities within its political space. The EU-based European complex of nation-state societies, whatever the different political histories and memories it contains, and however these differences may continue to be expressed in various cultural and socio-economic differences, nonetheless requires a conformity to and convergence on the liberal democratic model of statehood. This contemporary European situation is evidently not the product of some benign evolutionary or deterministic process unfolding over the period of modernisation, and we need to appreciate both its historical specificity and its fragility. To do this we need, among other things, to take account of Europeans' engagement with war-making and military organisation from the early modern period and to connect this with their development of types of state and of polity.

Various proposals have been made as to how best to conceptualise and visualise these connections, and some of the main approaches are what can be referred to as 'geopolitical', 'political economic' and 'politico-military' perspectives. The 'geopolitical' perspective focuses on epochal changes in the inter-state environments of European nation-states created by changes and conflicts in the small group of 'great power' states, together with the threatened and actual hegemony they exercised in relation to European politics and the wider world order. Issues relevant to this perspective have been noted throughout Chapter 4 and this chapter.[29] The 'political economic' perspective focuses on the role of combinations of the two factors of capitalism and military power in the development of nation-states, and issues relevant to this have been noted earlier in this section.[30] In what follows we focus on the 'politico-military' perspective.[31]

The rise of a Europe of differences: a politico-military perspective

The politico-military perspective addresses the fact that in spite of their commonalities European countries developed politically in different ways over the modern period. It explores the origins and early modern emergence of democratic and autocratic types of state by the 19th and 20th centuries in Europe, relating these developmental routes to differences connected with the common imperatives of the military revolution. In doing so it draws from and dialogues with the other perspectives. Conventional political economic understandings of European political differences refer to economic and class-based factors, such as the degree to which in early modern Europe agriculture was commercialised or the capacity of the middle class for political and economic innovation.[32] The politico-military perspective recognises these factors and links them to historical and war-related factors.

The historical factors are consistent with the 'continualist' perspective in the analysis of nationalism also considered earlier (see Chapter 4). They relate to differences in the nature of the medieval polities from which the early modern dynastic and absolutist states emerged. In particular, they relate to the degree of parliamentarianism, multiple power centres and rule of law that medieval proto-states involved prior to such early modern institutionalisation and centralisation. The war-related factors are perhaps a combination of the kinds of issue addressed by the geopolitical and political economic perspectives. On the one hand, relevant to the geopolitical perspective, there are the differences in the degree to which the states were threatened externally by international wars and needed to develop their military capacity because of this. On the other hand, relevant to the political economic perspective, they have to do with differences in the degree to which states' costly investments in military facilities and organisations needed to be met from a mobilisation of their own resources or from the use of other states' resources (whether those of allies or of defeated and exploitable enemies).

From a politico-military perspective, the historical imagination can help highlight the relevance of the war factor by envisaging its absence. If other things were equal, we could assume that the modern states that emerged from medieval proto-states that had a strong and established proto-parliamentary, pluralistic and legalistic constitutional character would tend towards becoming democracies in the modern era. The opposite could be assumed about medieval autocracies, namely that, other things being equal, they would tend to retain autocratic traditions and characteristics in modernity. However, these tendencies need to be assessed in terms of differences in the sort of experience of warfare each type of polity went through in the early modern period. As we have seen, the inter-state environment of most states in much of Europe throughout this period was particularly volatile and constituted a continuing threat to their security. In order to organise themselves as warfare states this led in most countries to develop forms of absolutist states and polities. These war-inspired and military-oriented forms of absolutism differed in terms of the factors of medieval constitutionalism and type of resourcing. Countries like Russia, France and Prussia, with autocratic medieval settlements, subject to high levels of military threat, and with a need for self-resourcing (e.g. from maximal development of their domestic agricultural economy) tended to generate what Downing (1992) refers to as 'military-bureaucratic absolutism'. This involved centralised repression of medieval parliamentarianism and feudal power centres and the long-term institutionalisation of autocratic forms of governance.

As against this, more transient forms of absolutism emerged in societies which had strong experiences of medieval constitutionalism and which could resource themselves from trade, the plunder of enemies and colonies, and the support of allies. Downing's argument is that they tended to develop ultimately, by the 20th century, into more democratic types of polity. In his view, this was particularly marked in societies which were relatively lightly affected by the draining experience of land-based warfare. A notable case here was that of England, whose main experience of absolutism occurred in the 17th-century in the relatively transient form of Cromwell's dictatorship, and whose traditions of medieval constitutionalism proved an important political resource in the subsequent development of a constitutional monarchy and later a formal democracy. Downing suggests that other relevant cases are those of Sweden and the Netherlands. Their status as dynamic democracies in the 20th century was achieved through an early modern experience of high levels of threat from war and, in response to this, forms of 'populist-military absolutism' which ultimately proved to be transitional rather than deeply institutionalised. Their transcendence of absolutism in the modern period was made possible partly by their traditions of medieval constitutionalism and partly by the fact that in each case the country had access to resources to support militarisation and war-making from elsewhere. In the case of the Netherlands, resources were available from foreign trade and plunder in its non-European colonies, and in the case of Sweden they were available from domination and plunder in its imperial adventures into northern Europe and Russia.

Conclusion

In this chapter, we first observed the nature and scale of European states' involvements with war-making over the course of the modern period. We then considered the implications of this in terms of the deep structures of time, space and technology in the general development of European society. In the main part of the discussion we considered the three societal dimensions of polity, economy and culture and the relevance of war for understanding changes in them in Europe over the course of the process of modernisation. The assumption that war played a major role as a catalyst and field of interdimensional connections and as a catalyst for their wider effects on Europe society in promoting both their commonalities and their differences was borne out.

The discussion indicated that in the early modern period transformational dynamics ('revolutions') in each of the three social dimensions – for instance, the military revolution in politics, the capitalist revolution in economics, and the Protestant Reformation in culture – tended to promote inter-state war independently in Europe. They did this even more so in the historical reality of their combination. From a sociological perspective, it was the combination of all of the three factors – galvanised in particular, and wittingly or not, by the cultural/religious factor – which fed Europe's inter-state war process, and this in turn intensified the modernisation of the European complex as a 'Europe of nations'. The European complex might appear as if it is a set of independent units and a mere juxtaposition of national differences. However, Europe is more and other than that. Its nation-states have emerged through the process of warfare in the modern period as a field and system of inter-connected and ultimately interdependent competitive nation-states. From the 16th century this already volatile and violence-prone system of warfare states would seek to dominate the world through imperialism, and ultimately, by the 20th century, it would risk destroying itself completely in its two 'world wars'. It is this complex of warfare states which provides the basis for under-standing broader socio-political developments in Europe in the 20th century, including both those of welfare states and of the EU, topics to be explored further in the following chapters.

The three main social dimensions of European societies were understood in socio-historical terms as, among other things, domains of agency and institu-tions. But they can also be understood as domains of social divisions, the identities, differences and inequalities that exist between classes, genders and ethnicities. Space inevitably limited our capacity to look into these aspects of the social implications of war. However, we touch on them in the following chapters in relation to considering Europe as a welfare complex. In Chapter 6 and Part 3, attention is shifted from European societies understood as warfare states and from issues in the sociology of war to European societies understood as welfare states and to issues in the sociology of welfare. However, in relation to this shift it is worth concluding with some observations on some of the more direct welfare implications of Europe's long commitment to war. In the course of this it needs to be borne in mind that these implications are to be understood in analytic and objective terms and not normative terms. (On the latter, see the discussion of the relevance of the lessons of Europe's war-torn history and of the values and principles of peace-keeping and peaceful coexistence to contemporary Europe in Chapter 9.)

As we noted earlier, the military revolution and the development of warfare states led to an increase in battle and related violent death. Ironically, this did not result in long-term reductions of population across Europe. On the contrary, populations tended to continue their long-term expansion throughout the centuries of modernisation. The development of the warfare state involved a continuous pressure to increase the size of infantry armies, and generally towards the deployment of large-scale drilled and organised armies as dynamic new factors in the geopolitical and strategic security interest of states. This, together with the new intensity and scale of killing and thus the need for reserves of military manpower, led to the reproduction and increase of their human populations becoming an increasingly strategic issue for states. But to achieve population buoyancy and growth to meet these military needs was only possible on the basis of growing economies and their variable but generally positive effects on standards of living and collective welfare. Thus the military need for larger fighting forces and the greater demands for their continuous replacement generated a need for states to support economies in order to provide the employment, income and food basis for this. In addition, the warfare state indirectly, unintentionally and equally counter-intuitively could be argued to have promoted the growth of the citizen state and also the welfare state in the course of the modernisation process.

The warfare state created situations and needs which helped to stimulate the embryonic development of citizenship and of the state as a citizen state. People performing war-related duties whether in war-time or (in forms of 'national service') in peace-time thereby effectively took part in what can be referred to as the warfare state's military 'social contract' or 'military covenant' among citizens and between citizens and the state. They came to be addressed by the state and to understand themselves as citizens possessing reasonable expectations about what the state might do for them given what they were doing for 'the nation' and for its state. At the very least this legitimised publics' expectations that states ought, to the extent that they could, to provide them with peace and security, and with effective rights for the protection of life and personal property. Relatedly, it tended to promote democratic politics by promoting the expectation that states could be held accountable for their sides of the military 'social contract' and further that people could reasonably expect to participate in law- and policy-making related to it.

The warfare state could also be argued to have contributed to the development of welfare in modern society, particularly the 'welfare state' in its various national versions. The idea of the welfare state refers to the state's role in securing key aspects of citizens' standard of living and quality of life, together with citizens' expectations about and social rights in this. The military need for a healthy and well-fed population generated an impetus towards the institutionalisation and formalisation of 'charity' and 'philanthropy'. This was initially provided through churches and local communities, and later through the national state, not least ultimately through the institutionalisation of various forms of primary schooling and physical education in the 19th century. It also generated a need for sickness and ill-health care, medical and nursing skills services, and pensions and allowances for war veterans and war widows (that is, for the generation that had performed their part of the military 'social contract' (above) and had made partial or ultimate sacrifices in the quality or very existence of their lives for the nation). Generally, the impact in the 20th century of the two world wars on the state provision of all manner of welfare benefits, including housing, income, health and education, cannot be underestimated (even if they often disappointed the political rhetoric of war leaders and the expectations of publics). This general and historically deep linkage between the demands of the modernising European warfare state and the development of the welfare capacity of Europe's capitalist economies, and later the welfare policies of their states, needs to be recognised, and we consider it further in the following chapters.

Notes

1 Mazower 1998.
2 Classical era sociologists and social theorists (with some exceptions, such as Weber and Sombart) tended to underplay or even substantially overlook the factor of warfare in the analyses of modern society. For discussions, see Giddens 1985, Chapter.1; and Shaw 1988. In the 20th century, early post-war sociology recognised the role of the military in relation to power, both in developed societies (see, for instance, Andreski 1968; and Aron 1968) but also particularly in the new wave of post-colonial nation-building at the time (see, for instance, Janowitz 1964).
3 In the last two decades or more there has been something of a revival of interest in the social and historical importance of the factor of warfare, particularly in relation to Europe. In general and political history this was initiated by responses to Michael Roberts' 'military revolution' analysis (Roberts 1967) and includes Bobbitt 2002; Downing 1992; Kennedy 1988; McNeill 1983; and Parker 1996; also Corvisier 1979. In sociology it includes Giddens 1985; Klausen 2001; Mann 1986; Shaw 1988; Skocpol 1995; and Tilly 1992. Relatedly, in gender studies it includes Ehrenreich 1997; Goldstein 2001; Lorenzten and Turpin 1998; also Hacker 1981; and Hacker and Vining 2001.

4   On the relevance of military institutions and orders to the structuring of elites and power in both developed and developing societies see references in this chapter, note 2 above and Willner 1970; on their relevance to gender identities, role and inequalities, see gender studies references in note 3 above.

5   For studies which emphasise the inter-state and the geopolitical see, for instance, Downing 1992; Giddens 1985; Kennedy 1988; and Mann 1986.

6   This refers to the war-making capacity of states from the early modern period onwards. It includes versions of what has come to be called 'the military–industrial complex'. These have been prevalent at many different stages in modernity, and not just in the recent and contemporary period (the Second World War to present) when they have been identified as such (e.g. Klausen 2001).

7   See, for instance, Tilly 1992, Chapter 3. On the development from early modernity of the key financial institutions of capitalism at the national and international level (including banking and credit, the organisation of companies on a joint stock basis, and crucially national and international markets in government bonds), together with their connection with the rising military demands of European states in particular, see Ferguson 2008.

8   Tilly 1992, Chapter 3 estimates war years as a proportion of all years per century in Europe as an initially very high, although declining, percentage over the course of the centuries of modernisation, as follows: 16th century – 95%, 17th century – 94%, 18th century – 78%, 19th century – 40%, 20th century – 53%. (Also see Goldstein 1988.) The apparent dip in the 19th century might be accounted for by the acceleration of European states' commitment to worldwide empire-building projects in this period. The military power and war-making this involved was to a significant extent externalised and 'exported' outside the European continent in the land grabs they made for territories and resources in other continents (see Bayly 2004; Hobsbawm 1999; and Sherlock and Bennett 1998).

9   Davies indicates that the population fell from 21 to 13 million because of this war (Davies 1997, p. 568).

10 See Bobbitt (2002, Chapter 19), Davies (1997, pp. 565–567) and Kennedy (1988, p.51), who discuss the treaty's varied outcomes. Bobbitt (2002) and Tilly (1992, p.51) also contribute to the conventional view that the treaty mainly entrenched Europe's emerging system of nation-states.

11 On Europe's experience of making peace treaties see Bobbitt 2002, Book II; and Tilly 1992, Chapter 6. On Europe as 'lawyer to the world', see Therborn 2002. For an influential sociological perspective on the connections between this and the growth of cultural inhibitions on violence and its motivations in medieval and early modern Europe as part of an alleged 'civilising process', see Elias 1983, 2000; for critiques of this perspective see Fulbrook 2007. On the EU's contemporary potential 'soft power' in this and other respects, see McCormick 2007; and Telo 2007; also Chapters 7 and 9 below.

12 Kennedy 1988, p.91.

13 Parker 1996. See, for instance, the review of criticisms of the military revolution thesis in Parker 1996, Chapter 6. For the original thesis see Roberts (1967) and for later applications see Downing (1992).

14 For Marxist and related social history and sociology on the role of capitalism and the bourgeois class in European modernisation see, for instance, Wallerstein 1974, 1980, 1989. With reference to warfare in this context, see Mann 1986; and Tilly 1992; and for a critique, see Downing 1992. For a review of most of the major classical sociological approaches to the rise of modern society as capitalist society, see Giddens 1971.

15   On this, see Wallerstein (1974) relating to the 16th century and on the preparation for this in the late medieval period see Abu-Lughod (1989).

16   See McNeill 1984, Chapter 3. For a relevant and illuminating case study of a leading condottiere, John Hawkwood, who was of significance in the history of the Florentine state in the 14th century, see Saunders 2004.

17   An interesting case in this context is that of the use of privateers and pirates by the English state to contest Spanish imperial power in the Caribbean in the 16th and 17th centuries. See Sherlock and Bennett 1998, Chapter 8.

18   See Weber 1970; also his discussion on the 'origins of discipline in war' (Weber 1967a, p.257); for an alternative view stressing the factor of nationalism, see Greenfeld 2003; and also Chapter 4 above.

19   See Schumpeter 1976; Goldstein 1988; Ruttan 2006a, 2006b.

20   Kennedy 1988, p.91.

21   For an influential view on the dynamics of capitalism as comprising cycles of economic and productive innovation and destruction, see Schumpeter 1976, Part 1, Chapter 7, where he argues that the 'process of Creative Destruction is the essential fact about capitalism' (p.83). Also see Ruttan 2006a, 2006b. This perspective has influenced contemporary work on techno-economic paradigms, policy and change, see Freeman and Soete 1987; also Green et al. 1999; and Hull et al. 1999. For a discussion of the connection between long-term economic change and war, see Goldstein 1988, 1991.

22   On the notion of a 'military–industrial complex', this has passed into common political and analytical discourse since US President Eisenhower first used it early in the Cold War (1961) to characterise and warn about the historically unprecedented scale of the US state-funded arms industry. For the development of earlier but analogous state–corporate developments in Europe (particularly in late 19th-century Britain and First World War France), see McNeill 1984. For a discussion of the US power elite in Eisenhower's time, see Mills 1959.

23   Versions of this view are supported in the work of historical sociologists such as Mann 1986; Therborn 1995 and Tilly 1992.

24   Religious fervour and conflict from the 16th century onwards, of course, also involved more conventional versions of intra-national civil war as in many German principalities and in France. In addition, the religious factor generated parallel campaigns of violence between the genders in the waves of persecutions of women for witchcraft during the Reformation and early modern period (see Levack 1995).

25   On the relevance of nation-building for the growth of capitalism, see Greenfeld 2003 and 2006.

26   On the connection between Protestantism and the rise of the European nation-state, see Chapter 4 above, also Hastings 2003. Weber was not unaware of the relevance of war and military organisation for organisational rationalism (and by implication for capitalism) in modernity; see his discussion the 'origins of discipline' (Weber 1967a). However, he did not refer to this in his *Protestant Ethic* thesis. On the role of religion and culture in the development of nation-states and ultimately welfare states in Europe see, for instance, Kaspersen 2004; van Kersbergen 1995; van Kersbergen and Manow 2009; and also the discussion later in Chapter 6.

27   On the role of nationalism, states and nation-states in European modernization, see Greenfeld 2003, 2006; Tilly 1992; also Anderson 1979; Flora et al. 1999; Giddens 1985; Moore 1966; and the discussions in section 2 above and Chapter 4.

28 Generally on the Rokkanian notion that Europe experienced a 'national revolution' in the period of modernisation, equivalent to but preceding the more familiar 'industrial revolution', and so developed nation-states as the modal type of modern social units, see Flora et al. (eds) (1999) and Flora 1983; Flora et al. 1983. Also see Parsons 1971; Giddens 1985; and the discussion in Chapter 4. On this development in relation to war and militarisation, see Downing 1992; and Giddens 1985; also McNeill 1984; and Parker 1996.

29 On the geopolitical perspective, see Kennedy 1988.

30 On the political economic perspective, see Tilly 1992; also see Mann 1986; and Moore 1966. Tilly (1992) observed a number of trajectories in early European state formation in the medieval period. All of them involved war, and they differed in terms of their balance and combination between coercive power (landlord/warlord-based) and capital (city/commercial-based), and the various different class and status-group alliances. He identified three main trajectories, namely 'coercion-intensive' (e.g. Prussia), 'capital-intensive' (e.g. Netherlands) and 'capitalised coercion' (e.g. France and Britain).

31 On the politico-military perspective, see Downing 1992; Bobbit 2002; also aspects of Shaw 1988; and Giddens 1985. Bobbitt (2002) focuses on the characteristics of state types and their changes, understood in terms of their bases of popular legitimacy and their institutional and military power.

32 See Moore 1966; and Tilly 1992.

6

THE MODERN EUROPEAN COMPLEX, WELFARE AND CITIZENSHIP

Introduction

So far we have considered the modern European social complex as an historically developed configuration of commonalities and differences among European societies which was importantly driven, both in the early modern period and later, by the dynamics of warfare and the building of nation-states as warfare states. In this chapter we take the exploration of the complex further in terms of the centrally important, but polar opposite, theme of welfare rather than ill-fare, and the way in which it has come to be socially constructed and organised in modern European nation-states. Welfare and social policy are central features not only of the organisation, but also of the meaning, of nation-states and their societies in the modern period, and this is particularly and distinctively so, out of all world regions, in the world region of Europe. Later we consider the relevance for the contemporary development of welfare and social policy in Europe of this world regionality and more generally the process of globalisation which pervades it, together with the EU-orchestrated Europeanisation which is coming to characterise it (Part 3 below). In this chapter we establish some terms of reference for that discussion by mapping out the current way in which welfare and social policy developed as an aspect of the building of nation-states and of the 'Europe of differences' in modernity.

Contemporary European societies tend to be self-consciously understood and organised by the governments, and often also understood by their publics, as being 'welfare states', organised around distinctive sets of welfare principles and traditions which can be referred to as 'social models'. The establishment of a state role and governmental responsibilities for the social conditions and quality of life of the mass of the people, albeit to varying extents and in varying ways between nations, was a key element in the development of democratic politics and of nation-state-building, particularly from the end of the 19th century in most European national societies. And this process was decisively renewed in the post-war period in the second half of the 20th century. In both periods the development of states' welfare roles coincided with new stages in the development and institutionalisation of national industrial capitalist economies. Thus they went hand in hand with the political imperatives influencing states to attempt to organise themselves as warfare states, to attempt to orchestrate and promote national economic growth, and to organise effective and efficient national markets in labour as well as in goods and capital in order to contribute to those ends.

The national development and organisation of industrial capitalism and capitalist economies provides one important context for understanding the effectively ubiquitous presence of versions of 'the welfare state' across contemporary Europe. Another important context is that of citizenship in European societies, a phenomenon whose development more or less paralleled the developments of modern national capitalism and welfare states from the late 19th century. Citizenship in the modern period typically refers, among other things, to the status of and individual's possession of 'nationality', a formal identity conferred by nation states, and of a variable and complex set of formal and informal civil, political and social rights, also conferred by nation-states.[1] The establishment of such individual rights was critical in institutionalising capitalism, in terms of such things as rights to private property and rights in the labour contract. It also came to be central to the institutionalisation of the welfare state, in terms of rights beyond the labour market to state guarantees and/or to the direct provision of such things as out-of-employment reliefs and benefits (against poverty and destitution, sickness and unemployment), post-employment old-age pensions, and pre-employment education and vocational training services. Thus, the development of the status of citizenship was central to the integration and solidarity of national societies in Europe in the modern period, both 'horizontally' and 'vertically'. 'Horizontally', the development of citizenship provided the medium to link together and mutually legitimate two of the core institutional sectors of the modern national social formation (i.e. national capitalist economies and national welfare states). 'Vertically', the development of citizenship operated to promote individuals' perceptions of belongingness, loyalty and identity with and within their overarching nation-states more generally.

These observations provide some background for exploring European society in the key field of welfare and social policy. However, to make progress in this discussion it is first necessary to outline some concepts to guide it.

Worlds of welfare capitalism: concepts and perspectives

The comparative study of welfare and social policy in European societies has become a mainstream element of sociological and social policy analysis over the last two decades, and we draw on some of the substantive findings in this field later. The work of Gosta Esping-Andersen has been central to, indeed seminal for, this field, particularly his landmark study *The Three Worlds of Welfare Capitalism* (1990).[2] For the purposes of the present discussion, at this stage it is worth taking note and adapting some elements of his conceptual framework, particularly the concepts of 'world of welfare capitalism' and 'social citizenship'.

Esping-Andersen sees 'worlds of welfare capitalism' as institutional complexes which combine together mainly political (class-based party democratic and state-based systems) and economic (capitalistic) dimensions in distinctive ways. He also refers to these complexes as 'welfare state regimes' to mark the distinctive ways in which capitalist economies have been embedded in social institutions in order to ameliorate their negative impacts, and to promote their positive potential impacts, on the welfare needs of individuals and communities.[3] The 'worlds' are mainly organised at the national level, but they can also be seen to be characteristic of clusters of nations which have historical and cultural affinities and some geographic proximity. Esping-Andersen identifies three such clusters among European societies, and these are discussed later. One of these clusters or 'worlds', namely that involving Scandinavian countries, is characterised using the concept of 'social citizenship'. This is intended to identify the distinctive commitment to universalism in state-based social rights systems in Scandinavia.[4] This 'world of welfare capitalism', by implication, is also what we can refer to as a 'world of (social) citizenship'.

The discussion in this chapter, particularly in the final section on European 'worlds of citizenship', aims to make use of these concepts. However, to do so it adapts Esping-Andersen's usage where necessary. For instance, like T.H. Marshall, Esping-Andersen focuses on rights and has very little to say about the responsibilities and obligations of citizenship, social or otherwise.[5] In addition, from the perspective of an adequate sociological and comparative analysis, it is necessary to maintain the integrity and multidimensionality of citizenship both as a concept and as a social reality. That is, citizenship encompasses civil and political dimensions as well as the social/welfare dimension, and the latter should not be addressed in a decontextualised way.[6] To adapt Esping-Andersen's usage, then, it is useful to understand the citizenship aspects of 'worlds of welfare capitalism' as having general rights features (i.e. as involving distinctive combinations of all of the three main dimensions of citizenship, and not just the social dimension), and also as involving responsibilities in each of the dimensions. The citizenship aspect of a 'world of welfare capitalism' can be referred to as a 'world of citizenship'.[7] The link between distinctive institutional complexes ('worlds of welfare capitalism') and distinctive citizenship complexes ('worlds of citizenship') does not hold, as in Esping-Andersen's perspective, only for the cluster of Scandinavian countries, as if other clusters and countries had no concept either of citizenship in general or social citizenship in particular. From the perspective of this chapter, and to maximise its analytic utility in sociological and comparative analysis, the citizenship concept and its relevance should be understood to hold for *all* 'worlds of welfare capitalism' and for the nations they encompass.

Recognising European Society and its Duality

The populations distributed across the sub-continent of Europe are evidently divided between and parcelled up by territorial states, much as they have been throughout the modern period, even if these spatial parcels have been subject to much (and often arbitrary) change. States' claims to sovereignty involve the claim to monopoly control of particular territories and the maintenance of boundaries to defend these particular territories against all other states. Also, as seen earlier (Chapters 4 and 5), the nationalist ideologies associated with state-building require that each nation and people be seen as having particular unique historical, cultural and often ethnic characteristics and identity. The social life of the people living in nation-states in Europe is thus perhaps best characterised, initially at least, in terms of a 'Europe of differences' model, given both the particularity of the territories they occupy and control access to, and the identities which they claim or aspire to.

However, the duality of Europe as a continental social formation, particularly as it bears on issues of welfare and social policy, can be seen in the co-presence of commonalities along with these differences. In the Introduction, some of the major structural commonalities involved in the modernisation process were briefly indicated, including the development of national capitalist economies and welfare state systems, albeit of variable kinds. So the particularity of European nation-states, and the image of Europe as a set of differences, needs at the very least to be put into context, and to be seen against such structural commonalities. As was seen in Chapters 4 and 5, it also needs to be put into context in terms of the development of Europe in the modern era as an organised environment (even arguably an inter-state system) for similarly structured nation-states, that is similarly sovereign 'containers' of population and territory.[8]

The duality of the European social formation, its differences and its commonalities, can be thought of in the too simplistic terms of either/or, or zero-sum.[9] To take the discussion further it is necessary to continue along the line of the argument followed in earlier chapters, namely that European social reality is characterised by both its commonalities and its differences simultaneously. A way of grasping this is to recognise the utility of seeing European nation-states in terms of types and/or clusters. Each cluster contains nations which share some key socially-relevant characteristic, and each is differentiated from other clusters and the nations they contain.

Evidently, there are type- or cluster-based commonalities (and related differences) between European nation-states in terms of such socially-relevant characteristics as scale (whether large- or small-scale in terms of territory controlled or population or both), location (whether in the north, south, west or east of the sub-continent), and historicality (including the duration of continuous self-government and occupation of their territory). Beyond this, and equally evidently among European nation-state societies, there are commonalities within and differences between categories along the socio-economic continuum from 'rich' to 'poor'. This is so even in the European Union, the 'integration' of which in other respects is having some standardising influences on member-state societies. Indeed, the fact of continued economic disparities even within the 'old' EU (EU 15) tells us that what we mean by Europeanisation needs to incorporate a process in which greater integration simultaneously provides a basis for renewed socio-economic differentiation of various kinds (e.g. regional differentiation). This is even more true when we attempt to take account of recent enlargements of the Union to include most of the eastern and southeastern European post-communist states. These are considerably poorer *vis-à-vis* the existing EU than any previous set of accession countries.[10] In this way, relating to basic criteria for differentiating countries, together with the categories of countries they imply, the European social formation can begin to be seen as involving simultaneously both commonalities and differences. We can illustrate some of these type and category commonalities and differences in Tables 6.1 and 6.2.

Table 6.1   European societies in the 21st century: socio-economic differences and commonalities

Nation	National economies		State tax and spend		Social problems	
	GDP (trillions US $)	GDP per capita (thousands US $)	Tax (%GDP)	Welfare spend (% GDP)	Unemployment (% labour force)	Poverty (% of work age)
	A	B	C	D	E	F
Sweden	0.3	28.1	50.7	32	7.3	5.14
Germany	2.7	26.3	34.8	29.4	10.6	8.00
UK	2.0	29.0	36.5	26.8	4.8	8.68
Italy	1.7	26.1	41.0	26.4	7.7	11.53
Czech Republic	0.2	16.7	37.8	19	7.9	3.76

Sources: Col. A: World Bank 2008. Data for 2007; Col. B: OECD 2005a, p.71. Data for 2003; Col. C: OECD 2005d, Finfacts Oct. 2007. Data for 2005; Col. D: Eurostat 2008. Data for 2005; Col. E: OECD 2005b. Data for 2005; Col. F: OECD 2005c. Data for 2000.

Table 6.2 European populations in the 21st century: socio-demographic differences and projected changes 2000–2050

Nation	Population (million)	Natural change (million)	Net migration (million)
UK	59.6	−0.3	+4.9
France	59.9	+2.9	+2.8
Germany	82.5	−17.3	+8.9
Spain	42.3	−6.0	+6.2
Sweden	8.9	+0.1	+1.0
East Europe (Bulgaria)	7.8	−2.5	−0.2

Source: Eurostat 2006a (*Eurostat in Focus, 3/2006*).

Tables 6.1 and 6.2 illustrate the current great variety of differences of population size, wealth, and living conditions between European national societies. They present information about representative countries for the five types of welfare regime to be discussed in the following section, including the three types mapped by Esping-Andersen (see below).

Table 6.2 illustrates some significant social differences and commonalities between European nations relating to population. The difference is that of the scale of the country as expressed in population size. The important structural commonality among European nations is that of underlying population decline. Of course there are other socially relevant commonalities: for instance, they are all organised politically as forms of liberal democracy; economically they have developed as generally fairly successful capitalist economies; and particularly in the centre and north of the sub-continent they have often developed substantial welfare state systems. However, in addition to these common achievements, they also have some fateful social conditions in common. These commonalities include long-term decline in their populations, and the projections through the first half of the 21st century contained in Table 6.2 indicate this.[11] This is likely to create weaknesses and problems for European economies in terms labour supply. This is particularly so in the context of the 21st-century global commonality of a plural world order of great powers and large states, such as China, India and Brazil, whose populations are increasing rather than declining.

The reasons for long-term population decline are various. Among the main factors are the long-established link between economic growth and family size (namely, that the latter typically tends to decline as the former rises). Also women's entry into the labour market implies more decision-making about whether and when to rear children. Understandably, given continuing patriarchal traditions and assumptions about the domestic division of labour, this has tended to be linked with women choosing to have fewer children and later in life.

The underlying decline in population is consequential because modern economies still depend on the maintenance of the quantity of labour supply to their national labour markets (in addition to the issue of the quality (skills and employability) of the labour force). Population decline is likely to be counter-balanced to a certain degree by net in-migration. However, this may not be sufficient to stem absolute decline in some cases (e.g. Germany, Table 6.2). This is particularly so in the Eastern European countries which are unlikely to experience much in-migration (e.g. Bulgaria). In-migration, whether from elsewhere in the EU or from non-EU countries, carries its own challenges and problems in terms of accommodating multicultures and managing problems of xenophobia.

Social Worlds in the European Complex: Multi-national Patterns of Commonality and Difference

The discussion in the first section above indicates that the duality of European society, its simultaneous commonalities and differences, can begin to be recognised in terms of the way that national societies can be initially clustered. That is, they can be simultaneously differentiated from some of their neighbours and categorised as similar to other of their neighbours in relation to geographical location, and also in relation to the rough-and-ready social criteria of population (small–large) and wealth (rich–poor). In principle, countries which are, say, large, rich and in the same general geographic location might be assumed to have features and interests in common, and to have significant collective differences from small, poor countries in a different location. However, this is a rather artificial, even superficial, basis for exploring the duality of the European social formation. What is needed are more organic (i.e. historical and sociologically realistic) ways of conceptualising and recognising country clusters, and this is what has begun to be provided in the comparative social policy analysis of the last two decades.

European 'worlds of welfare capitalism'

A key point of reference in this context is the argument initially proposed by Gosta Esping-Andersen and his colleagues on the basis of an extensive and intensive comparative analysis of social statistics relating to welfare in various European countries. This involved the claim that three 'worlds of welfare capitalism' can be identified in Europe, dependent on the 'mix' of countries' main welfare-relevant institutions and systems, particularly of social rights, namely those of state, market and civil society (particularly the family). The worlds were defined mainly in terms of the balance between state and market in the supply of welfare. The main empirical indicator which was used to differentiate and categorise societies into worlds of welfare capitalism was that of the degree to which state-based incomes and services could provide for a person's life needs where the market failed to provide for them, that is the degree of 'decommodification'. The degree of decommodification was checked for each country and analysed with respect to three sets of benefits, namely pensions, unemployment benefits and sickness benefits.

The three worlds of welfare capitalism were those of the liberal-market type, the conservative-continental type and the social-democratic type, defined in terms of whether the dominant element in the mix was, respectively, the market, the family or the state. These worlds were understood to be heuristic conceptual constructs or 'ideal types', and thus not fully realised empirically anywhere. In reality, most Western European countries may well be hybrids of two or more of these types, and increasingly so as the EU-coordinated process of Europeanisation proceeds (see Chapter 8). However, for Esping-Andersen and his associates, European countries could be seen as empirically approximating to one or another of the ideal types. So, for instance, Britain, and to a certain extent Ireland, could be seen as the main cases of the market-liberal type (at least, among European countries; internationally the USA is taken to be the main exemplar of this type). France and Germany could be seen as key cases of the conservative-continental type (along with Austria, Belgium and the Netherlands), and the Scandinavian countries – Sweden, Norway, Denmark and Finland – could be seen as the main cases of the social-democratic type. Esping-Andersen found differences in governance and coalition-building between social class-based political parties and interest groups to be associated with differences between the 'worlds'. National class politics, together with a 'path dependent' approach to nation-state institutions and their building and unfolding over time, in Esping-Andersen's view, helped to explain the emergence of and difference between the three worlds. We return to this issue of explanation in the following section.

The countries within each 'world' could be assumed to share 'family resemblances', while those in different 'worlds' could be assumed to differ from each other as do people from different and unrelated families. This analysis reveals commonalities and differences among the countries within and between each 'world'-cluster which go well beyond the kind of category-based clusters of population size and wealth noted earlier. 'World'-based commonalities and differences could be said to be much deeper and to be more 'organic' in a sociological sense. That is, they claim to relate to similarities between the central institutional structures of entire national societies, the systems which frame and guide both the everyday interactions and flows of social life within them, and also their intra- and intergenerational reproduction as societies.

The 'worlds of welfare capitalism' analysis has become mainstream, and as such it has been much discussed and criticised as well as replicated over the last decade.[12] One of the most authoritative replications in recent years was, ironically, originally based on a criticism. A multidisciplinary team involving Robert Goodin and his colleagues produced a study of the *The Real Worlds of Welfare Capitalism* in 1999.[13] Although it used the mainstream 'three worlds' analysis, it addressed itself to a relative weakness in Esping-Andersen's analysis, namely that he mainly focused on policy inputs (e.g. finance/expenditures and ideology/policy aims) without exploring their effects. Goodin et al. chose to focus on policy effects. Nevertheless, they demonstrate the utility of the analysis, and confirmed Esping-Andersen's estimation of the quality and adaptability of the social-democratic model.

An important question for the contemporary relevance of Esping-Andersen's 'three worlds' analysis is that of whether it adequately covers the full range of commonalities and differences presented by 21st-century European societies. Esping-Andersen's original analysis was first published in 1990 and addressed itself to the understanding of comparative social statistics for a particular set of countries gathered in or before the mid-1980s. Looked at from a vantage point nearly two decades later, the study now looks significantly limited in its scope, and utility, and perhaps also thereby in its validity, and this is for two main reasons.

On the one hand, with the exception of some passing references to Italy, the study simply does not address or account for forms of welfare capitalism in southern European countries, specifically Spain, Portugal or Greece. The reasons for this are not made clear, but it is possible that they had to do with either the lack of available and trustworthy social statistics, or with the relative weakness of state institutions for the provision of welfare, or both. These countries had only relatively recently made their historic breaks with authoritarian forms of government inherited from the inter-war period, and thus qualified for entry to the European Union (Common Market). Whatever the reason, these countries have long traditions of membership and welfare which are based on a range of civil society institutions, including local community, family, trade union and religion, which make them quite distinctive from any of the 'three worlds of welfare capitalism'. Commentators have thus argued that they constitute a fourth, southern European, 'world of welfare capitalism' or 'welfare regime'.[14]

On the other hand, and perhaps understandably given its period, the study refers exclusively to West European countries and contains no references to East European countries. Countries such as Poland, Hungary, Czechoslovakia (subsequently the Czech republic and the Slovak republic) and the Baltic republics (Latvia, Lithuania and Estonia) had barely begun their historic extrication from domination within the Soviet communist neo-imperial system and were *en route* as 'post-communist' and 'transitional' societies to a new but uncertain future. A decade or more later, they had begun to establish themselves as new nations, democracies and capitalist economies, and in 2004 they were in a position to be accepted into the European Union. However, they still retain many distinctive common socio-political characteristics and, together, remain marked and influenced by their relatively recent status as dominated provinces within the Soviet empire. The standardised features of this status for each of them had involved maximal and authoritarian state control not only of the economy, and thus of the nature and distribution of work, but also of all relevant aspects of welfare.

The construction of national markets in labour, together with their associated phenomena of unemployment of varying types and degrees and the adaptation of national welfare systems to support this, proved a jarring experience for all Eastern countries. This experience, particularly that of unemployment and the problem of its management, was amplified by initial disruptions and regressions in their national economic performance as state-based production systems were dismantled and falteringly replaced by market-based systems, and also, as a sectoral shift in employment got under way, of workers using their new rights of mobility to move away from labour-intensive agriculture and into work-search either in urban and industrial centres, or internationally. Given the family resemblances of these nations in terms of their communist heritages, their transitional experiences and adaptations, and their contemporary conditions, some commentators argue that they need to be addressed and understood as a fifth 'world of welfare capitalism' or 'welfare regime'.[15]

Although useful, the original worlds of welfare capitalism analysis may need to be adapted and extended in other ways also. Multinational 'regime' clusters have been identified beyond the field of welfare state analysis, in a range of welfare-related fields such as family and gender relations, migration, taxation, and intergenerational relations (the latter through policies in fields such as pensions and lifelong learning). From the mainstream multidimensional sociological perspective used in this study, relevant extensions to the 'worlds of welfare capitalism' analysis could reasonably take in the economic dimension and possibly also the cultural dimension.[16] Whether such extensions would reveal a deepening of the 'worlds of welfare capitalism' patterns through their replication in a range of additional areas, or the reverse, namely an increased fragmentation of our picture of Europe's differences, is as yet unclear.

One way to pursue the argument that the patterns may be replicated in other relevant areas is to consider the linkage between worlds of welfare capitalism and versions of citizenship across Europe (see this chapter's Conclusion below). Two questions guide inquiries in this field. First, what is the connection, if any, between 'worlds of welfare capitalism' and 'worlds of citizenship'? And secondly, what is the place of social responsibilities as well as social rights in Europe's worlds of welfare capitalism and citizenship? However, before we turn to these issues it is first necessary to appreciate something about how Europe's societies developed their social policies and in many cases institutionalised them in 'welfare states'. What were some of the main forces and factors driving and catalysing these developments? Have these also, in turn, left their mark on Europe's versions of citizenship?

Understanding European Worlds of Welfare Capitalism

So far we have focused on outlining the contemporary pattern of similarities and differences among nations within European society in the field of welfare and 'worlds of welfare capitalism'. This picture needs to be deepened further by a consideration of the connections between welfare and citizenship in European society, and we come to this later. However, first we need to consider why and how this pattern has developed and become institutionalised. This discussion aims to provide a basis from which it will be possible to assess how likely the current pattern and its institutions are to change and perhaps converge under the influence of contemporary forces such as globalisation and Europeanisation. We address these mainly *political-economic* dimension factors later when considering the contemporary EU-level of organisation of 'welfare capitalism' in Europe (see Chapter 8). In the present discussion we focus on the *cultural* and *political* dimensions of European society and their relevance for understanding the development of social policies. They are interwoven in history, and also in any concrete example of a nation-state society. However, they can be grasped separately analytically, and we can consider them in turn.

Culture and European worlds of welfare capitalism: the role of religion

An important aspect of contemporary globalisation in relation to European national societies is that of the long-term growth of international migration. This has economic impacts in terms of labour supply and wage levels in host-country labour markets. In addition, it also has cultural implications for host societies in terms of the *de facto* multicultural (often including new multi-religious) social contexts it produces, particularly in European cities. These impacts have meant that in the field of welfare, among others, the dimension of culture needs to be better identified and understood than it typically has been, for instance in social policy analysis.

In recent years, then, there has been something of a reaction against the long-standing overemphasis on political-economic (modernisation and class-based) analysis in the sociology and comparative study of social policy, and the beginnings of a 'cultural turn' in this field, which we will consider further in a moment.[17] In trying to restore the cultural factor to the understanding of the rise and operation of Europe's welfare states and the contemporary patterns of welfare capitalism they help to form, a number of major national and multinational cultural patterns of factors could be explored. These include commonalities and differences between families of languages, such as Latin, Germanic and Slavic. They also include the distinct ideologies, mythologies and cultures of nationalism (which have historically have often been connected with and dramatised by war, which we discuss later, see below). However, probably the most important cultural factor which needs to be considered is religion, and its social implications.

Major and long-established patterns of religious identities and differences can be readily seen to run not only between European nations but also within them. Nations can be seen, in terms of their dominant versions of Christianity, as Catholic (e.g. Italy, Spain, France, Portugal, also Ireland, and now Poland, Hungary, and the Czech republic), or as Protestant (e.g. Scandinavian countries and the UK), or as Orthodox (e.g. Greece, and now also Bulgaria and Romania), or as significantly mixed and multi-faith (e.g. the Netherlands and Germany). These kinds of religiously-based cultural patterns also, unsurprisingly, express themselves in relation to the development of welfare policies and states. To a certain extent they map on to Esping-Andersen's picture of Europe's 'three worlds' of welfare capitalism, and they help also with understanding the sources of aspects of the 'five worlds' pattern noted earlier.

Unfortunately, the interest of comparative sociologists and social policy analysts in the role of religion in understanding the origin of European welfare states in relation to their commonalities and differences has generally tended to be slight. This compares with their strong interest, on the one hand, in modernisation (and the logic of industrialism) or, on the other hand, in the logic of capitalism and the counter-capitalist agency of trade unions, workers parties and left politics.[18] However, this has begun to change in recent years, and there is a renewal of interest in cultural factors in general, and religion in particular in this field.[19] As we have noted (above), the crucial originary period for the simultaneous emergence of modern social policy and legislation across many leading European nation-states was the late 19th century, particularly from the 1880s to the First World War. The general politics of this period and the decades preceding it from the mid-19th century onwards were marked by the struggle for popular mass democracy, or at least the democracy of (and for) males. Whether in liberal or socialist forms, this often also involved the growth of secular and rationalist worldviews, whether of the pro-science variety or the anti-clerical power variety. In addition, and connected with this, in many particularly Catholic countries there were serious cleavages and conflicts between the institutions and ideologies of churches and national states. This was particularly so in relation to states' aspirations in the field of education through emerging public schooling systems and thus in relation to the knowledge, beliefs and value systems through which successive generations of nationals and citizens would be socialised. It also included conflicts over the accelerating ambitions of the state in other welfare-related fields, such as philanthropy, hospital care and anti-poverty work, in which the Catholic and other churches were traditionally prominent.

To hope to adequately understand the social conditions of, dynamics of and reasons for, these developments it is increasingly recognised that it is necessary to take both the presence and absence of religious politics, and the national particularities of those politics, into account. This is not least the case since the accelerating mobilisation and rising political power of urban industrial workers and the left had not yet formally manifested and institutionalised itself in democratically successfully parties, in electoral majorities and in the formation of governments. This was to really begin to happen in the post-First World War period and particularly in the post-Second World War period. However, the lack of this formal and substantial political presence in late 19th-century governance meant that, in order to press the case for amelioration and regulatory limitation of their national industrial capitalist economies, left politics and workers parties needed coalitions and alliances with other types of party and political interest group. The latter included in some cases (i.e. in most Nordic countries) coalitions with established parties of farmers and agrarian interests, and in other cases (i.e. Germany and some continental countries) coalition with powerful religiously-based organisations, both trade unions and parties.

Differences in the timing and nature of the social policies and welfare states which began to emerge in the early 20th century between particular European nations and families of nations were significantly influenced by the balance of forces in these contextual political conditions. These conditions notably included the role of religion and religiously-based politics. Manow and van Kersbergen (2006) have provided an innovative, insightful and authoritative analysis of this situation recently and what follows draws on their account. To summarise and simplify complicated processes in a complex field we can say that two key issues need to be clarified in relation to any given nation to help identify the role of religion in the development of its version of social policy and welfare state. First, there was the nature of the nation's dominant faith community and church, importantly whether it was Catholic, Protestant[20] or split. Secondly, there was the nature of the state's democratic electoral system, importantly whether based on (winner-take-all) simple majorities or on proportional representation.[21] We can consider these issues in turn.

By the late 19th century Lutheran Protestantism was a long-established, effectively unopposed and culturally unifying dimension, although a fading one, in the national life and state systems of most Nordic countries. It provided a shared resource of values to underpin collective and cross-sectoral (agrarian–urban) politics in the evolving democratic contexts. Also, it provided no serious doctrinal or effective institutional barriers to the development of the state's role in education or welfare on behalf of mass electorates. In addition, the electoral systems in these countries tended to be based on proportional representation, which helped the formation of parties around special interests and intra-party cleavages. There was no religious opposition (or inter-faith variety of religious interest) to be represented and the major political cleavage tended to be that between agrarian interests versus worker interests (a version of country versus city). Given the broad balance between agrarian and worker parties, as well as the socio-economic links and divisions of labour existing between country and city, national political and governmental processes required a capacity for searching for and making compromises. This led to a movement towards the universalisation of rights and benefits which also partially reflected egalitarian traditions deriving from the late medieval and early modern period. These included the intrinsic egalitarianism of Protestant religiosity as well as the *de facto* egalitarianism of agricultural traditions based around small-holdings rather than the large-scale estates of landed nobilities.[22] By comparison, in countries where Catholicism was dominant (e.g. Italy), or where Christians were split between Catholics and Protestants (e.g. Germany), religious ideologies and commitments, and inter-faith and church–state cleavages remained significant elements of national political life, and of the politics of welfare in particular, well into the mid-20th century. There was a heavy emphasis here on the family as a cornerstone of social organisation and welfare, and of course a more defended role for the church's organisations, alongside the state organisations, in the delivery of social care and services.[23]

We can now turn to the second issue, namely the nature of countries' electoral systems. The national democratic systems of most continental nations used proportional systems of representation from the end of the First World War, and this allowed for the formation of a range of parties and for governments to be formed through coalition-building. So the religiously-based parties (and their trade unions and philanthropic and other related institutions) could retain their identity and compromises needed to be done with them by workers' parties. In this case (unlike the Nordic case) such coalition-building led in a different direction from universalism, and in the direction of corporatist arrangements (which, for instance, tend to favour contributory social insurance principles). The move towards state-based welfare systems in Germany and Italy was led by Liberals, initially against the opposition of strong Catholic parties and interests. The resulting systems were compromises reflecting elements of these two types of political interest.

The British and liberal-market welfare regime fits this analysis mainly because its majoritarian system tended to prioritise the major capital–labour cleavage. All other social cleavages, particularly agrarian–urban and church–state were collapsed into the essentially two-party system which nonetheless retained a degree of representativeness given that the parties were themselves coalitions. It was not necessary for the parties to make compromises with each other in order to govern. So unless the left had been able to mobilise sufficient electoral support and form a government (which it could not do early in the 20th century), then the natural outcome would be very minimal social policy. The development of state welfare functions required redistribution and thus taxation, particularly of the middle class. They, in turn, were not able either to form a separate party or to go into compromise politics on this issue. Thus they were not able to explore the possible benefits to them as well as costs of investing in welfare systems, as happened in continental Europe's other two main social models.

Power and European worlds of welfare capitalism: the role of war

Politically (and in terms of the cultural politics of 'nation' and national identity-building), the role of war is central in all phases of European history. As we have already seen in Chapter 5, most European nation-states developed as types of warfare state before they went on to become industrial capitalist and welfare states from the 19th century and particularly in the 20th century. War influenced the kind of welfare states they became both from the early modern period and throughout the later modern period. This factor has been overlooked in the mainstream 'mature modernity' perspective and its sociology and comparative study of social policy. This has tended to produce narratives of liberal and/or left social progress, largely ignoring the role of death, violence and power in Europe's social affairs. However, studies on this aspect of the field have been accumulating in recent times and they indicate its importance.[24]

It is worth recalling that war not only marked European society in the early modern and industrialising periods from the 16th to the 19th centuries but also throughout the century of 'high modernity', the 20th century. Europe was marked by war or war-related processes effectively from the beginning to the end of the 20th century. Over the course of this century some of the key war-related aspects and turning points of European politics and international relations, which also relate to welfare, include the First World War and the flawed arrangements for international peace to which it led; the inter-war militarisation of societies and states' war preparations; the Second World War and its peace arrangements (notably including the division of Western and Eastern European societies, and of Germany into new Western and Eastern

German nations); the post-war 'Cold War'; the collapse of the Soviet communist system; and the re-unification both of Eastern and Western Europe and of the two Germanies in the late 20th century. In this section we briefly outline some aspects of the factor of war in relation to the various worlds of welfare capitalism we have been considering in this chapter.

War, society and welfare in general: war as social process
From some historical perspectives war can be seen as a singular event requiring a particular narrative. However, a sociological perspective on war, at the very least, requires a deeper temporal and a broader contextual approach. Analytically, it is necessary to view war in temporal terms and as a social process or cycle (albeit from a normative perspective an 'anti-social' process, see Chapter 9). If, as is sometimes said, 'war is politics by other means', we need to know something of the political, economic and social contexts and conditions which both prompt the process, enable it to unfold, and enable it to have its welfare-related effects.

From sociological and historical perspectives, 'war' in all eras needs to be understood as referring to much more than a set of physically violent events involving death and destruction. In the modern era, the event of war is a complex one, and can be seen in a cyclical way in terms of the temporal dimensions and sequence of typical sets of social activities and organisation in pre-war, in-war and post-war phases (with the latter phase sometimes including a formal peace but also the possibility of repeating the cycle). There are connections with social welfare and welfare policy in each of these stages. The 'pre-war' stage is typically one of societal preparation, which may be of a medium- or short-term kind and can include such things as the securing of food resources, attention to the nutrition, social disciplining and training of armies of fighting 'men' (and related gender divisions of labour). The 'in-war' stage is typically one in which governments attempt to take total control of the planning of many aspects of national social life, including its reproduction in terms of the distribution of such basics as food and healthcare.[25] There is also a militarisation of medicine and the development and application of new medical technologies to increase the usability of human military resources and to compensate for new military technology's destructive capacities on the part of enemies. In the 'post-war' (and possibly inter-war) stages there are typically efforts of social reconstruction, aimed at replacing destroyed national and urban communication systems, transport infrastructures, energy infrastructures, and accommodation. There are issues of war-exhaustion and low collective morale to be faced, in part through cultural policies (particularly in relation to losers, but also in relation to 'winners'). In addition, there are issues of compensation to citizen-soldiers to be faced through social and welfare polices in fields such as housing, disability benefits and health services, pension systems, and widows' benefits.

War and the worlds of welfare capitalism

War processes left their mark on European nations, and on their similarities and differences, not only in early modernity (as we have seen in Chapter 3) but also in the period of mature modernity, when their particular forms of social policy and welfare state formally originated (in the late 19th century) and developed to full institutionalisation (in the mid-20th century). This was both individually in terms of their particular paths to modern national state-hood and democracy, and also in terms of their participation in the three main 'worlds of welfare capitalism' we have been concerned with. Before we turn to consider the three main worlds, it is worth recalling, as noted earlier, the evident importance of war processes as being central to the political and welfare experiences of the two relatively recent additional 'worlds of welfare capitalism', namely the southern European and the Eastern European. The effects of the Second World War in particular were crucial in the experience of each.

Southern European countries suffered the effects, on the one hand, of association with the defeat of Nazism, and yet, on the other, the continued power of military elites and authoritarian governments throughout the early post-war decades. In this period this involved a continuation of traditional conservative emphases on the social role of the church, the family and local community in welfare, and the blocking of influences from other more progressive welfare models in Europe. This situation only began to change in the direction of a greater role for the state in welfare when democratisation processes were established in the 1970s, and later when countries from this region entered the EU in the 1980s.[26]

Eastern European countries were taken over by Soviet armies and authoritarian communist governments imposed by the USSR, and were integrated into the post-war Soviet empire and its 'Cold War' with the USA and Western Europe. The communist system's command economy model required full employment and provided significant support (albeit centrally determined, standardised and of relatively low quality) for mass housing, educational, health and welfare services. The fall of communism in 1989/90 encouraged these countries to move rapidly to establish capitalist economies. However, this meant they also had to face new social policy problems of poverty, unemployment and labour market management, and more generally with securing effective tax bases for government and fighting corruption in state administrative and legal systems. So their desire to break away from their war legacy, namely their communist statist welfare model, in order to experiment with liberal-market capitalist versions of social policy, has been tempered by the need to address these problems and to begin to provide a new institutional base for the development of both democracy and capitalism. Their more recent entry to the EU has underscored their need to address hangovers from the communist period, that is their war legacies, in all fields of politics and governance, including the field of social and welfare policy. Eastern European countries' war legacies need to be identified and addressed if they are to benefit from fuller participation in the development of the cross-European version of 'welfare capitalism' that the EU is currently attempting to orchestrate (see discussion in Chapter 8).[27]

We can now turn to the relevance of international war for understanding the development of the three core worlds of welfare capitalism. The background for any such assessment is the pervasive role of international war in the building (and destroying) of European nation-states throughout the overall period of modernity, from the early modern period (Chapter 4), and particularly in the main centuries of mature modernity, the 19th and the 20th centuries. This international war-oriented approach rejects the 'methodological nationalism' of perspectives such as those of Esping-Andersen, which stress 'path-dependency' and internal national class-based politics as the basis of welfare regimes. Most European countries from the 19th century onwards found themselves required to accommodate common processes of industrialisation and capitalistic development in their economies. Comparably, they were also periodically involved together in major cross-continental wars, particularly the Napoleonic wars of the early 19th century and the two world wars of the 20th century. These were common stimuli to which they were forced to react, albeit in ways particular to their political traditions and culture. In spite of these differences, commonalities in the development of workers' conditions and needs, and their level of trade union organisation and power in response to industrialisation, can be seen in the common wave of new social policies to insure and compensate industrial workers which were created in many European societies in the last two decades of the 19th century.[28] The development of the various versions of social policy and the welfare state in each of the three main worlds of welfare capitalism is inconceivable apart from a recognition that the worlds were intertwined together and influenced by the dynamics induced by major types of common conditioning factors, such as industrialisation. In addition to industrialisation, a major common factor has been that of international war (and the symbiosis of industrialisation and war in the growth of industrialised warfare) as a driver of social change.[29]

The 19th century in Europe was marked early on by Napoleon's ultimately failed project to export the French republican political model (and the influence of France as a neo-imperial nation) across the continent. Napoleon waged war on Europe's 'old regimes', and later the same republican political theme characterised many of the civil wars, wars of national liberation and wars of national unification which his project had helped to encourage.[30] The impacts of the alliances which were built and the wars which were undertaken to defeat the Napoleonic project were felt across Europe and left long-term marks on nations' politics, including their social politics. In terms of the core countries in the 'three worlds' analysis, they strengthened conservativism and delayed the growth of citizenship in Britain, they stimulated the growth of independent nation-states in Scandinavia and they provided a platform from which Prussian power would ultimately orchestrate the unification of Germany. In the 20th century, the two world wars and their unprecedented levels of death and destruction, particularly the Second World War, had even greater impacts on the nature and timing of political developments, including social policy, in each of the three worlds, as we have already noted in relation to southern and eastern Europe.

This was particularly so for the Scandinavian social-democratic model of welfare policy.[31] Welfare policies had been initiated in Sweden in areas such as ill health and pensions in the First World War period. Workers' unemployment insurance was introduced in 1934. Social-democratic governance involving, among other things, cooperative approaches to labour market regulation between employers and workers had been explored in the pre-war period in Sweden as a way of managing the effects of the international economic depression. Scandinavian countries took advantage of the imperatives of post-Second World War social reconstruction to consolidate and institutionalise the social-democratic model of welfare policy. In Sweden and elsewhere, such elements of the model as old-age pensions, health insurance and rent allowances were introduced on universalistic citizenship-based principles, together with child and family allowances.

In relation to the liberal-market model, its main European representative, Britain, well exemplifies the linkages between war and welfare.[32] The injuries to British soldiers during the Crimean War against Russia (1853–56) prompted the development and professionalisation of hospitals and nursing. Subsequently, initial British defeats in the Boer War against South African settlers (1899–1902) prompted studies which revealed the generally poor physical condition of working-class recruits due to poverty and poor nutrition. This in turn led to the introduction of physical education and a welfare aspect into the contemporary public schooling system as a means of boosting the quality of Britain's military manpower. The large-scale human sacrifices and suffering exacted from this manpower by Britain's participation in the First World War (1914–18) led to various examples of what was referred to earlier as the military 'social contract' in modern societies. Because of the war, the British state began to take on substantial responsibility for the housing conditions of the working class. This occurred through a campaign known as 'homes fit for heroes'. The government initiated the campaign in 1919 and it became a permanent fixture of the British welfare state, requiring and financing local authorities to build public (or 'council') housing, initially for returning soldiers and their families. In relation to what is the most evident linkage between war and welfare needs, government support for widows, orphans and veteran soldiers was provided in 1925. Similarly, a wide range of new welfare measures, in some cases operated by new ministries, was enacted in the immediate aftermath of the war as part of the social reconstruction effort, including in the fields of unemployment insurance, health, education, family allowances and urban planning. This pattern of a wave of new policies across a comparably broad range of welfare fields being stimulated by a war was repeated on a much grander scale following the Second World War, given the even greater scale of death, destruction and needs it involved, including major damage to the nation's housing stock. What effectively amounted to the creation of a welfare state, which was in some ways and for that period comparable to European models, occurred in the immediate post-war years. The main pillars of this were state-organised unemployment insurance, health services, family allowances and secondary education provided on a basis of public accessibility and in terms of what T.H. Marshall in 1950 was to refer to as 'citizenship' principles.

Linkages between war and welfare are also clear in the case of the continental corporatist model. In the early 19th century one of the consequences of the successful campaign to defeat the Napoleonic project was the emergence of Prussian power and of pan-German nationalism among the otherwise hitherto fragmented German principalities and states. Building on this, Bismarck's subsequent successful wars against Hapsburg Austria in 1866 and France in 1870–71 brought these two factors together to create a unified and modern German state. This major new European 'great power', rapidly became equally engaged, along with the other leading European states, in promoting national capitalism at home and seeking imperial expansion abroad. The implications of these war-related developments for the origins of European social policy and the notion of the welfare state were profound, as we noted earlier. As part of a programme of political pacification of left parties and in the context of a new, strong and autocratic nationalist politics, Bismarck introduced insurance and compensation schemes for workers for sickness (1883) and for work injuries (1884) and also worker old-age pensions (1889). These building blocks of the new German nation-state and welfare state also contributed to the national public solidarity, which would sustain the country's imperial projects in the pre-First World War period and ultimately the war effort itself. In turn, defeat in the First World War, together with an onerous peace settlement, had major implications for social policy along with all other aspects of politics in Germany in the inter-war period. Initially, the new Weimar Republic created a liberal constitution which embodied social rights. However, the rise of the Nazi party, its accession to state power in 1933, its militarisation of German society and preparation for war involved the nightmare of racist and eugenics-based social policies. The defeat of Nazism in the Second World War led to the re-establishment of a democratic polity and, in form of the Bonn Constitution, of a German state which regarded itself as a guardian of citizens' rights, including social rights, and thus as a 'social state'.

Conclusion: European 'Worlds of Citizenship' in the European Complex

So far we have seen that Europe is marked by distinct 'worlds of welfare capitalism' and that these have arisen in response to, among other things, the catalysing and causal role of religion and war in the history and development of modern European society. These patterns of commonality and differences can be seen in a wider and deeper sociological perspective by considering their connection with patterns in the development of citizenship, which can be referred to as 'worlds of citizenship'. As was noted earlier, Esping-Andersen established the case for this when he invoked T.H. Marshall's analysis of the civil, political and social rights dimensions of citizenship to help characterise 'worlds of welfare capitalism'.

Esping-Andersen focuses on the social dimension of citizenship, 'social citizenship', understood in terms of social rights, and he links this exclusively with one of the worlds of welfare capitalism, namely that of the Scandinavian social-democratic model. As was also noted earlier, it is possible, indeed necessary, to take a broader view of the relevance of citizenship to welfare capitalism than this. First, Esping-Andersen is unduly restrictive about the dimensions of citizenship he considers to be relevant to understanding welfare capitalism. Secondly, he is unduly restrictive about the countries he is prepared to see as having a conception of citizenship embedded in their versions of welfare capitalism. A more rounded and adequate view is needed. In relation to the first point, types of society and of welfare capitalism are connected with the full range of dimensions of citizenship, civil and political as well as social. This was the idea behind the concept of 'citizens' worlds' introduced earlier which comprise this full range of types of rights. In relation to the second point, the types of society and of welfare capitalism which can be usefully analysed in terms of citizenship should not be restricted to social-democratic countries (whether in Scandinavia or not). Rather, different types of society and of welfare capitalism can be differentiated by their particular versions of citizenship and 'citizen worlds', that is, by their particular combinations of citizenship dimensions, whether emphasising the social dimensions, as in Scandinavia, or the political or civil dimensions, as in other countries).[33]

A fuller use of the concept of citizenship can help to deepen and broaden the notion of 'worlds of welfare capitalism' by connecting it with particular variations in 'worlds of citizenship'. This is particularly clear when we turn to the role of social responsibilities as well as social rights in Europe's societies. This issue had remained latent in the original analysis of Western Europe into 'three worlds of welfare capitalism'. However, it becomes clearly visible, even if only in hindsight, once we recognise that there are additional worlds of welfare capitalism in Europe, namely the southern and eastern variants. These variants need a citizenship analysis which recognises the fact, which is both a sociological and a normative fact, that citizenship contains a responsibilities as well as a rights aspect. The importance of the responsibilities aspect is underscored when we consider what is involved in recognising and understanding many of the new socio-political changes and challenges facing societies in the changing world of the 21st century. Citizens' social movements, such as those concerned with children's rights or with safeguarding the environment, are attempting to address and engage with the societal problems generated by contemporary social change. They include rights in their discourses. However, these movements tend, in the main, to press governments and publics in Europe and in other world regions towards a greater recognition and acceptance of responsibilities. Such responsibilities can relate, for instance, to the need for a rebalancing of rights among citizens, a contemporary renewal of the traditional social contracts which can be claimed to normatively ground national societies and the international community (such as it is). They can also relate to the need for governments and publics to accept new welfare-relevant constraints on the development of capitalism and on the property rights and freedoms it institutionalises.

Worlds of welfare capitalism, then, that is distinctive 'mixes' of the welfare-relevant societal systems of state, market, civil society, are connected with worlds of citizenship, that is distinctive 'mixes' of both rights and responsibilities across the main citizenship-relevant dimensions – civil, political, and social. In the early 21st century Europe's worlds of welfare capitalism, as we have suggested, are at least five in number. Each of them is linked with a distinctive world of citizenship and none of these can be adequately characterised purely in terms of patterns of rights, whether social or not. That is, none of them can be understood in what is effectively a 'duty-free' way. It is necessary to recognise the responsibilities and obligations aspect of citizenship, in relation to the full range of social, civil or political citizenship dimensions. We can now look at this aspect, first, in relation to the additional southern and eastern European worlds and next in relation to western Europe's original three worlds.

The two additional worlds of European welfare capitalism briefly considered earlier each emerged from systems characterised to a significant degree by various authoritarian forms of the state, whether proto-fascist, as in the southern European case, or communist, as in the eastern European case. Each of them was traditionally influenced by dominant versions of the Christian religion in their spheres of national identity and civil society, and each remains so in their contemporary post-authoritarian period. Churches played different roles under communism and proto-fascism. Under communism they were a focus of opposition; under proto-fascism they were a part of the establishment and a core source of regime legitimation. However, in the contemporary period, which is both post-communist and post-fascist, churches form key elements in the civil society aspect of each of these clusters of societies.

The nations in each cluster have now achieved stability as democracies with a liberal and pluralistic culture and civil society. Nevertheless traces of these state-centric traditions no doubt remain in their political cultures. In addition, in each cluster national identities needed to be renewed in the post-authoritarian period. And large-scale communities of religious faith continue to be major presences in their national cultures and civil societies and contribute to the renewal of national collective identities (e.g. Catholicism in Poland and Spain, and Orthodox Christianity in Greece and Bulgaria).

Each of these political and cultural factors implies, *de facto*, that responsibilities have a significant presence in these countries' contemporary versions of citizenship and in their national cultures and public life. Their political heritages do not guarantee the dominance of patriotic duty in their public spheres, but they make it possible. They make probable a form of democratic politics which circles around the issues of governmental power and authority, and of the state's claims on the citizen through identity, loyalties and obligations. In relation to their cultural heritages of religion, faith, whether in the private sphere or the public sphere, expresses itself in attitudes, beliefs and practices which are typically much more likely to be oriented to responsibilities and obligations than to individual rights and liberties. Many of the societies of southern and eastern Europe may appear to be unaffected by this because they have secular constitutions. But formal secularism is consistent with major faith communities and institutions playing a significant public role in these societies, as they have traditionally done throughout the modern period, and are likely to continue doing so into the 21st century.

The cultural-religious factor and the responsibilities-oriented colour it casts over nation-state versions of citizenship is an important one to consider, not only in relation to the two additional European worlds, but also in relation to the original three worlds. Esping-Andersen's analysis of these three worlds is interesting and useful as far as it goes. But as we have noted earlier, it fails to engage with the sociological as well as the normative realities of citizenship, namely that systems of rights simply do not exist in a social and moral vacuum. They always come associated with systems of responsibilities whether or not we would welcome this from a normative perspective.

There is some limited recognition of this fact in Esping-Andersen's discussions.[34] For instance, he identifies one of the 'worlds of welfare capitalism' with reference to the importance of religion. The 'world' in question is the 'conservative corporatist' type, and the religion is Catholic Christianity. The version of democratic politics connected with this welfare regime typically involves a significant role being played by religiously-based political parties and governments. The welfare regime itself involves a significant but ultimately limited orchestrating and regulatory role for the state. It also involves a substantial role for the more formal and corporate elements of civil society, namely primarily organisations such as churches and trade unions, and secondarily families. The model involves the work ethic, employment-based social insurance, and a male 'bread-winner' family system. It at least permits dominant churches to operate major welfare and philanthropic systems, as they have done traditionally. As part of this, conservative corporatist societies' self-understandings are likely to be balanced towards versions of citizenship emphasising social responsibility, whether or not these versions retain the religious appearance of their origins.

We can assume that Esping-Andersen's conceptualisation of the conservative-corporatist model in terms of the political significance of the cultural (religious) factor implies a certain minimal recognition of citizenship and its responsibilities aspect. However, what is curious about his analysis is his failure to explore the cultural (religious) factor more generally beyond this model. We find out nothing at all about the religious influences on and context of the other two welfare models, and thus about the responsibilities that in social reality, they undoubtedly do involve as aspects of the regime institutions and also of the associated worlds of citizenship. The main responsibilities and duties which are relevant here are those relating to work and the family, key elements of which we can refer to as the work ethic and the family ethic. All welfare regimes need to concern themselves with work and with family life. Further, all of them may reasonably be assumed to make assumptions about responsibilities in these spheres and to institutionalise them – in their professional discourses and ideologies, in their organisational rules and practices, and in their assumptions and requirements concerning citizens as welfare claimants and clients. What do welfare regimes assume about citizens' responsibilities to work in formal paid employment, and what connections do they make between this and relevant benefits which might be provided by the welfare system (e.g. in relation to unemployment, sickness and retirement)? What do they assume about citizens' responsibilities to undertake informal and unpaid carework in the family for children and the dependent elderly? What do they assume about citizens' responsibilities to pay taxes to the state on their employment income or wealth? Welfare regimes can be usefully explored and characterised in terms of such questions, although they are effectively ignored in Esping-Andersen's original analysis. Of course the liberal-market and social-democratic worlds of welfare and their related worlds of citizenship as they developed over the course of the 19th and 20th centuries were traditionally marked by versions and patterns of social responsibilities, and they remain so in the contemporary period.

If the UK is taken to represent the liberal-market model in Europe, then we need to recognise the importance of the work and family ethics and related structures and distributions of social responsibilities.[35] The work ethic has been built into the UK welfare state, for instance, in the form of conditions for benefit, since its creation in the early post-war period. The family ethic was also a built-in feature of UK social policy in the inter-war period and since the creation of the post-war welfare state. The latter assumed a gendered division of labour, a male breadwinner model and the household (with a male head) as the unit of benefit. This has been modified somewhat in recent years in the direction of individualisation and reducing gender assumptions. Taxpaying duties to pay for the transfers involved in the welfare state are generally perceived as legitimate and thus capable of being effectively enforced on British citizens. There are relatively high rates of collection of levied taxes and low rates of tax evasion. However, this acceptance of citizen responsibilities is potentially contentious, and there has been a volatile politics focused around the levels and types of taxation in the UK in recent years.[36]

Although the Scandinavian social-democratic model and countries were Esping-Andersen's main example of rights-based social citizenship, and of his effectively duty-free conception of citizenship, nonetheless, in each of these areas these countries have nationally developed versions and patterns of citizen duties and expectations about at least the work ethic if not also the family ethic.[37] The work ethic has been built into the Swedish welfare state, for instance in the form of conditions for benefit, since its creation. The family ethic was a built-in feature of Swedish social policy in the inter-war period and since the creation of the post-war welfare state. Although this has been modified a lot in recent decades in the direction of individualisation and reducing gender biases, assumptions remain about the gendered nature of the division of labour. As in the other social models, the traditional version involved the standard male breadwinner model and household (with its assumed male head) as the unit of benefit. The more recent modifications make more egalitarian assumptions. These developments have been in a progressive direction for women and have been connected with a major expansion over time of female employment in the public sector. However, in terms of citizenship and the rights–responsibilities balance, one interpretation of this development might reasonably be that it effectively socially relocates women from being (social rights-claiming) clients of the welfare state into being (responsibility-performing) employees of the welfare state. Also, on the responsibilities side, in addition to work and family responsibilities, there is the issue of people's taxpaying responsibilities. Scandinavian publics have tolerated rates of taxation from employment incomes which are high in comparative international terms to pay for the costs of the extensive welfare state, its benefits, services and employees, although this has begun to be challenged and to change marginally in recent years under the pressure of wider social changes such as globalisation and Europeanisation.[38]

What social changes and common challenges have been affecting Europe's social complex of welfare capitalist and citizenship 'worlds' in the late 20th and early 21st centuries, and what policy challenges do they raise? What opportunities and barriers do they present to the future development of European society, particularly in the form of the EU and particularly in the field of welfare? These are issues we consider in the following two chapters.

Notes

1   On citizenship and modern society, see Roche 1996 and 2002; also Roche 1987, 1994, 1995, 2000b. Also see Barbalet 1988; Dwyer 2000; Faist 1995, 2000; Faist and Kivisto 2007; Heater 1990; Isin and Turner 2002; Isin and Wood 1998; Janoski 1998; Marshall 1992; Stevenson 2000; Turner 1986, 1993; Twine 1994. On citizenship in European and EU contexts, see Brubaker 1992; Delanty 2007; Ferrera 2003; Martiniello 1997; Meehan 1993; O'Leary and Tiilikainen 1998; Roche 1996, Chapter 8, 1997; Roche and van Berkel 1997a; Rosas and Antola 1995; and Wiener 1998.

2   For Esping-Andersen's work, see 1990, 1996a, 1996b, 1996c, 1999, 2002a, 2002b, 2002c; and Esping-Andersen et al. 2002; Esping-Andersen and Regini 2000.

3   Esping-Andersen 1990, Chapter 1. To characterise the worlds or regimes, Esping-Andersen draws on, among others, the ideas of the social policy analyst Richard Titmuss (1963). See Esping-Andersen 1990, p.20.

4   To explain this, Esping-Andersen draws on T.H. Marshall's early post-war analysis of citizenship into three dimensions of rights, namely civil, political and social (Marshall 1992).

5   On responsibilities, see Roche 1996, 2002; also Janoski 1998; and Dwyer 2000; also see final section of the chapter.

6   Such a rich multidimensional perspective is well illustrated in the notable work of Janoski 1998.

7   See Roche 1987 and 1996, Chapter 1; also Brubaker 1992; and Ferrera 2003.

8   See Chapter 4 earlier; Giddens 1985; and Mann 1986.

9   See Beck and Grande (2007) on the logic of both/and rather than either/or; also see Chapter 9 below.

10 On enlargement, see Nugent 2004; also the discussion of the East European world of welfare capitalism later in this chapter.

11 Also see long-term population projections in Eurostat 2008.

12 For studies of European welfare regimes and 'world of welfare capitalism' apart from Esping-Andersen, see Abrahamson 2000; Arts and Gelissen 2002; Bambra 2004, 2005, 2006; Bode 2006; Gallie and Paugam 2000; Ginsburg 1992; Gould 1993; J. Lewis 1992, 1997; Morissens and Sainsbury 2005; Orloff 1993; Roche and Annesley 2004; Palier and Sykes 2001; Prior and Sykes 2001; Sainsbury 1999, 2006; Sykes et al. 2001.

13   Goodin et al. 1999.
14   On the European southern welfare regime see, for instance, Ferrera 1996, 2005b; and Guillen and Alvarez 2001.
15   On East European welfare regimes see, for instance, Deacon 2000; Deacon and Stubbs 2007; Fajth 2000; Ferge 2001; Kaufman 2007; Kornai et al. 2001; Lendvai 2004; Outhwaite 2008, Chapter 5; Sotiropoulos 2005; Sotiropolous and Pop 2007; and Sotiropoulou and Sotiropoulos 2007.
16   In terms of the economic dimension and diversity in Europe's 'models of capitalism', see Schmidt 2002. In terms of the cultural dimension and European diversity in this context, see the following section. For a relevant sociological review of European and wider socio-economic models of capitalism, see Outwaite 2008, Chapter 3.
17   For discussions relevant to this 'cultural turn' see, for instance, Baldock 2000; Chamberlayne et al. 1999; Freeman and Rustin 1999; Pfau-Effinger 2005; van Kersbergen and Manow 2009; and van Oorschott 2007; also work on the factor of religion in relation to social policy, see below.
18   For instance, on modernisation, see Parsons 1971; Polanyi 2001; Rimlinger 1993; Flora et al. 1999; Wilensky 1975; and on class and power-resources approaches, see Korpi 2004 and Esping-Andersen (notes 2 and 3 above). For relevant reviews of long-term social and political economic change in modernity concerned with the development of welfare and social policy, see Ferrera 2005a, Chapter 2; Gough 2005; Lindert 2005; and Pierson 1991, Chapter 4.
19   For discussion of religion as a factor in the development of social policy in different welfare regimes, see Anderson 2009; Hornsby-Smith 1999; Korpi 2004; Manow and van Kersbergen 2006, 2009; Morgan 2002; van Kersbergen 1995; and van Kersbergen and Manow 2009. On religion as a general factor in the comparative sociology of European society, see Crouch 1999, Chapter 9.
20   Within Protestantism, the difference between two types needs to be recognised, namely Lutheranism and Calvinism. In their 16th-century origins these differed on a number of fronts, particularly in relation to the nature of the practices of worship, communion and Bible study. Lutheranism was willing to accommodate more to traditional Catholic-type practices such as celebrating the mass and regarding communion as being a sacrament. Calvinism held to a view which aimed to be based more on the New Testament and which could be iconoclastic in relation to such rituals and beliefs. Lutheranism became institutionalised in the national churches and state religions of the Nordic countries in the 16th century and is most relevant in this discussion.
21   Many European countries had proportional representation systems by 1919, although among the major EU member states this has not been taken up by France and the UK, which operate alternative electoral systems (respectively 'two round' and 'first past the post').
22   On the role of religion in the origins of the Danish welfare system, see Sorensen (1998) and on its indirect relevance in Sweden as creating the space for oppositional and secularised liberal and social-democratic social policies, see Anderson 2009; also Manow and van Kersbergen 2006, 2009.
23   On Catholicism and social policy in Europe, see Hornsby-Smith 1999; van Kersbergen 1995; also van Kersbergen and Manow 2009, Chapters 4 and 6.
24   Giddens 1985, Chapter 9 and *passim*; Downing 1992; Klausen 2001; Skocpol 1995; Kaspersen 2004; and Milward 1977.

25 On the influence of war on state governance capacities, see Klausen 2001; also Milward 1977.

26 On southern Europe, see note 14 above.

27 On post-communist Eastern Europe in general, see Brubaker 1996; Davies 2006; Judt 2005; Mazower 1998; and Schopflin 2000. On social policy aspects, see note 15 above.

28 See Ferrera 2005a, Chapter 2; and Korpi 2004.

29 On the history of the corporatist world of welfare capitalism, including in relation to the two 20th-century world wars, on Germany see Hong 1998; Klausen 2001, Chapter 7; Korpi 2004; and Steinmetz 1993; and on France, Ambler 1991; Downing 1992, Chapter 5; and Dutton 2002.

30 On the European context and influence of the Napoleonic wars, see Bobbitt 2002, Chapter 19; Davies 1997, Chapter 9; Kennedy 1988, Chapter 3; Tilly 1992, Chapter 4.

31 On war and the Scandinavian social-democratic world, on Denmark see Kaspersen 2004; on Sweden, see Downing 1992, Chapter 8; and Klausen 2001, Chapters 4 and 5; generally, see Jochem 2000; and Kautto et al. 1999.

32 On war and the liberal-market welfare regime see, on UK, Downing 1992, Chapter 7; Klausen 2001, Chapter 2 and 3; Milward 1977; and discussion in Chapter 5 above. On the USA, see Skocpol 1995.

33 Janoski (1998) provides a good example of an analysis of citizenship and worlds of welfare capitalism which takes this kind of view, although overall in his account he generally attests to the utility of Esping-Andersen's three worlds analysis.

34 Also Esping-Andersen's advocacy of a 'new social contractualist' perspective in his recent work on European social policy would seem to carry the implication that responsibilities need to be recognised as well as rights, since the logic of contracts is that they require both. On this perspective, see the discussions in Chapters 7 and 8.

35 On the ideological and social policy-relevance of the idea of the work/employment ethic (for instance, in the form of 'workfare' policy) in the American so-called 'liberal-market model', see Roche 1996, Chapter 6; also Handler 2004, 2005. On the ideological and the social policy-relevance of the related idea of the family ethic in the USA, see Roche 1996, Chapter 5. Generally, on work responsibilities in contemporary European social inclusion and employment policy, see Lind and Moller 1999; Lodemal and Trickey 2001; Roche and Annesley 2004; and van Berkel and Moller 2002. On the important but often neglected social context of informal work and its responsibilities, as for instance in relation to household and neighbourhood community divisions of labour in relation to carework, see Williams and Windebank 1998.

36 On the general issue of citizens' responsibilites to pay tax, see Twine (1994), and on 'tax regimes' as an aspect of and in their connection with welfare regimes, see Kemmerling (2002). The setting of tax levels and the acceptance and/or enforcement of responsibilities to pay tax as well as cross-border customs duties have, of course, been potentially highly contentious themes in politics throughout European history, linked with the establishment, authority and growth of the territorial state. The UK is a notable case of a European country in which these issues have remained highly contested through to the contemporary period. For instance, Prime Minister Margaret Thatcher's

introduction of a new and additional local 'poll tax' in the mid-1980s attracted public opposition in the form of large-scale and animated demonstrations and 'riots'. The tax ultimately had to be significantly altered and the public's negative reaction to it helped to end her premiership. Or again, in the mid-1990s the press helped create a public mood antagonistic to tax increases to influence the incoming New Labour government. Press pressure and the public mood was sustained throughout New Labour's decade or more in power from 1997, and influenced the UK government to keep tax increases to a minimum over the course of this period.

37 On the work ethic and welfare in Scandinavian social-democratic model, see Lindbeck (1995) on Sweden, and more generally Heinemann (2008); on the family ethic and approaches to women's rights in this model, see J. Lewis 1992; and Sainsbury 1999.

38 In 2007 Swedish tax rates and thus citizens' agreed tax responsibilities, both in terms of personal incomes and also in terms of corporate taxation, were comparable with and in some cases lower than those accepted by publics in corporate welfare regime countries; see OECD Tax Database (2008). For a relevant general discussion on the growth from the 18th century of modern states' economies and welfare spending, and also of tax levels and systems to pay for the latter, which in addition discusses the Swedish case in some detail, see Lindert 2005.

PART 3

The European Complex in the 21st Century: Contemporary Social Change and European Welfare Capitalism

7

CONTEMPORARY SOCIAL CHANGE AND EUROPEAN WELFARE CAPITALISM: THE CHALLENGES OF GLOBALISATION AND POST-INDUSTRIALISM

Introduction

From a sociological perspective, we have suggested that contemporary Europe can be usefully understood as a duality of commonalities and differences within the social complex formed by Europe's nation-state societies. In Chapter 6 we began to engage with this duality and with the European complex in terms of one of its core fields, welfare. We considered the social construction and reconstruction of differences within the welfare field of the European complex in terms of the five multinational clusters of types or 'worlds of welfare capitalism' and their related configurations or 'worlds' of citizenship. It was observed that these differences emerged in response to some relatively common socio-historical factors and experiences, particularly those of industrial capitalism, war and religion. Later we turn to look at another common factor which is also beginning to shape the European social complex in field of welfare, namely the European Union and its attempted reconstruction of welfare capitalism across the continent in ways which aim to promote commonality over difference (Chapter 8). This attempt, as we will see, has made only slow and fitful progress in the last two decades. It has encountered resistance from EU member states and their citizens' general support for retaining the kind of welfare state differences we discussed in Chapter 6.[1] The EU project of 'Europeanisation' in the welfare field, as in other fields, has made some headway and it is possible that it will to continue to do so into the future. However, its capacity to do this is conditioned by the continuing influence of these kinds of differences.

In Chapter 1 we outlined a framework to address social change in the modern era in terms of 'modernisation' and 'globalisation'. Common 'modernising' social changes from the 19th through to the mid-20th centuries in Europe, as we have seen, tended to promote the construction of a complex of warfare states, national-level industrial capitalist economies and ultimately welfare states and forms of welfare capitalism. The modernising phase of social change can be interpreted as involving the construction of nation-state societies and a variety of types of 'national functional' social order within them. National functionalist projects involved states attempting to control and integrate their societies by coordinating core 'national' institutions and regulation in the three societal dimensions of economy, culture and polity.[2] Common vectors and dynamics of social change have continued to influence and shape the European social complex in the late 20th and early 21st centuries. But, as indicated in Chapter 1, the dominant theme of these changes is that of globalisation. Globalising influences now challenge the very national functional systems which earlier versions of modernisation achieved and established. They pressure these systems to restructure themselves, and arguably they even threaten ultimately to significantly undermine and deconstruct them. The EU's attempt to promote more common approaches to welfare capitalism across Europe can be seen as both a symptom of these kinds of globalising changes and also as a way of responding to and managing them. To provide a basis for understanding and assessing the EU's project in the following chapter it is first necessary to look further into some of these contemporary common social changes, their structural impacts and the social and welfare problems to which they can be argued to give rise.

While common to all, the major trends and changes in European welfare capitalism we are concerned with in this chapter nevertheless reveal and embody themselves, to varying extents and in varying combinations, at the level of particular national societies and particular welfare regimes. In the discussion we need to consider both these common challenges and also the differentiated effects and responses they provoke. With this in mind, information about a range of major European countries that are representative of four of the five worlds of welfare capitalism (namely Germany, the UK, Spain and Sweden) considered in Chapter 6 will be presented to illustrate the discussion. The chapter consists of sections organised around three sets of issues and questions. First, what are the major social changes? Secondly, why are they happening? And thirdly, what are their social effects, and what social risks and problems do they cause? The three sections address these issues in turn.

Common Social Realities and Dynamics in the European Complex

Social and economic change has been endemic throughout the modern era, but it has qualitatively accelerated over the last generation. It affects the structures

Table 7.1   European socio-demographic trends and projections 1960–2050

Nation	Birth rates and population				Ageing and dependency rates			
	Birth rate trends		Population projections* (millions)		Ageing trends**		Dependency projections	
	A	B	C	D	E	F	G	H
	1960	1990	2004	2050	1960	1990s+	2004	2030
Sweden	2.17	2.00	8,976	10,216	1.94	4.69	26.4	38.5
Germany	2.27	1.39	82,532	74,201	1.46	4.32	26.8	46.0
UK	2.66	1.79	59,652	64,247	1.91	3.26	24.3	37.4
Spain	2.86	1.26	42,345	42,573	2.71	3.70	24.6	38.9

Sources: Cols A, B: Crouch 1999, Table A7.1, A7.2; Cols C, D: Eurostat 2006a Cols E, F: Crouch 1999, Table A2.1, A2.3; Cols G, H: Eurostat 2007.

Notes: *Includes immigration (net migration). Without immigration population declines are significant for all countries, except Sweden. ** People aged 80 years or more. + Various 1990s years (i.e. Sweden 1994, Germany 1990, UK 1993, Spain 1995).

and prospects of all European societies to some extent or another, and challenges them to respond and restructure themselves in order to adjust to and manage the changes. Before we consider some of the causes and drivers of contemporary social change (second main section below) we first need to get a picture of some of the main areas and characteristic of these changes. Two areas which need to be recognised immediately are those of socio-demographic and socio-economic change. The former involves a long-term underlying population decline and the ageing of the population across Europe. The latter involves an equally long-term decline in employment in industry and the shift from an industrial to a post-industrial form of capitalist economy across Europe. To illustrate the discussion, some key features of these sociologically common and politically challenging social changes are summarised in the social data presented in Tables 7.1 and 7.2.

Table 7.1 shows two of the main socio-demographic trends and 'revolutions' that are restructuring European societies. In the late twentieth century in advanced capitalist countries around the world, but particularly across Europe, the major population trends have been the decline in birth rates (columns A and B) and the extension of people's life spans into a longer old age (columns E and F), which is initially healthier and later (e.g. 75 years or more) more frail and dependent. Each of these trends can be understood as a product of a combination of social factors, but particularly cultural factors. The main cultural factors which can be pointed to are, respectively, the changing attitude of women to traditional forms of family and child-rearing in relation to the decline in birth rates (see later) and developments in medical science in relation to the ageing of populations. In turn, each of these trends has important social effects; in the former case on the capacity of national populations to reproduce themselves, and in the latter case on the capacity of countries to care for their dependent elderly. Evidently, when birth rates decline below two children per set of parents, as they have done across most of Europe over the course of the post-war period, then societies are no longer capable of maintaining their overall numbers and, without alternative action, national populations will decline.

The maintenance and indeed growth of their populations remains a vitally important condition for nations' economic growth in the modern era, irrespective of structural changes which may also have occurred in the uses made of labour in contemporary economies (which we will discuss in a moment). Long-term population decline in European societies threatens to undermine both their capacity for sustained economic growth and also their capacity to provide the labour and tax base to resource and service the needs of their dependents, particularly the increasing (and increasingly costly) group of dependent elderly. (The problem is indicated in the increases in the ratio of such dependents to working-age people projected for the coming generation in columns G and H).

One important solution to these socio-economic problems, and to the population problem causing it, is for countries to encourage sufficient immigration to have a net positive population impact. Of course, as European countries' experiences over the last generation have indicated, immigration is not a costless solution. It carries the possibility of major cultural and 'racial' problems along with it, relating to the adequate inclusion of culturally different immigrant groups into majority host populations and cultures. In addition, in some cases the underlying birth rate reduction trends may be so steep that even reasonable assumptions about substantial net migration may be incapable of ultimately rescuing national populations either from stasis (e.g. Spain) or from ultimate decline (e.g. Germany) (see the population information and projections in columns C and D in Table 7.1).

We now need to consider another set of social changes which have rolled through European societies and challenged them in the past generation or so, namely indicators of a major socio-economic transformation from the 'industrial society' version of modernity to a 'post-industrial society' version. Table 7.2 summarises some relevant information about socio-economic trends and changes affecting all types of European societies over the course of the post-war period. In this period large-scale and inevitably costly welfare states were established across most of northern and central Western Europe. The funding base for these developments lay in the successful long-term growth of Europe's capitalist economies, as indicated in the growth of gross domestic product (expressed in the indicator GDP per capita, column A). Of course GDP per capita is an abstract measure of the social character of real economies in which income distributions were and remain very unequal, only ameliorated somewhat

Table 7.2 European socio-economic change and restructuring 1: 1960–2006 – Economic growth and the shift to a post-industrial economy

Nation		Economic growth		Sector shifts	
		GDP per capita ($ 000s)	Labour Productivity*	Manufacturing sector (% employed)	Service sector (% employed.)
Sweden	Rows:	A	B	C	D
1960	1	10	58	34	20
1990s	2	25	81	24	73
2000s	3	32	88	23	75
Germany					
1960	4	91	39	36	19
1990s	5	20	94	31	67
2000s	6	26	92	27	70
UK					
1960	7	12	61	26	24
1990s	8	21	74	22	77
2000s	9	29	87	19	80
Spain					
1960	10	3	25	22	14
1990s	11	12	82	29	64
2000s	12	17	76	29	65

Sources: Cols A, B: Mishel et al. 2007, Tables 8.1 and 8.3; Cols C, D: 1960, 1995 data from Crouch 1999, Appendix A2.2 and A2.4; 2003 data from EC 2005c.

Notes: * Measured by GDP per work hour, as percentage of USA (100) at each period, earliest year here is for 1950 not 1960. Other data are for 1990 and 2004.

by the redistributive effects of welfare states and social policy in favour of various types of disadvantaged people, the poor, unemployed and elderly, among others. Nevertheless, it gives a rough, although telling, indication of the real long-term qualitative change (threefold increase) in the generality of post-war West European family incomes and standards of living, particularly given Europeans' preceding common experiences of depression, unemployment and war. No doubt since the mid-20th century there has often been political support across western European democracies for the critique and containment of capitalism, and even periodically for its overthrow. Nevertheless a latent legitimation of market economies has always been available in western European publics throughout this period. The experience of the real benefits of economic growth helps to explain this, just as the prospect of following along this trail has made such legitimation more manifestly available from eastern European publics since the fall of Soviet communism.

The long-term and continuing socio-economic transformation towards relative affluence within European societies in the late 20th century was associated with, and arguably driven along by, two significant, even 'revolutionary', economic changes. The first was the long-term growth in the productivity of labour (column B). This is connected in part with developments in (the partly cultural factors of) science and technological innovation, together with their institutional conditions in the development of education and research, and their applications in the modern economy. It implies that, on the one hand, labour has been being applied to increasingly productive capital assets and, on the other hand, that the information, knowledge and skills, and hence the education and training, required from much labour in the contemporary capitalist economy has increased qualitatively.

These changes are consistent with the second major economic change summarised in Table 7.2, namely that between the major sectors of contemporary European economies. It is conventional to analyse the main sectors of modern economies as being those of agriculture, industrial manufacturing and services. The modernisation process has long been recognised to require at least a process of industrialisation, even 'an industrial revolution', to shift traditional and early modern-type economies decisively away from their focus on agriculturally-based capital, production, trade and employment. This process rolled out in West Europe in the late 19th and early 20th centuries and has been rolling out as a wave through central, eastern and southeastern Europe ever since, accelerated by the accession of many countries in the latter regions to the EU in recent years. However, the process of the building up of the industrial sector in modern economies, with all of its massive implications for labour and for societal organisation more broadly (in particular for class, gender and family systems and social identities) peaked in West Europe and elsewhere in the world in the 1970s. Since that time apparently irreversible processes of 'deindustrialisation' have set in, which continue to be visible in many of Europe's great cities. European economies and their employment patterns have shifted inexorably towards a focus on the service economy and its various sub-sectors, both public and private, both high- and low-skilled (columns C and D).

Socio-economic change involving 'deindustrialisation' carries with it important implications and potentially major problems for the production and distribution of welfare in the forms of 'welfare capitalism' that have been established in the 20th century in Europe. These changes and problems are manifest most clearly in one of the core institutions of capitalist society, namely the labour market, and we look at this in a moment. First, we need to briefly consider some of the main causes of socio-economic changes in contemporary Europe outlined so far. They relate to the pervasive influence of globalisation and to the equally pervasive influence of 'post-industrialism' and the emergence in the 21st century of social and economic formations organised around 'information' and 'knowledge' and related technologies and services. We consider these interpretations and their implications in the following section and also later in Chapter 8.[3]

Understanding Contemporary European Social Change

What has been driving the socio-demographic and socio-economic changes outlined in the previous section? In relation to socio-demographic changes, some cross-national cultural factors were noted as playing a causal role. These include the fact that over the course of the recent generation women have made major changes in their gender roles in the family and labour market. They also include developments in scientific knowledge and medical technology and their impacts on populations' longevity and health. In this section we will focus more on exploring the socio-economic changes and their dynamics.

Earlier a general framework for analysing the nature of major social change in contemporary modern Europe was indicated (see Chapter 1 and also the Introduction to this chapter). This proposed seeing it as involving a shift beyond the mid-20th-century version of the European complex organised around 'national functionalist' societal systems and their typically state-dominated welfare systems. What the new post-functional situation might be is currently unclear, as the situation has not yet stabilised and structural changes continue. They create problems for European versions of welfare capitalism and the welfare state and challenge them to reconstruct and reform themselves. We consider these challenges and problems later. For the moment, we need to pause to consider the dynamics and drivers of these changes further.

Our general framework for analysing contemporary social change in general and socio-economic change in particular gives the main priority to the factor of globalisation. But this has been understood in broad and multidimensional terms, and in Chapter 1 it was seen as being associated with 'post-industrialism'. Although they are interconnected in socio-economic reality, the factors of globalisation and post-industrialisation can be distinguished analytically. It is relevant also that policy-making and governance systems at national and EU levels can often distinguish them in terms of the particular challenges they present and the policy responses they require. So for each of these reasons it is convenient to discuss them separately in turn. As dynamic factors they can be distinguished, among other ways, in terms of their internality or externality in relation to national economies. Post-industrialisation can be visualised as being an internal factor operating within European national economies and their modernisation trajectories. Globalisation can be visualised as being more of an external factor, bringing influences from the international economic environment to bear on these economies. The theme of post-industrial change is taken up later in connection with the new priority it attaches to skills and human capital in the labour force and, relatedly, the new social problems of marginalisation it creates for the unskilled manual working class. The theme of globalisation is also taken up again later when considering influences on changes in contemporary European welfare states and systems. Thus it would be useful at this stage in the discussion to provide some introductory observations about each of these factors, so we first turn to globalisation and then to post-industrialism.

Europe and globalisation: the EU in the global context

Europe and the EU's global context in general and the pervasive and relentless dynamics associated with globalisation in particular are external sources of change for nation-states and all social formations in the 21st century. This particularly includes in the contemporary EU as a social and policy complex. Arguably, in the 21st century we are witnessing the development of a 'new globalisation'.[4] The first phase in the contemporary reality of globalisation, and certainly in its recognition as such in policy and academic circles, was that of the 1990s, following the collapse of the USSR and its neo-empire in eastern Europe. 'First phase' globalisation coincided with the USA assuming sole global superpower status. In this phase much globalisation could be argued to have been effectively a process of Americanisation, connected with the domination of the global economy by capital markets, multinational companies, mass affluent consumer demand based in the USA and exerting influences of neo-liberal political ideology and cultural standardisation as well as economic power from that base.[5]

This situation has begun to change in the early years of the 21st century because of such dynamics as the widespread dissemination of the internet as a *de facto* world-wide real-time market place, and the newly recognised and accelerating rise of China as an economic and military superpower. On the basis of these dynamics, what can be referred to as a stage of 'new' or 'second phase' globalisation has emerged. This is a more complex form of globalisation.[6] It includes the notion that the world order which is emerging increasingly appears to be a multi-polar order, one which sees an EU-coordinated Europe as one of the global poles. We consider the implications of the global contexts involving the new globalisation for EU social and economic policy in the 21st century in outline in this section and then in more detail in Chapter 8. This initial brief outline makes use of the idea that globalisation can be helpfully viewed from the perspective of one of its poles, in this case that of the EU. It also makes use of the idea that the EU's global contexts and the influence of processes of globalisation have, of course, become objects of EU policy discourse as well as of social scientific discourse.

For a number of decades in the post-war period the precursor versions of the EU (e.g. the European Economic Community) were relatively inward-looking, and the organisation developed in a stuttering fashion. A new dynamism and a more outward-looking stance was imparted to the organisation in the 1980s by Jacques Delors, who was President of the European Commission for a consequential decade, 1985–95. The organisation moved towards a deepening of its economic rationale and structures through the Single European Act 1986 and the Maastricht Treaty 1992. These created the Single Market project and we will consider this again in the following chapter. While this project intensified the EU's inward-looking stance and its internal rule-creation and institution-building, the whole process was also simultaneously being connected with a more outward-looking stance.[7]

From this period onwards part of the policy discourse repertoire which the EU periodically used to encourage the elites and publics of the member states in the direction of greater economic integration, greater Europeanisation in this sense, was to draw their attention to the threats and opportunities presented by the EU's global context. This was particularly so in the 1990s following the fall of communism, which raised the profile of both market-based economic globalisation and also the new and problematic nature of global governance in a post-Cold War world. This has continued, indeed has escalated, through to the present (as we see later in this section). Reference to the global economy in EU policy discourse has tended to take two main forms: on the one hand, comparison with its perceived global economic competitors and, on the other hand, discussion of its role as a policy actor in global economic policy. The comparative theme implies a perception of the EU as open to being changed by the global economic realities, while the actor theme implies a perception of the EU as being capable of influencing and changing those realities. We can look briefly at each of these aspects.

The EU's global economic context

In the 1980s and 1990s the EU's global economic competitors were seen to be mainly the USA and Japan, with whom the EU formed a 'triad' of economic blocs. The success of these competitors was seen to threaten the EU's position. Thus it was assumed that, besides monitoring them, the EU had much to learn from them in terms of such things as the promotion of employment, labour productivity, the application of new technologies and economic growth. A notable example of the use of this comparison motif in EU policy discourse was that comparing the EU and USA, which was used in the preamble to the strategically significant Lisbon Agenda 2000, to explain why it was necessary. (We consider the Lisbon Agenda in more detail later in Chapter 8.) [8]

The 'comparison' motif in EU policy discourse, unlike some of the EU's more idealistic ways of conceiving the global order, at least has the virtue of making reference to some sociologically relevant economic realities relating to the EU's current and probable future economic position and context. Table 7.3 summarises some of these. What is notable is the scale of the EU's economy as measured by GDP (recognising that this a measure aggregated from the GDPs of its 27 member states). After a long period of dominance of the global economy by the USA in the post-war 20th-century period, the EU's economy has now surpassed it in aggregate terms and also as a share of world GDP. However, what is also clear from Table 7.3 is that India, and particularly China are on rapid economic growth trajectories and are making their

Table 7.3   The EU in the global economy

Nation/ region		GDP (2007)		Shares of world GDP (1995–2030)		
	Population (million)	GDP (trillion $)	GDP (per head $)	1995	2007	2030
EU	492	14.8	30,100	24.5	20.8	15.6
USA	302	13.8	45,820	21.7	19.4	16.6
China	1,323	7.1	5,420	5.5	10.1	22.7
India	1,110	3.0	2,730	3.1	4.3	8.7
Japan	127	4.2	33,630	8.3	6.0	3.6
Russia	142	2.0	14,460	2.8	2.9	2.7

Source: Grant and Barysch 2008, pp 2–3 (GDP figures are calculated in purchasing power parities).

presence felt in the global economy. From 1995 to the present, each of them has substantially increased their shares of world GDP. Chinese growth is particularly dramatic, having already overtaken Japanese GDP, and it is projected to overtake the EU and the USA in terms of share of world GDP by 2030.

The EU as a policy actor in the global order

In the 21st century most European nations (arguably all of them, even including UN Security Council nuclear powers France and the UK) are no longer realistically in the position to be able to sustain notions of being global-level actors capable of shaping the nature and direction of globalisation as well as merely adjusting and reacting to global forces. A question for Europeans might be, then, could the EU, representing them all collectively, aspire to become such an actor? It has generally been kept relatively weak politically and militarily compared with the USA by its member states' defence of their individual international positions and self-images, and also by the participation of most of them with the USA in the traditional Atlanticist military alliance of NATO. Consequently, the EU is not yet adequately resourced or organised to play a global role anywhere comparable with that of the USA (although it is possible to argue that the EU can be politically influential without great military capacity, as we discuss in the following chapter). However, within its limits the EU has achieved a globally leading role in the field of aid and related development policy[9] and it has begun to develop an influential policy profile in the field of international environmental policy.[10] Against this background, what has its role been in the global economic context?

Alongside the EU's perception of its comparative position in the global economic order there is also its perception of itself as a policy actor in the institutional machinery of global economic governance. The main institution here is the World Trade Organization (WTO), which emerged out of the previous post-war international economic regulatory system, the General Agreement on Tariffs and Trade (GATT). The EU represents its member states in the WTO and is the largest single actor in the organisation. It has seemed to be able to exert some influence on this organisation and it is relevant in this context that the EU's Commissioner for Trade, Pascal Lamy, a respected left-of-centre politician and Europhile, moved across to head the WTO in 2004/05. The organisation had earlier successfully expanded to incorporate China in 2001. However, beyond this the WTO (and the EU within it) has struggled to achieve very much in a world economy which has been effectively dominated by the USA's interests, problems and agendas, and which in other respects remains fairly anarchic.[11]

A significant part of the WTO's agenda has been to act to enable poor and developing countries to raise their standards of living and strengthen their economies beyond a dependency on aid, through a greater involvement in international trade (a process sometimes referred to as the 'Doha' round). However, its recent history is littered with international conferences (Seattle 1999, Doha 2001, Cancun 2003, Hong Kong 2004, Geneva 2006 and 2008) that have recurrently failed to produce relevant compromises and agreements in this and other policy areas.[12] Among the various complex reasons for this failure, the USA's unilateralist defence of its national interest during the period of the Presidency of George W. Bush loomed large. By 2008 the series of WTO failures culminated in 'the Doha round' project effectively being 'parked' in order to give the American electoral process time to generate a new President in 2009. It was hoped that this event might eventually enable the multilateral process of compromise-making required by the construction of global economic governance to resume.

In this policy hiatus, the EU has become involved in a series of 'trade wars' both with the USA and also increasingly with China.[13] The EU and its member states cannot hope to compete with China's low levels of labour costs. Chinese low-cost products threaten the home markets of European producers in a range of sectors from textiles to toys.[14] Their industries exert a downward pressure on wages in low-skilled European production sectors and indeed threaten their very existence by tempting European employers to relocate 'off-shore' and 'export' their jobs to China. This in turn, for the EU, has resulted in the growth of bilateral rather than multilateral trade agreements, including with China. As a practical gesture of social solidarity relevant to the intensified challenges created by 21st century 'new globalisation', the EU agreed in 2006 to create a Global Adjustment Fund (GAF). This aimed to provide a 'shock absorber' for unemployment in the EU which has been created by globalisation, in addition to whatever compensation strategies the EU's member states organise for themselves. It makes 500 million euro available to affected member states to finance job search allowances and retraining. Whether this is a substantial enough contribution to the potential scale of the problems Europe faces on this front, or is rather something of a policy gesture, remains to be seen.[15]

The global context as a rationale for further EU integration and change
The EU's global context in general, and the development of new factors and dynamics in the process of globalisation in the 21st century in particular, provide contemporary EU policy-makers with rationales both for further EU integration internally and for attempting to play a more influential role internationally. In their view, the global context involves increased threats but also increased opportunities for the EU. On the one hand, as noted above, globalisation's threats have become obvious and tangible to Europeans with the recent and continuing rise of the Chinese economy. On the other hand, globalisation appears to offer the EU new opportunities. First, it is currently argued that a globalised economy presents Europe with new incentives and opportunities for building high-skilled enterprises and employment, which need to be actively identified and coherently pursued.[16] Secondly, EU policy discourse on the EU's global context and the challenges of globalisation, and the EU's potential global role, now appears to be willing to move emphatically and optimistically beyond the economic dimension.

This development is evident, for instance, in the views of European Commission President José Manuel Barroso. He argues for the potential global role of the EU as an exemplar and bearer of peaceful international cooperation, and of political and social systems framed by the values of human rights, democracy and social justice. In his view, the EU 'needs a new core purpose', and this should be 'to help Europeans prosper in a globalised world' and to tackle the major cross-border 'challenges which no nation can tackle alone', for instance climate change, growing competition from China and India, mass migration and international terrorism. He argues that '[g]lobalisation makes the case for the EU' in terms of its size, its resourcefulness and its problem-solving capacity: '[S]ize matters in a globalised world ...[the]... actors of globalisation, the US, China, India, dwarf any single member (state) of the EU. ... But the EU has size, 500 million people, the world's biggest single market, the world's biggest aid donor. ... Globalisation has reduced the ability of the nation-state alone to provide solutions and has failed to provide a realistic alternative at global level. ... Europe with its shared values and diversity of expertise fills that gap.'[17] We return to consider some of these ideals and principles in relation to Europe and the EU, understood normatively as a cosmopolitan civil society, in Chapter 9. From the socio-economic dynamics of globalisation we can now turn to the related dynamics of post-industrialism.

Post-industrialism 'plus': from service industry to cultural capitalism

To help understand post-industrialism as a dynamic in social change it is useful to recall the industrialism to which it is 'post', as an analogy. The 'industrial revolution' was at the heart of the European modernisation process from the 19th century onwards. Among other things, it helped shape the economic dimension of the societal model, which stabilised across Europe in the early post-war period, in what we have referred to here as a 'national functionalist' form. Far from being a singular revolutionary moment, the 'industrial revolution' was a long-drawn out process, stretching over generations for all European countries, and particularly so for Britain, the country which pioneered it. Analogously, the 'post-industrial revolution', which is helping to shape contemporary post-national functional change, can also be visualised as a multi-generational process. It has been running for a generation or more, since what can be called its 'first phase' in the mid-1970s and 1980s, and was famously foreseen as early as the 1960s by the American sociologist Daniel Bell, whose work on this theme culminated in his study of *The Coming of Post-Industrial Society*.[18]

The process really set in, in what can be called the 'second phase' of post-industrialisation, during the 1990s, boosted by two developments (hence the expression 'post-industrialism "plus"'). On the one hand, there was the unheralded and rapid collapse of Soviet communism. This system was notoriously over-burdened by, among other things, its long-established commitment to the construction and development of an industrial economy and society, a societal model which in this version at least seemed to have run out of road. On the other hand, and by contrast, there was the equally unheralded and rapid acceleration of technological innovation which occurred in the western capitalist world in the 1990s. This was associated with the widespread diffusion in American, European and Japanese economies first of computerisation and then of the internet, which appeared to open up new possibilities and futures for economic and societal development. The two factors had begun to emerge together in the Cold War superpower competition and arms race between a post-industrialising USA and an industrially-tethered USSR in the 1980s. The USA was able to use its emerging leadership in the new techno-economy's military applications to increase to breaking point the economic costs to the USSR of attempting to maintain military parity, resulting in the Soviet regime's exhaustion of both economic resources and related political (legitimacy) resources and its collapse in 1989/90.[19]

Characterising socio-historical periods and changes as 'post' something, as in expressions like 'post-war', can be analytically useful. But inevitably they carry cognitive costs as well as benefits, to the extent that they conjure up and focus attention on a negative situation, the absence of the key factor in question. Post-industrialism (particularly the 'first phase' version) has been associated with other similar 'post-' expressions, including 'post-Fordism'. 'Fordism' referred to the industrial mass production and distribution system of the kind pioneered by Henry Ford's corporation in the automobile industry in the USA in the early 20th century, and which came to be the central and dominant form of organisation in national economies for much of that century. 'Post-Fordism', like post-industrialism, as a perspective on socio-economic change, indicated that this economic form had run its historical course and was being replaced by something different, without there needing to be a consensus about what exactly that something might be.[20] In the case of Bell's early and seminal analysis, the replacement was the service-based economy, and this undoubtedly remains highly relevant to understanding contemporary European economies and societies.[21] As we have seen in Table 7.2, services are now by far the dominant 'industrial' and employment sector. The contemporary service sector is complex and comprises various kinds of functions from state-based services (e.g. the welfare state) for citizens and clients, to market-based services for consumers, operating in personal and welfare fields as well as services to financial and business fields, and these, importantly, require low as well as high skills from employees.

In addition, by the 1980s it was becoming clear that developments in information and communication technologies (hereafter ICTs) held the promise of transforming the nature of industrial production, introducing a new capacity for flexibility and specialisation of products in the context of mass production systems. Analysts focused on emerging shifts in the 'techno-economic paradigms' institutionalised in the Fordist production systems of industrial societies.[22] In more recent times, the transformative potential of the take-up of ICTs as central features of the 'second phase' post-industrial economic landscape has become qualitative and undeniable. From the mid-1990s we have witnessed technological 'revolutions' and worldwide waves of diffusion of personal computers, mobile telephony, the internet and synergies between them; the construction of new national, international and global production and service production and distribution organisations and systems; and the evolution of major new popular uses and consumer markets. These developments in 'new media' have had major transformative impacts on the 'old' media technologies and related industries of modernity (which had been equally revolutionary in their days, earlier in the 20th century), namely those of the mass print industries (books, magazines, press), radio, recorded music and television, and cross-platform popular cultural industries such as news journalism, sport presentation and journalism, and advertising. These impacts have enhanced some aspects of the traditional mass popular cultural appeal and demand for the products produced by these industries. However, in other respect they have threatened both to overshadow and undermine them as distinct 'industrial' sectors. The processes of production, distribution and consumption of such traditionally pervasive and taken-for-granted goods in modern Europe and other developed societies, such as books, newspapers, films, recorded music and adverts, are being revolutionised by digitisation, the diffusion of personal computing and the internet. We can be sure that they will be produced and consumed in very different ways in later decades of the 21st century and that the patterns of employment and 'bread-winning' connected with them will be very different, even if we cannot yet be clear about the nature of the new patterns.

We can bring some of these developments together in a conception of a shift in the modern economy from 'industrial (and welfare) capitalism' to not only 'post – i.e. non – industrial capitalism', but, more positively to what might be called 'cultural capitalism'. Welfare will continue to be a major theme in the development of the cultural and political context of capitalism in the advanced societies in the 21st century, not least because of the ageing of the population. So we can elaborate the expression to 'cultural (and welfare) capitalism'. The expression 'cultural capitalism' does not only refer to the new priority being given to the economic exploitation of cultural phenomena. From my perspective, it refers more broadly to the techno-economic aspect of what is an historically new condition in which contemporary societies in the advanced world in Europe and elsewhere find themselves. This is that the continuing ICT revolution (the 'digital revolution'[23]) gives a massive new and dynamic role to what are essentially cultural phenomena, namely information and knowledge, and essentially cultural processes, namely communication, in all dimensions of society, including the economy. In addition, they refer to and interconnect both 'high culture' and 'popular cultural' aspects of the emerging society. Users of ICTs animate both high and popular culture in their own spheres, and also connect them both up in new ways with the economy, creating new (cultural) 'industries'. Whether taken independently or collectively, these represent major and growing sources of GDP and employment in contemporary advanced economies, both across Europe and around the world.[24]

On the one hand, in terms of high culture, the new ICT revolution is making possible new dynamics and interconnections both within knowledge production systems, and between these systems and the economy. This aspect has been focused on in contemporary academic and policy-makers' analyses and interpretations of 21st-century socio-economic change as involving developments towards an 'information economy and society' and more recently a 'knowledge economy and society'.[25] In this context, analysts rightly point to the qualitatively new position in contemporary capitalist economies now being occupied by 'human capital', that is the knowledge and high skills of the increasing cadres of professionals, technicians and others who have passed through higher education systems.[26]

On the other hand, there are the numerous new popular culture aspects of the emerging 'cultural capitalism' made possible by the mass, pervasive and continuing diffusion of ICTs, particularly the internet. The ICT revolution provides new communication and market-organising infrastructures. In addition (because of its linkage to knowledge systems and technologies, for instance satellite-based global positioning systems, and new energy and engine technologies), it also enables the qualitative and quantitative growth of new transport systems and infrastructures (e.g. high-density, high-speed air and rail travel). So it enables the comprehensive renewal and extension of mass popular 'cultural industries' such as tourism, sport, entertainment (film, music, etc.), socialising (wining and dining) and shopping. The idea that the shift to post-industrialism can usefully be seen involving a shift towards 'cultural capitalism' is intended to allow both these aspects of the cultural economy – both the knowledge-based aspect and the popular cultural aspect – to be grasped together and in their interconnection.

These post-industrial changes have positive as well as negative potential social and welfare impacts. Negatively, as with any structural shift in a techno-economic paradigm, they threaten established forms of employment and institutions. More positively, they also create opportunities for the creation of new industries and employment. In the next section we focus on the former, and in the following chapter, in the context of EU policy aspirations, on the latter. So next we consider the common social impacts on European society of the key globalisation-based and post-industrialism-based aspects of contemporary social change discussed so far, focusing on the social and welfare problems they generate.

Common Impacts of Social Change in European Society: Employment, Social Divisions and Welfare [27]

In the emerging capitalist socio-economic system of the late 20th and early 21st centuries the industrial and manual working class in Europe and other 'developed' world regions are in an increasingly structurally vulnerable situation. The emerging system's post-industrialising dynamic implies that unskilled industrial jobs can be readily automated, and its globalising dynamic implies that they can be readily relocated and 'exported' to developing countries. In this new system the realities of and relationships between capital and labour have become more complicated than they were in earlier periods of mature modernity and particularly in the late 19th- and early 20th-century industrial version of capitalism. No doubt the classical version of the underlying split, connection and conflict between capital owners and labour owners identified and explored by Marx at the time, in what we can see as the era of nation-state and industrial capitalism, can be argued to be still generally relevant in our times, an era marked more by globalising and post-industrialising forms of capitalism. Indeed, this may be particularly so when undertaking political economic analysis at the global rather than nation-state level. However, at the nation-state level and the continental level in the advanced capitalist societies of the West (and elsewhere, for instance Japan and Australia) the social nature and contexts of contemporary capitalism have become more structurally complex and enigmatic than they were in preceding eras.

Capital and labour are linked generally through labour markets, which we discuss further in a moment, and directly through enterprises and production organisations. In the contemporary period the relationships between capital and labour in production organisations have expanded to cover an enormous range of types. These run between two polar types of production organisation, each of which has become more prominent over the last generation. At one emergent pole are the large-scale multinational corporations organising production and assembly chains across nations and continents, and owned by stockholding individuals and companies, including pensions funds, through the operation of stock markets across the world. At the other opposite emergent pole are small-scale enterprises, including the self-employed, often the biggest sector in aggregate in terms of value of product and employment in contemporary European economies. In the former case, capital–labour relations are organisationally fragmented and socio-spatially radically distantiated and disconnected; while in the latter case they are the very opposite, they can even overlap in the same people, in the form of people who are simultaneously shareholders or owners and also employees in their enterprise.

Within the global–local network of economic relations linking these poles, at the conventional nation-state level, contemporary capital ownership within nation-state societies has tended to become polarised between two classes and strata. On the one hand there is the highly focused form of capital ownership among national and international elites and operating through multinational corporations. These strata are often culturally barely visible because of their international mobility, and they are statistically barely visible because of their small relative numbers.[28] On the other hand there is a range of diffuse and distributed forms of capital ownership. These are represented by home ownership and also by the dominant presence of occupational pension funds and their holdings in national and international stock markets. In addition, from a sociological perspective, capital as a concept has needed to be broadened to reflect emerging changes and social realities. Also, along with financial and economic capital, the post-industrialising nature of contemporary capitalism means that it is now necessary to take full account of 'human capital', namely the possession and distribution of knowledge and skills at all levels generated by education and training. In addition, it has proved analytically interesting and useful to extend the capital concept to include 'social capital', which refers to such relative intangibles as the pattern of trust, reciprocity and solidarity between people which is possessed by a community or nation and which is thereby available to its members as a resource for action, whether in the economy or beyond it.[29]

Relatedly, the labour side of the labour–capital relation has also become more complex in terms of the level of human capital it embodies and the quality of social capital it can draw on. The capitalist labour market was always polarised and unequal, but these characteristics are being renewed in distinctive ways in the contemporary period, particularly between people and strata deemed to be 'skilled' and those deemed to be 'unskilled'. That is, an important and new axis of polarisation within labour in the contemporary era of globalisation and post-industrialism is coming to be that between groups and classes representing labour which contains high human capital (high skills and educational qualifications) and those representing labour which contains low human capital (low skills and educational qualifications).[30]

The degree of possession of human capital by class strata can also be linked along the same axis, not only with incomes but also with their degree of possession of types of social capital. Strata possessing higher human capital also tend to live and operate in social contexts involving higher levels of 'bridging' social capital (favourable to personal network-building). Correlatively, strata possessing lower human capital tend to live and operate in social contexts and communities involving either lower levels of all forms of social capital or high levels of the inward-looking and constraining type of 'binding' social capital.[31] These structural trends are also connected with differences in the mobility of labour both in the sense of the capacity for the physical movement of economic migration and also the capacity for the social movement of improving income and status by changing employment. Each of these forms of mobility is strategically important in the new, globalised socio-economic system, and skilled people are more likely to be able to access each form of mobility as compared with unskilled people, who are more likely to be socio-spatially and socio-economically fixed in their locations.[32]

So far we have suggested that the main common contemporary drivers of the social changes experienced by European societies and reshaping the European social complex, particularly in the area of welfare, are sets of socio-economic and socio-demographic factors. The socio-economic factors of globalisation and post-industrialism are promoting, in Europe as elsewhere, a restructuring and diversification of the capitalist economy and the socio-demographic and cultural factors of changing gender roles and an ageing population are promoting a restructuring and diversification of households and family life. In this section we aim to fill out this picture of the nature and impacts of these kinds of changes for society generally and for welfare in particular by focusing on the emergence of new labour market dynamics and changing patterns of employment.

The labour market has been one of the core social institutions in modern societies since the development of mercantile, colonial and international capitalism in the early modernity and of industrial capitalism from the 19th century.[33] In its contemporary incarnations, no doubt the capitalist labour market generates dis-welfares – social inequalities, psychological stress and even in some cases the alienation and emiseration of which it was accused by Marx in its 19th-century incarnations. However, the sociological fact remains that for the main periods of people's adult lives in modern and contemporary society their participation in the labour market through work is a major source (arguably *the* major source, even when compared with the welfare roles of the state and the family) of welfare and identity (i.e. of income for welfare consumption, of agency through the exercise of choices, of status and recognition, etc.). Relatedly, lack of employment and absence or exclusion from the labour market is a principal cause of social problems, particularly of the dis-welfares of poverty and social exclusion.

Table 7.3 focuses on contemporary social changes in and restructurings in the labour market which, in significant part, are the products of the socio-economic and socio-demographic changes noted earlier. It summarises some of the main vectors of labour market change which both separately, and particularly in combination, carry with them new risks of social insecurity and welfare problems in European society. These social problems are illustrated in Table 7.4. They represent new and common challenges to European welfare states and welfare capitalist systems which require a rethinking and reform of European versions of welfare capitalism, and relatedly of citizenship and its social dimension, in the direction of such policies as 'flexicurity' and 'active labour market' policies.[34] In the following chapter we consider these directions of contemporary welfare reform in Europe, with particular reference to the role in this of EU-based Europeanisation processes and EU policies. However, we need to provide a background and basis for this later discussion. So in this section we first discuss the nature of contemporary labour market changes in European societies and then turn to the new generation of social risks and problems of poverty and social exclusion that they generate.

Labour market changes and employment problems

There are three main vectors of change affecting the contemporary labour market. They relate, first, to the gender balance of employment (the 'feminisation of work' process), secondly, to the nature of employment contracts (the 'flexibilisation of work' process), and thirdly, to the presence of structural unemployment in the emerging market order (the 'underemployment' problem), and we can look at each of them briefly in turn.

The feminisation of the labour market[35]
Table 7.4 (columns A and B) illustrates long-term changes in the participation of males and females in the labour market for a range of countries. In each of them there had undoubtedly occurred a 'feminisation' of the labour market. The scale and social implications of this vector of change (whether for the efficient operation of capitalist economies, the viability of welfare states, or the sustainability of communities, whether for the care of children or care of the elderly) cannot be overstated. Every society's capitalist market for paid labour in the formal capitalist economy throughout modernity has been symbiotically connected with the divisions of labour and work exchange systems for unpaid labour which exist in the informal economy constituted by families, networks of friends, communities and civil society.[36] The paid and unpaid spheres are mutually dependent: the former provides income for the latter, and the latter provides services for the former, not least in the everyday and also the intergenerational reproduction of paid labour force. A similar comment could be made about the third dimension of the 'welfare mix', the welfare state, which is also positioned between these two systems and

Table 7.4 European socio-economic change and restructuring 2: 1960–2006 – labour market changes and problems

Nation	Gender in employment		Labour market structure		Employment rate (F/T)	Unemployment + underemployment		
	Male employ.	Female employ.	Part-time employ.	Temp. employ.		Unemploy overall	Youth Unemploy	Long-term Unemploy.
Rows:	A	B	C	D	E	F	G	H
Sweden								
1960 1	85	35	10	–	60	0	–	–
1990s 2	67	64	10	–	66	6	16	2
2000s 3	74	69	25	15	71	8	13	1
Germany								
1960 4	89	44	7	–	64	0	–	–
1990s 5	71	48	8	–	59	5	9	4
2000s 6	71.4	61	26	14	66	11	11	6
UK								
1960 7	87	38	9	–	62	2	–	–
1990s 8	69	54	12	–	61	7	13	2
2000s 9	77	66	25	6	71	5	12	1
Spain								
1960 10	92	19	0	–	54	0	–	–
1990s 11	62	25	3	–	43	14	31	6
2000s 12	75	52	12	33	64	9	23	2

Sources: Cols A, B, C, D, E, F: 1960 and 1995 data from Crouch 1999, pp. 428–439, Appendix A2.1, A2.3; 2006 data from Eurostat 2006b, Tables 4, 6, 10, 14; Col. G: Data is for 1998 and 2003 from EC 2005c; Col. H: Data for 1999 from EC 2005c and for 2006 from Eurostat 2006b, Table 16.

related to them symbiotically. The mainstream socio-economic model which evolved across Europe in the post-war period involved to one extent or another a 'male breadwinner' model of households and families, in which women specialised in unpaid domestic work connected with the reproduction of the male worker, care for children and care for the elderly. This model is clearly represented in Table 7.4 in the 1960 information for the countries concerned (columns A and B, rows 1, 4, 7 and 10). The massive priority at that time given by all types of society to males as forming the bulk of the workforce is evident. It provides a background against which to recognise the extent of the shift towards the more similar, and still converging, pattern of labour market participation that now prevails a generation later in all types of European society.

There have been social benefits and costs to this structural change. On the benefits side, the mass of women's potential life choices (as between employment careers, domestic work, or both) appear to have been significantly broadened compared with previous generations, together with their access to politico-cultural contexts (the public sphere, beyond the private sphere) previously overwhelmingly dominated by males. On the costs side, the feminisation of the labour market still has a long way to run to achieve full equality in this respect with males. Whether through choice or force of circumstance, many women across Europe carry a heavy 'double burden' of work in both paid and unpaid spheres. Little in the way of a 'masculinisation' of domestic labour has occurred so far to compensate for the reduction in care-work in the domestic sphere which the change has carried with it. Generally, the capacity for, and interest in, the work of child-bearing and child-rearing on the part of partners, particularly women, together with the capacity for the performance of care-work for the elderly, has been reduced over the course of the post-war period in societies across Europe. This, in turn, as we have seen in the comments on Table 7.1, has led to a decline in the birth rate, a population replacement problem and pressure to increase immigration. It has also contributed to strains in the capacity of welfare systems across Europe to provide the care-work needed by increasingly ageing and dependent cohorts of elderly people.

Flexibilisation and the labour market[37]

In addition to the feminisation of the labour market, and related to it, there have been major long-term changes in the nature of employment in the direction of institutionalising greater flexibility. In the early post-war period, expectations about employment, by both employees and employers, were that it tended to be full-time and also to be long-lasting, often lifelong. This consensus assumed a fairly stable categorisation of labour skills and organisation of work, assumptions which have not proved to be tenable in more dynamic and volatile contemporary economic conditions. As indicated in columns C and D, there has been a rise of part-time work to around a quarter of all employment in countries representing the three original 'worlds of welfare capitalism'. This form of work has tended to be taken up mainly by women, and to a certain extent it has been a positive factor in some societies in providing some scope and resources for child-rearing and in easing women's 'double-burden'. In the contemporary period this has been accompanied by significant rates of employment on the basis of temporary contracts. The rise of part-time and temporary forms of employment and labour market participation may have some social benefits to offer in the context of easing the work–family balance and increasing the availability of low-wage entry-level work for young people. But generally they carry social costs in that the part-time work reduces long-term career and promotion prospects, and also pension entitlements, while temporary work effectively disconnects workers from careers and pensions. In recent years this would seem to be a notable problem for Spain (Table 7.4, column D, row 12) and more generally for the southern European 'world of welfare capitalism'.

Underemployment and the labour market

Finally we can turn to what appears to be an emerging and endemic under-employment problem in the order of contemporary European capitalist societies and their labour markets. The early post-war period was not only one in which European capitalism began to grow strongly and in which sophisticated welfare state systems were developed. It was also one in which socio-economic policy appeared to be realistically capable of aiming at 'full employment', and in which there appeared to be relatively little unemployment to be recorded (Table 7.4, column F, rows 1, 4, 7 and 10). The situation has changed considerably through to the present across all types of European society. Employment rates for males in all types of society declined considerably from the 1960s for decades through to the 1990s. They have picked up since then, but they remain a long way off what they once were. Female employment rates have been increasing, as indicated above, but they remain depressed both relative to male rates and more generally in relation to what they might be. The era of full employment as a concept and a realistic policy aspiration appears to have gone. For instance, unemployment has stubbornly remained at historically relatively high rates (around 10%) over the last decade in continental corporatist and southern European welfare capitalist regimes and long-term unemployment remains relatively high there also (Table 7.4, columns F and H, rows 5, 6, 11 and 12). Youth unemployment, meanwhile, remains over 10% in the original three welfare capitalist regimes and double that in the southern European regime (Table 7.4, column G).[38]

Poverty and social risks in the new social order

The underlying socio-demographic changes and socio-economic changes, together with the labour market changes considered so far, create a qualitatively new situation and socio-economic order in contemporary European societies, whatever their 'welfare capitalist' type. They have led to changes in primary elements of European social structures, namely in the social divisions of social classes and class relations, and of gender roles and relations, and in the inter-connections of these. In addition, but in a more secondary position, there have been changes in the cultural mix of European societies due to immigration, and this has carried particular kinds of social and cultural risks with it.

In terms of *class*, we have noted the growth of service sector workers and, crucially, the decline of the industrial working class. This has implications for the reconstruction and social marginalisation of European traditional work-ing classes as now largely 'unskilled' (i.e. irrelevantly skilled relative to emerging technological and occupational requirements). In terms of *gender*, the chang-ing role and status of women in contemporary European society is central. We have noted the rise of female employment, the decline in the birth rate, and the development of the 'double (work) burden'. We now need to add a related development to this picture, namely a fragmentation of household patterns (see later). The interconnections between these changes in work-related social status and resource include the facts that the growth of service and part-time work has mainly operated to provide women with some new access to the labour market, and that declines in manual and full-time work have reduced male labour market participation.

These two factors and their connection have also impacted on immigra-tion-based groups and communities in European societies, and thus on *ethnic* social divisions and relations. First-generation economic migration into European societies occurred in the early post-war period in response to the demand for both skilled and unskilled manual labour in industrial economies operating at full employment capacity. The decline in this kind of employ-ment not only has damaged the resource base and status recognition of first-generation immigrant males, but has also carried social exclusion risks and poor employment prospects through to immigration-based communities and to their second and later generations. In addition, since sections of the new service economy demand low-skilled labour, new waves of migrants orient to and get absorbed into this low-wage economy.[39]

The underlying changes and their implications for the restructuring of class, gender and ethnic relations create serious new potential social problems among vulnerable and 'at risk' social groups and categories. The latter are either new (e.g. the new cohorts of the very dependent elderly, new immigrant groups attracted into national labour markets, people in new types of house-hold, people in part-time and temporary employment) or are newly publicly and officially visible as such (e.g. working women and unskilled workers). The new social problems are partly those of 'poverty' (in 'relative' sense of low income, typically under half of median income), and partly those of 'social exclusion' (that is multiple disadvantage, e.g. membership of a number of the categories of problem mentioned above, resulting in a lack of participation, isolation and even discrimination in terms of employment and other aspects of the life of a society). New forms, sources and risks of poverty and social exclusion

Table 7.5 New social risks and poverty in 21st-century European societies

Nation	Poverty in general + in dependent groups			No-work households			Single-parent households		
								Poverty rates and employment in these families	
	Poverty in general (%)	Elderly poverty	Child poverty	No-work households as % of all households	Low income in these households	% of all child families	Poverty rates in these families	If not in work	If in work
	A	B	C	D	E	F	G	H	I
Sweden	6	8	4	8	59	18	7	24	4
Germany	8	10	9	12	57	16	41	49	32
UK	12	20	15	13	56	21	49	69	26
Italy	13	14	17	10	51	21	48	49	25

Sources: Cols A, B, C: Data from Mishel et al. 2007, Table 8.17; Cols D, E, F, G: Data from Esping-Andersen 2002b, Table 3.2; Cols H, I: Data from Esping-Andersen 2002b, Table 3.3.

create new challenges and priorities for contemporary welfare states and social policy-makers across Europe, both at nation-state and EU levels. How they have responded to these challenges we need to consider later.[40] First, it is necessary to take a look at the problems and their sources in a little more detail and to discuss them in relation to two strategically important social groups or categories, namely the unskilled working class and women.

Table 7.5 summarises the scale of the problem of poverty facing different types of European society both in general and for key vulnerable groups of dependents, namely the elderly and children. It is noteworthy that even in the relatively successful 'social democratic' world of Swedish welfare capitalism the rate of relative income poverty, while low, has not been eradicated, particularly among the elderly (Table 7.5, column B). For the other worlds of welfare capitalism, poverty remains at least around 10%, and significantly higher for the British liberal-market model and for the Italian southern European model.

As we have noted earlier, the balance in women's lives as between domestic and familial roles and work, and employment in labour markets, has been restructured in all types of European society, albeit to varying extents in recent decades. This has had implications for the formation of families and households, with more diversity now possible than was the case traditionally in the post-war period. On the one hand, the new degree of volatility and fragmentation of partnerships and marriages can be said to represent gains in the exercise of freedom in relation to lifestyle for the adults involved, although not necessarily for any children involved. On the other hand, these processes can present significant risks of non-employment, resulting in both poverty and dependency on welfare state systems, and particularly so for women.

The long modernisation processes European societies went through from the 19th century involved the evolution of a fairly standard 'nuclear' pattern of two-person households and, where children were involved, two-parent families, each being single-earner economic units. This pattern became widely institutionalised across Europe in the 20th century and particularly during the post-war period. However, social change and diversification over the last generation has added at least three notable extra types to the landscape and repertoire of European household and family types, namely dual-earner, no-earner households, and single-parent households.

Dual-earner households register the long-term growth in women's employment which we have already considered. Apart from their general potential for promoting women's 'double-burden', they do not present urgent new social risks and in many ways could be said to represent a functional adaptation and contribution to the emerging new service sector-led economy. Single-parent households tend to be mainly (although not exclusively) headed by women. They have grown to being a significant proportion, around a fifth, of all family households with children across all types of European society (Table 7.5, column F). Where they are well identified and supported by social and employment policy, as in social-democratic model societies such as Sweden, they represent a positive lifestyle option, particularly for women (Table 7.5, column G). However, in the other three welfare capitalist regimes, that is to say in most European societies, including all of the biggest societies, single-parent households run very high risks of poverty. These risks are amplified if the single parent chooses to concentrate on parenting rather than involving themselves in the labour market, a situation which has been allowed to become severe in the case of the UK (partly for welfare/workfare policy reasons) (Table 7.5, columns G and H). No-earner households represent the final newly emerging household and family type carrying most social risks of achieving only low incomes (see Table 7.5, column E). This type of household is connected particularly with the rise of social vulnerability and marginalisation of the unskilled sector of the working class which we noted earlier.

Within any given national society in Europe in the contemporary period people with low human capital and skills carry high risks of recurrent bouts of unemployment, income poverty and the multiple disadvantages or 'social exclusion'. Of all social groups, they have the greatest likelihood of gaining their incomes either from low-skilled, low-waged employment or from state-based unemployment or welfare benefits. They also have the greatest likelihood of living in households and relationships vulnerable to social risks, in which both partners are unemployed or where they live as single parents. If they have children in these situations, then their children are at greater than ordinary risk of living in poverty. The social risks of self-damaging lifestyles, social isolation and welfare dependency are greatest for this group, together with the likelihood of relatively early permanent withdrawal from labour market because of disability or, if formally retired, living on only a basic state pension.[41]

Conclusion

In this chapter we have reviewed some of the main common structural social dynamics and changes affecting European societies in the contemporary period and shaping the European social complex they form. These involved the socio-economic changes of globalisation and post-industrialisation, and the socio-demographic changes involving a restructuring of gender roles, among other things. We also considered the implications of these developments for changes in the social nature and distribution of welfare and dis-welfare in these societies. Generally, the changes can be captured, as indicated in the Introduction, in the structural shift which began in the late 20th century from a national functionalist societal model of capitalism and welfare to a post-national functional model. This involves changes in the social nature and relationship of capital and labour, and in the social divisions of class and gender.

Economic growth in European capitalist society over this period has generally benefited the standards of living and thus the welfare of most Europeans. In addition, some of the structural changes have benefited some categories and strata, including relevantly skilled professionals and workers in particular, and many women in general. However, they have also resulted in the growth of new problems and levels of risk relating to unemployment or underemployment, poverty and social marginalisation or exclusion for various social categories and strata. These social categories include women working the 'double shift' (of formal employment and domestic care-work), immigrant 'newcomers', traditional working-class males, young people, children in no work or single-parent households, and generally people designated as 'unskilled'.

These common structural changes in European society and this new generation of common social problems have evidently begun to create new policy challenges for the various established but diverse 'worlds of welfare capitalism' we discussed in Chapter 6. Have these challenges and the rethinking they require resulted in changes and reforms in welfare policy and institutions? If so, do these responses tend in a common and convergent direction or do they maintain the existing range of diversity? To address these kinds of questions requires a recognition of the two distinct but increasingly interconnected policy levels which are now relevant to understanding the European social complex, namely both the national level and also (for the core and majority of European states) the EU level.

Answers to the questions at the national level have been offered by a range of empirical comparative sociology and social policy studies. A weakness of such studies is that they tend to operate with relatively decontextualised and methodologically nationalist assumptions. However, a strength is that they sometimes reach beyond European societies and imply comparisons with other world regions. The answers they have produced have been various, but they have often confirmed that significant changes have occurred in many nations' welfare policies over the last decade or more and that the common factor of globalisation has played a major role in stimulating these changes in welfare policies.[42] The changes have often commonly involved attempts to cut the levels of states' expenditure and they have tended to be towards a greater targeting of social assistance and benefits, together with a greater degree of conditionality and individual contractualism in the relation between welfare clients and welfare states, which has been aimed at promoting clients' participation in the labour market and their employment.[43] However, while studies confirm that globalisation has generated a degree of convergence among states' welfare policies in the ways indicated, including among European states, nonetheless there is also much evidence to indicate that many European and non-European nations have so far been relatively successful in maintaining the distinctiveness of their approaches to welfare policy.[44]

In the following chapter we focus on the EU level and the Europeanisation associated with it. The EU has, at the very least, attempted to promote a common recognition of, diagnosis of and discourse about contemporary European social problems. It has also attempted to coordinate a common process of labour market and welfare reform among its member states. This has aimed at, among other things, promoting employment and ameliorating social exclusion by means of polices referred to as involving 'active labour markets' and 'flexicurity'. In the following chapter, then, we explore the EU level of policy response to the challenges posed by new structural and welfare problems discussed in this chapter.[45] We consider what these policies involve and whether they are likely to promote real commonality at the level of member states.

Notes

1   See Fligstein 2008; and Ferrera 2005a.
2   For an account and application of this analysis in the field of the sociology of citizenship, see Roche 1996.
3   On the information society and knowledge-based economy, see Chapter 2 note 20, and also Chapter 8. In particular, see Axford and Huggins 2007; Benkler 2006; Castells 2002; Mansell and Steinmuller 2000; and Rodrigues 2002.
4   See the discussion of globalisation in Chapter 1. The notion that there is a 'new' or 'second phase' of globalisation refers to the idea that following the initial recognition and analysis of globalisation in relatively simplistic and standardising terms in the 1990s an understanding of the intrinsic complexities of the process has begun to emerge. This has been associated with a willingness to address such phenomena as glocalisation, world regionalisation and the emergence of a multi-polar world order noted in Chapter 1 and discussed further in this chapter.
5   On American-based global cultural standardisation, see Ritzer's influential analysis of 'McDonaldization' (Ritzer 2008). For alternative views of cultural globalisation, see Ritzer 2005; also Bryman 2004; Lechner and Boli 2005; Roche 2000a; and Tomlinson 1999.
6   On 'global complexity', see Urry (2003) for a wide-ranging interpretation; for a brief analysis and application of the concept of 'complex globalisation', see Roche 2006b; for a relevant interpretation of globalisation as involving a polycentric world order, see Scholte 2005.
7   See Delors 1989 speech 'A Necessary Union' (Delors 1998).
8   We consider the Lisbon Agenda in more detail in Chapter 8. The comparison motif in EU discourse resonates with political economic analyses of the EU and the USA as globally competitive 'trade blocs', see Hirst and Thompson 1999; and also Gamble 2001.
9   On the EU in relation to international aid and development policy, see Bretherton and Vogler 1999; relatedly, on the EU's role in the promotion of 'socially responsible globalisation', see Deacon 2007.
10   On the development of the EU's role in international environmental policy, see Bretherton and Vogler 1999, Chapter 3.

11   To address both US dominance and the otherwise generally anarchic character of what passes for 'global governance' in the contemporary period (dramatically illustrated in the 2008/09 global economic crisis), analysts have proposed various institutional developments embodying 'cosmopolitan democracy' and a new social 'covenant' between developed and underdeveloped countries. See, for instance, Held 1995, 2004; and Held et al. 2005.

12   On the WTO and EU's role in it, see Bretherton and Vogler 1999, Chapter 2; and McCormick 2007, Chapter 4.

13   On China and the EU, see Barysch 2005; Grant and Barysch 2008.

14   For an indication of the range of relevant industries, see Barysch 2005.

15   On China and globalisation, see Guthrie 2006; Barysch 2005; and Grant and Barysch 2008; on the Global Adjustment Fund, see EU 2006c.

16   See, for instance, the report of the High-Level EU Social Policy Group and the Aho Report, respectively EC2004 and EC2006a.

17   All quotations are from Barroso 2006b.

18   Bell 1973. Apart from Bell, it tended to be popular 'futurology' (sadly, rather than Western sociology) which initially led the exploration of this first (pre-globalisation and pre-internet) phase of post-industrial structural social change in contemporary capitalist society. See, for example, Toffler 1970, 1980, 1985. For a discussion of the 'first phase' post-industrialism and the challenges it posed (and poses) to forms of national social citizenship established in terms of industrial society, see Roche 1996, Chapter 7.

19   On the collapse of communism see, for instance, Judt 2005, Chapter 19; and Mazower 1998, Chapter 11.

20   For a seminal study in 'first phase' post-industrialism and 'post-Fordism', see Piore and Sabel 1984. They pointed to advanced capitalism's emerging new technological capacity for flexible specialisation in its production process as opposed to the standardisation involved in mass production processes. For a discussion of the kind of new political economy implied by post-Fordism, see Bob Jessop's (1994) analysis of what he referred to as 'the Schumpeterian workfare state', and on post-Fordism's implications for the welfare state and employment policy see the various contributions collected in Loader and Burrows (1994).

21   On the relevance of such a services-based and basically 'first phase' understanding of post-industrialism for contemporary European social policy, see Esping-Andersen 1990, Chapter 8 and 1999; and also Begg et al. 2008.

22   Freeman and Soete 1987; and Piore and Sabel 1984.

23   On the digital revolution and its social implications, see Benkler 2006; Castells 2002; and Wessels 2009a; on the related theme of the knowledge and information technology-based society, see references in this Chapter's note 3 above.

24   On the new cultural and creative industries, see Brinkley and Lee 2007; Florida 2002; Florida and Tinagli 2004; Hesmondhalgh 2002; Scott 1999, 2000, 2004; also European Commission reports EC 2005b, 2006c. Also see sociological analysis of these kinds of phenomena, including Bryman 2004; Ritzer 2005; and Roche 2000a, 2000b. Critical theorists propose that to attempt to grasp the class and political economic implications of these kinds of changes, the traditional category of labour needs to be rethought, for instance in Lazzarato's (1996) case in terms of its 'immaterial' aspects.

25   On the information society and knowledge-based economy, see note 3, Chapter 7: note 24, Chapter 1; note 20, Chapter 2; and note 31, Chapter 8.

26   On the key role of 'human capital' and thus skills and thus, in turn, education and training in the new knowledge and information-based economy, see Benkler 2006; Giddens 2007; and Rodrigues 2002; also EC 2005b, 2006c. On the corollary, namely the social problems of unemployment, poverty and social exclusion associated being 'unskilled', see the following section.

27   Social changes connected with new globalisation and new post-industrialism create restructuring dynamics and situations of semi-permanent 'transition' in contemporary social formations. An aspect of this is a further entrenchment and acceleration of long-term trends in modernity favouring greater individualisation. This can have benefits in human rights and citizenship rights terms, but it can also be associated with costs in terms of the erosion and dissolving of traditional social bonds, institutional and community structures and identities. Relevant and influential general discussions of these and other aspects of contemporary society are provided in, among others, Beck (1992) and Putnam (2000), respectively, seeing these trends as creating a new 'risk society' and as undermining 'social capital' (see later). Esping-Andersen et al. (2002), Manning and Shaw (2000a) and Taylor-Gooby (2004) pursue the theme of new social risks associated with structural change, individualisation and erosion of social capital in the context of contemporary social problems and welfare policies; also see Gallie and Paugam 2000.

28   See, for instance, Sklair 2001.

29   Two types of social capital, namely bridging and binding, are particularly significant in this context. The former involves open and weak links, and the latter closed and strong links. The former is more connected with human capital than the latter. On this, see Putnam 2000, Chapter 1 and *passim*.

30   What the content of skills are and who has the power to define this in any given society at any given time is, of course, another (social and political) story.

31   The phenomenon of the emerging urban 'underclass' associated with the development of post-industrial society is relevant here; for an analysis, see Roche 1996, Chapters 5 and 6. The great socio-psychological problems associated with modern industrial capitalist society in Durkheim's and Marx's perspectives were respectively 'anomie' (people's disconnection from norms, literally de-moralisation) and 'alienation' (including worker's dispossession of the products of their labour). In post-industrial society, people and communities which possess low human and social capital tend to be socially excluded from employment, and more generally from the labour market *per se*. In this context, the analysis of the problems and situation of this class fraction (whether or not understood as an 'underclass') in terms of the concept of anomie (non-participation) is more useful and appropriate than in terms of the concept of alienation (exploited participation).

32   An influential analysis of the implications of globalisation and post-industrial change for polarising social classes in terms of the international mobility of middle- and upper-class groups and the urban locatedness of working and underclass groups is provided in Castells 1996. The implications of the new importance of mobility in contemporary society are explored in terms of social theory in Bauman (1998, 2000) and Urry (2000), and empirically in terms of middle-class mobility across Europe in Favell (2003b and 2008), and Fligstein (2008). Contrary views abut the continuing importance in the new 21st-century social context of social locatedness, 'state spaces' and 'enclaves' are offered by Brenner (2004) and Turner (2007).

33   On the sociology and social policy of European labour markets in relation to issues of (i) unemployment and the link to social isolation, social exclusion, see Gallie and Paugam (2000); (ii) informal work and social capital, see Williams and Windebank (1998); and (iii) employment and social inclusion policy in their links both with welfare benefit conditionality and 'workfare', and also with 'active' labour market policy, see Lind and Moller (1999); Lodemal and Trickey (2001); Roche and Annesley (2004); and van Berkel and Moller (2002).

34   For some early discussions, see Roche 1996, Chapters 7 and 9; and Huws 1997; for contemporary discussions and policies relating to 'flexicurity', see Chapter 8.

35   On the feminisation of the European labour market and some of its social implications, see Esping-Andersen 2002a; and Larsen et al. 2003. On the differential response of Europe's welfare regimes to this phenomenon, see Bambra 2004; J. Lewis 1992, 1997; Orloff 1993; and Sainsbury 1999.

36   On informal work and the informal economy, which importantly are systems that build social capital rather than running it down, see Williams and Windebank 1998.

37   On flexibilisation in relation to labour and the labour market see, for instance, Standing 1999; and for a critique in the context of Europe, see Gray 2004.

38   See, for instance, Barysch et al. 2008.

39   According to some analyses, the economic dynamics of this situation tend to pressure low-skilled workers' wage rates down towards welfare state-based legally guaranteed minimum wage rates, see Sinn 2007. This, together with pressures towards undeclared employment, helps create and entrench new problems of inequality, poverty and exclusion in relation to first- and second-generation immigrant and ethnic minority communities in European countries. For social policy responses to this situation, see Bay and Pederson 2006; Commander et al. 2006; Kofman et al. 2000; and Sainsbury 2006.

40   On national level responses see the third section in this chapter, and on EU level responses, see Chapter 8.

41   See, for instance, Esping-Andersen 1999; Esping-Andersen et al. 2002; and Gallie and Paugam 2000.

42   On globalisation and social policy see, for instance, Castles 2004; Castles and Pierson 1996; Palier and Sykes 2001; Sykes et al. 2001; also Begg et al. 2008; Adelantado and Calderon 2007; and Deacon 2000, 2007; Deacon et al. 1997; and Navarro et al. 2004.

43   These trends were indicated at least in the 1990s, see Eardley et al. 1996; Gough et al. 1997; also Sykes et al. 2001.

44   See, for instance, Castles 2004; and Navarro et al. 2004.

45   Also see Roche 1996, Chapters 7, 8 and 9, and 1997; Roche and van Berkel 1997a; and Roche and Annesley 2004.

8

THE EU AND THE EUROPEAN SOCIAL COMPLEX: THE EUROPEANISATION OF WELFARE STATES AND WELFARE CAPITALISM?

Introduction

From a sociological perspective it might be argued that a distinctive European society is beginning to emerge in the contemporary period, and that the EU is at the heart of this process. The EU is not a nation-state type of society, but rather is a unique, complex and changing social formation linking its numerous (currently 27) member states. It links them as a societal complex which is multidimensional in terms of economy, polity and culture, and multi-levelled in terms of supra-national, national and sub-national/regional levels, and which can be analysed in terms of the analogies of networks and neo-empires (Chapter 2). It also links them as a sociological duality. That is, viewed from one perspective, the European complex that the EU is beginning to orchestrate is composed of societies of a common political type being challenged by common social changes in a common globalising environment (as we saw in Chapter 7). On the other hand, viewed from a different perspective, it is a complex which is also simultaneously structurally multinational and multicultural, composed of societies which not only are distinct sovereign states, but also are different in many cultural and other ways (as we saw in Chapters 5 and 6). So far we have considered the late 20th- and early 21st-century processes of change and reconstruction of European society and 'welfare capitalism' in terms of the differences and commonalities of European national societies. In this chapter we now need to explore these processes in terms of the role of the EU within them, and, relatedly, as processes of the 'Europeanisation' of member-state societies.

The fact that an EU-orchestrated social formation may be said to be emerging through processes of Europeanisation does not necessarily entail either that it is doing so in a manner which is coherent, effective, or sustainable. Nor does it necessarily entail that such a development is very positive or progressive in terms of whatever normative criteria we may wish to apply to it. Evidently, given the nationalist resurgence across Europe in the early 21st century, it is potentially highly controversial for many citizens. In addition, in the contemporary period the EU, which had long been criticised for its democratic and other deficits, has entered a crisis-ridden phase in which its progress in a range of constitutional, organisational and socio-economic fields has, at the very least, been significantly delayed. We discuss some of these normative and political issues relating to the EU later (see Chapter 9). In this chapter the main socio-logical task we are concerned with is not primarily a normative one, however important that may ultimately be for academic perspectives as much as for citizen perspectives. Rather, the primary task is the more preliminary and basic analytic work of attempting to identify some key developments of the EU-orchestrated social complex and to understand something of their nature and prospects.[1]

In this chapter the focus, in terms of our analytic framework of societal dimensions, is on the political and economic dimensions of the EU and on EU economic and social policies. This is partly for practical reason of limited space, but also because the period in which the EU has developed, from the mid-20th century to the present, is a very unusual one in terms of the histor-ical perspectives on Europe discussed earlier (Chapters 4 and 5). It is one in which two of the key cultural and political factors fuelling and driving the development of European welfare states and world of welfare capitalism, namely religion and war, have practically ceased to operate. Post-war Europe has been fortunate enough to experience two generations of peace. In addi-tion, it has become largely disenchanted with and disconnected from the version of Christian religiosity which used to dominate the continent, and with the secular religions of nationalism, fascism and communism which supplanted them. In the evident absence of an alternative cultural factor, such as a simple cultural unity and common identity across Europe, what remain in terms of factors energising the development and transformation of welfare capitalism are political factors connected with changing nation-state interests and economic factors connected with the changing dynamics of capitalism.

The discussion is organised in two main sections. First, it introduces the two main ways in which the EU can be said to be relevant to the general development of welfare capitalism in Europe. These are the EU's economic project to construct a unitary EU-wide market, and also its related interest in influencing and framing member states' social policies, particularly in the field of employment, in terms of a 'European social model'.[2] Secondly, it explores the relevance of the EU to the contemporary reconstruction of European welfare capitalism in the early 21st century in relation to contem-porary social changes. On the one hand we look here at the emergence of a new economy influenced by globalisation and post-industrialism, which emphasises knowledge and culture. On the other hand, and related to this, we look at the emergence of new welfare challenges and social policy approaches. These aim to combine social security with the promotion of flexibility and activism within the context of policy perspectives emphasising the life-course and the social rights of citizenship.

The EU and European Welfare Capitalism

In this section we consider the EU's development of its role, first, in relation to promoting the European capitalist economy and, secondly, in relation to attempting to frame and shape Europe's social model(s).

The EU's Common Market: building the European capitalist economy

Two sets of issues need to be considered here. First, what is the general nature of the EU's role *vis-à-vis* EU member states' roles in economic policy-making, and how is it institutionalised? Secondly, why and how was it developed, and what were some of the main stages in the process?

The EU and the European economy 1: EU's general policy role [3]
Apart from its general contribution to keeping the peace in post-war Europe in it various manifestations since the Treaty of Rome in 1957, the EU has always been principally an organisation concerned with the mission of promoting the economies of its member states in the context of the promotion of a wider European 'common market'. We will consider the nature and development of this mission in a moment. First, it is useful to recognise what this mission has generated in terms of the EU's contemporary institutional capacity to influence economic policy across Europe.

EU member states have 'pooled' their sovereignty in the economic field more than in most others. They have granted the EU's central institutions – primarily the European Council (that is the member states themselves, albeit in a collective form) and the European Parliament – the authority (that is the legal 'competence') to make law and policy which is often binding on the member states. This is particularly so for that (majority) sub-set of EU member states which has adopted the common currency of the euro. Some of the main mechanisms and instruments of the EU's economic policy are connected with its two major long-term economic projects: the building of its Single Internal Market across the EU and the development of its Economic and Monetary Union (EMU) project, at the heart of which is the management of the single EU currency and euro-zone affairs.

Before we consider these projects further it is worth noting that some additional economically relevant institutions were central to the early development of the EC/EU. These included the common organisations set up to support and to some extent to share in what were then regarded as strategic industries, namely iron, steel and coal, atomic energy and, of course, agriculture. However, for various reasons they have each become less central over time as we approach the contemporary period, with the lingering exception of agriculture. The Common Agricultural Policy (CAP) is a system to subsidise product prices and thereby incomes and employment in Europe's main agricultural regions for strategic reasons in order to protect their food production capacity on behalf of European security. The policy centrality of CAP has been reflected in the fact that it has tended to consume around half of the EU's total budget for decades since its creation in 1962. This is of continuing relevance to the EU as an economic policy-maker. The EU's main power has been exerted through regulation (and deregulation in relation to nation-states) rather than spending. Its capacity to spend in support of its policies has always been extremely limited in that the member states have legislated to keep the EU's budget very low, currently (2008) below a maximum of 1.24% of EU (member states') aggregate gross national income (GNI). This pales in comparison with member states' budgets, which average between 40 and 45% of their GNIs. In addition, what little is available to spend in support of the EU's economic, social and other priorities is further limited by the enormous proportion which has traditionally had to be consigned to the support of the EU's agricultural production system. Although the EU is making efforts to reduce it over time, the CAP still consumed 40% of EU spending in 2008. It is sobering to recognise that this was on behalf of an economic sector which accounts on average for only miniscule proportions of the employment and production of member states' national economies. These basic problems of the budget's extreme limitation in general and also its skewing towards support for the agricultural sector are likely to remain into the medium term. We can now return to the EU's two main economic policy projects, which, it is worth noting, are mainly regulatory rather than expenditure-based programmes.

First, there is the euro currency and euro-zone project.[4] Countries using the euro currency participate more deeply than the other member states in the EMU project. For them, the EU institution of the European Central Bank (ECB), together with the Stability and Growth Pact connected with it, is particularly influential. Drawing on deep European experiences of the political and social catastrophes which are possible when rampant inflation decimates economies, the ECB's goals give priority to the control of inflation through the control of the exchange rate of the euro and associated interest rates. Its rules also prescribe the limits allowed for participating member states in terms of the degree of public debt they can incur in order to finance counter-cyclical spending programmes, including in such areas as social and welfare policy. The system has proved to be reasonably robust. For instance, it weathered the global economic problems of 2007/08 better than the dollar and sterling, appreciating in value against each of these currencies over this period.

Secondly, there is the project to construct the Single Internal Market.[5] Generally, this economic project has been most influential on the whole membership of the EU. It aims at reducing the costs to profitability, employment and consumers traditionally produced by international barriers to free trade in Europe. It aims at thereby generating a new order of benefits from economic organisation within one of the largest and wealthiest markets in the world. It is a long-term process involving the progressive removal of national barriers to the free movement of goods, capital and ultimately also capital and labour creation in all economic sectors across Europe. It is managed and executed principally by the European Commission's various relevant Directorates General (DGs) or ministries, particularly DG Competition, which are answerable to the European Council and Parliament, the ultimate authors of the project. And it can be enforced by the European Court of Justice (ECJ), which is the ultimate interpreter and enforcer of EU laws and rules in the economic as well as all other fields. DG Competition monitors the operation and evolution of the Single Internal Market in order to try to ensure that market forces are free to operate to their maximum. So its main aims are to prohibit the formation of cartels and also to limit member states' abilities to protect particular public or private sector industries in their own national self-interest. Nonetheless it is prepared to occasionally recognise the necessity and/or the justice of retaining nation-states' roles in particular economic areas.

The EU and the European economy 2: developing the EU's policy role [6]

To help understand why and how the EU developed its contemporary influential position in the coordination and thus Europeanisation of its member states' economic policies it is useful to begin in the 1980s and note some of the main steps along the way. The French politician Jacques Delors became President of the European Commission in 1985, a post he held for the following decade. He was an influential figure, representing an interesting combination of principle and pragmatism, the principles relating to his general commitments both to European federalism and also to a social market. He aimed to make further progress with the process of developing the EU and European integration after a period in which the impetus which had been provided by such steps as enlargement, involving the UK in the 1970s, had faded away.

The contemporary context of the mid-1980s was a challenging period. On the one hand, this was because of a wave of structural change which visibly worked its way through the West's industrial economies, involving sometimes rapid processes of de-industrialisation, recession and unemployment affecting particular economically important cities and regions in the USA and across Europe. On the other hand, simultaneously pro-market neo-conservative leaders and governments came into the ascendancy in the USA and UK, threatening cut-backs in taxation and state spending, particularly in social policy fields.[7] Similarly ideologically based governments were soon, albeit unexpectedly, to come to power in a range of nations in Eastern Europe also with the fall of communism in 1989/90.

In the mid-1980s the EU was digesting the implications of the progression to membership of Spain and Portugal, which was confirmed in 1986. This was a boost to the organisation politically. Each of these countries had recently emerged from decades of authoritarian government which had necessarily required their exclusion from the EU as an organisation committed to respecting democracy. The EU had become bigger and could associate itself with the resurgence of freedom and democracy in its new member states. On the other hand, economically there were concerns about the potential for the new members to engage in 'social dumping', namely promoting the mass migration of their low-wage labour to the higher wage labour markets of the established member states of the EU. In addition, by 1989 and 1990 the EU was confronted with the fall of the USSR, and the emergence of numerous new and unstable democratic nations on its eastern borders.

The period from the mid-1980s to the early 1990s, then, was one of international structural socio-economic change and ideological challenge, of possible socio-economic problems within the EU and later of political challenges and socio-economic instability on its borders. It was against this background that Delors helped to reanimate the organisation and its fortunes. He encouraged the member states to recommit themselves to common actions and projects in two important treaties, the Single European Act (SEA, Rome) 1986 and the Treaty on European Union (TEU, Maastricht) 1992. Principal among the common projects was that of the construction of the Single Internal Market, a project calculated to appeal to the UK's pro-market and otherwise Euro-sceptic leadership. Also, the new political status of 'Citizen of the European Union' was created in the TEU, potentially opening up a new trajectory for political developments in the EU, and likely to appeal to more idealistic and Europhile member states and their leaderships. In addition, the TEU 1992 also established the EMU process, moving to create the common currency.

In addition, there was the question of the possible need for a common approach to social policy to manage the apparent threats to national employment and wage levels represented by the accession of Spain and Portugal. In the event, these threats did not materialise. Mass migration did not occur and the two countries began long-term processes of economic growth which have since transformed their societies and standards of living. However, the issue of the possible socio-economic problems which might be associated with further developments and extensions of the EU's 'common market', and of their implications for social policy, had been raised and needed some response. This need was accentuated by the liberation of the Eastern European nations from 1990 onwards. Delors helped to orchestrate this response by leading the production of a visionary White Paper report on *Growth, Competitiveness, Employment: The Challenges and Ways Forward into the Twenty-first Century.*[8]

This was published in 1993 and effectively became the EU's strategic guide in the general field of socio-economic policy-making for the rest of the decade. The Delors White Paper represented an early and influential recognition of the economic problems and opportunities of globalisation, and also of contemporary technological development. It proposed a new generation of investments in trans-European transport and information and communication technology (ICT) networks. It recognised the importance of the emerging information economy and society for Europe, how progress might be made towards it in priority techno-economic sectors such as biotechnology and the audio-visual sector, and the necessity, to support this, of steering public and private spending and investment towards research and development, human capital, education and training.

After Delors' departure in 1995 the EU's growing concern for employment policy as the bridge between economic and social policy was given a boost in the Amsterdam Treaty in 1997. The member states gave the EU new competences in the field of employment and policies to promote it. The Single Market project was taken further by a proactive Competition Directorate, enforcing anti-state aid and anti-cartel rules in notable cases in a variety of sectors.[9] However, in spite of this the Single Internal Market remained very far from completion. In addition, the challenges and opportunities presciently identified in the Delors White Paper continued to gather momentum. Each of these two issues of the completion of the Single Market and responding to globalisation and technological development received further consideration by the EU at what turned out to be a strategically important EU intergovernmental conference (IGC) at Lisbon in 2000. Agreements were reached in the Lisbon Strategy (which we will consider in a moment). In the EU's post-Delors period in the late 1990s the political and economic needs of the newly democratised but economically weak Eastern European countries intensified. And Germany, a bulwark of the EU, embarked on its ambitious, but costly and also (at least from an EU perspective) possibly distracting, process of unification. To address the question of the future of the Eastern nations an accession programme and process to enable them to enter the EU in 2004 was agreed in 1993 at Copenhagen. The organisational (e.g. voting) mechanics needed to make this work were put in place in the Nice Treaty 2001.

Three positive boosts were given to the EU in this period in terms of the economic aspect of its socio-economic policy interests. First, the euro currency and euro-zone arrangements were successfully established in the late 1990s and became active from 2000. Most of the EU member states, with the notable exceptions of the UK, Sweden and Denmark, made the move from their national currencies to the new common currency system. This activated new binding institutional connections among the participating member states, gave some elements of concreteness to the aspiration to build a single transcontinental market, and gave a new basis of connection between the EU and national publics, now emerging as at least a community of consumers.

Secondly, in 1996 two Nordic countries, Sweden and Finland (along with Austria), entered the EU as members. With these countries joining Denmark in the EU it was now possible to argue that the EU was in a position to benefit substantially from the Nordic countries' unique experience in the construction of their 'social-democratic' version of 'welfare capitalism'. As we have seen earlier (Chapter 6), this involves the creation of a social model which has consistently in recent decades been capable of successfully marrying together a universalistic citizen-oriented approach to a high-quality welfare system with a globally highly competitive, technologically innovative and high productivity economy, albeit on the basis of relatively high taxation levels. The model, as we have seen, has also enabled women to be maximally used in the labour market and has enabled them to achieve the highest levels of equality and autonomy in Europe. This model began to have considerable impact on EU socio-economic strategic thinking and policy-making, not least in helping to shape the Lisbon Agenda and its recent revision (see later).

Thirdly, the Amsterdam Treaty, constructed in 1997, came into force in 1999. This gave the EU some significant new competences in the field of regulation and the promotion of European labour markets and employment. As we have seen, from a sociological perspective the labour market and employment constitute the crucial link between social and economic policy and the central hinge around which they jointly turn. On the basis of the Amsterdam Treaty the EU began to aspire to, and to explore, the development of a more common approach in the fields of employment policy and social inclusion policy. Although the member states could not agree to cede their sovereign legal powers to the EU in these fields, they did agree to the development of a notable form of 'soft law'. This was a policy process known as the 'open method of coordination' (OMC), involving a system of annual national employment reports and biennial national social inclusion reports. This involved the member states actively in the development of a common policy vision and discourse, and in policy learning and transfer, through such things as best practice sharing, benchmarking, peer group pressure and even 'naming and shaming'. These developments were incorporated into the Lisbon Strategy in 2000 and in its successor versions, which we consider later.

The EU's social model: framing Europe's 'worlds of welfare capitalism'

The European social complex, from the perspective of an interest in welfare and social policy, as we saw in Chapter 6, is composed of a range of 'social models', national models and multinational 'regimes' and 'worlds of welfare capitalism'. The EU operates within the social and policy environment of this diversity. The diversity makes it difficult to speak straightforwardly of a singular or common 'European social model' existing in the past, present, or arguably, anytime soon in the future. In spite of this fact, the notion of *the* 'European social model' is often used in European policy-making circles.[10] This usage can serve to conflate ideals, hopes for the future and arguable assumptions about social realities in the present. In spite of its possible ambiguities, it can be used as part of the discourse the EU has developed to frame its initiatives in the field of social policy and to attempt to influence and shape member states' social policies.

The EU has limited political and economic resources to make social policy. In terms of political resources, and unlike the situation in relation to the single market and competition policy, the EU does not have very much legal competence in this field. EU member states, consistent with the principle of 'subsidiarity', have been able to largely reserve to themselves the authority to determine policy in areas such as unemployment benefits, pensions, health and education. However, given the objective overlap between economic and social policy at national and EU level in the area of employment and labour market policy, it has been possible for the EU to attempt to extend its influence from the former to the latter using this bridge.

In terms of economic resources the EU spends little on 'substantive' (e.g. redistributive) social and welfare policies. Unlike national taxation systems, the EU has little capacity, independent of member states' contributions to it, to raise funds to finance significant 'substantive' social policy spending. In any case, as we saw earlier, the member states have kept the EU's overall budget, from which any substantive social policies might be financed, very small. Given this, EU policies which could be regarded as an example of substantive/ redistributive social policy are few and far between. The main cases are the Common Agricultural Policy (CAP), discussed earlier, and Regional and Structural Policies. The latter are two policy fields which have some capacity to provide financial compensation to EU regions and economic sectors which have been negatively affected by the process of EU economic integration, particularly de-industrialising areas in northern Europe and newly industrialising areas in southern Europe. Expenditures in these fields have been growing and together are now beginning to match the level of spending on the CAP. Finally, it should be mentioned that the EU has a limited budget to finance relatively small-scale anti-poverty and anti-'exclusion' 'actions' and programmes for reasons of policy-piloting, policy-learning, and the sharing of 'good practice'.

The EU has been able to develop its main role in social policy, as in other policy spheres, in the form of regulation. This includes the 'soft' regulation of voluntary coordination, such as the 'open method of coordination' mentioned earlier, and to a lesser extent the 'hard' regulation of legally binding directives. The EU attempts to build in and orchestrate 'social dialogue' between representatives of employers, employees and civil society in relation to policy formation in the fields of industrial relations and social policy more generally. As the central level in a multi-level governance system, the EU has readily available organisational and policy space to develop its regulatory role. As a result, as Leibfried and Pierson (1995) suggested over a decade ago, national welfare states are becoming effectively only 'semi-sovereign' within this EU governance system. The diversity of substantive social policy delivery and social models that member states retain on this perspective can be referred to as effectively being an 'EU-licensed' diversity, activities which happen to be permissible within the EU's policy environment and legal framework.

The EU's regulatory role in social policy was taken further significantly in recent years, particularly in the EU's 1997 Amsterdam Treaty and its 2000 Lisbon intergovernmental conference. These developments paved the way for a new wave and a new level of EU-orchestrated policy coordination among member states in the fields of employment, social exclusion and social rights, policy fields central to the idea of a 'social model'. The Amsterdam Treaty in particular outlawed gender and race discrimination across the EU. This enabled connections to begin to be made between the morally and legally powerful sphere of human, civil and citizenship rights and social policy interests in areas such as employment policies and welfare benefits and services policies.

The EU's employment policy is the main interface between its macro-economic policy and its social policy. The EU's macro-economic policy addresses issues of international competition, price stability, the knowledge economy, and also the promotion of flexibility and adaptability. The Employment Guidelines policy (agreed at Luxembourg in 1997 and first implemented in 1998) requires EU member states to submit employment action plans and attempts to promote 'best practice' policy-sharing and a coordinated approach between the member states. The system was further institutionalised in 2000 by the creation of an intergovernment EU Employment Committee charged with the annual monitoring of member states' National Action Plans and the coordination of them in relation to the EU's overall Employment Action Plan policy. Key themes of the Guidelines are attempts both to improve the quality of labour supply and also to promote demand for labour. Promoting the demand for labour connects with general EU macro-economic policy to promote non-inflationary economic growth, pursuing 'high levels' of (but not 'full') employment within the EMU project. The project to improve the quality of the labour supply pursues a 'preventative' approach to unemployment and emphasises the new and long-term state obligation to support citizens' (working) lifelong 'employability', and generally a society of 'full' or 'secure employability', through education and training opportunities and 'active' rather than 'passive' approaches to the distribution of welfare benefits and services.[11] These policy approaches, particularly the preventative and employability approaches, have been reflected in employment policy discourses and practices of EU member states undertaking reforms in their mainstream work and welfare systems.[12]

This development of EU-level employment policy ran parallel to existing agreements in the social rights field. These included agreements (from Maastricht) to monitor social policy convergence and (from Amsterdam) to exercise an increased competence for EU institutions in the sphere of social inclusion policy actions. They also included, as we noted earlier, new commitments to human rights and to the European Social Charter's social rights agreed in the Amsterdam Treaty, commitments which are now embodied in the movement for a EU Charter of Fundamental Rights which was given Declaration status in the Nice Treaty 2000. Taken together, these developments began to amount to the construction of an EU framework for socio-economic policy-making and for the addressing of citizens' socio-economic rights at an EU level. They may be said to amount to the beginning of what can be referred to as a process of Civil and Social Union. While this has undoubtedly lagged behind the EMU process, it could be argued to be both logically and sociologically required by it (see the discussion in Chapter 9).

The EU and the Reconstruction of European Welfare Capitalism in the 21st Century

The EU and a new European economy?: the Lisbon strategy and its context

By 2000 the EU seemed to be entering a positive new phase of development and integration in its socio-economic policy. A common currency was being launched for the majority of the EU's member states, binding participating states together in policy areas such as exchange rates, interest rates and the regulation of state borrowing and changing the habits of hundreds of millions of consumers across the continent. New policy mechanisms had been created to coordinate the progressive convergence of employment and social inclusion policies. In addition, the Scandinavian social model, which as we saw in Chapter 6 has been impressively effective on both economic and welfare fronts, had become better known and more influential with the accession of two Nordic countries, Sweden and Finland, into the EU in 1995. Along with established member state Denmark, they offered substantial new policy experiences and ideas beyond the familiar market-based or state-based polarities visible in previous debates and conflicts between British and continental policy-makers and governments. However, the reality behind the appearance around 2000 was not so positive. As discussed earlier, common problems were being caused in the 1990s across Europe and the EU by globalisation and negative socio-demographic trends. Here we can add to this list Europe's share of the global ecological problems and costs of the development and operation of intensive industrial and mass consumerist economies since the 19th century and particularly in the late 20th century. These common problems accelerated from the mid-1990s and continue to challenge the EU through the present and into the future. In addition, EU member states began to recognise and position themselves in differing ways to face the looming and major new challenge of the likely costs of and competition from a large number of incoming Eastern European states, which would create a new and in some respects negative economic environment of influences on the EU-15 from 2004 onwards. In the face of these pressing problems, the socio-economic policies of the major continental and southern EU states (France, German, Italy and Spain) seemed to be structurally inadequate. They consistently failed to boost persistently low levels of economic growth, failed to reduce persistently high levels of unemployment, and seemed to be inflexible and incapable of constructive adaptation or reform.[13]

We now need to consider the EU's current framework for socio-economic policy, namely the Lisbon Strategy. While recognising that the Strategy attempts to integrate the EU's social policy and economic policy, nevertheless its economic aspects will be given greater emphasis in the section below, and its social aspects will be emphasised more in the following section. Here, then, we first consider some of the features and also some of the weaknesses of the Strategy, and then we consider its potential relevance and strengths in terms of the realities of economic change and the emergence of a new economy and new contexts of employment in Europe in the 21st century.

The Lisbon Strategy: elements, problems and revision

Approaching millennium year 2000, EU socio-economic policy could be characterised as being beset by a significant and persistent disjuncture. On the one hand, there were the apparent aspirations recurrently expressed in its policy discourse about the value of greater integration in all fields, including those of social and economic policy, together with some positive policy and institutional achievements in these fields. On the other hand, there were the realities of the major challenges it was increasingly facing, together with the limits and weaknesses of the responses to these challenges by some of its core and largest member states. It was out of this somewhat uncertain, late 1990s context that the Lisbon Strategy emerged, a version of which currently aims to promote and guide EU socio-economic policy into the medium term.

The EU heads of state at their intergovernmental conference at Lisbon in 2000 agreed a new strategic goal or vision, together with a timetable, some new objectives to substantiate the goal, and some policy means to achieve it. We can briefly consider each of these in turn. The strategic goal was that the EU should aim to become the world's 'most competitive and dynamic knowledge-based economy capable of sustainable growth, with more and better jobs and greater social cohesion'.[14] This vision aspired to be timely, relevant and innovative. It aspired to be timely and relevant in that it recognised and oriented to the newly emerging complex of interconnected and economically-relevant ecological and social as well as economic changes, challenges and opportunities characterising societies in the late 20th and early 21st centuries. It aspired to be innovative in that it attempted to link Europe's economic progress and policy in a positive way with Europe's social policy and also its environmental progress and policy. Social policy has traditionally often been seen negatively as a cost and a burden to the performance and growth of European countries' economies. Lisbon proposed that, on the contrary, it should be seen in positive terms as an investment in the economy and, indeed, as a precondition for its success in the new 21st-century context. The period that EU leaders allocated to themselves and their countries to turn the vision into a reality was a decade, with the target date of achieving the goal set at 2010.

Progress to the goal was to be made tangible in terms of a set of objectives and measured by associated indicators. The objectives included a number in and related to the social policy field. The social policy-related field of citizens' general rights was to be promoted by further support for gender equality ('mainstreaming', Rees 1998), by action against discrimination and by the reinforcement of fundamental human rights. Objectives more directly in the social policy field included the promotion of social inclusion, improvement in the quality of social policy, and the modernisation of social protection systems, particularly by the promotion of flexibility and security. We will consider these social policy aspects of the Lisbon Strategy at greater length in following section.

Economic objectives included the further development of the knowledge-based economy, not least by boosting national research and development spending towards 3% of GDP by 2010. Also the Strategy aimed at increasing the EU's pool of human capital available for economic production. The labour pool was to be improved by raising the proportion of eligible adults in employment, and also by promoting what were at the time very low levels of labour mobility across the EU. Notoriously low and variable European labour force participation rates (see Chapter 7) were to be raised by 2010 to an EU average of 70% for men and 60% for women. Development towards the overall goal would be promoted, steered and managed to a significant extent by means of innovative policy processes. That is, the Lisbon Agreement endorsed policy processes such as the 'open method of coordination'. As we saw earlier, this had been trialled for a few years prior, apparently with some success, in the fields of EU employment and social inclusion policy. Overall the Lisbon Agreement provided a new impetus, strategic policy framework and strategic coordination for these fields of policy.

The EU's Lisbon Strategy in the socio-economic policy field, however, ran into problems almost as soon as it had been agreed. By 2004 these problems had become clear enough to be the subject of various critical reports.[15] This situation led to a further agreement on a revised and renewed version of the strategy (referred to here as Lisbon–2) in 2005, which we will look at in a moment. The difficulties with Lisbon–1 were in some respects predictable from the underlying and ongoing uncertainties and disjunctures noted earlier. Predictable difficulties included the disjuncture between EU policy discourses and their aspirations and the member states' motivation and capacity to deliver practical outcomes. In particular, the target deadline for world leadership in the knowledge-based economy of 2010 was always ambitious and, as it turned out, became completely unrealistic. In other respects, particularly in terms of events in the wider world beyond Europe, the difficulties Lisbon–1 faced were unexpected. Major unexpected international events affecting Europe included the collapse of a speculative international investment boom based on internet companies and also the Islamist terrorist assault on the USA in 2001.

Overall there was some progress on some of the Lisbon objectives in the years immediately following. For instance, the general employment rate has grown particularly among women and older workers.[16] However, research and development spending did not rise on track for 3% by 2010, net job creation was slowing by 2004, and generally Europe was losing ground in terms of economic growth, employment and productivity, not only to the USA but also to Asia, including China.[17] The Kok Report commented: 'the risk is apparent that the 2010 target of 70% employment rate will not be reached' and that Lisbon might become 'a synonym for missed objectives and failed promises'.[18] In the report's view, the reasons for the possible failure of the Lisbon Strategy included, at the EU level, an 'overloaded agenda ('Lisbon is about everything and thus about nothing'), together with 'poor coordination' and 'conflicting priorities'.[19] At the level of the member states, the reasons include the familiar ones of poor economic performance because of structural weaknesses, together with what would appear also to be a lack of appreciation and urgency about, and possibly even of genuine commitment to, the collective goal.

Assessments of the first version of the Lisbon Strategy generally agreed on support for its ambition and vision, notwithstanding their implications of the need for greater realism about the possibility of world leadership in the knowledge-based economy as opposed to being 'among the best in the world', as the Kok Report put it.[20] However, they tended to be much more critical of the EU in relation to such things as the Strategy's timetable, its focus and the policy means needed to deliver it. Two influential reports proposed that in any revision the Strategy should be focused even more than it originally had been on the economic rather than the social dimensions of Europe, and in particular on market rather than public sector aspects of the EU and member state economies. Thus, the Strategy needed to be focused on promoting investment in research and, in particular, it needed to be concerned with this issue in terms of the market and enterprise conditions which were likely to stimulate growth in the private sector's share of research as opposed to the various public sectors' shares.[21] One of the reports argued for a more realistic approach to the research and development objective, and the need to lower the target to an average 2.5% of aggregate EU GDP (as opposed to 3%) and to stage the target date back from 2010 to 2015.[22] In terms of policy processes, the Kok Report suggested that the EU needed better frameworks which both recognise national differences of interest and attempt to bring them all together in a coordinated way behind a common strategy. In addition, it argues that the 'open method of coordination' needed to have more impact and should be more prepared to use techniques such as the 'naming and shaming' of member states which under-performed in terms of the Strategy.

The Lisbon Strategy was reviewed in 2004 and relaunched in 2005 as *The Community Lisbon Programme* (hereafter Lisbon–2).[23] It proposed a new tighter Strategy focus, a new understanding of the governance system needed to deliver the Strategy and a series of key actions in selected areas. The new focus was to be on economic growth and employment. In line with the Aho Report (EC 2006a), it aimed to promote the former through a better articulation of the connection between knowledge and innovation. Responding to various critiques in terms of employment, it argued for the need to promote Europe as a more attractive place to both invest and work (among other things, to counter the problem of Europe's 'brain drain' to the USA), and generally reasserted the need for the creation of 'more and better jobs. The new understanding of governance involved clarifying the different roles and responsibilities of the EU and the member states in developing and delivering the Strategy. This included a new coordinated packaging of the fields and topics addressed by the open method of coordination, collecting them together and focusing them as National Reform Programmes (NRPs), with the states committing to produce annual NRPs and the EU committing to provide an annual summary and assessment.

Areas to be particularly focused on within this relaunch of the Lisbon Strategy, areas for 'key actions' promising most in terms of 'European value added', included the following: a new willingness to tolerate state aid for particular economic sectors provided this was targeted to support knowledge and innovation; a commitment to the simplification of business regulation and 'red tape'; a programme and commitment to complete the Internal Market in terms of all the main categories of services to help promote the EU's service-based economy; a plan to remove remaining obstacles to intra-EU labour mobility and also to develop a common approach to non-EU inward economic migration; and the introduction of policies to help manage and ameliorate the negative social effects of economic restructuring.

Whether or not this relaunch of the Lisbon Strategy has made it more credible and realistic remains an open question. In spite of it, commentators continue to stress the scale and urgency of the challenges facing the EU in the economic field and related social fields, and the changes which continue to be needed (and thus which, by implication, are currently lacking).[24] Some progress is being made in relation to both the economic aspect and also, as we discuss in the following section, the social aspects of the strategy. However, particularly on the economic front, this continues to risk being 'too little, and too late'. This is not only in relation to the self-imposed, and thus somewhat artificial, timetable of 2010, but also, and more substantially, in relation to the pace of development of the EU's global trading partners and competitors, particularly the USA and Japan, and also increasingly, in some relevant aspects, China and India. Indeed, progress in some areas of the EU's economic strategy as a whole and the Lisbon Strategy in particular remains stubbornly minimal.

In terms of the EU's economic strategy as a whole it is sobering to realise that a decade and a half after the launch, in the 1992 Maastricht Treaty, of the Single Internal Market this project still will only be completed in 2009 in respect of the dominant economic sector in European societies of services.[25] Even then it will only be formally completed, that is it will only be an econo-legal space, a market place, an economic potential. From that time onwards the EU will enable the development of service industries on a border-free Europe-wide basis, and it is reasonable to expect that some such will occur. But this is, of course, a far cry from the EU being able to guarantee that such developments will happen in practice, or what shape they will take, or at what pace they will occur.

In terms of the Lisbon Strategy in particular, limited and inadequate progress is evident in a number of areas. These include the failure to boost public and private investment in research, noted earlier. They also include the long-term persistence of relatively high rates of unemployment across the EU (e.g. an 8.8% EU average in 2005). In addition, they include the long-term record (from the 1980s) of low growth in labour productivity compared to major competitors (e.g. in 2005 the EU average was only 0.9% per annum, compared with double that in the USA (1.8% p.a.) and Japan (2.2% p.a.)).[26] Against this kind of a background the EU Lisbon Strategy's aspirations to world leadership in knowledge economy terms, whether by 2010 or even by some other later deadline, or indeed even to parity with world leaders rather than continuing loss of ground to them, continues to look unrealistic. It is hard to see how recent developments in EU socio-economic policy centring on the Lisbon Strategy and its revisions could be argued to have closed the long-established disjuncture or gap between, on the one hand, EU aspirations and their supporting policy discourse and, on the other hand, EU policy delivery, achievements and realities. The gap remains, and its negative impacts on the EU's credibility and legitimacy remain also.

The EU and the European post-industrial economy in the 21st century: New economy? New jobs?

The EU as an economic community is facing new challenges in the 21st century in sustaining the employment, income and livelihoods of the 500 million people within its borders. As we have seen in previous discussions, the EU is being challenged to a new degree by internal changes and also by incoming factors and forces, particularly globalisation and enlargement. Globalisation in the 21st century is now no longer the force it initially appeared to be in the 1990s, that is as something which could be viewed in abstract terms, its impacts a matter of the future and of debate, a force perhaps seen as bearing the mask of the USA, which was at least a familiar competitor, and otherwise a long-term ally. Now it has taken much more tangible and urgent form, in the shape of the relatively recent, unexpectedly rapid and clearly long-term rise of China in the global economy. China is a less familiar competitor than the USA and is organised through an authoritarian political system and ideology rejected in principle by Europeans and the EU. The EU–China trade wars of 2005/06, which we noted earlier (Chapter 7),[27] prompted the EU to adopt a short-term economic protectionist position to attempt to defend against immanent job losses in particular sectors, and led to the creation of its Globalisation Adjustment Fund in 2006. Diplomatic agreements to the contrary notwithstanding, these trade wars may be harbingers of more economic difficulties to come for the EU in this relationship. The EU is also facing potential economic difficulties and over-stretch in its attempt to come to terms with the large-scale accession of twelve relatively economically undeveloped and socially struggling Eastern European countries in 2004–07. Beyond this there is the prospect that the EU might enlarge itself significantly over the coming decade, potentially amplifying the social and economic problems and costs it faces.

Each of these processes is generating concerns and doubts about the ability of the EU to generate employment and to thrive economically in the world of the 21st century. Perhaps its historical moment was the late 20th century and its potential for further development has already been used up. Employment has always been central to both economic and social policy, the axis around which each turns, and this is even truer in the contemporary period given the new centrality of human capital in the emerging knowledge-based society and economy. On a pessimistic reading of the runes, the early 21st-century world seems to promise little but competitive failure, sectoral unemployment and general underemployment. So are there realistic prospects for new and sustainable jobs being created in Europe in the contemporary period and going forward, and in what sectors might they grow?

In Chapter 7 we outlined some very long-term economic trends relating to sector changes connected with post-industrialism. Extrapolating these trends there is every reason at least to anticipate a continued growth of the services sector in Europe. This is not only to be expected at the high-skilled, high-value-added end of the economy, but it can also be reasonably anticipated at the low-skilled end. In terms of relatively low-skilled jobs this is particularly so in sectors such as personal and social care, involving face-to-face services by cultural familiars which cannot be provided at a distance and/or through ICTs, including the internet. This effectively protects them against international competition, although the funding for them would be expected to come significantly from states rather than local markets. In terms of higher ends of the skill spectrum, employment in the European knowledge economy has grown rapidly, by nearly a quarter in the recent decade (23.9% in 1995–2005), the fastest growth experienced in any sector in this period.[28] Employment in the cultural economy (creative industries, audio-visual, etc., see below) has also grown strongly in recent years (e.g. 12.3%, 1999–2003).[29] Table 8.1 reviews some information provided in a recent EU experts' report on the future of EU social policy in a globalised world and also in the current (2007–09) EU directive on the service economy, which suggest some possible sources of employment growth for the future in the European economy.[30]

Table 8.1 The European service economy in the 21st century: growth sectors in the EU

EU market-based services EU-wide service sectors + employment opportunities	EU polity-licensed services National public service sectors + employment opportunities	EU integration-based services Employment opportunities	Societal change-based services Public-private service employment opportunities
Electronic communications	Postal sector Electricity + gas sectors Water + waste sectors	Indirectly via EU policies for:	Environmental services Family care Pre-school education
Financial services	Maintenance of order Justice	EU enlargement Regional development	Lifelong learning Health
Business services Management consultancy, facilities management, advertising, legal and/or tax advice, etc.	Social policy Consumer and worker protection Social protection Prevention of fraud Town and country planning Cultural policy objectives	Internal market completion EMU-based support for national public Investments European Research Area, etc.	Social integration Urban management Cultural management, etc.
Land, building services Real estate agents, construction, architects, etc.	Amateur sport activities Animal welfare, etc.		
Distribution services			
Popular cultural sector services Tourism and travel, leisure services, sports centres, amusement parks, etc.			
Household support services Family services, welfare services, etc.			

Sources: EU 2006b and EC 2004.

New structures in the European economy: from welfare capitalism to cultural capitalism?

As far as the economic aspect of EU policy goes, so far we have noted the depth and urgency of the economic problems the EU and its member states face in the 21st century. In spite of this, there seem to be some grounds for optimism about Europe's capacity to sustain its economic position, employment base and standards of living. That is, we have noted that there are positive employment growth trends in terms of services, knowledge-based activities and in the cultural field. What is the basis for these trends and prospects? The EU's Lisbon Agenda and many commentators propose that one of the necessary conditions to enable these sorts of employment trends to thrive is the reform and integration of member states' economic and social policies. We will consider the social aspect of this attempt to promote the reconstruction of European 'welfare capitalism' and a new 'European social model' in the following section. However, other conditions for such employment growth might be more straightforwardly economic and require more directly economic or economy-related policies to address them.

Relevant policy intervention in the European economy, at EU level, or national level, or both, draws on some general understanding and conception of economic structure and development dynamics. Such general understandings, whether in the form of conceptual frameworks, theories or 'visions' which can provide a grounding for policies, have been in play in EU policy-making circles for a number of years. For instance, we recall that the Delors White Paper in 1993 provided an early policy-relevant recognition both of the notion that a knowledge economy/society might be emerging in Europe, and also that this might be occurring against the challenging background of globalisation. These notions are, of course, even more relevant and important analytically and in policy terms over a decade later. For instance, as we have seen, the Lisbon Agenda 2000 aimed at making Europe the leading knowledge-based economy in the world by 2010. We need to consider whether the EU's approach to supporting the European economy and employment, particularly in its Lisbon Agenda process, is well grounded in a moment.

However, it is worth observing at this point that it is evident that there is more to contemporary services economies than knowledge-based activities, enterprises and skills. This is indeed a massive (around 40% of GDP and employment) and growing sector in the 21st-century European economy, but there are no doubt limits to its potential. And in any case at various points in our discussion we have also noted that European societies and labour markets are also marked by the rise of low-skilled and insecure zones of employment as well as the persistence of large-scale welfare states and public sector employment. So in addition to this we also need to recognise the significance of new and growing, but often overlooked, sectors and employment in the general field of popular culture. These include the cultural and creative industries (such as audio-visual, arts, etc.), but also sport, and the massively important although complex sector of tourism (see Table 8.2). Taken together, which

Table 8.2   The European cultural economy in the 21st century

Sectors	Row	GDP (%)	Jobs (%)	Jobs growth rate (pa)
Creative/cultural	1	2.6	2.5	12.3
Tourism	2	11.5	12.1	4
Sport	3	3.7	5.4	–
Knowledge	4	38	41.4	23.9
Totals		55.8	61.4	–

Sources: Row 1: Data from EC 2005b (Marcus Report), EC 2006c (KEA Report), also Florida and Tingali 2004; Row 2: Data from KMU 2006; Row 3: Data from EC 2007a, also Arnaud 2006; Row 4: Data from Brinkley and Lee 2007, Table 1, p. 7, Table 3, p. 10, also Brinkley 2008, Fig.10, p. 50.

these areas rarely are, they currently provide around one in five of all jobs across Europe and are growing rapidly, and they often involve relatively low-skilled employment.

Strategies focused either on the new knowledge economy or on the new welfare economy, or both (such as the Lisbon Agenda) simply do not pick up and address this important structural dimension of the contemporary European economy. Along with a strategy for the reform, reconstruction and promotion of European society in its 'welfare capitalist' aspects, arguably perhaps what is needed in addition is a comparable strategy in relation to European society in its 'cultural economic' and 'cultural capitalist' aspects.[31]

The EU and a new European social model?: flexicurity and citizenship

The EU and its member states are entering a new situation in terms of both economic and social policy at the beginning of the 21st century. The rapid development externally of a global capitalist economy and internally of an EU-wide capitalist economy together constitute a new, dynamic and challenging economic context. These two orders of change and challenge imply that national versions of 'welfare capitalism' and social models are likely to be subject to pressure and to change. The radical social changes and new social problems affecting European societies, as we saw in Chapter 7, include the health and care problems associated with increasing longevity, and new forms of unemployment, partial and insecure employment affecting women, the young, older people and ethnic minorities. These changing factors, forces and contexts have manifested themselves in influential ways to one degree or another in all EU member states in recent years. In response to this there has been considerable activity and effort at the level of EU policy and related discourse, particularly in the Lisbon–2 Strategy and also in the EU's Social

Agenda, to map out a coherent vision of a new social model, namely a renewal of social and welfare policy thinking.

EU policies and discourses in this context can be interpreted as having three main interests and aims. First, they aim to promote change in its member states' national welfare and social models. The purpose of such change is not exercise of proto-federal power for its own sake, nor to fatally undermine these models on behalf of a neo-liberal political economic agenda. Rather it is to encourage member states to recognise that the rigidities of their traditional welfare systems could contribute to the possibility that they might be overwhelmed by the new and growing economic tides rising and flowing around them in global and European contexts, and to help them to act to sustain welfare principles in ways which prevent this. Secondly, EU policies aim to coordinate and orchestrate member state changes in terms of their content and timing so as to avoid policy fragmentation in the EU, and to maintain at least a minimum of inter-state policy communication and coherence across the organisation. Thirdly, they aim to begin the building-up of a new EU-wide social framework intended to provide a social safety net for the evolving new EU-wide market and its economy, and to support the cross-border and border-free movements and activities of this economy's massive pool of consumers and workers.

The new vision of the European social model involves a number of interconnected key ideas and ideals, together with a recognition that they need to be explicitly and actively tailored in order to apply to the particular circumstances of different nation-states and their distinctive welfare regime. There are two main sets of new social model ideas and ideals, relating on the one hand to the economic relevance of social policy and the other to what can be referred to as its human relevance. Thus, on the one hand, as we have already seen, the general idea that contemporary national social policy needs to be developed and reformed as a social investment in the promotion of national economies, and in their capacity to create employment, is a major theme in current EU socio-economic policy, particularly in the Lisbon Strategy. On the other hand, there is the major theme in policy relating to the new social model concerning the human relevance of social policy, and this consists of a number of interrelated strands.[32]

First, there is the idea that in their theory and practice national welfare systems need to recognise and build in a 'life-course' perspective on their citizens' and clients' needs, contributions and benefits. In some respects this could be said to be a 21st-century reinterpretation of the post-war 'cradle to grave' ideal in welfare policy, which was associated, among others, with the British welfare state architect William Beveridge.[33] Secondly, and taking the life-course perspective into account, there is the idea that the various implicit and explicit 'social contracts' and settlements between sections of national societies which underpin and legitimate their traditional welfare systems need to be reviewed and renewed in changing circumstances. These include inter-gender and intergenerational settlements in particular, but also include inter-class and inter-ethnic settlements. This contractarian approach has been taken in recent EU social policy thinking on the future of EU social policy.[34] For instance, the European Union (EU 2004) argues that the present intergeneration pact is focused on the elderly and based on fears – fears of ageing and of its consequences on the pension system and on the labour force. The new intergenerational pact should be focused on the young and based on confidence. The aspiration is to turn these fears into a win-win process based on a positive perception of the future and a new intergenerational balance.[35] It argues that the EU could contribute through the next social agenda to the emergence of this new intergenerational pact and that this should involve member states, the social partners and civil society.[36]

Thirdly, there is the idea of so-called 'flexicurity'.[37] This is that contemporary welfare systems need to promote both security, as they always have aspired to, but in ways that are positively adapted to the new socio-economic conditions of the 21st century, which require flexibility, particularly on the part of workers, but also on the part of corporations and public agencies. The key elements of 'flexicurity' relate to the nature of employment contracts (namely, that they should be both reliable and flexible), the need to ensure the availability of lifelong learning, the need for active labour market policies, on the basis of an approach to social security which guarantees an adequate income, promotes employment and mobility to get it, and which also encourages improvement in the balancing of work and life, including family commitments. Different countries need to consider the promotion of flexicurity in different parts of their welfare systems and currently face different kinds of problem in that respect. Thus there are different 'flexicurity pathways' which need to be followed by different countries. Southern European countries (such as Italy and Spain) face and need to overcome the problems of rigidities and segmentation (e.g. in terms of qualifications) in labour markets. Continental countries (such as Germany) face and need to overcome the problem of low job-flows in and between enterprises. Liberal-market countries, specifically the UK, face and need to overcome the problem of low skills in workforce. Eastern European countries need to face and need to overcome the problem of working-age people being in receipt of benefits on a long-term basis.

Finally, and normatively knitting together all of the preceding themes, there is the perspective that national welfare systems need to be conceptually framed and practically oriented in terms of the idea and ideal of 'the citizen', and thus relatedly in terms of the notions implied by this of individualism, rights and responsibilities. Formal EU citizenship was introduced in the 1992 Maastricht Treaty, and was intended to complement and not conflict with national citizenship.[38] The individual rights the EU supported were expanded to include a range of human rights in the 1997 Amsterdam Treaty and a range of social rights in the EU's Charter of Fundamental Rights, which was given declarative (symbolic, non-legally enforceable) status in the Nice Treaty 2001. The EU's general commitment to individual rights, through its treaty commitments, charter and court system, together with the Council of Europe and its European Charter of Human Rights and related court system, has been important in the development of rights for two classes of people in Europe, namely women and children.[39] The EU's Charter of Fundamental Rights is currently being moved towards a legally enforceable status in the Reform Treaty, which is planned to be agreed in 2009.

In relation to workers, the Charter endorses workers' rights to such things as fair and just working conditions, to information and consultation within the undertaking, to collective bargaining and action, to employment place-ment services, and to protection in the event of unjustified dismissal. It also prohibits child labour and requires that young people at work be properly protected. In relation to the family, the Charter supports the view that family life should enjoy legal, economic and social protection, and that there should be a right to paid maternity leave and to parental leave. In relation to general social protection, the Charter recognises and respects the range of rights typ-ically associated with European welfare states, namely entitlement to social security benefits and social services providing protection in cases such as maternity, illness, industrial accidents, dependency or old age, and in the case of loss of employment, and the right to social and housing assistance in order to combat social exclusion and poverty. Finally, in relation to people who are mobile beyond their nations within and across the EU, the Charter supports the 'portability' of social and health care rights. That is it supports the rights of those who reside and move legally within the Union to social security ben-efits and social advantages in accordance with Community law and national laws and practices. And it also supports people's rights of access to preventa-tive health care and to benefit from medical treatment under the conditions established by national laws and practices.[40]

There are EU-based Europeanisation trends operating in the social policy field in the 21st century which could be said to have some capacity to extend a common influence across national borders, and to begin lowering national borders in this field. Perhaps ultimately these trends may bring Europe's differing worlds of welfare and of welfare capitalism in Europe's social and welfare complex into a greater degree of harmony.[41] For instance, in the field of social insurance, nation-based contributions and benefits services are now 'portable' and usable across the EU. Also in the field of health care, various processes of Europeanisation are underway to one extent or another.[42] An example in this field is the fact that all EU citizens, if they are in the position of being medical patients in emergency situations, have a right of access to any national public hospitals in EU member states. This is on the standard-ised basis of these services being free at the point of delivery (whatever the national variations in subsequent coverage of the providing hospital's costs). Also, all EU citizens, in the position of consumers of medical services, have a right of access to health markets across the EU, whether services are made available for purchase by private or national public health providers. Finally, an EU-wide health labour market is beginning to operate, supported by processes of mutual recognition of qualifications. All qualified EU citizens have a right to be treated equally, to be able to offer their services and apply for employment in member states' national health systems. In the field of pensions, all EU citizens have rights as consumers to invest in private pensions funds across the EU and also as private pensions providers to advertise for and work for clients across the EU. Finally, in the field of higher education, there is the long-established student exchange scheme (Erasmus, etc.). In addition there are processes of Europeanisation underway in the general field of higher education teaching (the Bologna process) and to a lesser extent in the research field (the Research Framework programmes and also European Research Area policy).

In spite of all of this, it remains the case, as we discussed earlier, that the EU has limited formal competence and remains relatively weak in the social policy field. By contrast, traditional and unreformed national social models and welfare systems remain massive presences in many EU member states and across the European social complex. Given the contemporary uncertain and stalled nature of EU decision-making, they are likely to continue to do so beyond the Lisbon Agenda's 2010 target date and into the medium-term future.

Conclusion

In this chapter we have reviewed the EU's relevance for the development of the European social complex, particularly understood as a welfare complex (welfare capitalism) and as a policy complex (an EU-regulated multi-level and multinational system). The EU was seen to be relevant in two main ways: through its economic project to construct a unitary, EU-wide market, and also its related interest in promoting a version of 'the European social model', particularly in the field of employment. Arguably, a new economy is beginning to emerge in the early 21st century in Europe and in other world regions, influenced by the continuing dynamics of globalisation and post-industrialisation. We have suggested that these dynamics create new economic and employment opportunities in knowledge-based industries and also, importantly, for the low-skilled in the under-recognised popular cultural industries. They also create new challenges (both in terms of quality and quantity) for the future of employment in Europe and, relatedly, for social and welfare systems and models established to address the problems of preceding eras. The EU has attempted to encourage member states to reform their welfare systems in order to better combine the provision of social security with the promotion of flexibility and activism, in its new 'flexicurity' version of the European social model. We have suggested that perspectives emphasising the life-course and the social rights of citizenship are needed to adequately elaborate and contextualise this model.

The EU's single market project has made progress and contributes a Europeanising dynamic to the contemporary European complex. However, the single market remains incomplete in the strategically important area of services. In addition, the EU's economic aspirations announced in the Lisbon Strategy remain largely unfulfilled. This raises questions about the credibility of the Lisbon Strategy, and arguably about the EU more generally. Its related employment and social model policies, together with the voluntaristic methods used to promote reform in these areas, can be argued to have succeeded in promoting a greater degree of cross-European policy exchange, learning and consensus about the nature and need for reform than ever before.[43] But so far they have had little practical effect in changing the structure of established social welfare institutions, particularly in the bigger EU countries (Barysch et al. 2008). It may be that a longer timeframe is needed over which to assess these developments. Or it may be that problems and crises elsewhere in the EU system (for instance, in relation the major issues of further eastward enlargement or constitutional reform) need to be resolved before it would be reasonable to expect much in the way of further integrative developments.

One way or another, the EU's social and economic policy agendas appear increasingly challenged. Much the same can be said for the agendas involved in studying them, which are facing the embryonic sociology of Europe. This field of sociology has yet to seriously recognise and investigate Europe's experience of the 21st-century social changes and the structural dynamics lying behind the policy challenges facing the EU which we have outlined in this and the previous chapter. In the final chapter we reflect on some of the political and normative issues raised for the sociology of Europe by the EU's agendas and problems. We consider how they might be usefully understood and interpreted by sociological and social theoretical perspectives addressing the development of cosmopolitanism and civil society in Europe.

Notes

1   For relevant analyses relevant to these issues, also see Roche and van Berkel 1997a; Roche and Annesley 2004; Ferrera 2005a; also Kvist and Saari 2007a.
2   On the idea of a European social model and the problem of the convergence or lack of it among European social polices, see Aiginger 2005; Annesley 2007; Giddens 2007; Jepson and Pascual 2005; Kleinman 2002; Leibfried and Pierson 1995; Sapir 2006; Streeck 1996; Threlfall 2002, 2003; Wincott 2003; also the discussions in Chapters 6 and 7. For overviews of EU social policy, see Hantrais 2000; and Geyer 2000.
3   On the political economy of the main versions of the European capitalist economy, see Schmidt 2002; for general background on the EU's main economic policies, see Dinan 2005, Part 3; also generally Bromley 2001; Lintner 2001; and Thompson 2001.
4   On the euro and EMU policies, see Dyson 2002; also Thompson 2001.
5   See Delors 1998; also Nelsen and Stubbs 1998, Chapters 10 and 11.
6   For the general political context, see Nelsen and Stubbs 1998, Chapters 7–11.
7   On relevant aspects of US and UK socio-economic change and policy in this period, see Roche 1996; and Handler 2004.
8   See EC 1993a.

9   See, for instance, Dinan 2005, Chapter 14. For a discussion of the promotion of a single market and a single policy space in relation to the mass media, particularly television, see Harcourt 2002, 2003. On the EU's 'Television without frontiers' Directive and its audio-visual policy, see Harrison and Woods 2000, 2001; and generally Harrison and Wessels 2009.

10   See, for instance, the evolution of policies and discourses in the EU social policy field in EC 1993b, 1995b, 2004, 2005c; also note 2 above.

11   On EU employment policy, see EC 1999; also Bosco and Chassard 1999; De la Porte and Pochet 2004; Jacobsson 2004; and Mosher and Trubek 2003.

12   See Heikkila 1999; and Roche and Annesley 2004; also see Barysch 2008; Begg et al. 2008; and Daly 2006, 2007.

13   See Giddens 2007 on what he calls the 'blocked societies' of the continental corporate social model.

14   EU 2000a, section 1, para 5.

15   Some reports were official (for instance, the Kok Report, see EU 2004) and some were more varied and independent (for instance, the Sapir Report (see EC 2003) and the Aho Report (see EC 2006a). Also see EC 2004; Barysch et al. 2008; and Begg et al. 2008.

16   EC 2007e, p.4; and Barysch et al. 2008, p.81.

17   See EC 2006a (Aho Report). On the research and development expenditure front, Brinkley and Lee observe that in 2004 this only managed 1.92% of GDp. In their view, the Lisbon target of 3% is unachievable by 2010 or even 2015 (Brinkley and Lee 2007, pp.26, 28).

18   EU 2004, p.11 and p.10.

19   EU 2004, p.16 and p.6.

20   EU 2004, p.16.

21   EC 2006a (Aho Report); and Brinkley and Lee 2007.

22   Brinkley and Lee 2007.

23   On the relaunch of the Lisbon Agenda, see EC 2005a; also Barroso 2006a.

24   The Aho Report (EC 2006a) argues that a 'huge effort' is needed. Brinkley and Lee (2007) are sceptical about the research target (above) and Barysch et al. (2008) are sceptical about the NRP process.

25   See EU 2006b.

26   Information in this paragraph come from EU 2007b, p.7.

27   See Chapter 7, pp. 169–72 and endnotes 13 and 14; also Barysch 2005; Grant and Barysch 2008.

28   Brinkley and Lee 2007, table 3, p.10.

29   See EC 2005b.

30   See EC 2004 and EU 2006b, respectively.

31   The main popular cultural industries and forms of cultural consumption are commonly understood to include such sectors as media, retail, entertainment and sport. On the sociological analysis of some of these cultural industries in modern European and American societies see, for instance, Bryman 2004; Hesmondhalgh 2002; Ritzer 2005, 2008; and Roche 2000a, 2000b. This diverse field is not always well connected analytically to developing understandings of either the all-pervasive post-industrial structural shift to an information and knowledge-based economy, or the massive and growing presence of the tourism industry in all contemporary societies at all levels. A limited exploration of the overlaps between popular culture and the knowledge-based economy is beginning in the field recognised as 'creative industries', but there is very little connection being made currently between the tourism field and the other two. In my view this is

a mistake, since tourism provides an economic context and a source of creative hybridisation for most of the recognised cultural industries. The current and potential connections between each of these three fields needs to be fully explored in any sociologically adequate characterisation of the new cultural economy and its current and potential impacts on contemporary societies. On the knowledge-based economy in Europe, see Brinkley 2008; and Brinkley and Lee 2007. On the cultural economy in general, see Florida 2002; Scott 1999, 2000, 2004; and in Europe see EC 2005b (the Marcus Report); EC 2006c (the KEA Report); also Florida and Tingali 2004. On the sociology and analysis of tourism, see Urry 1990 and (in relation to Europe) 1995; also Shaw and Williams 2004; and Roche 2000a, Chapters 3, 4 and 5; on tourism in Europe, see KMU 2006.

32   On this normative analysis, see Begg et al. 2008; Giddens 2007; also Roche and Annesley 2004; also see the contractarian approach in Chapter 7, see note 34 below.

33   On a 'life course' perspective in European social policy analysis, see European Foundation 2007; Giddens 2007; and Leisering and Leibfried 1999.

34   On 'new social contractualist' approaches in international and European social policy analysis, see Esping-Andersen 2002b; EU 2004; Ferrera 2005a; Giddens 2007; and Roche 1996, Chapters 9, and 2002.

35   This is in line with, here, the idea of the improvement of family policy and of the work–life balance, and also with the 'new social contractualism' (see note 34 above).

36   EC 2004, pp.89–90. For relevant discussions, see Esping-Andersen 2002b; and Myles 2002; also generally Esping Andersen et al. 2002; Giddens 2007; and Jenson 2006.

37   On the EU's approach to flexicurity, see EC 2007b and 2007c.

38   On EU citizenship see, for instance, Martiniello 1997; Meehan 1993, 1997; Roche 1996, Chapter 8, 1997; Roche and van Berkel 1997a; and Rosas and Antola 1995; also EC 1996b.

39   On EU supports for rights relating to women and children, see Euronet 2005; and the European Charter of Fundamental Rights (European Parliament 2007). On the Amsterdam Treaty, see Duff 1997.

40   The European Charter of Fundamental Rights refers to social rights and thus social and welfare policy in various places, particularly (Chapter IV Solidarity, Articles 27–35) (see European Parliament 2007). The Charter was included as a non-justiciable declaration in the Nice Treaty 2001, and was contained in justiciable form in Part II of the failed EU Constitutional Treaty 2004 (see European Convention 2003). It is contained in this form in the proposed EU Reform Treaty 2007–09 the status and future of which is unclear at the time of writing (see EU 2007a).

41   See Kvist and Saari 2007a, 2007b; Ferrara 2005a; and Ferrera et al. 2000; also see Barysch et al. 2008; and Begg et al. 2008.

42   See EC 2008a, which is connected both with the EU's promotion of social welfare harmonisation and also with its policy to promote the single market in services (EU 2006b).

43   See Bosco and Chassard 1999; also Daly 2006, 2007; and Barysch et al. 2008.

9

THE EUROPEAN CIVIL COMPLEX: COSMOPOLITANISM AND THE SOCIOLOGY OF EUROPE

Introduction

The exploratory discussion of the sociology of Europe and the EU in this book has revolved around responses to two main questions. First, how might this relatively undeveloped field of sociology be conceptualised and approached analytically and, secondly, what are some important substantive areas in this field? As regards the first question, the book has proposed the usefulness of seeing Europe as a complex social formation, and of interpreting this in terms of forms of complexity connected with: (i) Europe's duality (between a formation of commonalities and one of differences); (ii) its societal dimensions (political, economic and cultural); (iii) its deep structures (of social space, time and technology); and (iv) its social divisions (its hierarchies of class, gender and ethnicity). As regards the second question, it has looked into a number of substantive areas in the field of the European complex, particularly historical and politico-cultural aspects (Part 1) and welfare and socio-economic aspects (Part 2).

Exploratory discussions being what they are, this discussion has done little more than push at a door which is already beginning to open, and to point to the fact that there is much more work to do in the rooms and spaces beyond. Of course, on the one hand, the approaches to the field of the sociology of Europe and the EU to which we have pointed can be conceptualised in more and different ways than those presented here. On the other hand, equally clearly, the field is a potentially vast one, and encompasses far more than the substantive areas we have been able to look into. Given these observations, the purpose of this final chapter, then, is not to exhaustively rehearse and connect each of the book's themes in order to terminate the discussion in a conclusive way. On the contrary, rather than making a conclusion, it aims to say that what discussions and work in this field need to do is to move on and to make progress. Further perspectives on the field need to be developed and further areas need to be studied within it.

New developments in the study of Europe and the EU, new conceptualisations and area studies, have begun to occur in recent sociology, and its close family relative social theory. For instance, a number of writers have begun to explore the social nature and implications of contemporary Europeanisation from social theory perspectives (e.g. Delanty and Rumford 2005; Beck and Grande 2007; and Rumford 2002, 2007).[1] Others have begun to provide substantial new empirical studies of contemporary European society which particularly aim to take account of intra-EU migration. Included here are studies – of the nature and wider social implications of class differences across European countries, of the strategically important phenomena of professionals' migration within the EU and its evolving labour market (see, respectively, Fligstein 2008 and Favell 2008), and of developments in European public attitudes (e.g. Medrano 2003[2]).

Such studies, while not explicitly adopting the kind of 'complexity' perspective developed in this book, nevertheless can be read as implicitly operating with a version of it. For instance, Fligstein's analysis of European society focuses on what he refers to as 'social fields', namely 'arenas of social interaction where organised individuals or groups such as interest groups, states, firms, and non-governmental organisations routinely interact under a set of shared understandings' relating to such things as goals, rules, and power.[3] Using this concept, he argues that 'Europe-wide social fields are being built', which involve horizontal interpersonal and communicative ties between people across borders as well as vertical ties from the national to the EU level. In the 1950s, fields tended to be mainly organised at a national level, but since then 'whole new sets of fields have emerged', for instance in such areas as policy domains, economic markets, trade associations, professional organisations and common leisure interests. Fligstein illustrates the analysis, which is resonant with earlier socio-political studies of European economic and policy sectors and institutions, with reference to detailed studies of social fields in the defence, telecommunications and sport sectors.[4] In Fligstein's view, although they can also generate contradictory ('euroclash') attitudes among some sectors of the European public, these fields may ultimately have the potential to generate a common 'European culture, identity and … politics'. Currently, a relatively small proportion of people participate in these social fields and in the EU projects connected with them. However, he suggests that these people's interactions in these European fields has the potential to affect identities, and 'make … them Europeans'.

Innovative studies of this kind and quality undoubtedly deserve careful as well as critical consideration both for their intrinsic merits and limitations, and also in their role as potential models for the further work which is needed to develop the sociology and social theory of Europe. That said, this final chapter is not the right place to undertake an intensive engagement with such work. Rather, the exploratory and illustrative spirit of our discussion will be better served at this stage by a brief and hopefully suggestive response to an important theme which marks some of these new developments. This is the theme of the relevance claimed for the sociology of Europe and the EU of an interest in the social theory of 'cosmopolitanism' and a 'cosmopolitan' perspective, not only in analytical terms but also, importantly, in normative terms.

Since the inception of sociology as an academic discipline, normative ideologies and arguments from across the political spectrum have been part of its discourse, whether identifying and offering solutions to perceived social problems, or criticising conventional wisdom, or advocating versions of the good society. On the whole, in terms of both its knowledge base and its social relevance as a form of responsible public intellectualism, the discipline should be judged to have benefited from the often noisy dialogues between its analytic and normative wings. For the moment, we can provisionally understand the cosmopolitan perspective as one which addresses and values humanity's political and cultural differences in the context of an interest in and valuation of moral universals. This perspective, which aims to bypass the 'methodological' and normative nation-statism common in work in humanities and social sciences disciplines, has been much debated and applied over the past decade. It offers both explicitly normative frameworks of moral and political judgement as well as analytic frameworks to guide research.[5]

In the case of the emerging sociology of Europe and the EU it offers a balanced normative support for and critical assessment of the development of the EU, and it promises to contribute significantly to the analytic understanding of the EU. That said, as currently understood, it has its weaknesses as well as its strengths. This concluding chapter aims to discuss some key aspects of each of these, drawing on both the analytic and normative resources of the 'social complexity' perspective outlined in this book. Before we characterise the cosmopolitan perspective any further and review some of its strengths and weaknesses (second section below), it is first useful to consider why sociologically oriented academics in the field of European studies could be argued to have become interested in it (first section). We then conclude by considering how the relevance of normative cosmopolitanism for the sociological understanding and critique of European society and the EU can be strengthened by drawing on normative aspects which can be referred to as the 'European civil complex' and interpreted as being implied by the 'European social complex' analytic perspective outlined in this book (third section below).

Enigmatic Europe: Public Attitudes and Academic Reflections

What makes cosmopolitanism appear to be a relevant perspective for understanding Europe and the EU? One response to this question might be to refer to the intrinsic merits of a perspective which is not yet part of the familiar discursive repertoire in European studies, and we will consider these merits and this response further in the following section. Another response might be to cite the contemporary political situation in relation to Europe, the troubled, uncertain and arguably enigmatic nature of public attitudes to the EU. In this context a cosmopolitan perspective can be seen as offering academics a way of intellectually reflecting the European enigma as well as reflecting upon it. We have reflected on enigmatic aspects of European society, its duality and complexity, throughout the discussion in this book. In this section we focus more on the idea that intellectualisation can be interpreted as reflecting as well as reflecting on its social conditions.

The political situation regarding the EU in the early 21st century, as we indicated in Chapters 1 and 2, has increasingly become one of crisis, and thus one of questioning and uncertainty, not only about the organisation's immediate future but also about its very *raison d'être* and nature. The EU's progress is stalled or risks stalling on a number of fronts simultaneously, particularly in terms of its capacity to reform its constitution and organisation, to justify and manage further enlargement, and to justify and implement its Lisbon socio-economic aspirations. European political leaderships struggle to understand or resolve the crises, and European publics exacerbate them by periodically withdrawing their interest, support and legitimacy, as in the cases of the initial Irish rejection of the Nice Treaty in 2001, the French and Dutch rejection of the proposed Constitutional Treaty in 2005, and the Irish rejection of the proposed Reform Treaty in 2008. Given that the EU requires that its treaties have unanimous support from the member states, such rejections operate as absolute vetoes and are potentially terminal for the particular policies they are concerned with.

The Nice Treaty (on which the strategically important 2004 enlargement depended) only survived because the Irish re-ran their referendum and happened to produce a majority in favour. The Constitutional Treaty failed and the outcome for the Reform Treaty (at least at the time of writing, summer 2008) is not positive. European publics have reflected the uncertainty about the EU which their votes have periodically helped to create in their ambiguous attitudes to the EU. The 2001 Irish rejection of Nice led the European Commission to comment that, in spite of the EU's significant political and economic achievements, 'Many people are losing confidence in [the] poorly understood and complex system [of the European Union] to deliver the policies that they want. The Union is often seen as remote and at the same time too intrusive.'[6] Since then cross-European public and political debate has been dominated by, among other things, the high-profile instances of public negativity to major EU initiatives indicated above. However, ironically, general attitudes towards the EU within the publics of its member states over the same period, particularly in the pre-2004 enlargement group of fifteen, appear to have remained largely positive, although that support has no doubt become increasingly instrumental, discriminating and volatile.[7]

In a period in which nations and their welfare states have become increasingly subject to influences from processes of economic globalisation, the EU's single market-building project can be perceived as a Trojan horse of global welfare-free neo-liberalism, as well as an attractor of barely controllable flows of EU and non-EU economic migrants. The uncertainty and volatility in public understandings and normative assessments of the EU project in general among majorities is no doubt connected with these sorts of perceptions and suspicions about some of the Europeanisation dynamics it has engendered. However, in some cases the same sort of perceptions and suspicions have led to a re-awakening, albeit among minorities, of the certainty and identity-claiming politics of nationalism, anti-Europeanism and xenophobia in some member states.[8] The general contemporary political situation surrounding the EU project in many member states, then, consists of a mix of, among other things, perceptions of EU institutional crisis, public uncertainty and volatility in relation to the EU project on the part of majorities, and the rise of ethno-nationalism and anti-Europeanism among minorities. These aspects of the contemporary situation have found resonances as well as responses in the academic contexts of European studies, including in the interest of the sociology and social theory of Europe and the EU in exploring the potential of a cosmopolitan normative and analytic perspective.[9]

When European political studies originally developed it was marked by a stark difference between intergovernmentalism and federalist theories and perspectives on European integration. These could be interpreted to represent more than academic differences about analytic understandings of reality. Such theories also offered political analysts opportunities to express and propose different normative visions of what Europe 'ought' to be, whether a loose association respecting and renewing the sovereignty of nationalism and nation-states or a supra-national regime decisively transcending nationalist moral principles and nation-state-level political organisation. Academics' engagement with the alternative analytic and normative perspectives of nationalist intergovernmentalism and federalism in the early post-war and Cold War contexts resonated with and arose from the particularities and problems of their political situation. There was a pressing need, recognised among western European publics, politicians and academics to rediscover and re-animate, or to re-invent, humane and liberal polities and political processes, beyond the reach of the left and right versions of authoritarianism which had so recently, in the inter-war fascist period and in the Second World War, helped to destroy the continent and which continued to threaten it.

Western Europe is now a generation or more further on and has experienced decades of relative peace and economic growth. Against this background in more recent years political studies of Europe, in implicit or explicit concert with sociological, social theoretical and other related studies, have begun to evolve more nuanced analytical perspectives. These often attempt to bridge the earlier more starkly dichotomous theories, to provide ways of reconciling, or at least linking, national-level perspectives with supra-national-level perspectives, and generally to substitute 'both/and' approaches (explicitly acknowledged to be equivocal) for 'either/or' approaches to Europe.[10] As with those earlier theories, the more recent views can also carry normative implications for value-based visions of the EU and its possibilities. Such visions attempt to reconcile (or at least link rather than see as mutually negating), on the one hand, aspects of nation-state society seen as normatively positive (e.g. the national institutionalisation of democracy and of citizens' rights) with, on the other hand, aspects of the EU seen as normatively positive (e.g. international cooperation and free movement across national borders).

Normative perspectives in European studies, which presented ethico-political interpretations of one or another wing of the earlier dichotomous analysis, always risked being proved irrelevant by history, and subsequently they have been. Nationalism may have become increasingly fashionable among publics, but, along with its opposite, supra-national federalism, it has faded back in use in the academic circles of social and political studies. Late 20th- and early 21st-century history has presented publics and academics alike with increasingly complex and sometimes enigmatic forms of inter-national and transnational connection in contemporary processes of Europeanisation and within the EU. Sociologists and social theorists in particular have attempted to recognise and understand this, and cosmopolitanism, to which we turn next, has appeared to offer useful intellectual resources for doing this.

Cosmopolitanism and Europe

As with many other sociologically-relevant perspectives, cosmopolitanism has a normative as well as an analytic aspect. The two aspects may well be inter-connected for many proponents of the perspective, nevertheless in principle they need to be distinguished. Our discussion aims to relate them to equivalent normative and analytic aspects of the 'social complex' perspective in relation to the study of Europe, so for this reason also they can be addressed separately in turn.

Normative aspects of the cosmopolitanism perspective

The idea that Europe ought to be a cosmopolitan society, and indeed that Europeans ought to see themselves as cosmopolitans, is an important normative conception which characterises much of the contemporary sociology and social theory of Europe and the EU. Normative cosmopolitanism, among other things, refers to perspectives which give a priority to moral and political universals over what, by comparison, appear as the moral and political particularities associated with perspectives such as communitarianism and nationalism. In earlier periods it was formulated in terms of such concepts as 'world citizenship' and expressed in terms of interests in internationalism in ideology and political practice.[11] In our period, in addition, it can be formulated in terms of the concept of human rights and expressed in terms of interests in the theory and practice of global governance.[12] However, in spite of its underlying universalism, normative cosmopolitanism, at least in sociology and social theory and related studies, has a somewhat ambiguous character in that it tends to be presented, and even conceived, as a critique of such things as moral and political universals. That is it tends to be presented through a positive valuation and openness to local and national differences, and by a critical attitude to the cultural standardisation and particularistic versions of universalism typically institutionalised in modern nationalism.[13]

An exception here is Fine's normative understanding of cosmopolitanism.[14] He focuses, as I do in this chapter, on what might be called 'negative cosmopolitanism' and in what is effectively a universalistic way. 'Negative utilitarianism' advocates the moral imperative to promote the minimisation of the greatest pain of the greatest number rather than the more familiar 'positive' (and arguably utopic) imperative to maximise the greatest happiness of the greatest number.[15] In my view, comparable with this (and perhaps analytically connectable with it), we can conceive a 'negative cosmopolitanism'. This is particularly relevant to understanding European society for reasons I discuss in the following section connected with Europe's deep traditions and potential for 'incivility'.

In the normative perspective of 'negative' or 'minimalistic' cosmopolitanism I am envisaging here, priority, both in theoretical and practical terms, needs to be assigned to the attempt to understand, address and ameliorate the causes and conditions of the denials of otherness, difference and peaceful coexistence involved in many kinds and levels of physically violent and abusive behaviour between people. This includes violence of the inter-state kind (war), of the inter- and intra-community kind (particularly that associated with xenophobia and 'racism'), and of the domestic kind (particularly that inflicted by males on women and children). The EU has aspired to play a role at each of these levels, and thus can be interpreted as developing and being guided by a particular version of negative or minimalistic normative cosmopolitanism.[16] This way of understanding cosmopolitanism provides for a degree of theoretical and practical clarity and focus which can too often be eschewed by more positive but also more ambiguous alternative versions.

What Fine refers to as the cosmopolitan 'outlook' (to differentiate it from a more ideological type of doctrine or '-ism') can be argued to exemplify a version of negative or minimalistic cosmopolitanism in that it particularly advocates the morality of promoting the minimisation of war and violence. This is seen to be a greater imperative than that associated with more familiar 'positive' (and arguably also utopic) cosmopolitan ideals about world society and citizenship. Fine does recognise that cosmopolitanism in our times needs to be understood as involving ambiguity and ambivalence. But this is not between universalism and localism within a positive understanding of cosmopolitanism. Rather, it is within the 'negative cosmopolitan' compass of the kinds of choices people, nations and humanity all too regularly face in relation to the realities and problems of global society in the 21st century. In extreme cases these can be between organising military force to intervene, pacify and police situations of war, genocide and mass violence, and trusting only to persuasive communication and diplomacy, eschewing the use of military force in such situations.

Ambiguity in the more conventional and positive normative cosmopolitan discourse about the value of universality as against particularity may derive from at least two sources. First, there is the need to grasp and accommodate important characteristics and contradictions of contemporary world society as it changes and develops. These include the reality of the historically deep and culturally valuable diversity of humanity's cultural and political traditions and the reality of globalisation, which can be argued to be promoting economic and cultural standardisation and thus in some respects concrete versions of universalism. In addition, there is the reality of the echoing absence (*pace* the contemporary UN and UNESCO) of a functioning world government which could be counted on to control economic globalisation, to defend human cultural diversity or generally to defend universal human rights.[17] Secondly, there is the intellectual persuasiveness of post-modern perspectives in epistemology, ontology and ethics, which value various types of difference and particularity over and above a range of 'ideological', 'essentialist' and otherwise allegedly fatally flawed 'grand narratives', including those of 'human identity' and of the moral universality typically connected with it.[18]

Normatively ambiguous cosmopolitanism, when applied to Europe, can be argued both to reflect and to reflect upon the enigmatic and uncertain character of the contemporary European social and political situation. Normative cosmopolitanism has been associated with an interest in and practice of internationalism (and an underlying interest in the promotion of politics and governance at a global level) and at the same time with a critical view of nation-states (as socio-cultural environments and in so far as they claim to standardise cultural identity and institutionalise universalistic-seeming rights and related concepts within those environments). As we have noted, the current period is one in which European publics' and politicians' criticisms of the EU have been growing, the EU's progress has been stalling and its future is becoming uncertain. The study of Europe is likely to reflect this as well as to reflect on it.

Normative cosmopolitanism, then, as interpreted here, appears to offer intellectual resources to the sociology and social theory of Europe and the EU. It can claim to help to develop and maintain the field's critical distance from, and normative critique of (the limitations of) Europeans' periodic capacities for excessive nationalism and also the EU project's recurrent capacities for excessive supra-national aspiration. Normative cosmopolitanism offers a discursive contextualisation and grasp of contemporary Europe and the EU, bridging from the perspective's conventional interpretation in terms of universalistic and global politics over to its sociological interpretation in terms of local and national cultural diversity. In spite of its ambiguities, the perspective offers particular support for the normative interpretation and critique of the EU as a potentially cosmopolitan form of society on two fronts simultaneously. On the one hand, on the internal front, a cosmopolitan perspective sensitises analysis to the possibility that, in spite of its policy rhetoric to the contrary, the EU has proved weak in defending intra-European national and cultural diversity in Europe. Rather, the Europeanisation and consumer cultural processes the EU has unleashed through its single market project can be argued to fundamentally undermine at least traditionalistic versions of diversity. On the other hand, on the external front, a cosmopolitan perspective sensitises analysis to the possibility that, although undoubtedly promising much, so far the EU cannot be said to have 'punched its weight' and achieved very much concretely in terms of the promotion of internationalism in global politics and the institutionalisation of global-level governance.[19]

Analytic aspects of the cosmopolitan perspective

However, perhaps it is more useful, from the viewpoint of the sociology of Europe and the EU, to regard cosmopolitanism as an analytic perspective with normative implications rather than as a fully-fledged normative perspective. Writers on cosmopolitanism refer as often to analytic conceptions, such as 'banal' and 'actually existing' forms of cosmopolitan, as to normative conceptions.[20] By the former, they refer to empirical and existential realities of cultural diversity and hybridity, and to processes of the change and adaptation of local factors to global forces. In addition, there is the presence in Europe's history and identity of various less than ideal but once definitely 'actually existing' forms of cosmopolitanism, in the morally highly problematic histories and heritages of European empires.[21] Arguably, to attempt to understand Europe sociologically is, among other things, to be willing to get to know and to engage with the 'actually existing' cosmopolitan realities and cross-continental reach of such culturally mixed and hybrid social phenomena as empires and their heritages, trading cities and their networks, religions, high cultures and popular cultures.

Analytic cosmopolitanism, like the social complexity perspective, guides sociological and social theoretical analysis in very different directions from the well-trodden paths mapped out in European academia under the pervasive influence of official and popular ideologies of nationalistic modernisation and its associated mythologisation of unmixed ('pure') ethnicities and monocultures. Rather, it guides sociology towards the study of Europe's pervasive social realities of mixture and hybridity, sometimes known about and intended, most often barely known about and/or unintended. These social realities and their ethical implications no doubt vary according to time and place, but they are extensive and comparable enough for us to be able to refer to them as constituting a 'condition' in European society.[22] Europe's analysable 'cosmopolitan condition(s)' can be seen as a set of situations of mixed but shared fate which underpin and motivate normative and ideological reflection and expression, conflict and debate (Roche 2007).

Cosmopolitanism may be a more helpful and heuristic concept when used in this mainly analytical but also normatively sensitive way rather than when used as if it constituted a ready-made, clear and coherent normative theory. As indicated earlier, it can be interpreted in both universalist and anti-universalist ways and is generally open to normative formulations and applications which can be ambiguous and thus potentially unreliable. In addition, in my view, it is a weakness that normative cosmopolitanism applied to Europe, as to any other field, tends to locate the field too vaguely and to argue too loosely between the moral 'micro' (the ideas and actions of individuals and groups) and the moral 'macro' (the 'cosmos', the world). Normative cosmopolitanism can ultimately appear relatively indifferent about its field of application, in this case the moral particularities, the moral achievements, disasters and lessons, of European history and society. To better engage with the European experience, in my view, the cosmopolitan perspective needs to be added to and strengthened, not least in terms of the concerns of what we have referred to as 'negative' or 'minimalistic' cosmopolitanism and reflection on the normative implications of 'the cosmopolitan condition'. In this way it might be better able to engage with Europe as a deep and distinct moral field and source of inspiration, and on this basis to promote a dialogue with the sociology and social theory of Europe and the EU. However, to guide and develop this engagement we need to reflect on the analytic relevance and normative implications of the 'social complexity' perspective on Europe, to which we now turn.

Civil Europe: Cosmopolitanism and the European Civil Complex

The discussions of European society in this book have touched on a number of normatively significant topics, such as citizenship, war and welfare, among other things, as well as analysing them as a set of social complexes. In my view, this kind of social complex analysis can be interpreted to bring with it normative implications which offer some focus and purchase to the application of analytic and normative cosmopolitan ideas to Europe. Some of the main implications are outlined in this section using the concepts of 'civil Europe' and 'the European civil complex' to refer to what is normatively distinct and valuable in Europe's experience and characteristics. First, 'civil Europe' is discussed with reference to 'European civilisation', together with its moral costs, and the more mundane civilisation of 'European civility and incivility'. This particularly refers to the civility of peaceful coexistence and Europe's struggle to achieve this. In each of these cases the fragility of civil Europe, the threats posed by European 'incivility' and the normative relevance, indeed priority, of this is emphasised. Secondly, we consider the idea of the 'European civil complex' and address two aspects of this. These correspond to two conceptual components in the analytical framework which was used to analyse the European social complex. On the one hand, and corresponding to the 'societal dimensions' (polity, economy and culture) component, there is the aspect of 'civil society'. On the other hand, and corresponding to the 'deep structures' (time, space, technology) component, there is the aspect of 'civil space'. It is suggested that cosmopolitan perspectives on Europe, in their analytic and normative aspects, can benefit from taking account of these kinds of social complex-based ideas.[23]

Normative aspects of the European complex: civilisation, civility, and incivility in Europe

European civilisation

Through the modern era Europeans have celebrated and publicised the normative values and 'civilisational' achievements of their continent to the rest of the world as well as to themselves. 'European civilisation' can be taken to refer to achievements institutionalised in the main societal dimensions of the European historical and social complex.

As we have seen in Part 2, the cultural achievements include those of such periods as classical Greece and Rome, medieval Christianity and Reformation Protestantism, the Renaissance and the Enlightenment, and their contribution to the promotion of the influence of knowledge and rationality in human affairs in Europe and more widely. The political and economic achievements include those of industrialisation and material 'progress' in the standards of living of mass publics, and of liberal and parliamentary democracy. The historical list of Europe's positive normative and civilisational achievements could evidently be extended, and they are real enough.

However, these achievements of 'European civilisation' have often tended to be viewed by Europeans, whether by elites or publics, through complacent, idealising or ideological Eurocentric distorting lenses. That is, as we also saw in Part 2, such mainstream interpretations of Europe by Europeans tend to simultaneously underplay two historical facts. First, there is the fact of the frequent major contributions made to Europe's normative and civilisational achievements from the non-European world (particularly from the Middle East and the Far East). Secondly, there is the fact of Europe's potential for incivility and barbarism. That is, over the course of history Europeans readily and recurrently used normatively negative means, including war, destruction and slavery, to accomplish their ends.

Modern Europe, the terrain of the 18th-century 'Enlightenment', was always a moral enigma. It developed, in the 19th and 20th centuries in particular, as we saw earlier, in Mazower's telling phrase, as 'the dark continent'.[24] Europe was characterised throughout the modern era, as we have seen in Part 2, by deep traditions and memories of the ethno-national and religiously-national war and violence associated with the building of warfare states and the export and reproduction of this in empire-building worldwide. The Second World War added to Europe's 'dark continent' experiences and memories, those of the modern barbarism of the 'democratisation' of death involved in 'total war' and genocide, particularly the Holocaust. These were fuelled by struggles within and between nationalist and communist ideological political movements promoting competing 'revolutionary' and utopian normative visions of the possible future of European society. In the shadow of these experiences and memories, the politics of post-war Western Europe (apart from occasional idealistic interludes, in particular the cultural politics of the 1960s) was marked more by pragmatic interests in social reconstruction, economic growth and the rebuilding of liberal democracies than any further adventures in utopianism.

As with its cultural civilisational achievements, Europe's political achievements in the recent and contemporary period are also real enough. Positive normative values, versions of such principles as freedom, justice, democracy, equality, and welfare have come to be embedded in the constitutions and institutions of polities and states across Europe in the post-war period. However, evidently institutionally embedding these principles is not the same as implementing them. As we saw in relation to welfare in Part 3, it would be complacent and mistaken to assume that the values they proclaim actually structure and pervade most contemporary Europeans' everyday lives. They remain normative ideals which Europeans need to stay ever vigilant about both in historical reflection, and also in the democratic practices involved in both the critique of contemporary social realities and the promotion of social change and political reform.

European civility and incivility

Europe's post-war political leaderships, supported by their publics, have attempted to learn lessons from the history of European capacities for barbarism and incivility. By means of various international organisations, but principally by means of the EU, European governments have attempted as far as possible to construct conditions of peaceful coexistence among the continent's nation-states as well as among it stateless nations, religions and ethnic groups. In this project, the EU, its member states and its allied organisations could be argued to have been largely successful. The dark continent's ancient and modern propensities towards violence and war appear to have been 'civilised'. But then there are the 'exceptions which prove the rule', or which, more accurately, prove the essential fragility of the rule. The list of exceptions is not insubstantial, and it continues to be added to in the 21st century. It includes the flourishing of violent national liberation movements in Northern Ireland and the Basque lands from the 1960s (and now we should probably add in the Kurd lands of eastern Turkey and arguably also in the breakaway provinces of Georgia), the post-communist Balkan wars of the 1990s, and contemporary international Islamist terrorist threats across Europe. It also includes the vulnerability of ex-Soviet bloc European border-land and 'neighbourhood' states, particularly Ukraine and Georgia but also including EU Baltic states, to intimidation and even invasion by a militarily resurgent Russian Federation claiming its place in the new 21st-century multipolar world order.[25]

It is clear that in contemporary Europe, the mundane form of European civilisation expressed in the civility of peaceful coexistence, in these and other social contexts, remains a fragile and vulnerable achievement. However, it remains, both sociologically and normatively, a fundamental precondition for the more sophisticated aspects of life in societies and polities normatively committed to values of freedom and democracy and the promotion of equality and welfare. The reproduction of these civil conditions can be too easily taken for granted. They require as much recognition, vigilance, conservation and resource as do the higher profile values and practices of freedom, democracy, equality and welfare.

The European civil complex: civil institutions and civil space

So far we have considered some normatively relevant 'civil' aspects of European history and society, and we have also recognised the social reality of their fragility and of the traditions of European incivility by which they have been recurrently threatened and periodically overwhelmed. These observations prefigure and illustrate the normative perspective that, arguably, is implied in the sociological and analytic perspectives developed in this book, which view Europe as a social complex and, relatedly, as a particular version of the contemporary cosmopolitan condition. This normative perspective can be referred to as one which sees Europe as a 'civil complex', and in this section we will explore it further.

The realities and contradictions of European civility and incivility noted in the previous section, can be understood from a normative perspective as offering, or better reminding, contemporary Europeans of versions of what people ought to value and seek to promote, both within and also outside Europe. Arguably, the cross-European commonalities and agreements are stronger and the issues more practically pressing on normatively negative aspects than on positive aspects. So perhaps, more importantly than the normatively positive aspects, these realities and contradictions can also be understood as reminding Europeans of versions of what people ought to reject and seek to prevent, again both within but also outside Europe. The concept of Europe as a 'civil complex' provides a way of referring to this kind of normative perspective, and identifying it in a sociologically recognisable way.

The sociological conceptual framework used to discuss the European social complex throughout this book involved analysing the complex at at least two levels – that of the social dimensions of polity, economy and culture, and that of the deep structures of social time, space and technology, which in some respects can be understood as contextualising and embedding dimensional institutions and their configurations. Relatedly, then, the European civil complex can be understood as consisting of normatively valued and valuable elements at each level, namely the sphere of European 'civil society' at the dimensional and institutional level, the sphere of European 'civil space' at the deep structural level, with the latter in some respects providing a context for the former. The European civil complex, understood particularly in terms of its two main spheres and their relationship, should be understood as providing contexts for the theory and practice of citizenship, that is for people's everyday struggles to construct personal and group identities, to recognise responsibilities and to claim rights in Europe. We can now briefly consider what might be involved in the sphere of civil institutions and the sphere of civil space.

The European civil complex 1: civil society

Any normative perspective on Europe must involve a positive valuation of Europe's distinct experiences and struggles for people's rights and freedoms, which are summarised in the histories of such things as the development of citizenship and democratic nation-state-building in Europe.[26] At the core of such developments and valuations have been Europeans' experience and valuation of 'civil society'. We have noted the socio-political importance of this version and aspect of European societies at a number of points in this book. These include its significance in relation to the history of European political communities in Part 2, the understanding the modern European welfare complex in Part 3, and the EU as a contemporary policy complex in Chapters 2 and 8.

For the purposes of this discussion, civil society can be taken to refer to the field of relatively free interaction, communication and association which exists in modern forms of society and particularly in the links and interstices between the key institutions of the main societal dimensions, namely, the state, the market and the family. Analytically and normatively, civil society can be understood as referring to a range of types of social field. On the one hand, types of civil society can be differentiated in terms of the greater or lesser degree of overlap, and the cooperation and/or conflict they have, with their societal and institutional environment. On the other hand, they can be differentiated in terms of the degree to which they are themselves organised and reproduced through their own institutions. The growth of civil society, initially among the middle class and increasingly among the working class, was central to western European societies' experiences of the modernisation process as being normatively 'progressive', and remains central to their self-definition as being relatively free societies. In recent decades the reanimation of civil society, and political and cultural movements and network-building it involved, was central in Eastern Europe to the undermining of authoritarian communism from within and to their transition to freer post-communist societies.

The European civil complex, then, can be understood, at the very least, as the aggregate of European states' national civil societies, which, in their national societal environments, operate at levels which range from the community and urban level though the regional to the national level. In addition, there are the vertical and horizontal civil society networks reaching beyond national social environments, which the fact of the growth of the EU as a policy complex has helped to stimulate (Part 1). The European civil society complex in this aspect includes networks in a great range of fields.[27] They link intra-national and inter-national levels both 'horizontally' (for example in interest associations), and also 'vertically' (as lobbies and feedback circuits linked to EU decision-making and regulatory power centres).

The European civil complex 2: civil space

The European civil complex's civil society networks can be understood as themselves constituting a version of European social space, and also from a deep structural and related normative perspective as being grounded in what can be referred to as 'European civil space'. This aspect of the European civil complex as a normative perspective refers to the valued and valuable aspects of European commonalities in the interconnected deep structures of social space, time and technology. In turn, and in line with the notion of 'negative' or 'minimalistic' cosmopolitanism outlined earlier, a core element within the normative idea of European civil space is the principle of valuing and promoting the experience and practice of peaceful coexistence.

The principle of peaceful coexistence involves moral agents in the toleration of the actual or potential embodied co-presence of non-threatening others and of their participation in a sharable world. Equally, if not more importantly in terms of the practice of the principle, is its negative corollary, namely the prohibition for moral agents of the incivilities involved in either the coercive exclusion of others from participation in a sharable world or, worse, the infliction on them of violence, injury or death. The principles have their most visible application to Europe's nation-states and to international relations within and in the neighbourhood of its world region, here prohibiting and seeking to prevent war and violent conflict. But they can also be usefully applied to the prohibition and prevention of violence among Europe's stateless nations and regions, its ethnic and religious minorities, and its migrants and diasporas. Further, the principle can be usefully extended, individualised and universalised to apply to all of Europe's people, whether citizens or 'denizens', in the context of their everyday efforts to build lives and identities in the often fragmented, effectively segregated and physically threatening conditions which are all too common features in contemporary European cities.

The considerable and ongoing normative and political significance of these principles of peaceful coexistence can all too often be taken for granted or underplayed in the political and sociological study of Europe and the EU, including in cosmopolitan perspectives. For instance, it is commonly observed about the EU and its early post-war precursor organisations that they were originally significantly driven by the goal of organising peaceful coexistence initially between the nations of western Europe. In such observations it may be conceded that the EEC/EU succeeded in substantially contributing to bringing a very long history of war and conflict to what now appears to be an end. Such views can, nonetheless, present this achievement as if this only was a matter of fading historical significance and of little relevance in the 21st century. Or again, contemporary critical perspectives on the EU can regard some of its current policy aspirations relevant to the goal of peaceful coexistence to be unnecessary or little more than rhetoric. Such aspirations include the EU's goal of creating a cross-European 'area of freedom, security and justice', its crisis-ridden efforts to promote cross-European human and citizens' rights in its constitutional project, and its efforts to create more resourced and dynamic policy profiles in the fields of defence and foreign affairs. They also include the EU's efforts to combat racism and xenophobia and to create a common immigration policy for asylum-seekers and migrants.[28]

Earlier we noted the depth of Europe's traditions of incivility and the fragility of its contemporary achievements in the field of civility. This suggests that these EU policies, in connection with the activities of European civil society in areas such as these, need to be more clearly recognised and given a more explicit and higher ethical and political priority than they have been hitherto in both sociological and normative perspectives on Europe. The civil complex and civil space approach to developing a normative perspective does not require unrealistic assumptions to be made about European nations or individuals sharing some set of common European values (never mind about some mythical underlying common European identity[29]). Nor, unlike 'public sphere'-based approaches to the analysis and assessment of contemporary European society and its politics and culture, does it require too much to be assumed about European individuals' interests in and capacities for elaborated and rationalistic discursive communication and for cooperation and decision-making based on this.[30] Rather, in relation to individuals, the principle ethically prioritises the achievement and maintenance of a peaceful sharing of embodied social space and time. This is consistent with practices which might require only minimal communication and the kind of tolerance represented by mutual indifference. Nevertheless it can be held to reproduce mundane forms of civility and to provide a base of solidaristic experiences which might be understood to provide some degree of security against at least the farther reaches of incivility.

The analytic sociology of Europe and its research effort could reasonably be guided by aspects of this normative perspective, which is in line with the negative or minimalistic cosmopolitan perspective outlined earlier. This suggests that we need to know more about, as well as to value more, everyday forms of life in Europe involving routine co-presence and mundane forms of civility in the 'actually existing' versions of cosmopolitanism which characterise individualised and culturally fragmented populations, particularly in cities. These include those involved in life in local city neighbourhoods, the use of public transport, everyday consumption practices, and participation in public cultural fields such as those of leisure, tourism and sport. They also include sharable public and popular events and event calendars, whether of a political, commemorative, festive or sporting kind, and the reconstruction and evolution of such calendars either within European nations (in order to reflect their multinational, multi-ethnic or multi-religious composition) or beyond the level of the nation and at an international, European or EU level.[31] In political and policy terms, at each of these levels the normative perspective based around the idea of European civil space suggests a new priority for actions and strategies, particularly in the EU oriented to 'Civil Europe', to monitor and prevent or minimise incivility, and to actively conserve and promote mundane civility. Such actions and strategies would need to be sociologically imaginative in addressing the interpersonal practices, popular cultural forms and social conditions of civility and incivility in contemporary Europe.

For reasons of space, the discussion of the European civil complex and its analytic and normative relevance to the development of the sociology of Europe's interests and agendas, as sketched here, has been angled to highlight the 'internal' (intra-European) aspect rather than the 'external' (global context) aspect. A final word is needed on this latter aspect. The sociology of Europe in principle could expect to contribute to the broader sociology and social theory of globalisation and global society. However, for it to make progress on this front, in my view, work would need to elaborate on the kind of multi-polar world-order analysis noted in Chapters 3 or 4. Interpreted in an externalist outward-looking way, the notions of civil society and civil space implied by the European social complex, understood in normative terms, involve principles of hospitality and welfare. On the one hand, the principle of hospitality[32] would be needed to normatively guide the field's studies of migrants, border-crossers and incomers of various kinds. Prominent on the agenda here are studies of intra-EU economic migrants and, in this context in particular, of non-EU economic migrants and asylum-seekers. However, the agenda also includes other potential 'incomer' cases, such as those of aspirant EU member states, in particular Turkey, but also (given the evolving geopolitical situation in Europe's 'neighbourhood') those of Ukraine and Georgia. On the other hand, there is the principle of welfare, and of the importance of a welfare model in European politics and policy-making, which we have discussed in Part 3. This will continue to be an important element in sociological and social sciences research agenda in relation to the future of Europe understood in terms of its internalist aspect. However, this principle, and the area it indicates, also needs to be understood in terms of Europe's external aspect. That is, it is likely that Europe's increasing differentiation from but also integration within the globalising economy raises perspectives and issues for Europeans of the welfare, employment and income problems of non-Europeans, particularly in the developing world. Europe's social model, both analytically and normatively, will increasingly demand to be interpreted in terms of human rights and needs and in terms of Europeans' ('negative') cosmopolitan and internationalist responsibilities in relation to global welfare.[33]

For Hegel, philosophy (here sociology) always comes too late for the world – the owl of Minerva only flies when 'life has grown old', and when night and the dark approaches.[34] The contemporary version of the European social complex is uncertain, unsettled and in the process of formation. At the heart of it the EU, the 'unidentified flying object' too often appears to be flying in the dark. It needs whatever light it can get, from new as well from old forms of inquiry.

In the 21st century humanity and its societies, including Europe and its social complex, will be increasingly shaped by a range of global-level factors and changes. No doubt these will include humanity's responses to the century's pressing global ecological crisis, together with the continued development of the increasingly all-pervasive media-sphere, particularly the internet. In addition, these factors are likely to include further developments in globalisation, now structured by the resurgence of the historic and civilisation-scale societies of China and India, and by the emergence and consolidation of a multi-polar geopolitical world order involving them as poles. Europe may become another pole in this world. Along with the other social sciences and humanities, the discipline of sociology will increasingly attempt to engage with and make sense of such factors, together with their influences not only at the global level but at all relevant levels below, including those of the world region and the nation. Hopefully, the sociology of Europe and the EU, as a new and developing field, will come to be an established part of these efforts. The self-understanding not only of Europe but of each of Europe's national societies can only benefit from such an exercise of the sociological imagination.

Notes

1   For other relevant studies in the sociology of Europe, see Chapter 1 note 1, and Chapters 1 and 2 *passim*; also studies in Rumford 2009. In this context it is worth noting the relatively recent institutionalisation if not of the Sociology of Europe, then at least of the professional community of European sociologists and their disciplinary project in the form of the European Sociological Association (created in 1992) and also of relevant journals (e.g. the *European Journal of Social Theory*, created in 1998).

2   Also see Roudemetof and Haller 2007. Public attitudes and opinions are formed in contexts analysable as 'public spheres' (Habermas 1989; Calhoun 1992) which are traditionally organised almost exclusively at nation-state level and studied by sociologists and others on a 'methodological nationalist' basis at that level. However, the slow and patchy development of a mass communications environment, elements of which can be interpreted as contributing to the emergence of a 'European public sphere', has been an additional and notable topic of study in the embryonic sociology of Europe in recent years (see Chapter 2, note 21).

3   See Fligstein 2008, p.8, all other quotes in this para are from p.9. For various interpretations of the complexity theme in sociological analysis, see Chapter 1, note 20; for my interpretation see Chapters 1 and 2.

4   Generally see Sandholz and Stonesweet 1998; and Schneider and Aspinwall 2001; on Europeanisation in the tecommunications and media sector, see Harcourt 2002, 2003; and in the sport sector, see King 2001; Milward 2006; Millward and Levermore 2007; and Roche 2007.

5   In Chapter 2, the concepts of network and (neo)empire were discussed as potentially useful models for analysing the nature and dynamics of the European complex. In terms of our interest in the normative and analytic aspects of cosmopolitanism in this chapter, these models can be interpreted in terms of their normative cosmopolitan implications, for instance see Beck and Grande 2007, Chapters 3 and 8. On analytic and normative cosmopolitanism in social theory and sociology, typically with some explicit concern for its relevance for understanding European society, see Baban and Keyman 2008; Beck 2006; Beck and Grande 2007; Boon and Delanty 2007; Calhoun 2002; Delanty and He 2008; Fine 2003, 2006; Habermas 2001; Roche 2007; Rumford 2007; Schlesinger 2007; Stevenson 2007; van der Veer 2002; and Vertovec and Cohen 2002. On cosmopolitanism in general terms and in varied applications, see Cheah and Robbins 1998; Harvey 2000; Held 1995, 2002, 2003; Kaldor 2002; Keane 2003, pp.92–128; Mouffe 2005; and Nussbaum 1994.

6   See EC 2001, p.3, my inserts.

7   See Eurobarometer 2008, tables in Chapters 2 and 3.

8   On the contemporary development of right-wing and populist nationalism and its attractions for elements of Europe's working class, see Oesch 2008; and on contemporary problems of racism and xenophobia in Europe, see European Agency 2007. Relevant contemporary political sociological background is reviewed in Fligstein 2008, Chapter 7; and relevant historical political and sociological context is reviewed in Chapters 4 and 5 above. Cultural factors connected with the construction and defence of national identity figured prominently in the historical review, and Oesch's study indicates that contemporary versions of these

factors are particularly significant in helping to explain current support for right-wing parties across Europe.

9   See note 5 above.

10 For instance, see Beck and Grande 2007, pp.29–30; on the need to move from what they call a 'logic of unequivocalness' to a 'logic of equivocalness'.

11 Kant 1967 (originally published 1784–95); also Marx and 19th-century socialism; and see references in Roche 2007. Durkheim lectured on 'Patriotism and Cosmopolitanism' at the 1900 Paris Expo. He later took the view that: 'Doubtless, we have towards the country in its present form, ... obligations that we do not have the right to cast off. But beyond this country, there is another in the process of formation, enveloping our national country: that of Europe, or humanity.' (Quoted in Lukes 1975, p.350.)

12 See Held 1995 and 2004.

13 See Delanty and Rumford 2005; and Rumford 2007 (Introduction); also generally see note 5 above.

14 See, for instance, Fine 2003 and 2006; also Kaldor 2002.

15 A negative utilitarian approach to ethics and politics has attracted support from various quarters, notably including that from the critical rationalist perspective of the philosopher of science Karl Popper. See, for instance, Popper 1962, Vol. 1, Chapter 5.

16 In terms of international peace-keeping, and more broadly the promotion of peaceful coexistence and cooperation between nations and world regions, see, for instance, McCormick 2007; and Telo 2007. In terms of monitoring and attempting to counter xenophobia and 'racism' see, for instance, the European Agency 2007. (On these problems see Modood and Werbner 1997; and Wrench and Solomos 1993.) In terms of recognising and countering domestic violence see, for instance, Euronet 2005; and EC 2005e.

17 For alternative discussions and ideals of global governance influenced by conceptions of cosmopolitanism, see Held 1995, 2004; and Keane 2003.

18 On 'post-modernism' see, for instance, Lyotard's seminal discussion (Lyotard 1991) and Harvey's critical analysis (Harvey 1989). On debates around universalistic and localist interpretations of cosmopolitan views, see Nussbaum 1994; and Harvey 2000; Cheah and Robbins 1998 on 'cosmopolitics'; and also Boon and Delanty 2007; and Jones 2007.

19 On the promise of the EU and its 'soft' or 'civilian' power in international/global politics and governance see, for instance, McCormick 2007; Rifkin 2004; and Telo 2007.

20 See Beck and Grande 2007; and Calhoun 2002.

21 On this, see Roche 2007; also Stevenson 2007; and van der Veer 2002.

22 For comparable types of use of the notion of 'condition', see Harvey 1989; and van Steenbergen 1994; also relatedly Lyotard 1991.

23 The earlier outline of the normative perspective of negative cosmopolitanism needs to be seen in relation to the discussion of a normative conception of Europe as a civil complex in this section. It is also relevant to mention that the discussion in this section derives from my general normative perspective, in its connection with sociological analysis. This was outlined in a previous study of citizenship (see Roche 1996, particularly Chapter 9, also Roche 2002, and related items listed in the References). It was developed further in relation to the analysis of Europe in Roche (1997) and in my contribution to Roche and Annesley (2004) (particularly Chapter 1).

24 Mazower 1998; also Mann 2005; and see Chapter 5 earlier.

25 On the concept of a multi-polar world order, see Chapter 1, Chapter 2 (notes 35 and 36), and Chapter 7 (notes 11–15). In relation to Russia's contemporary aspirations to be a pole in this order, it is relevant to note the range and scale of the threats it made to ex-USSR and Eastern bloc countries Estonia and Poland (now EU states) and Ukraine and Georgia (potential candidates for EU accession) in the course of the single year of 2008. It is also relevant to note its membership of the Shanghai Cooperation Organisation, formed in 2001, which links Russia with China and also with a number of post-communist central Asian countries and involves cooperation in terms of border control and in some military and security matters.

26 In Chapters 4 and 6 we reviewed aspects of the history of 'civil society' and citizenship in Europe from early modernity through to the contemporary period. In Chapter 5 we also reviewed aspects of the history of 'incivility' in Europe in the form of war and xenophobic attitudes in terms of religion and the secular religion of nationalism and their connections. On civil society in general terms, see Cohen and Arato 1997; Keane 1998, 2003; and on the related concept of 'the civil sphere', see Alexander 2006. On civil society in relation to Europe in general, see Janoski 1998; also Eder and Giesen 2001; Outhwaite 2006b; and Smismans 2003. And in relation to East European post-communist societies, see Chapter 6, note 27, also note 15. On the related concepts of national citizenship, see Chapter 6, note 1, and EU citizenship see Chapter 8, note 38. Although it contains little recognition of the ongoing dialectic of civility and incivility in the European experience through to the contemporary period, Elias's concept of 'the civilising process' points to some of the long-term historical conditions underlying the emergence and insitutionalisation of civil society and civility (such as they are) in European society (Elias 1983, 2000; also Fulbrook 2007).

27 On networks, see EC 2001; and Fligstein 2008; also Chapter 2 on network spaces in relation to urban and infrastructural, media and policy discursive versions of European networks.

28 The concept of civil space is a significant one in contemporary EU policy and discourse. It had its origins in the mid-1990s' policy work, which built the principle of anti-discrimination and human rights into the purpose and structure of the EU through the Amsterdam Treaty 1997 (implemented in 1999). See, for instance, EC (1996b) on the project to develop the EU as a sphere of 'civic and social rights'. The civic aspect of the project was pursued by means of the 2004 Hague programme for the 2005–10 period. This aimed to promote the EU as an 'area of freedom, security and justice' and involved the implementation of a number of objectives relating to these fields. Progress on these objectives is monitored annually (see, for instance, EC 2008b). One key area in terms of the civil values of citizenship and cosmopolitanism in Europe is that of the effort to identify and combat racism and xenophobia. For a report on the limited progress being made in this area, see the European Agency 2007.

29 For EU-oriented discourses on the concept of European identity, see Michalski 2006; and Biedenkopf et al. 2004. For questioning and critical discussions of the concept from sociological or related perspectives, see Balibar 2004; Checkel and Katzenstein 2008; Garcia 1993a, 1993b, 1997; Moxon-Browne 2004a; Schlesinger 2003; Shore 2000; and Strath 2002. For social theoretic perspectives on the relation between identity and social space, particularly that of

Europe, see Beck and Grande 2007, Chapter 4; and Delanty and Rumford 2005, Chapter 7; also generally Chapter 2, note 21.

30   On the public sphere in these communicative and rationalistic terms, see Habermas 1989, 1992; and Calhoun 1992; also, relatedly, see the discussion of the 'civil sphere' in Alexander 2006. For studies of the European public sphere, see Chapter 2, note 21.

31   'Actually existing' versions of the negative cosmopolitanism of physical co-presence and peaceful coexistence are core elements both in the experience of popular cultural forms and event, whether performative or spectatorial, and also in the strategies of the 'cultural industries' which produce and serve them. For instance, on the general history and continuing social significance of festival culture mainly in Europe, see Ehrenreich 2007. For studies and interpretations of festivals in Europe and elsewhere in the context of the contemporary period's touristically-oriented version of cosmopolitanism, see Picard and Robinson 2006. On cultural events and their strategic sociological and political role in structuring national and international public culture in Europe in the modern period, see Roche 2000b, 2003, 2006a.

32   On the ethics of hospitality, see Silverstone 2007; and Kant 1967. These ethics call for a sociologically aware interpretation in the socio-spatial terms of places, boundaries and movements, and in the 'banal' cosmopolitan terms of the co-presence of others and differences, including mediated versions of each of these things. A corollary of this, protecting the privacy of people in situations of co-presence, including mediated versions, is the principle of 'proper distance', which is also interpretable in socio-spatial and cosmopolitan terms (see discussion in Wessels 2009c). This set of principles potentially informs a normative version and vision of a 'civil Europe'. This chapter suggests that social research into contemporary European society and the European complex needs to take account of this vision.

33   On these issues, see Doyal and Gough 1991; Deacon et al. 1997; and Turner 2006; also in cosmopolitan terms, see Beck and Grande 2007.

34   Hegel 1942, p.13.

BIBLIOGRAPHY AND REFERENCES

This list mainly contains items cited either in the main text or Endnotes. It also contains some items relevant as resources in the writing of the book but which are not cited in it.

Abrahamson, P. (2000) 'The welfare modelling business', ch.4 in Manning and Shaw (eds) (2000a).

Abu-Lughod, J. (1989) *Before European Hegemony: The World System AD 1250–1350*. Oxford: Oxford University Press.

Addonino Report (see EC 1985).

Adelantado, J. and Calderon, E. (2007) 'Globalisation and the welfare state: the same strategies for similar problems?', *Journal of European Social Policy*, 16 (4): 374–386.

Aho Report (see EC 2006a).

Aiginger, K. (2005) 'Towards a new European model of a reformed welfare state', ch.7 in *United Nations Economic Survey of Europe*, 1. UN Economic Commission for Europe (UNECE), Geneva.

Alber, J. and Standing, G. (2000) 'Social dumping, catch-up or convergence? Europe in a global context', *The Journal of European Social Policy*, 10 (2): 99–119.

Albrow, M. (1999) *The Global Age*. Cambridge: Polity Press.

Alexander, J. (2006) *The Civil Sphere*. Oxford: Oxford University Press.

Ambler, J. (ed.) (1991) *The French Welfare State*. New York: New York University Press.

Amin, S. (1989) *Eurocentrism*. London: Zed Books.

Anderson, B. (1991) *Imagined Communities*. London: Verso.

Anderson, K. (2009) 'The Church as nation? The role of religion in the development of the Swedish welfare state', ch.8 in van Keesbergen and Manow (eds) (2009) (forthcoming).

Anderson, P. (1979) *Lineages of the Absolutist State*. London: New Left Books.

Anderson, P. and Weymouth, A. (1999) *Insulting the Public? The British Press and the European Union*. London: Longman.

Andreski, S. (1968) *Military Organization and Society*. London: Routledge.

Annesley, C. (2007) 'Lisbon and social Europe: towards a European "adult worker model" welfare system', *Journal of European Social Policy*, 17 (3): 195–205.

Ansell, C. (2000) 'The networked polity: regional development in Western Europe', *Governance: An International Journal of Policy and Administration*, 13 (3): 303–333.

Archer, C. (2004) 'The European Union as a international political actor', ch.16 in Nugent (ed.) (2004).

Archer, C. (2008) *The European Union*. London: Routledge.

Archibugi, D. and Coco, A. (2005) 'Is Europe becoming the most dynamic knowledge economy in the the world?', *Journal of Common Market Studies*, 43 (3): 433–459.

Armstrong, J. (1982) *Nations before Nationalism*. Chapel Hill, NC: University of North Carolina Press.

Arnaud, J. (2006) *Independent European Sport Review* (initiated by the EU, European Council), www.independentfootballreview.com (accessed on xx/xx/2008).

Aron, R. (1968) *Peace and War: A Theory of International Relations*. London: Weidenfeld and Nicolson.

Arts, W. and Gelissen, J. (2002) 'Three worlds of welfare capitalism or more? A state-of-the-art report', *Journal of European Social Policy*, 12 (2): 137–158.

Atkinson, T. (2002) 'Social inclusion in the European Union', *Journal of Common Market Studies*, 40 (5): 625–644.

Axford, B. (2006) 'The dialectic of borders and networks in Europe: reviewing "topological presuppositions"', *Comparative European Politics*, 4: 160–182.

Axford, B. and Huggins, R. (1999) 'Towards a post-national polity: the emergence of the network society in Europe', in Smith, D. and Wright, S. (eds), *Whose Europe? The Turn Towards Democracy*. Oxford: The Sociological Review/Blackwell.

Axford, B. and Huggins, R. (2007) 'The European information society: a new public sphere?', ch.7 in Rumford (ed.) (2007).

Axtmann, R. (ed.) (1998) *Globalisation and Europe*. London: Pinter.

Baban, F. and Keyman, F. (2008) 'Turkey and postnational Europe: challenges for the cosmopolitan political community', *European Journal of Social Theory*, 11 (1): 107–124.

Bache, I. (2005) 'Multi-Level governance and European Union regional policy', ch.10 in Bache and Flinders (eds) (2005).

Bache, I. and Flinders, M. (eds) (2005) *Multi-level Governance*. Oxford: Oxford University Press.

Baldock, J. (2000) 'Culture: the missing variable in understanding social policy?', ch.8 in Manning and Shaw (eds) (2000a).

Baldwin, P. (1990) *The Politics of Social Solidarity: Class Bases of the European Welfare States 1875–1975*. Cambridge: Cambridge University Press.

Balibar, E. (1998) 'The borders of Europe', pp. 216–232 in Cheah and Robbins (eds) (1998).

Balibar, E. (2004) *We, the People of Europe: Reflections on Transnational Citizenship*. Princeton, NJ: Princeton University Press.

Bambra, C. (2004) 'The worlds of welfare: illusory and gender blind?', *Social Policy and Society*, 3: 201–211.

Bambra, C. (2005) 'Worlds of welfare and the health care discrepancy', *Social Policy and Society*, 4: 31–41.

Bambra, C. (2006) 'Decommodification and the worlds of welfare revisited', *Journal of European Social Policy*, 16 (1): 73–80.

Barbalet, J. (1988) *Citizenship: Rights, Struggle and Class Inequality*. Milton Keynes: Open University Press.

Barenholdt, J. and Simonsen, K. (2004) *Space Odysseys: Spatiality and Social Relations in the Twenty-first Century*. Aldershot: Ashgate.

Barney, D. (2004) *The Network Society*. Cambridge: Polity Press.

Barroso, J.M. (2006a) 'Moving up a gear for growth and jobs: progress on implementing the new Lisbon strategy', SPEECH/06/569. European Commission, Brussels.

Barroso, J.M. (2006b) 'You don't have to love Europe, but do you want to lead or be dragged along?' Hugo Young Lecture, edited version, 18 October 2006. London: The Guardian newspaper.

Bartlett, R. (1994) *The Making of Europe: Conquest, Colonization and Cultural Change 950–1350*. London: Penguin.

Barysch, K. (2005) *Embracing the Dragon: The EU's Partnership with China*. London: Centre for European Reform.

Barysch, K. (2006) 'East v. West? The European economic and social model after Enlargement', ch.3 in Giddens et al. (eds) (2006).

Barysch, K., Tilford, S. and Whyte, P. (2008) *The Lisbon Scorecard VIII*. London: Centre for European Reform.

Bauman, Z. (1998) *Globalisation: The Human Consequences*. Cambridge: Polity Press.

Bauman, Z. (2000) *Liquid Modernity*. Cambridge: Polity Press.

Bauman, Z. (2004) *Europe: An Unfinished Adventure*. Cambridge: Polity Press.

Bay, A. H. and Pedersen, A. (2006) 'The limits of solidarity: minimum income, immigration and welfare', *Acta Sociologica*, 49 (4): 419–436.

Baylis, J. and Smith, S. (eds) (2008) *The Globalisation of World Politic* (4th edn). Oxford: Oxford University Press.

Bayly, C. (2004) *The Birth of the Modern World 1780–1914: Global Connections and Comparisons*. Oxford: Blackwell.

Beck, U. (1992) *Risk Society: Towards a New Modernity*. London: Sage.

Beck, U. (2000) *What is Globalization?* Cambridge: Polity Press.

Beck, U. (2006) *Cosmopolitan Vision*. Cambridge: Polity Press.

Beck, U. and Grande, E. (2007) *Cosmopolitan Europe*. Cambridge: Polity Press.

Beck, W., Maessen, L. and Walker, A. (eds) (1997) *Social Quality in Europe*. The Hague: Kluwer Law International.

Begg, I., Draxler, J. and Mortensen, J. (2008) *Is Social Europe Fit for Globalisation?* Brussels: European Commission (DG Employment).

Bell, D. (1973) *The Coming of Post-Industrial Society*. New York: Basic Books.

Bellamy, R. and Warleigh, A. (eds) (2001) *Citizenship and Governance in the European Union*. London: Continuum.

Bellier, I. and Wilson, T. (eds) (2000) *The Anthropology of the European Union*. Oxford: Berg.

Bendix, R. (1964) *Nation-Building and Citizenship*. New York: John Wiley.

Benkler, Y. (2006) *The Wealth of Networks: How Social Production Transforms Markets and Freedom*. New Haven, CT: Yale University Press.

Benko, G. and Strohmayer, U. (eds) (1997) *Space and Social Theory: Interpreting Modernity and Postmodernity*. London: Blackwell.

Bertola, G., Boeri, T. and Nicoetti, G. (2001) *Welfare and Employment in a United Europe*. Cambridge, MA: MIT Press.

Biedenkopf, K., Geremek, B. and Michalski, K. (2004) *The Spiritual and Cultural Dimension of Europe*. Vienna/Brussels: Institute for Human Sciences/European Commission.

Blaut, J. (2000) *Eight Eurocentric Historians* New York: Guilford Press.

Bloom, J. and Blair, S. (2001) *Islam: The Empire of Faith*. London: BBC Books.

Bobbitt, P. (2002) *The Shield of Achilles: War, Peace and the Course of History*. London: Penguin.

Bode, I. (2006) 'Disorganized welfare mixes: voluntary agencies and new governance regimes in Western Europe', *Journal of European Social Policy*, 16 (4): 353–359.

Bondeberg, I. and Golding, P. (eds) (2004) *European Culture and the Media*. Portland, OR: Intellect Books.

Boon, V. and Delanty, G. (2007) 'Cosmopolitanism and Europe: Historical Considerations and Contemporary Applications', Chapter 2 in C. Rumford (ed.) (2007) *Europe and Cosmopolitanism*. Liverpool: Liverpool University Press.

Borneman, J. and Fowler, N. (1997) 'Europeanization', *Annual Review of Anthropology*, 26: 487–514.

Bosco, A. and Chassard, Y. (1999) 'A shift in the paradigm: surveying the European Union discourse on welfare and work', in Heikkila (ed.) (1999).

Braudel, F. (1993) *A History of Civilizations*. London: Penguin.

Brenner, N. (2004) *New State Spaces: Urban Governance and the Rescaling of Statehood.* Oxford: Oxford University Press.

Bretherton, C. and Vogler, J. (1999) *The European Union as a Global Actor.* London: Routledge.

Briant, P. (1996) *Alexander the Great.* London: Thames and Hudson.

Brinkley, I. (2008) *The Knowledge Economy: How Knowledge is Reshaping the Economic Life of Nations.* London: The Work Foundation.

Brinkley, I. and Lee, N. (2007) *The Knowledge Economy in Europe.* London: The Work Foundation.

Brodsgaard, K. and Heurlin, B. (eds) (2002) *China's Place in Global Geopolitics.* London: Routledge.

Bromley, S. (ed.) (2001) *Governing the European Union.* London: Sage.

Brotton, J. (2002) *The Renaissance Bazaar: From the Silk Road to Michaelangelo.* Oxford: Oxford University Press.

Brubaker, R. (1992) *Citizenship and Nationhood in France and Germany.* Cambridge, MA: Harvard University Press.

Brubaker, R. (1996) *Nationalism Reframed: Nationhood and the National Question in the New Europe.* Cambridge: Cambridge University Press.

Bunce, V. (2005) 'The national idea: imperial legacies and post-communist pathways in Eastern Europe', *East European Politics and Societies,* 19 (3): 406–442.

Burgess, M. and Vollaard, H. (eds) (2006) *State Territoriality and European Integration.* London: Routledge.

Burke, P. (2005) *History and Social Theory* (2nd edn) Cambridge: Polity Press.

Bryman, A. (2004) *The Disneyization of Society.* London: Sage.

Calhoun, C. (ed.) (1992) *Habermas and the Public Sphere* Cambridge, MA: MIT Press.

Calhoun, C. (1997) *Nationalism.* Buckingham: Open University Press.

Calhoun, C. (2001) 'The virtues of inconsistency: identity and plurality in the conceptualisation of Europe', ch.2 in Cederman (ed.) (2001).

Calhoun, C. (2002) 'The class consciousness of frequent travellers: towards a critique of actually existing cosmopolitanism', ch.6 in Vertovec and Cohen (eds) (2002).

Campbell, J. (2005) 'Fiscal sociology in an age of globalisation: comparing tax regimes in advanced capitalist countries', pp. 391–418 in Nee, V. and Swedborg, R. (eds), *The Economic Sociology of Capitalism.* Princeton, NJ: Princeton University Press.

Cameron, E. (ed.) (2001) *Early Modern Europe: An Oxford History.* Oxford: Oxford University Press.

Caporaso, J. and Jupille, J. (2001) 'The Europeanization of gender equality policy and domestic structural change', ch.2 in Cowles et al. (eds) (2001).

Casey, E., Paasi, A., Shapiro, M. and Mayer, M. (2008) 'Comments on "Theorizing sociospatial relations"', *Environmental and Planning D: Society and Space,* 26 (3): 402–419.

Castellani, B. and Hafferty, F. (2007) Sociology and Complexity Science: A New Area of Inquiry. Available online: www.personal.kent.educ/~bcastel3/SACS.html. (accessed on xx/xx/2008).

Castells, M. (1996) *The Rise of the Network Society* (The Information Age, Vol. 1). Oxford: Blackwell.

Castells, M. (1997) *The Power of Identity* (The Information Age, Vol. 2). Oxford: Blackwell.

Castells, M. (1998) *The End of Millennium* (The Information Age, Vol. 3). Oxford: Blackwell.

Castells, M. (2002) *The Internet Galaxy: Reflections on the Internet, Business and Society.* Oxford: Oxford University Press.

Castle-Kanerova, M. and Jordan, B. (2001) 'The social citizen', Chapter 7 in Bellamy and Warleigh (eds) (2001) *Citizenship and Governance in the European Union*. London: Continuum.

Castles, F. (2004) *The Future of the Welfare State: Crisis Myths and Crisis Realities*. Oxford: Oxford University Press.

Castles, F. and Pierson, C. (1996) 'A new convergence?', *Policy and Politics*, 24 (3): 233–245.

Cederman, L. E. (ed.) (2001) *Constructing Europe's Identity: The External Dimension*. Boulder, CO: Lynne Rienner.

Chamberlayne, P., Cooper, A., Freeman, R. and Rustin, M. (eds) (1999) *Welfare and Culture in Europe*. London: Kingsley.

Cheah, P. and Robbins, B. (eds) (1998) *Cosmopolitics: Thinking and Feeling beyond the Nation* (Cultural Politics Vol. 14) Minneapolis, MN: University of Minnesota Press.

Checkel, J. and Katzenstein, P. (eds) (2008) *The Politics of European Identity Construction*. Cambridge: Cambridge University Press.

Chesters, G. (2004) 'Global complexity and global civil society', *Voluntas: The International Journal of Voluntary and Non-profit Organizations*, 15 (4): 323–342.

Chesters, G. and Welsh, I. (2005) 'Complexity and social movement(s)', *Theory, Culture and Society*, 22 (5): 187–211.

Christiansen, T., Jorgensen, K. and Wiener, A. (eds) (1999) *The Social Construction of Europe*. London: Sage.

Chrysochoou, D. (2001) *Theorizing European Integration*. London: Sage.

Cohen, J. and Arato, A. (1997) *Civil Society and Political Theory*. Cambridge, MA: MIT Press.

Colley, L. (2003) *Britons: Forging the Nation 1707–1837*. London: Pimlico.

Commander, S., Heitmueller, A. and Tyson, L. (2006) 'Migrating workers and jobs: a challenge to the European social model?', ch.4 in Giddens et al. (eds) (2006).

Corvisier, A. (1979) *Armies and Societies in Europe, 1494–1789* Bloomington, IN: Indiana University Press.

Cowles, M., Caporaso, J. and Risse, T. (eds) (2001) *Transforming Europe: Europeanization and Domestic Change*. Ithaca, NY: Cornell University Press.

Cram, L., Dinan, D. and Nugent, N. (eds) (1999) *Developments in the European Union*. Basingstoke: Macmillan.

Crang, M. and Thrift, N. (eds) (2000) *Thinking Space*. London: Routledge.

Crossley, N. (2007) 'Social networks and extraparliamentary politics', *Sociology Compass*, 1 (1): 222–236.

Crouch, C. (1999) *Social Change in Western Europe*. Oxford: Oxford University Press.

Chryssochoou, D. (2001) *Theorizing European Integration*. London: Sage.

Cunliffe, B. (1997) *The Ancient Celts*. Oxford: Oxford University Press.

Cunliffe, B. (2005) *Iron Age communities in Britain* (4th edn). London: Routledge.

Dahrendorf, R. (1997) *After 1989: Morals, Revolution and Civil Society*. Basingstoke: Macmillan.

Daly, M. (2006) 'EU social policy after Lisbon', *Journal of Common Market Studies*, 44 (3): 461–481.

Daly, M. (2007) 'Whither EU social policy? An account and assessment of developments in the Lisbon social inclusion process', *Journal of Social Policy*, 37 (1): 1–19.

Davidson, R. (1998) *Travel and Tourism in Europe* (2nd edn). Harlow: Addison-Wesley Longman.

Davies, N. (1997) *Europe: A History*. London: Pimlico/Random House.

Davies, N. (2006) *Europe East and West*. London: Jonathan Cape.

De la Porte, C. and Pochet, P. (2004) 'The European employment strategy: existing research and remaining questions', *Journal of European Social Policy*, 14 (1): 71–78.

De Vreese, C. (2003) *Framing Europe: Television News and European Integration*. Amsterdam: Aksant.

De Vreese, C. (2007) 'The EU as a public sphere', *Living Reviews*, http://European governance.livingreviews.org/Articles/Ireg-2007-3/ (accessed 01/05/2009.)

Deacon, B. (2000) 'Eastern European welfare states: the impact of the politics of globalization', *Journal of European Social Policy*, 10 (2): 146–161.

Deacon, B. (2007) *Global Social Policy and Governance*. London: Sage.

Deacon, B., Hulse, M. and Stubbs, P. (1997) *Global Social Policy*. London: Sage.

Deacon, B. and Stubbs, P. (eds) (2007) *Globalization and the Making of Social Policy in South Eastern Europe*. Aldershot: Edward Elgar.

Dear, M. and Flusty, S. (eds) (2002) *The Spaces of Postmodernity* Oxford: Blackwell.

Delanty, G. (1995) *Inventing Europe: Idea, Identity, Reality*. London: Macmillan.

Delanty, G. (2000) *Citizenship in a Global Age*. Buckingham: Open University Press.

Delanty, G. (2005) 'The idea of a Cosmopolitan Europe: on the cultural significance of Europeanization', *International Review of Sociology*, 15 (3): 405–421.

Delanty, G. (2006) 'Borders in a changing Europe: dynamics of openness and closure', *Comparative European Politics*, 4: 183–202.

Delanty, G. (2007) 'European citizenship: a critical assessment', *Citizenship Studies*, 11 (1): 63–72.

Delanty, G. and He, B. (2008) 'Cosmopolitan perspectives on European and Asian transnationalism', *International Sociology*, 23 (3): 323–344.

Delanty, G. and Jones, P. (2002) 'European identity and architecture', *European Journal of Social Theory*, 5 (4): 453–466.

Delanty, G. and Kumar, K. (eds) (2006) *Handbook of Nations and Nationalism Studies*. London: Sage.

Delanty, G. and Rumford, C. (2005) *Rethinking Europe: Social Theory and the Implications of Europeanization*. London: Routledge.

Delors, White Paper (see EC 1993a).

Delors, J. (1998) 'A Necessary Union' (original 1989), ch.9 in Nelsen and Stubbs (eds) (1998).

Diez, T. (2006) 'The paradox of Europe's borders', *Comparative European Politics*, 4: 235–252.

Dinan, D. (2005) *Ever Closer Union: An Introduction to European Integration* (3rd edn). London: Palgrave.

Dobb, M. (1963) *Studies in the Development of Capitalism*. London: Routledge and Kegan Paul.

Downing, B. (1992) *The Military Revolution and Political Change: Origins of Democracy and Autocracy in Early Modern Europe*. Princeton, NJ: Princeton University Press.

Doyal, L. and Gough, I. (1991) *A Theory of Human Needs*. London: Macmillan.

Duff, A. (ed.) (1997) *The Treaty of Amsterdam*. London: Federal Trust.

Duncan, S. and Edwards, R. (1999) *Lone Mothers, Paid Work and Gendered Moral Rationalities*. London: Palgrave.

Dunkerley, D., Hodgson, L., Konopacki, S., Spybey, T. and Thompson, A. (2002) *Changing Europe: Identities, Nations and Citizens*. London: Routledge.

Dutton, P. (2002) *Origins of the French Welfare State (1914–1947)*. Cambridge: Cambridge University Press.

Dwyer, P. (2000) *Welfare Rights and Responsibilities: Contesting Social Citizenship*. Bristol: The Policy Press.

Dyson, K. (ed.) (2002) *European States and the Euro*. Oxford: Oxford University Press.

Eardley, T., Bradshaw, J., Ditch, J., Gough, I. and Whiteford, P. (1996) *Social Assistance in OECD Countries*. London: HMSO.

Eder, K. (2006) 'Europe's borders: the narrative construction of the boundaries of Europe', *European Journal of Social Theory*, 9 (2): 255–271.

Eder, K. and Giesen, B. (eds) (2001) *European Citizenship: Between National Legacies and Postnational Projects*. Oxford: Oxford University Press.

Ehrenreich, B. (1997) *Blood Rituals: Origins and History of the Passions of War*. New York: Owl Books/Holt.

Ehrenreich, B. (2007) *Dancing in the Street: A History of Collective Joy*. London: Granta.

Eisenstein, E. (2005) *The Printing Revolutions in Early Modern Europe*. Cambridge: Cambridge University Press.

Elias, N. (1983) *The Court Society*. Oxford: Blackwell (originally published 1969).

Elias, N. (2000) *The Civilising Process* (rev. edn). Oxford: Blackwell (originally published 1939).

Eluere, C. (1993) *The Celts: First Masters of Europe*. London: Thames and Hudson.

Eriksen, E. (2007) 'Conceptualizing European Public Spheres: General, Segmented and Strong Publics', Chapter 2 in Fossum and Schlesinger (eds) (2007) *The European Union and the Public Sphere*. London: Routledge.

Esping-Andersen, G. (1990) *The Three Worlds of Welfare Capitalism*. Cambridge: Polity Press.

Esping-Andersen, G. (ed.) (1996a) *Welfare States in Transition: National Adaptations in Global Economies*. London: Sage.

Esping-Andersen, G. (1996b) 'After the Golden Age? Welfare state dilemmas in a global economy', ch.1 in Esping-Andersen (ed.) (1996a).

Esping-Andersen, G. (1996c) 'Welfare states without work: the impasse of labour-shedding and familialism in Continental European social policy', ch.3 in Esping-Andersen (ed.) (1996a).

Esping-Andersen, G. (1999) *The Social Foundations of Post-Industrial Economies*. Oxford: Oxford University Press.

Esping-Andersen, G. (2002a) 'A new gender contract', ch.3 in Esping-Andersen et al. (2002).

Esping-Andersen, G. (2002b) 'A new European social model for the twenty-first century?', ch.3 in Rodrigues (ed.) (2002).

Esping-Andersen, G. (2002c) 'A child-centred social investment strategy', ch.2 in Esping-Andersen et al. (2002).

Esping-Andersen, G. and Regini, M. (eds) (2000) *Why Deregulate Labour Markets?* Oxford: Oxford University Press.

Esping-Andersen, G., Gallie, D., Hemerijk, A. and Myles, J. (2002) *Why We Need a New Welfare State*. Oxford: Oxford University Press.

European Agency (2007) *Report on Racism and Xenophobia in the Member State of the EU*. Vienna: European Agency for Fundamental Rights.

Eurobarometer (2008) *Eurobarometer 68: Public Opinion in the European Union*. Brussels: European Commission (DG Communication).

Euronet (2005) *What about Us? Children's Rights in the European Union: Next Steps* (Ruxton Report). Brussels: European Children's Network.

European Commission (this authorship is indicated in this Reference list by EC)

EC (1985) 'A People's Europe' (Addonino Report, Parts I and II), *Bulletin of the European Communities*, Supplement 7/85. Luxembourg: EC.

EC (1988) *Europe without Frontiers: Completing the Internal Market* (2nd edn). European Documentation. Luxembourg: EC.

EC (1992) *Treaty on European Union*. Luxembourg: EC.

EC (1993a) *Growth, Competitiveness, Employment: The Challenges and Ways: Forward into The Twenty-first Century* (The Delors White Paper). Luxembourg: EC.

EC (1993b) *European Social Policy: Options for the Union* (The Green Paper). Luxembourg: EC.

EC (1995a) *Social Protection in Europe*. Directorate-General Employment, Industrial Relations and Social Affairs. Brussels: EC.

EC (1995b) *European Social Policy: The Medium Term Action Plan*. Luxembourg: EC.

EC (1995c) Intergovernmental Conference 1996: Commission Report for the Reflection Group. Luxembourg: EC.

EC (1996a) Intergovernmental Conference 1996: Commission Opinion – Reinforcing Political Union and Preparing for Enlargement. Luxembourg: EC.

EC (1996b) *For a Europe of Civic and Social Rights: Report by the Comite des Sages*. Luxembourg: EC.

EC (1997) *The Globalising Learning Economy*. Brussels: EC.

EC (1999) *Implementing the European Employment Strategy*. Luxembourg: EC.

EC (2001) *European Governance: A White Paper*. COM (2001) 428. Brussels: EC.

EC (2003) *An Agenda for a Growing Europe: Making the EU Economic System Deliver*. (The Sapir Report – A report of an Independent High-level Study Group, chaired by A. Sapir). Brussels: EC.

EC (2004) *Report of the High-level Group on the Future of Social Policy in an Enlarged Union*. DG Employment. Brussels: EC.

EC (2005a) *Common Actions for Growth and Employment: The Community Lisbon Programme*. COM (2005) 330. Brussels: EC.

EC (2005b) *The Future of Creative Industries* (Report by C. Marcus). DG Research, EUR 21471. Brussels: EC.

EC (2005c) *Joint Report on Social Protection and Social Inclusion*. COM (2005) 14. Brussels: EC.

EC (2005d) *European Values in the Globalised World*. COM (2005) 525 final. Brussels: EC.

EC (2005e) *The Daphne Experience 1997–2003: Europe against Violence towards Children and Women*. DG Justice, Freedom and Security. Brussels: EC.

EC (2006a) *Creating an Innovative Europe* (The Aho Report). EUR 22005. Brussels: EC.

EC (2006b) *Social Inclusion in the New Member States*. SEC (2004) 848. Brussels: EC.

EC (2006c) *The Economy of Culture in Europe* (Report by KEA, Berlin). Brussels: EC.

EC (2007a) *A White Paper on Sport*. COM (2007) 391. Brussels: EC.

EC (2007b) *Towards Common Principles of Flexicurity: More and Better Jobs through Flexibility and Security*. COM (2007). Brussels: EC.

EC (2007c) 'Flexicurity in Europe: modernising the European labour market in the twenty-first century' (Spidla, V.), SPEECH/07/421, European Commission, Brussels.

EC (2007d) *Strategic Report on the Renewed Lisbon Strategy for Growth and Jobs: Launching the New Cycle (2008–2010)*. COM (2007) 803 final, PART III. Brussels: EC.

EC (2007e) *Integrated Guidelines for Growth and Jobs (2008–2010)*. COM (2007) 803 final, PART V. Brussels: EC.

EC (2008a) *Proposal for a Directive of the European Parliament and of the Council on the Application of Patients' Rights in Cross-border Healthcare*. COM (200) 414 final, 2008/0142 (COD). Brussels: EC.

EC (2008b) *Report on Implementation of the Hague Programme for 2007*. Brussels: EC.

European Convention (2003) *Draft Treaty Establishing a Constitution for Europe*. Luxembourg: European Communities.

European Foundation (2007) *First European Quality of Life Survey: Time Use and Work-life Options over the Life Course*. Dublin: European Foundation for the Improvement of Living and Working Conditions.

European Parliament (2007) *The European Charter of Fundamental Rights* (Draft). Brussels: European Parliament.

European Union (this authorship is indicated here in this Reference list by EU).

EU (1993) 'European Council in Copenhagen 21–22 June 1993, Conclusions of the Presidency'. SN 180/1/93 REV 1. Brussels: European Council.

EU (2000a) 'Lisbon European Council, Presidency Conclusions'. Brussels: European Parliament. Available online: www.europarl.europa.eu/summi?redirected=1/lis1_en.htm (accessed on 20/07/2009).

EU (2001) *Treaty of Nice* (10/3/2001, pp.C80/1–C80/87). Brussels: Official Journal of the European Communities.

EU (2004) *Facing the Challenge: The Lisbon Strategy for Growth and Employment* (The Kok Report, the report by the High-level Group chaired by Wim Kok). Brussels: European Council.

EU (2006a) *Joint Report on Social Protection and Social Inclusion* (7294/06). Brussels: European Council.

EU (2006b) Directive 2006/123/EC of the European Parliament and of the Council on Services in the Internal Market (27/12/2006, pp.L376/36-L376/68). Brussels: Official Journal of the European Union.

EU (2006c) Regulation (EC) No. 1927/2000 of the European Parliament and of the Council of 20 December 2006 on establishing the European Globalisation Adjustment Fund. L48/82–L48/88. Luxembourg: Official Journal of the European Union.

EU (2007a) *The Reform Treaty* (or Lisbon Treaty), 'Treaty amending the Treaty on European Union and the Treaty establishing the European Community', IGC (Conference of the representatives of the governments of the member states) CIG 1/07. Brussels: Presidency of the IGC.

EU (2007b) *Joint Employment Report 2006/7* (6706/07). Brussels: European Council.

Eurostat (2006a) *Eurostats in Focus 3/2006*. Luxembourg: Eurostat.

Eurostat (2006b) *Eurostats in Focus 17/2006*. Luxembourg: Eurostat.

Eurostat (2007) *Eurostats in Focus 28/2007*. Luxembourg: Eurostat.

Eurostat (2008) 'From 2015, deaths projected to outnumber births in the EU27', Eurostat News Release 119/2008. Available online: http://epp.eurostat.ec.europa.eu/portal/page/publications/collections/news_releases (28 August 2008, accessed on 20/07/2009).

Faist, T. (1995) *Social Citizenship for Whom?* Aldershot: Avebury.

Faist, T. (2000) 'Social citizenship in the European Union: nested membership', *Journal of Common Market Studies*, 39 (1): 39–60.

Faist, T. and Kivisto, P. (2007) *Citizenship: Theory, Discourse and Transnational Prospects*. Oxford: Blackwell.

Faist, T. and Ozveren, E. (eds) (2004) *Transnational Social Spaces: Agents, Networks and Institutions*. Aldershot: Avebury.

Fajth, G. (2000) 'Social security in a rapidly changing environment: the case of post-communist transformation', ch.5 in Manning and Shaw (eds) (2000a).

Farrell, M., Fella, S. and Newman, M. (2002) *European Integration in the 21st Century: Unity in Diversity?* London: Sage.

Favell, A. (2003a) 'Games without frontiers? Questioning the transnational social power of migrants in Europe', *Archives Europeennes de Sociologie*, Winter, XLIV, (3): 106–136.

Favell, A. (2003b) *Eurostars and Eurocities: Towards a Sociology of Free-moving Professionals in Western Europe*. Working Paper 71. Center for Comparative Immigration Studies, University of California, San Diego.

Favell, A. (2004) 'Eurostars and Eurocities: free-moving professionals and the promise of European integration', Council for European Studies, Columbia University, New York.

Favell, A. (2006) 'After enlargement: Europe's new migration system', DIIS Brief, Migration Research Unit, Danish Institute for International Studies, Copenhagen.

Favell, A. (2008) *Eurostars and Eurocities: Free Movement and Mobility in an Integrating Europe*. Oxford: Blackwell

Featherstone, K. and Radaelli, C. (eds) (2003) *The Politics of Europeanization*. Oxford: Oxford University Press.

Ferge, Z. (2001) 'Welfare and 'ill-fare' systems in Central-Eastern Europe', ch.7 in Sykes et al. (eds) (2001).

Ferguson, N. (2008) *The Ascent of Money: A Financial History of the World*. London: Allen Lane.

Fernandez-Armesto, F. (2001) *Civilisations*.London: Pan.

Ferrera, M. (1996) 'The 'southern model' of welfare in Social Europe', *Journal of European Social Policy*, 6 (1): 17–37.

Ferrera, M. (2003) 'European integration and national social citizenship', *Comparative Political Studies*, 36 (6): 611–652.

Ferrera, M. (2005a) *The Boundaries of Welfare: European Integration and the New Spatial Politics of Social Solidarity*. Oxford: Oxford University Press.

Ferrera, M. (ed.) (2005b) *Welfare State Reform in Southern Europe*. London: Routledge.

Ferrera, M., Hemerijk, A. and Rhodes, M. (2000) *The Future of Social Europe: Recasting Work and Welfare in the New Economy*. Oeiras: Celta.

Fiddler, C. (2003) 'Citizenship and the Euro: an analysis of British perceptions and attitudes to the process of European economic integration'. Unpublished PhD thesis, Available at: University of Sheffield Library, Sheffield (www.shef.ac.uk/library/).

Fildes, A. and Fletcher, J. (2004) *Alexander the Great*. London: Duncan Baird.

Fine,R. (2003) 'Taking the "ism" out of Cosmopolitanism', *European Journal of Social Theory*, 6 (4): 451–470.

Fine, R. (2006) 'Cosmopolitanism and violence: difficulties of judgement', *British Journal of Sociology*, 57 (1): 49–67.

Fine, R. (2007) *Cosmopolitanism*. London: Routledge.

Fligstein, N. (2008) *Euroclash: The EU, European Identity and the Future of Europe*. Oxford: Oxford University Press.

Flora, P. (1983) 'Stein Rokkan's macro-model of Europe', Introduction, in Flora et al. (1983).

Flora, P. (ed.) (1986) *Growth to Limits: The Western European Welfare State since World War II*. Berlin: de Gruytes.

Flora, P., with Kuhnle, S. and Urwin, D. (eds) (1999) *State Formation, Nation Building and Mass Politics in Europe: The Theory of Stein Rokkan*. Oxford: Oxford University Press.

Flora, P., Alber, J., Eichenberg, R., Kohl, J., Kraus, F., Pfenning, W. and Seebohm, K. (1983) *State, Economy and Society in Western Europe 1815–1975*. Vol. 1: *The Growth of Mass Democracies and Welfare States*. London: Macmillan.

Florida, R. (2002) *The Rise of the Creative Class*. New York: Basic Books.

Florida, R. and Tingali, I. (2004) *Europe in the Creative Age*. London: Demos.

Fossum, J. and Schlesinger, P. (eds) (2007) *The European Union and the Public Sphere*. London: Routledge.

Freeman, C. and Soete, L. (eds) (1987) *Technical Change and Full Employment.* Oxford: Blackwell.

Freeman, R. and Rustin, M. (1999) 'Introduction: Welfare, culture and Europe', pp. 9–22 in P. Chamberlayne et al. (1999) *Welfare and Culture in Europe.* London: Kingsley.

Friedrichs, J. (2001) 'The meaning of new medievalism', *European Journal of International Relations,* 7 (4): 475–502.

Fulbrook, M. (ed.) (2007) *The Un-Civilising Processes? Excess and Transgression in German Society and Culture: Perspectives Debating with Norbert Elias.* Amsterdam and New York: Editions Rodopi.

Gallie, D. and Paugam, S. (eds) (2000) *Welfare Regimes and the Experience of Unemployment in Europe.* Oxford: Oxford University Press.

Gamble, A. (2001) 'Regional blocs, world order and the new medievalism', ch.1 in Telo (ed.) (2001).

Gamble, A. and Payne, A. (eds) (1996) *Regionalism and World Order.* London: Macmillan.

Garcia, B. (2005) 'De-constructing the City of Culture: The long-term legacies of Glasgow 1990', *Journal of Urban Studies,* 42 (5/6): 1–28.

Garcia, S. (ed.) (1993a) *European Identity and the Search for Legitimacy.* London: Pinter/The Royal Institute for International Affairs.

Garcia, S. (1993b) 'Europe's fragmented identities and the frontiers of citizenship', ch.1 in Garcia (ed.) (1993a).

Garcia, S. (1997) 'European Union identity and citizenship: some challenges', ch.13 in Roche and van Berkel (eds) (1997a).

Geary, P. (2002) *The Myth of Nations: The Medieval Origins of the Europe.* Princeton, NJ: Princeton University Press.

Geddes, A. (2003) *The Politics of Migration and Immigration in Europe.* London: Sage.

Gellner, E. (1983) *Nations and Nationalism.* Oxford: Blackwell.

Gellner, E. (1988) *Plough, Sword and Book: The Structure of Human History.* London: Paladin.

Gellner, E. (1998) *Nationalism.* London: Phoenix/Orion.

George, S. (2005) 'Multi-level governance and the European Union', ch.7 in Bache and Flinders (eds) (2005).

Geyer, R. (2000) *Exploring European Social Policy.* Cambridge: Polity Press.

Gibson, C. and Kong, L. (2005) 'Cultural economy: a critical review', *Progress in Human Geography,* 29 (5): 541-561.

Giddens, A. (1971) *Capitalism and Modern Social Theory.* Cambridge: Cambridge University Press.

Giddens, A. (1981) *A Contemporary Critique of Historical Materialism* (Vol. 1). London: Macmillan.

Giddens, A. (1984) *The Constitution of Society.* Cambridge: Polity Press.

Giddens, A. (1985) *The Nation-State and Violence.* Cambridge: Polity Press.

Giddens, A. (1999) *Runaway World: How Globalisation is Reshaping Our Lives.* London: Profile Books.

Giddens, A. (2000) *The Third Way and its Critics.* Cambridge: Polity Press.

Giddens, A. (2007) *Europe in the Global Age.* Cambridge: Polity Press.

Giddens, A., Diamond, P. and Liddle, R. (eds) (2006) *Global Europe, Social Europe.* Cambridge: Polity Press.

Giddens, A. and Hutton, W. (eds) (2000) *On the Edge: Living with Global Capitalism.* London: Jonathan Cape.

Ginsburg, N. (1992) *Divisions of Welfare: A Critical Introduction to Comparative Social Policy*. London: Sage.

Glatzer, M. and Rueschemeyer, D. (eds) (2005) *Globalization and the Future of the Welfare State*. Pittsburgh, PA: University of Pittsburgh Press.

Goldstein, J. (1988) *Long Cycles: Prosperity and War in the Modern Age*. New Haven, CT: Yale University Press.

Goldstein, J. (1991) 'A war-economy theory of the long wave', ch.12 in Thygesen, N., Velupillai, K. and Zambell, S. (eds), *Business Cycles: Theories, Evidence and Analysis*. London: Macmillan.

Goldstein, J. (2001) *War and Gender*. Cambridge: Cambridge University Press.

Goodin, R., Headey, B., Muffels, R. and Dirven, H.-J. (1999) *The Real Worlds of Welfare Capitalism*. Cambridge: Cambridge University Press.

Goodwin, J. (1999) *The Lords of the Horizon: A History of the Ottoman Empire*. London: Vintage.

Goody, J. (2000) *The European Family: An Historico-anthropological Essay*. Oxford: Blackwell.

Goody, J. and Watt, I. (1975) 'The consequences of literacy', pp. 27–68 in Goody, J. (ed.), *Literacy in Traditional Societies*. Cambridge: Cambridge University Press.

Gorski, P. (2006) 'Pre-modern nationalism', ch.12 in Kumar and Delanty (eds) (2006).

Gough, I. (2005) 'European welfare states: explanations and lessons for developing countries'. Unpublished conference paper, 'New frontiers of social policy', World Bank, Arusha (12–15 December). Available online: http://siteresources.worldbank.org/INTRANETSOCIALDEVELOPMENT/Resources/Gough.rev.pdf (accessed on 01/05/2009.)

Gough, I., Eardley, T., Bradshaw, J., Ditch, J. and Whiteford, P. (1997) 'Social assistance in OECD countries', *Journal of European Social Policy*, 7 (1): 17–43.

Gough, I. and Olofsson, G. (eds) (1999) *Capitalism and Social Cohesion: Essays on Exclusion and Integration*. London: Macmillan.

Gould, A. (1993) *Capitalist Welfare Systems: A Comparison of Japan, Britain and Sweden*. London: Longman.

Gowan, P. (2002) 'The EU and Eastern Europe: diversity without unity?', in Farrell et al. (2002).

Grant, C. and Barysch, K. (2008) *Can Europe and China Shape a New World Order?* London: Centre for European Reform.

Gray, A. (2004) *Unsocial Europe: Social Protection or Flexploitation?* London: Pluto Press.

Green, K., Hull, R., McMeekin, A. and Walsh, V. (1999) 'The construction of the techno-economic: networks vs. paradigms', *Research Policy*, 28: 777–792.

Greenfeld, L. (2003) *The Spirit of Capitalism: Nationalism and Economic Growth*. Cambridge, MA: Harvard University Press.

Greenfeld, L. (2006) 'Modernity and nationalism', ch.13 in Kumar and Delanty (eds) (2006).

Gripsrud, J. (2007) 'Television and the European public sphere', *European Journal of Communication*, 22 (4): 479–492.

Guibernau, M. (ed.) (2001) *Governing European Diversity*. London: Sage.

Guibernau, M. and Hutchinson, J. (eds) (2001) *Understanding Nationalism*. Cambridge: Polity Press.

Guillen, A. and Alvarez, S. (2001) 'Globalization and the southern welfare states', ch.6 in Sykes et al. (eds) (2001).

Guillen, A. and Matsaganis, M. (2000) 'Testing the 'social dumping' hypothesis in Southern Europe', *The Journal of European Social Policy*, 10 (2): 120–145.

Guthrie, D. (2006) *China and Globalization: The Social, Economic and Political Transformation of Chinese Society*. London: Routledge.

Habermas, J. (1989) *The Structural Transformation of the Public Sphere* (German original, 1962). Cambridge: Polity Press.

Habermas, J. (1992) 'Further reflections on the public sphere', ch.17 in Calhoun (ed.) (1992).

Habermas, J. (1994) 'Citizenship and national identity', ch.3 in van Steenbergen (ed.) (1994).

Habermas, J. (2001) *The Postnational Constellation*. Cambridge: Polity Press.

Hacker, B. (1981) 'Women and military institutions in early modern Europe', *Signs*, 6 (4): 643–671.

Hacker, B. and Vining, M. (2001) 'From camp follower to lady in uniform: women, social class and military institutions before 1920', *Contemporary European History*, 10 (3): 353–373.

Hall, J. (ed.) (1998) *The State of the Nation: Ernest Gellner and the Theory of Nationalism*. Cambridge: Cambridge University Press.

Halsall, G. (2003) *Warfare and Society in the Barbarian West 450–900*. London: Routledge.

Handler, J. (2004) *Social Citizenship and Workfare in the United States and Western Europe*. Cambridge: Cambridge University Press.

Handler, J. (2005) 'Myth and ceremony in workfare: rights, contracts and client satisfaction', *The Journal of Socio-Economics*, 34 (1): 101–124.

Hantrais, L. (2000) *Social Policy in the European Union* (2nd edn). London: Macmillan.

Harcourt, A. (2002) 'Engineering Europeanisation: the role of European institutions in shaping national media regulation', *Journal of European Public Policy*, 9 (5): 736–755.

Harcourt, A. (2003) 'Europeanisation as convergence: the regulation of media markets in the European Union', ch.8 in Featherstone and Raedelli (eds) (2003).

Hardt, M. and Negri, A. (2000) *Empire*. Cambridge, MA: Harvard University Press.

Harrison, J. and Wessels, B. (eds) (2009 forthcoming) *Mediating Europe: European Media, Mass Communications and the European Public Sphere*. Oxford: Berghahn.

Harrison, J. and Woods, L. (2000) 'European citizenship: can audio-visual policy make a difference?', *Journal of Common Market Studies*, 38 (3): 471–495.

Harrison, J. and Woods, L. (2001) 'Defining European public service broadcasting', *European Journal of Communications*, 16 (4): 477–504.

Harvey, D. (1989) *The Condition of Post-Modernity*. Oxford: Blackwell.

Harvey, D. (2000) 'Cosmopolitanism and the banality of geographical evils', *Public Culture*, 12 (2): 529–564.

Hastings, A. (2003) *The Construction of Nationhood: Ethnicity, Religion and Nationalism* (originally published 1997). Cambridge: Cambridge University Press.

Heater, D. (1990) *Citizenship: The Civic Ideal in World History, Politics and Education*. London: Longman.

Hechter, J. (2001) *Containing Nationalism*. Oxford: Oxford University Press.

Hegel, G. (1942) *Philosophy of Right* (originally published 1821). Oxford: Clarendon Press.

Heikkila, M. (ed.) (1999) *Linking Welfare and Work*. Dublin: European Foundation.

Heinemann, F. (2008) 'Is the welfare state self-destructive? A study of government benefit morale', *Kyklos: International Review for Social Sciences*, 61 (2): 237–257.

Held, D. (1995) *Democracy and the Global Order: From the Modern State to Cosmopolitan Governance*. Cambridge: Polity Press.

Held, D. (2002) 'Culture and political community: national, global and cosmopolitan', ch.5 in Vertovec and Cohen (eds) (2002).

Held, D. (2003) *Cosmopolitanism: A Defence*. Cambridge: Polity Press.

Held, D. (2004) *Global Covenant: The Social Democratic Alternaive to the Washington Consensus*. Cambridge: Polity Press.

Held, D., McGrew, A., Goldblatt, D. and Perraton, J. (1999) *Global Transformations: Politics, Economics and Culture*. Cambridge: Polity Press.

Held, D., Barnett, A. and Henderson, C. (eds) (2005) *Debating Globalization*. Cambridge: Polity Press.

Hesmondhalgh, D. (2002) *The Cultural Industries*. London: Sage.

Hill, M. (1996) *Social Policy: A Comparative Analysis*. London: Prentice Hall/Harvester Wheatsheaf.

Hilson, C. (2008) 'The unpatriotism of the economic constitution? Rights to free movement and their impact on national and European identity', *European Law Journal*, 14 (2): 186–202.

Hirst, P. and Thompson, G. (1999) *Globalization in Question* (2nd edn). Cambridge: Polity Press.

Hix, S. (1998) 'The study of the European Union–2: The new governance agenda and its rival', *The Journal of European Public Policy*, 5 (1): 38–65.

Hobden, S. and Hobson, J. (eds) (2002) *Historical Sociology of International Relations*. Cambridge: Cambridge University Press.

Hobsbawm, E. (1984) 'Mass-producing traditions: Europe, 1870–1914', ch.7 in Hobsbawm and Ranger (eds) (1984).

Hobsbawm, E. (1992) *Nations and Nationalism since 1870: Programme, myth, reality*. Cambridge: Cambridge University Press.

Hobsbawm, E. (1999) *Industry and Empire: from 1750 to the present day*. London: Penguin.

Hobsbawm, E. and Ranger, T. (eds) (1984) *The Invention of Tradition*. Cambridge: Cambridge University Press.

Hobson, J. (2004) *The Eastern Origins of Western Civilisation*. Cambridge: Cambridge University Press.

Holland, T. (2005) *Persian Fire: The First World Empire and the Battle for the West*. London: Little, Brown.

Hong, Y.-S. (1998) *Welfare, Modernity and the Weimar State 1919–1933*. Princeton, NJ: Princeton University Press.

Hooghe, L. and Marks, G. (eds) (2001) *Multi-level Governance and European Integration*. Oxford: Rowman and Littlefield.

Hornsby-Smith, M. (1999) 'The Catholic Church and social policy in Europe', ch.9 in Chamberlayne et al. (eds) (1999).

Hoskyns, C. (2004) 'Gender perspectives' (on European integration), ch.11 in Wiener and Diez (eds) (2004).

Hull, R., Walsh, V., Green, K. and McKeekin, A. (1999) 'The techno-economic: perspectives for analysis and intervention', *Journal of Technology Transfer*, 24: 185–195.

Huntington, S. (2002) *The Clash of Civilizations and the Remaking of World Order* (originally published 1997). London: Free Press.

Hutton, W. (2008) *The Writing on the Wall: China and the West in the 21st Century*. London: Abacus.

Huws, U. (1997) 'Flexibility and security: towards a new European balance', Citizens Income Trust Discussion Paper 3. London: Citizens Income Trust.

Huysmans, J. (2001) 'European identity and migration policies', ch.8 in Cederman (ed.) (2001).

Isin, E. and Turner, B. (eds) (2002) *Handbook of Citizenship Studies*. London: Sage.

Isin, E. and Wood, P. (1998) *Citizenship and Identity*. London: Sage.

Jacobsson, K. (2004) 'Soft regulation and the subtle transformation of states: the case of EU employment policy', *Journal of European Social Policy*, 14 (4): 355–370.

James, C.L.R. (1980) *The Black Jacobins: Toussaint L'Ouverture and the San Domingo Revolution*. London: Allison Busby.

James, S. (1999) *The Atlantic Celts: Ancient People or Modern Invention?* Madison, WI: University of Wisconsin Press.

Janoski, T. (1998) *Citizenship and Civil Society*. Cambridge: Cambridge University Press.

Janowitz, M. (1964) *The Military in the Political Development of New Nations*. Chicago: University of Chicago Press.

Jensen, O. and Richardson, T. (2004) *Making European Space*. London: Routledge.

Jenson, J. (2006) 'The European social model: gender and generational equality', ch.8 in Giddens et al. (eds) (2006).

Jepsen, M. and Pascual, A. (2005) 'The European social model: an exercise in deconstruction', *Journal of European Social Policy*, 15 (3): 231–245.

Jessop, B. (1994) 'The transition to post-Fordism and the Schumpeterian workfare state', ch.2 in Loader and Burrows (eds) (1994).

Jessop, B. (2005) 'Multi-level governance and multi-level metagovernance', ch.4 in Bache and Flinders (eds) (2005).

Jessop, B., Brenner, N. and Jones, M. (2008) 'Theorizing sociospatial relations', *Environment and Planning D: Society and Space*, 26: 389–401.

Jochem, S. (2000) 'Nordic labour market policies in transition', *Western European Politics*, 23 (3): 115–138.

Jones, P. (2007) 'Cosmopolitanism and Europe: Describing elites or challenging inequalitiea?', Chapter 5 in C. Rumford (ed.) (2007) *Europe and Cosmopolitanism*. Liverpool: Liverpool University Press.

Jonsson, C., Tagil, S. and Tornqvist, G. (2000) *Organising European Space*. London: Sage.

Jordan, W. (2002) *Europe in the High Middle Ages*. London: Penguin.

Judt, T. (2005) *Postwar: A History of Europe since 1945*. London: Heinemann.

Kaldor, M. (2002) 'Cosmopolitanism and organized violence', ch.17 in Vertovec and Cohen (eds) (2002).

Kant, I. (1967) *On History* (originally published 1784–95). New York: Bobbs-Merrill.

Kaspersen, L. (2004) 'How Denmark became democratic: the impact of military reforms', *Acta Sociologica*, 47 (1): 71–89.

Katzenstein, P. (2005) *A World of Regions: Asia and Europe in the American Imperium*. Ithaca, NY: Cornell University Press.

Kaufman, R. (2007) 'Market reform and social protection: lessons from the Czech Republic, Hungary and Poland', *East European Politics*, 21 (1): 111–125.

Kautto, M., Hekkila, M., Hvinden, B., Marklund, S. and Ploug, N. (1999) *Nordic Social Policy: Changing Welfare States*. London: Routledge.

Keane, J. (1998) *Civil Society: Old Images, New Visions*. Cambridge: Polity Press.

Keane, J. (2003) *Global Civil Society*. Cambridge: Cambridge University Press.

Kemmerling, A. (2002) 'The employment effects of different regimes of welfare state taxation: an empirical analysis of core OECD countries', MPiFG Discussion Paper 02/8, Cologne: Max-Planck Institut für Gesellschaftsforschung (available online: www.mpfi-fg-koeln.mpg.de). (accessed on xx/xx/2008).

Kennedy, H. (2002) *Mongols, Huns and Vikings: Nomads at War*. London: Cassell.

Kennedy, P. (1988) *The Rise and Fall of the Great Powers: Economic Change and Military Conflict 1500–2000*. London: Fontana.

Keohane, R. and Hoffman, S. (1991) 'Institutional change in Europe in the 1980s', ch.1 in Hoffman, S. and Keohane, R. (eds), *The New European Community*. Boulder CO: Westview Press.

Kern, P. (2007) *Cultural and Creative Industries in Europe: Coherent Policy in a Globalised World*. Berlin: KEA European Affairs.

Khanna, P. (2008) *The Second World: Empires and the Influence in the New Global Order*. London: Penguin.

King, A. (2001) *The European Ritual: Football in the New Europe*. Aldershot: Ashgate.

Klausen, J. (2001) *War and Welfare: Europe and the United States 1945 to Present*. London: Palgrave.

Kleinman, M. (2002) *A European Welfare State? EU Social Policy in Context*. London: Palgrave.

KMU (2006) 'The Importance of Tourism in Europe' (European Tourism Ministers' conference: 'Tourism – Key to Growth and Employment', Background material). Vienna: KMU Forschung Austria.

Koenigsberger, H. (1987) *Medieval Europe 400–1500*. London: Longman/Pearson.

Kofman, E., Phizacklea, A., Raghuram, P. and Sales, R. (2000) *Gender and International Migration in Europe: Employment, Welfare and Politics*. London: Routledge.

Kok Report (see EU 2004).

Kolsto, P. (ed.) (2005) *Myths and Boundaries in South-Eastern Europe*. London: Hurst and Company.

Koopmans, R. and Erbe, J. (2003) 'Towards a European public sphere? Vertical and horizontal dimensions of Europeanised political communication', EUROPUB F5 project, Berlin. Available online: http://conferences.en.htm//europub.wz-berline.de (accessed on 01/05/2009).

Kornai, J., Haggard, S. and Kaufman, R. (eds) (2001) *Reforming the State: Fiscal and Welfare Reform in Post-Socialist Countries*. Cambridge: Cambridge University Press.

Korpi, W. (2004) 'Changing class structures and the origins of welfare states: the breakthrough of social insurance 1860–1940'. Unpublished paper. Stockholm: Swedish Institute for Social Research.

Kostakopolou, T. (2001) 'Invisible citizens?' ch.10 in Bellamy and Warleigh (eds) (2001).

Kristiansen, K. (1998) *Europe before History*. Cambridge: Cambridge University Press.

Kumar, K. and Delanty, G. (eds) (2006) *Nations and Nationalism*. London: Sage.

Kvist, J. (2004) 'Does EU enlargement start a race to the bottom? Strategic interaction among EU member states in social policy', *Journal of European Social Policy*, 14 (3): 301–318.

Kvist, J. and Saari, J. (eds) (2007a) *The Europeanisation of Social Protection*. Bristol: The Policy Press.

Kvist, J. and Saari, J. (2007b) 'The Europeanisation of social protection: domestic impacts and national responses', ch.13 in Kvist and Saari (eds) (2007a).

Laffan, B., O'Donnell, R. and Smith, M. (2000) *Europe's Experimental Union*. London: Routledge.

Lake, M. (2005) *The EU and Turkey: Glittering Prize or a Millstone?* London: Federal Trust.

Larner, W. and Walters, W. (2002) 'The political rationality of "new regionalism": towards a genealogy of the region', *Theory and Society*, 31: 391–432.

Larsen, T., Taylor-Gooby, P. and Kanane, J. (2003) 'The myth of a dual earner society: new policy discourses in European welfare states'. Available online: www.kent.ac.uk/wramsoc/conferencesandworkshops/conferenceinformation/berlinconference/themythofadualearnersociety.pdf. (accessed on 01/05/2009.)

Lash, S. and Urry, J. (1987) *The End of Organised Capitalism*. Cambridge: Polity Press.

Lash, S. and Urry, J. (1994) *Economies of Signs and Space*. London: Sage.

Law, J. (1992) 'Notes on the theory of the Actor Network: ordering strategy and heterogeneity', Centre for Science Studies, Lancaster University, Lancaster. Available online: www.lancs.ac.uk/fass/sociology/papers/law-notes-on-ant.pdf (accessed on 01/05/2009.)

Law, J. and Hassard, J. (eds) (1999) Actor Network Theory and After. Oxford: Blackwell/Sociological Review.

Lazzarato, M. (1996) 'Immaterial labour', pp.133–147 in Hardt, M. and Virno, P. (eds), Radical Thought in Italy. Minneapolis, MN: University of Minnesota Press.

Le Goff, J. (2005) The Birth of Europe. Oxford: Blackwell.

Lechner, F. and Boli, J. (2005) World Culture: Origins and Consequences. Oxford: Blackwell.

Lefebvre, H. (1991) The Production of Space (originally published 1974). Oxford: Blackwell.

Leibfried, S. and Pierson, C. (eds) (1995) European Social Policy. Washington, DC: Brookings Institute.

Leisering, L. and Leibfried, S. (1999) Time and Poverty in Western Welfare States: United Germany in Perspective (originally published 1995). Cambridge: Cambridge University Press.

Lendvai, N. (2004) 'The weakest link? EU accession and enlargement: dialoguing EU and post-communist social policy', Journal of European Social Policy, 14 (3): 319–333.

Leonard, M. (1999) Network Europe: The New Case for Europe. London: The Foreign Policy Centre/Clifford Chance.

Levack, B. (1995) The Witch-hunt in Early Modern Europe (2nd edn). London: Longman/Pearson.

Lewis, B. (1992) The Arabs in History. Oxford: Oxford University Press.

Lewis, B. (2002) The Emergence of Modern Turkey (3rd edn). Oxford: Oxford University Press.

Lewis, J. (1992) 'Gender and the development of welfare regimes', Journal of European Social Policy, 2 (3): 159–173.

Lewis, J. (1997) Lone Mothers in European Welfare Regimes. London: Jessica Kingsley.

Lewis, P. (2001) 'The Enlargement of the European Union', ch.9 in Bromley (ed.) (2001).

Lind, J. and Moller, I. (eds) (1999) Inclusion and Exclusion: Unemployment and Non-Standard Employment in Europe. Aldershot: Ashgate.

Lindbeck, A. (1995) 'Welfare state disincentives with endogenous habits and norms', Scandinavian Journal of Economics, 97 (4): 477–494.

Lindert, P. (2005) Growing Public: Social Spending and Economic Growth since the Eighteenth Century. Cambridge: Cambridge University Press.

Lintner, V. (2001) 'EU and European economy', ch.2 in Thompson (ed.) (2001).

Lister, R. (1997) Citizenship: Feminist Perspectives. London: Macmillan.

Loader, B. and Burrows, R. (eds) (1994) Towards a Post-Fordist Welfare State? London: Routledge.

Lodemal, I. and Trickey, H. (eds) (2001) 'An Offer You Can't Refuse': Workfare in International Perspective. Bristol: The Policy Press.

Lorentzen, L. and Turpin, J. (eds) (1998) The Women and War Reader. New York: New York University Press.

Lukes, S. (1975) Emile Durkheim: His Life and Work. A Historical and Critical Study. London: Penguin.

Lyotard, F. (1991) The Postmodern Condition: A Report on Knowledge (originally published 1979). Manchester: Manchester University Press.

MacCullough, D. (2004) *Reformation: Europe's House Divided 1490–1700*. London: Penguin.

MacDonald, S. (1993) *European Identities: Ethnography in Western Europe*. Oxford: Berg.

MacDonald, S. (ed.) (2000) *Approaches to European Historical Consciousness*. Hamburg: Edition Korber-Stiftung.

Mahoney, J. and Rueschemeyer, D. (eds) (2003) *Comparative Historical Analysis in the Social Sciences*. Cambridge: Cambridge University Press.

Maizey, S. (ed.) (2000) *Women Power and Public Policy in Europe* (A special issue of a journal, *The Journal of European Public Policy*, 7 (3).)

Man, J. (2004) *Genghis Khan: Life, Death and Resurrection*. London: Bantam Books.

Mann, M. (1986) *The Sources of Social Power. Vol. 1: A History of Power from the Beginning to AD 1760*. Cambridge: Cambridge University Press.

Mann, M. (1993) *The Sources of Social Power. Vol. 2: The Rise of Classes and Nation-States*. Cambridge: Cambridge University Press.

Mann, M. (1998) 'Is there a society called Euro?', ch.11 in Axtmann (ed.) (1998).

Mann, M. (2003) *Incoherent Empire*. London: Verso.

Mann, M. (2005) *The Dark Side of Democracy: Explaining Ethnic Cleansing*. Cambridge: Cambridge University Press.

Manning, N. and Shaw, I. (eds) (2000a) *New Risks, New Welfare*. Oxford: Blackwell.

Manning, N. and Shaw, I. (2000b) 'The Millennium and social policy', pp.1–11 in Manning and Shaw (eds) (2000a).

Manow, P. and van Kersbergen, K. (2006) *The Impact of Class Coalitions, Cleavage Structures and Church–State Conflicts on Welfare State Development*. Working Papers in Political Science, No. 2006/03, Department of Political Science. Amsterdam: Vrije Universiteit.

Manow, P. and van Kersbergen, K. (2009) (forthcoming) 'Religion and the western welfare state: the theoretical context', ch.1 in van Kersbergen and Manow (eds) (2009).

Mansell, R. and Steinmuller, E. (2000) *Mobilizing the Information Society: Strategies for Growth and Opportunity*. Oxford: Oxford University Press.

Marks, G. and Hooghe, L. (2005) 'Contrasting visions of multi-level governance', ch.2 in Bache and Flinders (eds) (2005).

Marks, G., Scharpf, F., Schmitter, P. and Streeck, W. (1996) *Governance in the European Union*. London: Sage.

Marozzi, J. (2004) *Tamerlane: Sword of Islam, Conqueror of the World*. London: Harper Collins.

Marshall, T.H. (1992) 'Citizenship and social class', in Marshall, T.H. and Bottomore, T., *Citizenship and Social Class* (originally published 1950). London: Pluto.

Martiniello, M. (1997) 'The development of European Union citizenship', ch.3 in Roche and van Berkel (eds) (1997a).

Massey, D. (2005) *For Space*. London: Sage.

May, J. and Thrift, N. (2001) *Timespace: Geographies of Temporality*. London: Taylor and Francis.

Mazower, M. (1998) *Dark Continent: Europe's Twentieth Century*. London: Penguin.

McCormick, M. (2002) *Origins of the European Economy: Communications and Commerce AD 300–900*. Cambridge: Cambridge University Press.

McCormick, P. (2007) *The European Superpower*. London: Palgrave.

McIntosh, P. (1968) *Physical Education in England since 1800*. London: Bell and Hyman.

McNeill, D. (2004) *New Europe: Imagined Spaces*. London: Arnold.

McNeill, W. (1974) *The Shape of European History*. New York: Oxford University Press.

McNeill, W. (1984) *The Pursuit of Power: Technology, Armed Force and Society since AD 1000*. Oxford: Blackwell.

McNeill, W. (1998) *Plagues and Peoples*. New York: Anchor Books.

Medrano, J. (2003) *Framing Europe: Attitudes to Integration in Germany, Spain and the United Kingdom*. Princeton, NJ: Princeton University Press.

Meehan, E. (1993) *Citizenship and the European Community*. London: Sage.

Meehan, E. (1997) 'Citizenship and social inclusion in the European Union', ch.2 in Roche and van Berkel (eds) (1997a).

Meyer, C. (2005) 'The Europeanization of publicised debates: a study of quality press coverage of economic policy coordination since Amsterdam', *Journal of Common Market Studies*, 43 (1): 119–146.

Michalski, K. (ed.) (2006) *What Holds Europe Together?* Budapest/New York: CEU Press.

Miles, D. (2005) *The Tribes of Britain*. London: Weidenfeld and Nicolson.

Mills, C.W. (1959) *The Power Elite*. London: Oxford University Press.

Mills, C.W. (2000) *The Sociological Imagination* (originally published 1959). Oxford: Oxford University Press.

Milward, A. (1977) *War, Economy and Society, 1939–1945*. London: Allen Lane.

Milward, A. (2000) *The European Rescue of the Nation-State* (2nd edn). London: Routledge.

Millward, P. (2006) 'Networks, power and revenue in contemporary football: an analysis of G14', *International Review of Modern Sociology*, 32 (2): 199–216.

Millward, P. and Levermore, R. (2007) 'Official policies and informal transversal networks: creating 'pan-European identifications' through sport?', *The Sociological Review*, 55 (1): 144–164.

Mishel, L., Bernstein, J. and Allegretto, S. (2007) *The State of Working America 2006/7*. Ithaca, NY: Cornell University Press.

Mishra, R. (1999) *Globalization and the Welfare State*. Cheltenham: Edward Elgar.

Modood, T. and Werbner, P. (eds) (1997) *The Politics of Multiculturalism in the New Europe*. London: Zed Books.

Moore, B. (1966) *The Social Origins of Dictatorship and Democracy*. London: Penguin.

Morgan, G. (1986) *Images of Organisation*. London: Sage.

Morgan, K. (2002) 'Forging the frontiers between state, church and family: religious cleavages and the origins of early childhood education and care policies in France, Sweden and Germany', *Politics and Society*, 30 (1): 113–148.

Morley, D. (2000) *Home Territories: Media, Mobility and Identity*. London: Routledge.

Morley, D. and Robins, K. (1995) *Spaces of Identity: Global Media, Electronic Landscapes and Cultural Boundaries*. London: Routledge.

Morissens, A. and Sainsbury, D. (2005) 'Migrants' social rights, ethnicity and welfare regimes', *Journal of Social Policy*, 34 (4): 637–660.

Mosher, J. and Trubek, D. (2003) 'EU social policy and the European employment strategy', *Journal of Common Market Studies*, 41 (1): 63–88.

Mosse, G. (1975) *The Nationalisation of the Masses: Political Symbolism and Mass Movements in Germany*. New York: Howard Fertig.

Mouffe, C. (2005) *On the Political*. London: Routledge.

Moxon-Browne, E. (ed.) (2004a) *Who Are the Europeans Now?* Aldershot: Ashgate.

Moxon-Browne, E. (2004b) 'Eastern and Western Europe: towards a new European identity?', ch.10 in Moxon-Browne (ed.) (2004a).

Munkler, H. (2007) *Empires: The Logic of World Domination from Ancient Rome to the United States*. Cambridge: Polity Press.

Myles, J. (2002) 'A new social contract for the elderly?', ch.6 in Esping-Andersen et al. (2002).

Navarro, V., Schmitt, J. and Astudillo, J. (2004) 'Is globalisation undermining the welfare state? The evolution of the welfare state in developed capitalist countries during the 1990s', *International Journal of Health Services*, 34 (2): 185–227.

Nelsen, B. and Stubbs, A. (eds) (1998) *The European Union: Readings on the Theory and Practice of European Integration*. London: Macmillan.

Norwich, J. (1998) *A Short History of Byzantium*. London: Penguin.

Nugent, N. (2003) *The Government and Politics of the European Union* (5th edn). Basingstoke: Palgrave.

Nugent, N. (ed.) (2004) *European Union Enlargement*. Basingstoke: Palgrave.

Nussbaum, M. (1994) 'Patriotism and cosmopolitanism', *The Boston Review*. Available online: www.soci.niu.edu/~phildept/Kapitan/nussbaum1.html. (accessed on 01/05/2009.)

OECD (2005a) *Education Policy Analysis*. Paris: OECD.

OECD (2005b) *Standardised Unemployment Statistics*. Paris: OECD.

OECD (2005c) *Income Distribution and Poverty in OECD Countries in the Second Half of the 1990s*. Available online: www.oecd.org/els/workingpapers. Paris: OECD.

OECD (2005d) 'Tax revenue 2005', in *'OECD Countries' Tax Burdens Back up to 2000 Historic Highs*. Dublin: Finfacts. Available online: www.finfacts.com/.

OECD (2008) *OECD Tax Database 2007*. Available online at: www.oecd.org. Paris: Organisation for Economic Cooperation and Development.

Oesch, D. (2008) 'Explaining workers' support for right-wing populist parties in Western Europe', *International Political Science Review*, 29 (3): 349–373.

O'Leary, S. and Tiilikainen, I. (1998) *Citizenship and Nationality Status in the New Europe*. London: IPPR/Sweet Maxwell.

Oppenheimer, S. (2006) *Origins of the British*. London: Constable and Robinson.

Orenstein, M. and Haas, M. (2005) 'Globalisation and the future of welfare states in the post-communist East-Central European countries', ch.6 in Glatzer and Rueschemeyer (eds) (2005).

Orloff, A. (1993) 'Gender and the social rights of citizenship: the comparative analysis of gender relations and welfare states', *American Sociological Review*, 58 (June): 303–328.

O'Shea, S. (2006) *Sea of Faith: Islam and Christianity in the Medieval Mediterranean World*. London: Profile Books.

Ostner, I. and Lewis, J. (1995) 'Gender and the evolution of European social policies', ch.5 in Leibfried and Pierson (eds) (1995).

Outhwaite, W. (2006a) 'Social structure' (of Europe), ch.6 in Sakwa and Stevens (eds) (2006).

Outhwaite, W. (2006b) 'Is there a European civil society?', ch.5 in Rogowski and Turner (eds) (2006).

Outhwaite, W. (2008) *European Society*. Cambridge: Polity Press.

Pagden, A. (ed.) (2002) *The Idea of Europe: From Antiquity to the European Union*. Cambridge: Cambridge University Press.

Palier, B. and Sykes, R. (2001) 'Challenges and change: issues and perspectives in the analysis of globalization and the European welfare states', ch.1 in Sykes et al. (eds) (2001).

Palmer, R. (ed.) (2004) *European Cities and Capitals of Culture* (Vol. 1). Brussels: Palmer/RAE Associates.

Parker, G. (1996) *The Military Revolution: Military Innovation and the Rise of the West, 1500–1800* (2nd edn). Cambridge: Cambridge University Press.

Parker, P., Clark, C. and Moore, T. (2004b) *The Collins Atlas of Military History*. London: Collins.

Parsons, T. (1966) *Societies: Evolutionary and Comparative Perspectives*. Englewood Cliffs, NJ: Prentice-Hall.

Parsons, T. (1971) *The System of Modern Societies*. Englewood Cliffs, NJ: Prentice-Hall.

Pestieau, P. (2006) *The Welfare State and the European Union*. Oxford: Oxford University Press.

Peters, B. and Sifft, S. (2003) *The Transnationalisation of Public Spheres: A Public Discourse Approach*. INIIS, University of Bremen.

Peters, B., Sifft, S., Bruggeman, M., Kleinen-von Konigslow, K. and Wimmel, A. (2005) 'Segmented Europeanisation: Exploring the Legitimacy of the European Union from a Public Discourse perspective', *Journal of Common Market Studies*, 45 (1): 127–155.

Pfau-Effinger, B. (2000) 'Changing welfare states and labour markets in the context of gender arrangements', in Duncan, S. and Pfau-Effinger, B. (eds), *Gender, Work and Culture in the European Union*. London: Routledge.

Pfau-Effinger, B. (2004) *Development of Culture, Welfare States and Women's Employment in Europe*. Aldershot: Ashgate.

Pfau-Effinger, B. (2005) 'Culture and welfare state policies', *Journal of Social Policy*, 34 (1): 3–20.

Picard, D. and Robinson, M. (eds) (2006) *Festivals, Tourism and Social Change*. Clevedon, UK: Channel View Publications.

Pierson, C. (1991) *Beyond the Welfare State? The New Political Economy of Welfare*. Cambridge: Polity Press.

Pieterse, J. (ed.) (2000) *Global Futures: Shaping Globalization*. London: Zed Books.

Pinder, J. (2001) *The European Union*. Oxford: Oxford University Press.

Piore, M. and Sabel, C. (1984) *The Second Industrial Divide*. New York: Basic Books.

Polanyi, K. (2001) *The Great Transformation: The Political and Economic Origins of Our Time* (originally published 1944). Boston: Beacon Press.

Popper, K. (1962) *The Open Society and Its Enemies* (Vols 1 and 2) (4th edn). London: Routledge.

Prior, P. and Sykes, R. (2001) 'Globalisation and the European welfare states: evaluating the theories and the evidence', ch.10 in Sykes et al. (eds) (2001).

Pryor, F. (2004) *Britain AD: A Quest for Arthur, England and the Anglo-Saxons*. London: Harper-Collins.

Putnam, H. (2000) *Bowling Alone: The Collapse and Revival of American Community*. New York: Simon & Schuster.

Rees, T. (1998) *Mainstreaming Equality in the European Union: Education, Training and Labour Market Policies*. London: Routledge.

Rhodes, M. (1996) 'Globalization and West European welfare states: a critical review of recent debates', *Journal of European Social Policy*, 6 (4): 305–327.

Richards, G. (ed.) (2001) *Cultural Attractions and European Tourism*. Wallingford, Oxfordshire: CABI Publishing.

Richardson, T. (2006) 'The thin simplification of European space: dangerous calculations', *Comparative European Politics*, 4: 203–217.

Rietbergen, P. (1998) *Europe: A Cultural History*. London: Routledge.

Rifkin, J. (2004) *The European Dream*. Cambridge: Polity Press.

Rimlinger, G. (1993) *Welfare Policy and Industrialization in Europe, America and Russia* (originally published 1971). Aldershot: Gregg Revivals, Gower.

Risse, T. (2003) 'An emerging European Public Sphere? Theoretical clarifications and empirical indicators', IDNET F5 project (EUI), and Center for Transatlantic Foreign and Security Policy, Free University, Berlin.

Risse, T. (2004) 'Social constructivism and European integration', ch.8 in Wiener and Diez (eds) (2004).

Ritzer, G. (2005) Enchanting a Disenchanted World: Revolutionizing the Means of Consumption. Thousand Oaks, CA: Pine Forge Press.

Ritzer, G. (2008) The McDonaldization of Society (5th edn). Thousand Oaks, CA: Pine Forge Press.

Roberts, J. (1996) The Penguin History of Europe. London: Penguin.

Roberts, M. (1967) 'The Military revolution: 1560–1660', in his Essays in Swedish History. Minneapolis, MN: University of Minnesota Press.

Robertson, R. (1992) Globalisation: Social Theory and Global Culture. London: Sage.

Roche, M. (1973) Phenomenology, Language and the Social Sciences. London: Routledge.

Roche, M. (1987) 'Citizenship, social theory and social change', Theory and Society, 16: 363–399.

Roche, M. (1994) 'Citizenship and social change', ch.5 in Turner, B. and Hamilton, P. (eds), Citizenship: Critical Concepts (Vol. 1). London: Routledge.

Roche, M. (1995) 'Citizenship, obligation and anomie: themes in the analysis of contemporary political ideologies and social movements', pp.41–62 in Edgell, S. (ed.), Debating the Future of the Public Sphere. Aldershot: Avebury.

Roche, M. (1996) Rethinking Citizenship, Welfare, Ideology and Change in Modern Society. Cambridge: Polity Press.

Roche, M. (1997) 'Citizenship and exclusion: reconstructing the European Union', pp.3–23 in Roche and van Berkel (eds) (1997a).

Roche, M. (2000a) Mega-Events and Modernity: Olympics and Expos in the Growth of Global Culture. London: Routledge.

Roche, M. (2000b) 'Citizenship, popular culture and Europe', pp.74–98 in Stevenson (ed.) (2000).

Roche, M. (2002) 'Social citizenship: grounds of social change', pp.69–86 in Isin and Turner (eds) (2002).

Roche, M. (2003) 'Mega-events, time and modernity', Time and Society, 12 (1): 99–126.

Roche, M. (2006a) 'Nationalism, mega-events and international culture', ch.22 in Delanty and Kumar (eds) (2006).

Roche, M. (2006b) 'Mega-events and modernity revisited: globalisation and the case of the Olympics', ch.2 in Horne, J. and Manzenreiter, W. (eds), Sports Mega-Events: Social Scientific Analyses of a Global Phenomenon. Oxford: Blackwell.

Roche, M. (2007) 'Cultural Europeanisation and the "cosmopolitan condition": EU regulation and European sport', ch.8 in Rumford (ed.) (2007).

Roche, M. and Annesley, C. (eds) (2004) Comparative Social Inclusion Policies in Europe. Brussels: European Commission.

Roche, M. and van Berkel, R. (eds) (1997a) European Citizenship and Social Exclusion. Aldershot: Avebury.

Roche, M. and van Berkel, R. (1997b) 'European Union and social exclusion: an introduction', in Roche and van Berkel (eds) (1997a).

Roche, M. and van Berkel, R. (2002) 'Activation policies as reflective social policies', ch.5 in van Berkel and Moller (eds) (2002).

Rodrigues, M. (ed.) (2002) The New Knowledge Economy in Europe. Cheltenham: Edward Elgar.

Rodriguez-Pose, A. (2002) *The European Union: Economy, Society and Polity*. Oxford: Oxford University Press.

Rogowski, R. and Turner, C. (eds) (2006) *The Shape of the New Europe*. Cambridge: Cambridge University Press.

Rosamund, B. (2000) *Theories of European Integration*. London: Palgrave.

Rosas, A. and Antola, E. (eds) (1995) *A Citizen's Europe*. London: Sage

Rossiter, N. (2006) *Organized Networks: Media Theory, Creative Labour, New Institutions*. Rotterdam: NAi Publishers.

Roudemetof, V. and Haller, W. (2007) 'Social indicators of cosmopolitanism and localism in Eastern and Western Europe: an exploratory analysis', ch.11 in Rumford (ed.) (2007).

Rovisco, M. (2007) 'Cosmopolitanism, collective belonging and the borders of Europe', ch.12 in Rumford (ed.) (2007).

Roxburgh, D. (ed.) (2005) *Turks: A Journey of a Thousand Years 600–1600*. London: Royal Academy of Arts.

Rumford, C. (2002) *The European Union: A Political Sociology*. Oxford: Blackwell.

Rumford, C. (2006) 'Rethinking European spaces: territory, borders, governance', *Comparative European Politics*, 4: 127–140.

Rumford, C. (ed.) (2007) *Europe and Cosmopolitanism*. Liverpool: Liverpool University Press.

Rumford, C. (2008) 'Theorizing borders', *European Journal of Social Theory*, 9 (2): 155–169.

Rumford, C. (ed.) (2009) *The Sage Handbook of European Studies*. London: Sage.

Ruttan, V. (2006a) *Is War Necessary for Economic Growth? Military Procurement and Technology Development*. Oxford: Oxford University Press.

Ruttan, V. (2006b) 'Is war necessary for economic growth?', *Historically Speaking* (The Bulletin of the Historical Society, Boston University), 7 (6): 17–19.

Sainsbury, D. (ed.) (1999) *Gender and Welfare State Regimes*. Oxford: Oxford University Press.

Sainsbury, D. (2006) 'Immigrants' social rights in comparative perspective: welfare regimes, forms of immigration and immigration policy regimes', *Journal of European Social Policy*, 16 (3): 229–244.

Sakwa, R. and Stevens, A. (eds) (2006) *Contemporary Europe* (2nd edn). Basingstoke: Palgrave.

Sandholtz, W. and Sweet, A. (eds) (1998) *European Integration and Supranational Government*. Oxford: Oxford University Press.

Sapir, A. (2006) 'Globalisation and the reform of European social models', *Journal of Common Market Studies*, 44 (2): 369–390.

Sapir Report (see EC 2003)

Saunders, F. (2004) *Hawkwood: Diabolical Englishman*. London: Faber & Faber.

Scharpf, F. (2000) 'Globalization and the welfare state', conference paper, The Year 2000 International Research Conference on Social Security, Helsinki, 25–27 September 2000.

Scharpf, F. (2002) 'The European social model', *Journal of Common Market Studies*, 40 (5): 645–670.

Schimmelfennig, F. and Sedelmeier, U. (eds) (2005) *The Europeanization of Central and Eastern Europe*. Ithaca, NY: Cornell University Press.

Schirm, S. (2002) *Globalization and the New Regionalism: Global Markets, Domestic Politics and Regional Cooperation*. Cambridge: Polity Press.

Schlesinger, P. (2003) 'The Babel of Europe? An essay on networks and communicative spaces', *ARENA Working Paper 22/03*. Oslo: University of Oslo, Centre for European Studies.

Schlesinger, P. (2007) 'A cosmopolitan temptation', *European Journal of Communication*, 22 (4): 413–426.

Schmidt, V. (2002) *The Futures of European Capitalism*. Oxford: Oxford University Press.

Schmitter, P. (2000) *How to Democratize the European Union ... and Why Bother?* New York: Rowman and Littlefield.

Schneider, G. and Aspinwall, M. (eds) (2001) *The Rules of Integration: Institutionalist Approaches to the Study of Europe*. Manchester: Manchester University Press.

Scholte, J. (2005) *Globalisation: A Critical Introduction* (2nd edn). London: Palgrave.

Schopflin, G. (2000) *Nations, Identity Power: The New Politics of Europe*. London: Hurst and Company.

Schumpeter, J. (1976) *Capitalism, Socialism and Democracy* (5th edn). London: Allen and Unwin.

Schutz, A. and Luckmann, T. (1974) *The Structures of the Life-World*. London: Heinemann.

Scott, A. (1999) 'The cultural economy: geography and the creative field', *Media, Culture and Society*, 21: 807–817.

Scott, A. (2000) *The Cultural Economy of Cities*. London: Sage.

Scott, A. (2004) 'Cultural-products industries and urban economic development', *Urban Affairs Review*, 39 (4): 461–490.

Seamon, D. (1979) *A Geography of the Lifeworld: Movement, Rest and Encounter*. London: Croom Helm.

Shaw, G. and Williams, A. (2004) *Tourism and Tourist Spaces*. London: Sage.

Shaw, M. (1988) *Dialectics of War: An Essay on the Social Theory of Total War and Peace*. London: Pluto Press.

Sherlock, P. and Bennett, H. (1998) *The Story of the Jamaican People*. Kingston: Ian Randle, and Princeton, NJ: Markus Wiener.

Shore, C. (2000) *Building Europe: The Cultural Politics of European Integration*. London: Routledge.

Silverstone, R. (ed.) (2005) *Media, Technology and Everyday Life in Europe: From Information to Communication*. Aldershot: Ashgate.

Silverstone, R. (2007) *Media and Morality*. Cambridge: Polity Press.

Sinn, H.-W. (2007) 'The welfare state and the forces of globalization', *CESifo Working paper 1925*. Munich: University of Munich.

Sklair, L. (1991) *Sociology of the Global System*. London: Harvester/Wheatsheaf.

Sklair, L. (2001) *The Trans-National Capitalist Class*. Oxford: Blackwell.

Skocpol, T. (ed.) (1984) *Vision and Method in Historical Sociology*. Cambridge: Cambridge University Press.

Skocpol, T. (1995) *Protecting Soldiers and Mothers: Political Origins of Social Policy in the United States*. Cambridge, MA: Belknap Press.

Smismans, S. (2003) 'European civil society: shaped by discourses and institutional interests', *European Law Journal*, 49 (4): 473–495.

Smith, A. (1995) *Nations and Nationalism in a Global Era*. Cambridge: Polity Press.

Smith, A. (1998) *Nationalism and Modernism*. London: Routledge.

Smith, A. (2004) *The Antiquity of Nations*. Cambridge: Polity Press.

Smith, A. (2005) *Chosen Peoples: Sacred Sources of National Identity*. Oxford: Oxford University Press.

Smith, A. (2006) 'Ethnicity and nationalism', ch.14 in Kumar and Delanty (eds) (2006).

Sorensen, A. (1998) 'On kings, pietism and rent-seeking in Scandinavian welfare states', *Acta Sociologica*, 41: 163–175.

Sotiropoulos, D. (2005) 'Poverty and the safety net in Eastern and South-eastern Europe in the post-communist era', pp.266–296 in Ferrera (ed.) (2005b).

Sotiropoulos, D. and Pop, L. (2007) 'International actors and social policy in Bulgaria and Romania, 1996–2006', ch.4 in Deacon and Stubbs (eds) (2007).

Sotiropoulou, V. and Sotiripoulos, D. (2007) 'Childcare in post-communist welfare states: the case of Bulgaria', *Journal of Social Policy*, 37 (1): 141–155.

Spybey, T. (1999) *Globalization and World Society*. Cambridge: Polity Press.

Standing, G. (1999) *Global Labour Flexibility*. London: Macmillan.

Steinmetz, G. (1993) *Regulating the Social: The Welfare State and Local Politics in Imperial Germany*. Princeton, NJ: Princeton University Press.

Stevenson, J. (ed.) (2002) *The History of Europe*. London: Mitchell Beazley.

Stevenson, N. (ed.) (2000) *Culture and Citizenship*. London: Sage.

Stevenson, N. (2007) 'Cosmopolitan Europe, post-colonialism and the politics of imperialism', ch.4 in Rumford (ed.) (2007).

Strath, B. (2002) 'A European identity: to the historical limits of a concept', *European Journal of Social Theory*, 5 (4): 387–401.

Strath, B. and Triandafyllidou, A. (eds) (2003) 'Representations of Europe and the nation in current and prospective member states: media, elites and civil society', EUR 20736, (Euronat, The collective state of the art and historical reports). Brussels: European Commission (DG Research).

Strathern, P. (2005) *The Medici: Godfathers of the Renaissance*. London: Pimlico.

Streeck, W. (1996) 'Neo-voluntarism: a new European social policy regime?', ch.4 in Marks et al. (1996).

Stringer, C. (2006) *Homo Brittanicus*. London: Allen Lane.

Sunstein, C. (2007) *Republic.com 2.0*. Princeton, NJ: Princeton University Press.

Sutton, I. (1999) *Western Architecture: A Survey*. London: Thames and Hudson.

Sykes, R., Palier, B. and Prior, P. (eds) (2001) *Globalization and European Welfare States*. Basingstoke: Palgrave.

Taylor-Gooby, P. (ed.) (2001) *Welfare States under Pressure*. London: Sage.

Taylor-Gooby, P. (2004) *New Risks, New Welfare: The Transformation of the European Welfare State*. Oxford: Oxford University Press.

Taylor-Gooby, P. and Daguerre, A. (2004) 'The new context of welfare: welfare reform and the management of societal change', Welfare reform and the management of societal change programme (WRAMSOC). Luxembourg: European Commission (DG Research).

Telo, M. (ed.) (2001) *European Union and New Regionalism: Regional Actors and Global Governance in a Post-hegemonic Era*. Aldershot: Ashgate.

Telo, M. (2007) *Europe: A Civilian Power? European Union, Global Governance and World Order*. Basingstoke: Palgrave.

Therborn, G. (1995) *European Modernity and Beyond: The Trajectory of European Societies 1945–2000*. London: Sage.

Therborn, G. (2002) 'The world's trader, the world's lawyer: Europe and global processes', *European Journal of Social Theory*, 5 (4): 403–417.

Thompson, G. (ed.) (2001) *Governing the European Economy*. London: Sage.

Threlfall, M. (2002) 'Social integration in the EU: towards a single social area?', ch.8 in Farrell et al. (eds) (2002).

Threlfall, M. (2003) 'European social integration: harmonization, convergence and single social areas', *Journal of European Social Policy*, 13 (2): 121–139.

Thrift, N. (1999) 'The place of complexity', *Theory Culture and Society*, 16 (3): 31–69.

Tilley, C. (1994) *A Phenomenology of Landscape: Places, Paths and Monuments.* Oxford: Berg.

Tilly, C. (1992) *Coercion, Capital and European States, 990–1990.* Oxford: Oxford University Press.

Tilly, C. (1993) *European Revolutions 1492–1992.* Oxford: Oxford University Press.

Titmuss, R. (1963) *Essays on the Welfare State.* London: Allen and Unwin.

Toffler, A. (1970) *Future Shock.* London: Pan.

Toffler, A. (1980) *Third Wave.* London: Pan/Collins.

Toffler, A. (1985) *Previews and Premises.* London: Pan.

Tomlinson, J. (1999) *Globalization and Culture.* Cambridge: Polity Press.

Townsend, A. (1997) *Making a Living in Europe.* London: Routledge.

Tsoulakis, L. (2006) 'Economic reform, further integration and enlargement: can Europe deliver?', ch.13 in Giddens et al. (eds) (2006).

Twine, F. (1994) *Citizenship and Social Rights.* London: Sage.

Turner, B. (1986) *Citizenship and Capitalism.* London: Allen and Unwin.

Turner, B. (ed.) (1993) *Citizenship and Social Theory.* London: Sage.

Turner, B. (2006) *Vulnerability and Human Rights.* University Park, PA: Pennsylvania State Press.

Turner, B. (2007) 'The enclave society: towards a society of immobility', *European Journal of Social Theory*, 10 (2): 287–304.

Urry, J. (1990) *The Tourist Gaze.* London: Sage.

Urry, J. (1995) 'Tourism, Europe and identity', ch.11 in his *Consuming Places.* London: Routledge.

Urry, J. (2000) *Society Beyond Societies: Mobilities for the 21st Century.* London: Routledge.

Urry, J. (2003) *Global Complexity.* Cambridge: Polity Press.

Urry, J. (2005a) 'The complexity turn', *Theory, Culture and Society*, 22 (5): 1–14.

Urry, J. (2005b) 'The complexities of the global', *Theory, Culture and Society*, 22 (5): 235–254.

van Berkel, R. and Moller, I. (eds) (2002) *Active Social Policies in the EU.* Bristol: The Policy Press.

van de Steeg, M. (2002) 'Rethinking the conditions for a public sphere in the European Union', *European Journal of Social Theory*, 5 (4): 499–519.

van de Steeg, M. (2005) 'The public sphere in the European Union: a media analysis of the public discourse on EU enlargement and the Haider case', unpublished PhD thesis. Florence: European University Institute.

van der Veer, P. (2002) 'Colonial cosmopolitanism', ch.10 in Vertovec and Cohen (eds) (2002).

van Dijk, J. (1999) *The Network Society.* London: Sage.

van Kersbergen, K. (1995) *Social Capitalism: A Study of Christian Democracy and the Welfare State.* London: Routledge.

van Kersbergen, K. and Manow, P. (eds) (2009) (forthcoming) *Religion, Class Coalitions and Welfare States.* Cambridge: Cambridge University Press.

van Oorschott, W. (2007) 'Culture and social policy: a developing field of study', *International Journal Social Welfare*, 16 (2): 129–139.

van Steenbergen, B. (ed.) (1994) *The Condition of Citizenship.* London: Sage.

Vertovec, S. and Cohen, R. (eds) (2002) *Conceiving Cosmopolitanism: Theory, context, practice.* Oxford: Oxford University Press.

Walby, S. (2004) 'The European Union and gender equality: emergent varieties of gender regime', *Social Politics*, 11 (1): 4–29.

Walby, S. (2007) 'Complexity theory, systems theory and multiple intersecting social inequalities', *Philosophy of the Social Sciences*, 37 (4): 449–470.

Wallerstein, I. (1974) *The Modern World-System: Capitalist Agriculture and the Origins of the European World Economy in the 16th Century* (Vol. 1). London: Academic Press.

Wallerstein, I. (1980) *The Modern World-System: Mercantilism and the Consolidation of the European world-Economy 1600–1750* (Vol. 2). London: Academic Press.

Wallerstein, I. (1989) *The Modern World-System: The Second Era of Great Expansion of the Capitalist World-Economy 1730–1840s* (Vol. 3). London: Academic Press.

Walters, M. (2002) 'Mapping Schengenland: denaturalizing the border', *Environment and Planning D: Society and Space*, 20: 561–580.

Warleigh, A. (2002) *Flexible Integration: Which Model for the European Union?* London: Sheffield Academic Press.

Weber, M. (1967a) 'The origins of discipline in war', ch.10.1 in Gerth, H. and Mills, C.W. (eds), *From Max Weber*. London: Routledge.

Weber, M. (1967b) 'Class, status and party', ch.7 in Gerth, H. and Mills, C.W. (eds), *From Max Weber*. London: Routledge.

Weber, M. (1968) *Economy and Society: An Outline of Interpretive Sociology* (Vols 1, 2 and 3). New York: Bedminster Press.

Weber, M. (1970) *The Protestant Ethic and the Spirit of Capitalism* (originally published 1904–05). London: Unwin.

Webster, F. (ed.) (2004) *The Information Society Reader*. London: Routledge.

Weil, P. (2006) 'Immigration: a flexible framework for a plural Europe', ch.12 in Giddens et al. (eds) (2006).

Wessels, B. (2009a) *Internet as Socio-Cultural Form: Understanding the Internet and Contemporary Society*. Basingstoke: Palgrave.

Wessels, B. (2009b, forthcoming) 'Exploring the role of European information society developments in the Europeanization of public spheres', in Harrison and Wessels (eds) (2009 forthcoming).

Wessels, B. (2009c) 'Exploring the notion of the Europeanization of public spheres and civil society in fostering a culture of dialogue through the concept of "proper distance"', *Sociology: Thought and Action*, 3 (23): 28–46.

Wheatcroft, A. (2004) *Infidels: A History of the Conflict between Christendom and Islam*. London: Penguin.

Wheatcroft, A. (2008) *The Enemy at the Gate: Hapsburgs, Ottomans and the Battle for Europe*. London: The Bodley Head.

White, H. (2002) *Markets from Networks: Socio-economic Models of Production*. Princeton, NJ: Princeton University Press.

Wiener, A. (1998) *'European' Citizenship Practice: Building Institutions of a Non-State*. Boulder, CO: Westview Press.

Wiener, A. and Diez, T. (eds) (2004) *European Integration Theory*. Oxford: Oxford University Press.

Wilensky, H. (1975) *The Welfare State and Equality*. Berkeley, CA: University of California Press.

Williams, C. and Windebank, J. (1998) *Informal Employment in the Advanced Economies*. London: Routledge.

Williams, K. (2005) *European Media Studies*. London: Hodder Arnold.

Williams, R. (1961) *The Long Revolution*. London: Penguin.

Willner, A. (1970) 'Perspectives on military elites as rulers and wielders of power', *Journal of Comparative Administration*, November: 261–276.

Wilson, K. and van der Dussen, J. (eds) (1996) *The History of the Idea of Europe*. London: Routledge.

Wincott, D. (2003) 'The idea of the European social model: limits and paradoxes of Europeanisation', ch.12 in Featherstone and Radaelli (eds) (2003).

Wistrich, E. (1994) *The United States of Europe*. London: Routledge.

World Bank (2008) *World Development Indicators Database* (revised 10/09/2008). Washington, DC: World Bank.

Wrench, J. and Solomos, J. (eds) (1993) *Racism and Migration in Western Europe*. Oxford: Berg.

Zetterholm, S. (ed.) (1994) *National Cultures and European Integration: Cultural Diversity and Common Problems*. Oxford: Berg.

Zielonka, J. (2006) *Europe as Empire: The Nature of the Enlarged European Union*. Oxford: Oxford University Press.

Zimmer, O. (2003) *Nationalism in Europe 1890–1940*. Basingstoke: Palgrave Macmillan.

AUTHOR AND NAME INDEX

(Note: excludes most names in the set of Tables)

SUBJECT INDEX